FOR POWER

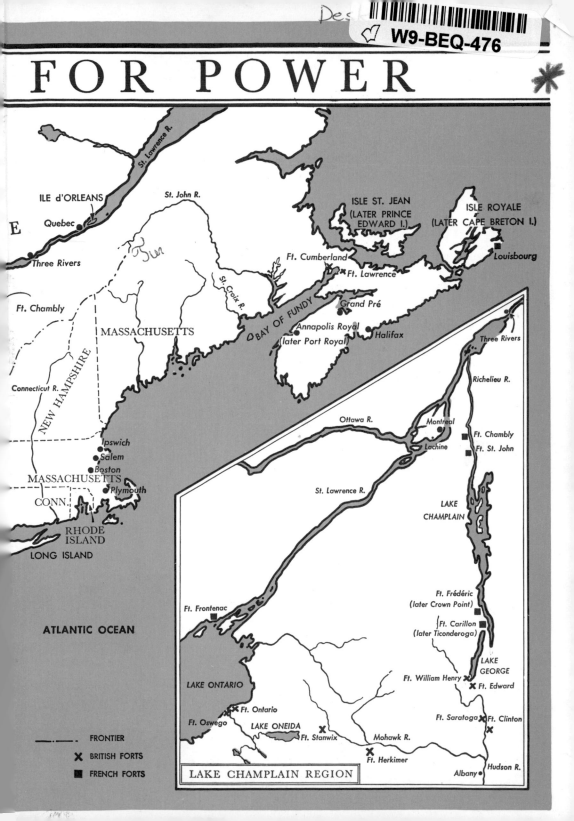

ILE d'ORLEANS

St. Lawrence R.

St. John R.

E

Quebec

Three Rivers

ISLE ST. JEAN
(LATER PRINCE
EDWARD I.)

ISLE ROYALE
(LATER CAPE BRETON I.)

Ft. Cumberland

Louisbourg

Ft. Lawrence

Ft. Chambly

St. Croix R.

MASSACHUSETTS

Grand Pré

Annapolis Royal
(later Port Royal)

Halifax

BAY OF FUNDY

Three Rivers

Richelieu R.

Connecticut R.

NEW HAMPSHIRE

Ottawa R.

Montreal

Ft. Chambly

Lachine

Ft. St. John

Ipswich

Salem

Boston

Plymouth

MASSACHUSETTS

CONN.

St. Lawrence R.

LAKE
CHAMPLAIN

RHODE
ISLAND

LONG ISLAND

Ft. Frédéric
(later Crown Point)

ATLANTIC OCEAN

Ft. Carillon
(later Ticonderoga)

Ft. Frontenac

LAKE
GEORGE

Ft. William Henry

Ft. Edward

LAKE ONTARIO

Ft. Ontario

Ft. Saratoga

Ft. Clinton

Ft. Oswego

LAKE ONEIDA

Ft. Stanwix

Mohawk R.

Ft. Herkimer

Albany

Hudson R.

— ·· — FRONTIER

✕ BRITISH FORTS

▪ FRENCH FORTS

LAKE CHAMPLAIN REGION

Fair Domain

The Ryerson Press — Toronto

Fair Domain The story of Canada
from earliest times to 1800

By GEORGE E. TAIT *Professor of Education, University of Toronto*

Illustrated by
VERNON MOULD *Head of the Art Department, Upper Canada College*

V. MOULD

SBN 7700 3055 6

Acknowledgments

The author is indebted to a host of historians, living
and dead, whose names are so numerous that they cannot
be mentioned here. For patient and skilful guidance in
the writing and production of this book, I offer my
deepest thanks to three members of The Ryerson Press—
Mr. Campbell B. Hughes, until recently the Textbook Editor;
Mr. James K. Smith, Assistant Editor; and Mr. Arthur G. Steven,
Art Director. I particularly wish to thank my friend, Vernon
Mould. The attractiveness and usefulness of this publication
has been immeasurably enhanced by his artistry.

Maps by **ROBERT KUNZ**

PRINTED AND BOUND IN CANADA BY THE RYERSON PRESS, TORONTO

To The Teacher

Fair Domain is a chronological history of Canada from earliest times to 1800.

Much attention has been paid to the arrangement of the material in this book. To assist pupils in locating information, such aids as unit headings, unit summaries, marginal headings and an index have been included.

A collection of stories from the past, fanciful tales and legends of North America's early years, has been placed in the Appendix.

In the creation of *Fair Domain* the author and the artist have made every effort to provide material that is interesting, informative and historically accurate. Illustrations have been designed to supplement the text, special care being given to the historical development of costume, arms, architecture, watercraft and household articles. The captions appearing below the illustrations have been prepared with the purpose of providing a maximum of information.

G.E.T.

Map List

Title   *Page*

THE RIVALS FOR POWER. *This is a large over-view of the scene of the Seven Years' War together with an inset giving details of the Lake Champlain-Mohawk River region.* . . . . . END PAPER

ICE INVASIONS OF NORTH AMERICA 4

INDIAN GROUPS OF CANADA 8

INDIANS OF THE PACIFIC COAST 9

INDIANS OF THE PLAINS 16

INDIANS OF THE EASTERN FORESTS 22

THE IROQUOIANS 28

EXPLORATIONS OF JACQUES CARTIER 48

EXPLORATIONS OF SAMUEL de CHAMPLAIN 74

JESUIT MISSIONS IN HURONIA 100

FIRST SETTLEMENTS IN NORTH AMERICA 125

THE WEST INDIES, 1600-1700 157

EXPLORATION OF THE MISSISSIPPI 208

EARLY HUDSON'S BAY COMPANY POSTS 221

NEW FRANCE IN FRONTENAC'S TIME 228

THE ACADIAN PENINSULA 258

THE LA VÉRENDRYES AND ANTHONY HENDAY 273

SIEGE OF LOUISBOURG, 1758 292

QUEBEC, 1759. THE SIEGE AND THE BATTLE 307

NORTH AMERICA, 1763-1775 321

BRITISH COLONIES IN NORTH AMERICA, 1763-1775 . . 326

THE WAR OF INDEPENDENCE, 1775-1783 359

NORTH AMERICA IN 1783 366

THE UNITED STATES IN 1783 367

LOYALIST SETTLEMENTS BEFORE 1800 384

EXPLORATIONS OF COOK AND VANCOUVER 403

EXPLORATIONS OF ALEXANDER MACKENZIE 407

EXPLORATIONS OF SIMON FRASER AND DAVID THOMPSON . 411

Contents

		Page
	Introduction	xi
ONE/ *The First Inhabitants*	1. The New World and Its People . .	3
	2. Indians of the Pacific Shores . .	9
	3. Indians of the Plains	16
	4. Indians of the Eastern Forests . .	22
	5. The People of the Long House . .	28
	6. The Eskimos	34
TWO/ *Early Expeditions to North America*	7. Europeans Reach North America .	41
	8. The English and French Re-discover North America	4(
	Summary of Section Two . .	52
THREE/ *The Beginnings of New France*	9. The French in Acadia	55
	10. The Founding of Quebec . . .	64
	11. Trade, Travel and Indian Warfare .	71
	12. Slow Growth at Quebec . . .	79
	13. The Last Days of Champlain . .	86
	14. The Founding of Montreal . . .	93
	15. The Huron Missions	99
	16. Adam Dollard at the Long Sault . .	108
	Summary of Section Three . .	113

FOUR / *The English Colonies in North America*

17. Newfoundland 117
18. Virginia 124
19. The Pilgrim Fathers 133
20. The New Netherlands 142
21. Maryland 148
22. Pennsylvania 151
23. The West Indies 156
    Summary of Section Four . . 160

FIVE / *Growth in New France*

24. Bishop Laval 163
25. War Against the Iroquois . . . 168
26. Monsieur Jean Talon 173
27. Life in New France 179
28. Radisson and Groseilliers . . . 187
29. Count Frontenac 194
30. The Empire of the Mississippi . . 201
31. Frontenac Recalled 210
    Summary of Section Five . . 215

SIX / *The Struggle for Power*

32. The Hudson's Bay Company . . 219
33. The Last Days of Frontenac . . 227
34. A Second War in North America, 1702-1713 237
35. The Founding of Louisbourg . . 242
36. A Third War in North America, 1744-1748 246
37. The Founding of Halifax . . . 252
38. The Expulsion of the Acadians . . 256
39. Furs and the Western Sea . . . 264
40. Henday Reaches the Rocky Mountains . 271
41. Conflict on the Ohio Frontier . . 275
    Summary of Section Six . . 281

SEVEN / *The Seven Years' War in North America, 1756-1763*

42. Major-General Montcalm . . . 283

43. The Fall of Louisbourg . . . 290

44. Weakness at Quebec 298

45. Major-General Wolfe 304

46. The Plains of Abraham . . . 312

47. The End of New France . . . 319

48. Results of the War 323

Summary of Section Seven . . 332

EIGHT / *The American Revolution*

49. Life in the Thirteen Colonies . . 335

50. The Road to Revolution . . . 342

51. The War of Independence . . . 352

52. The States Win Independence . . 365

53. The Formation of the United States . 369

Summary of Section Eight . . 375

NINE / *Growth in British North America*

54. The United Empire Loyalists . . 379

55. The Fur Empire of the West . . 389

56. The Pacific Coast 398

57. Through the Rockies to the Pacific . 405

58. The Two Canadas 414

59. Life in the Northern Colonies . . 423

60. British North America in 1800 . . 432

Summary of Section Nine . . 439

Appendix

Stories from the Past 445

Index of Illustrations . . . 456

Index 459

Introduction

The early story of Canada is a complex, vivid tale, covering ages of time and ranging across vast regions of the North American continent. Perhaps our history may be thought of as an endless drama played out against a gigantic background of rivers, lakes, forests, prairies and mountains. As for the characters involved, they are a more robust and exciting group than ever appeared on a real stage. The cast includes roving Indians, bold French adventurers, gentle, black-robed priests, the hardy *coureurs de bois,* haughty noblemen, humble settlers, wealthy traders, proud army officers, singing *voyageurs,* and last but not least, the patient pioneer women. They played their parts in one of the most thrilling stories in world history. These are the people who found North America, explored and settled it, and laid the foundations of the nation we call Canada.

The opening scenes of this drama show the struggle between several European nations to secure land, trade and power in the New World. For a long time the question of which nation will win hangs in the balance. Then, as the actors meet in battle after battle, terrible events succeed each other on the great stage. The first climax of this drama comes as two rivals for power meet and fight in the forests of North America. After the smoke of the last battle dies away and the final peace treaty is signed, the victor and the vanquished settle down together to develop a transcontinental empire. We see the fur brigades paddling further and further into the western lands, leaving behind them the blue smoke of many fires in clearings where pioneers are burning the spruce and pine in order to plant crops.

Fair Domain is a description of the long Canadian drama which began in the days before the coming of Europeans, and reached one thrilling climax on the summit of the tall, dark cliff that overhangs Quebec.

Fair Domain

ONE / *The First Inhabitants*

INDIAN MIGRATIONS FROM ASIA

THE ICE AGES

ARRIVAL OF THE INDIANS IN NORTH AMERICA

WHAT THE INDIANS TAUGHT US

HOW THE INDIANS LIVED

INDIANS OF THE PACIFIC COAST

INDIANS OF THE PLAINS

INDIANS OF THE EASTERN FORESTS

THE LEAGUE OF THE IROQUOIS

THE ESKIMOS

1

THE NEW WORLD AND ITS PEOPLE

The first known inhabitants of North and South America were copper-skinned, dark-haired people who lived in various regions of the two continents. Christopher Columbus, meeting some of these people, made the original error of thinking them the natives of the Indies he was seeking and named them "Indians." Jacques Cartier saw their faces daubed with red ochre and in consequence called them *peaux-rouges,* "redskins." To this day we speak of *Red Indians* and though both words have long been known to be a mistake, they are still used.

Indians bear a marked resemblance to the natives of Siberia, and it is reasonable to suppose that our first settlers came originally from northern Asia. They probably crossed the short distance of the Bering Strait in primitive boats and gradually spread through North and South America. They may also have crossed over on an ice bridge, or followed the Aleutian islands to Alaska. They continued to arrive over a long period of time, looking for new land and game. The Eskimos may have been the last to arrive, and some of them still live in Stone Age conditions.

No one knows when these migrations began. It is unlikely Ice Ages that men inhabited North America before the Ice Ages, periods when gigantic glaciers covered the northern part of the continent. For perhaps a million years or more large sections of North America (and Europe) were covered by glaciers which moved slowly down from the Arctic regions toward the south. In places the ice was comparatively shallow, but elsewhere it attained a thickness of 1200 feet. This enormous sheet ground onward over forests and grasslands. This mass of ice pushed on into what is now the United States, reaching a southerly point near where St. Louis, Missouri, now stands.

3

With the power of a million bulldozers, the ice wore down
mountain tops, removed hills, wiped out forests, filled up lakes,
changed river valleys and gouged deep holes in the landscape.
The ice was so heavy in certain places that it depressed the ground
with sheer weight by as much as 400 feet.

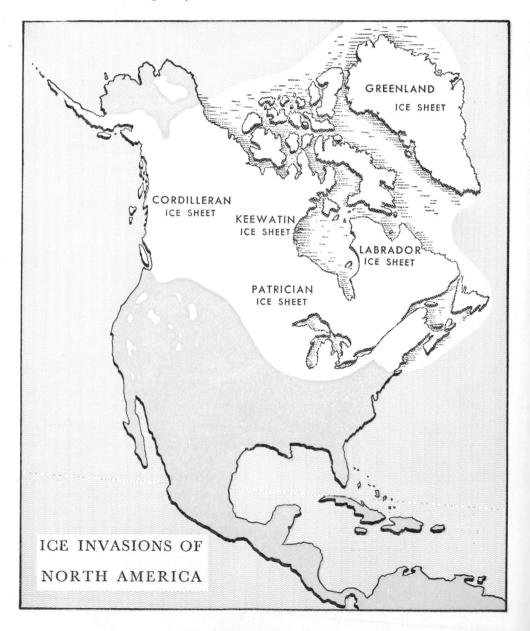

GREENLAND
ICE SHEET

CORDILLERAN
ICE SHEET

KEEWATIN
ICE SHEET

LABRADOR
ICE SHEET

PATRICIAN
ICE SHEET

ICE INVASIONS OF

NORTH AMERICA

Scientists have found it difficult to estimate the time at which the Ice Ages began and ended, but about 20,000 years ago, a weather change occurred in the northern latitudes and the great ice cap began to melt as the climate became warmer.   Then, through the course of centuries, the glaciers gradually melted and retreated toward the north, leaving a battered landscape marked by ugly gashes and strewn with boulders and rubble.

The Ice Ages not only altered the appearance of the northern **Animal life** half of the continent, but they also brought remarkable changes in animal life.   Before the coming of the ice, trees, plants and animals flourished in areas close to the North Pole.   Among the animals were large cats resembling tigers, wild dogs, tapirs, llamas, camels, bison, sheep, elephants and other strange beasts.   Some of them may have made their way north from South America while others probably crossed over from Europe and Asia by means of an ancient land bridge.   Most of these animals became extinct with the coming of the ice.   Thus, in later years, horses, camels and elephants were found only in the Old World, although ancient skeletons occasionally turn up in North America.

The melting ice turned depressions into lakes; mosses, **Migrations** grasses, plants and trees began to grow and birds and animals **from Asia** moved northward from the warmer regions.   Thousands of years passed before the land was freed of its icy armour.   Following this climatic change, the first migrations of people from Siberia took place, but in what year we do not know.   We have to assume that some time between 15,000 and 20,000 years ago the first inhabitants arrived on this continent.

The Indians probably arrived in bands over long periods of time.   There may have been a heavy traffic of people across Bering Strait in years when game was scarce in Siberia.   It is also possible that some groups, dissatisfied with North America, moved back again to Siberia.

Scientists think that many of the migrants pushed on southward or southeastward into the heart of the vast continent. Some settled permanently in favourable districts, while the more restless moved on to the south, across what is now the United States, Mexico and Central America until they eventually entered

Historians think that between 15,000 and 20,000 years ago bands of hardy Asiatic hunters made their way from Siberia across the Bering Strait to North America. Satisfied with the new land, they spread out, making little settlements here and there in favourable places. Their descendants, whom we call Indians, gradually pushed southward and eastward, finally occupying scattered regions throughout the entire continent.

the continent that lies below. After thousands of years, these migrations resulted in Indian populations scattered all the way from the Arctic to Cape Horn.

Appearance of Indians
Although we often speak of "red men" or "Red Indians," as already mentioned, this term is by no means accurate. The colouring of the Indians is actually brown, but a great many shades of this hue are found among various groups. Skin tones range all the way from a light yellowish-brown to a deep reddish-brown. The remarkable variety of hair colour found among European peoples does not exist among Indians. They have straight, thick, black hair (which in former times was worn long), and unlike Europeans have little or no beard. As a general rule, Indians have broader faces than Europeans.

Indians varied in appearance from one region to another, and varied even more in their ways of living. Some remained primitive wanderers, living a hand-to-mouth existence, while others built up remarkable civilizations. Some were hunters and fishermen; others became skilled farmers. Some dressed in the crudest of clothing; others created costumes of beauty and magnificence. Some tended to be quiet and peaceful; others became fierce and powerful warriors.

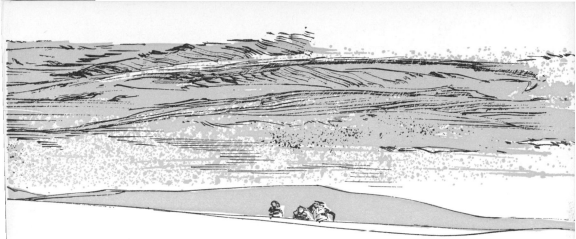

The outstanding Indian civilizations were those established by the Aztecs and Mayans of Mexico and by the Incas of Peru. In these amazing empires the tribesmen created woven cloth, costumes, carved woods, jewellery, pottery, masonry, architecture, bridges and highways. Their accomplishments appeared nothing less than astonishing to the first Spaniards who met them.

From the Indians we have gained much. The early European traders, adventurers and settlers soon discovered that many Indian ways were admirably suited to life in the rugged New World. From the Indians they soon learned how to build and paddle a canoe, hunt and trap wild animals, tan hides, make moccasins and snowshoes, travel silently and how to fight in the forest. Indeed, some of the wilder European spirits found native ways so attractive that they preferred the life of the wilderness to that of their own communities. Indian guides led the way to the northern and western regions of North America and played a vital role in the discovery of rivers, lakes, plains and mountain passes.

If Europeans gained knowledge from the hunters and warriors, they gained even more from the Indian farmers who cultivated corn, beans, pumpkins, squash, cocoa beans, peanuts, strawberries, pineapples, potatoes and tomatoes. In addition, they were introduced to several other products that cannot be classified as foods. These include tobacco, quinine and cocaine.

Settled in regions scattered from the Pacific to the Atlantic, the Indians shaped their lives to the conditions they encountered. Climate, waterways, plains, mountains, forests and wild animals all played a part in their daily living. From nature they obtained

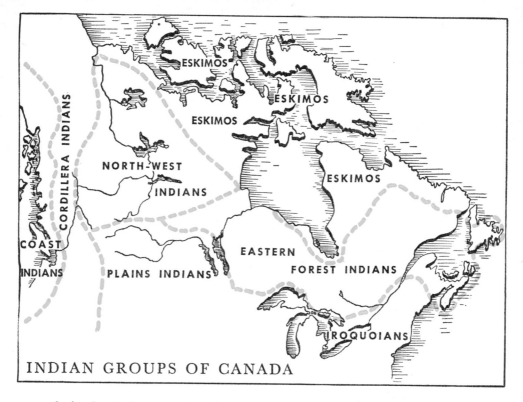

INDIAN GROUPS OF CANADA

their food, homes, clothing, weapons and decorations.   From earth, sky and water were derived their customs and many of their gods.   So close were they to nature that some Indians believed wild animals were their brothers, that spirits dwelt in the streams and that gods took the form of sun, moon and stars.   Spirits spoke in the lapping of the waves, and the roaring of thunder was the angry shouting of the gods.

The tribes living in various areas gradually developed their own peculiar means of hunting, travelling, working, building, decorating and worshipping.   Since these activities differed so widely from place to place, it is best to examine them separately in the following chapters.

2

INDIANS OF THE PACIFIC SHORES

In the regions where mountain ranges meet the Pacific Ocean and on some of the large off-shore islands lived groups of stocky Indians whose tribes bore such pleasant sounding names as Bella **Tribes** Coola, Tlinkit, Tsimshian, Coast Salish, Nootka, Kwakiutl and Haida. Their lives were governed by the sweeping sea and the damp, lush forests. More than mere fishermen, these people were skilled craftsmen, artists and woodcarvers who developed the magnificent totem pole and the graceful dugout canoe.

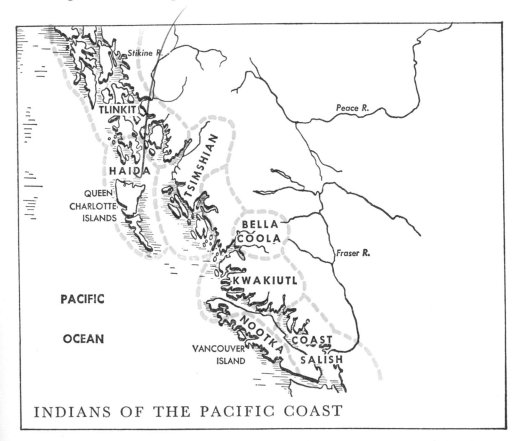

INDIANS OF THE PACIFIC COAST

The coastal and island tribes had much the same appearance. They were short in stature and had thick chests and powerful arms. Oriental features are still so noticeable among their descendants that they have sometimes been mistaken for Chinese.

A curious custom, occasionally practised by two of the tribes, resulted in the development of peculiarly-shaped heads. This odd moulding of the skull was accomplished by bandaging the heads of the children at a very early age. In consequence, some of the Coast Salish had flattened foreheads that sloped back sharply from the eyes to the crown of the head. The Kwakiutl people, using the same method, achieved another grotesque shape that can only be described as a pointed head. It appears that these deformities were considered a mark of honour, for they were found only among high-ranking families.

Food The Indians obtained most of their food from the ocean in which they caught salmon, cod, halibut, sea-lion, sea-otter, whale and such other eatables as clams, cuttlefish and sea urchins. The forests, too, offered an abundance of game in the form of elk, moose, bear, caribou, mountain-sheep and mountain-goat. Although these Indians were not farmers, they utilized certain vegetable products that grew in a wild state, among these being berries, the inner bark of trees, seaweed and various roots.

Being expert fishermen, the tribesmen used a variety of methods to obtain their catches. For still-fishing they employed long lines of seaweed to which were attached hooks made from bone or wood. They knew something of trolling, too, for the fishermen trailed lines as they paddled along the coast. Other methods of fishing included the use of the spear, the net, traps and an odd instrument shaped like a rake. At times the herring swam so thickly and in such teeming shoals that they could be scooped into the canoes by the basketful. Another small fish, the candle-fish, came up the rivers during the spring. These, too, swam in their millions and catching them was a simple matter. The remarkable feature of this fish was that when it was dried it could be lit and burned like a candle. Oil from the candle-fish was highly-prized, since it could be employed as we use butter and cooking oil.

Winter supplies of food were carefully prepared. Large quantities of fish, meat and vegetable products were stored away. Salmon, clams and meats were smoked for preservation, and berries were dried in the sun. Vast stores of food were necessary not only for family use but to provide hospitality during the entertainment and feasting of the winter months.

Beautifully-carved masks, employed for ceremony or war, were relatively common among the Indians of the Pacific coast. Members of the Tlinkit tribe sometimes wore a wooden battle helmet similar to the one illustrated above. The grotesque wooden face, decorated by tufts of hair, was designed to terrify the enemy. In order to absorb the shock of head blows suffered during battle the Tlinkit warrior donned a wooden collar directly below the helmet.

In mild weather men did not bother to wear any clothing, **Clothing** but the women wore aprons. Even on cool days the Indians went about with very little to protect their bodies. It was only during heavy rains or on cold days that they found it necessary to don warm garments made from dog-hair, mountain-goat wool or shredded cedar bark. This last material scarcely seems a suitable fabric, but, because it rubbed gently against the body of the wearer, it created warmth.   Aprons, hats, cloaks and complete dresses were created from woven cedar bark.   On ceremonial occasions, the men sometimes wore magnificent robes made from the glossy skin of a water animal, the sea-otter.   These furs were so beautiful that they astonished and attracted the first Europeans who visited those regions.

Homes   The Indian homes were called clan houses because the people in them belonged to the same clan, a group of persons closely

A Tsimshian village with its inhabitants dressed for a *potlach*.   The Tsimshians lived in villages of cedar lodges, each large enough to house many families.   The ceremonial masks worn by the Indians were carved in cedar or alder wood, and were often painted in bright colours.   Some masks had moving parts, which were manipulated by pulling strings, thus changing the expressions on the carved faces. In the foreground is one of the long, graceful dugout canoes used for fishing, travelling and fighting.   The dugout canoe was constructed by hollowing out a huge cedar log, pouring water into it, heating the water with hot stones, and then covering the whole log to let the steam soften the wood.   While still softened, the sides of the log were spread outwards and held apart with wooden stretchers until the wood hardened again.   The additional width thus gained made the craft roomier and more seaworthy.   Separate wooden sections were later added to create the high graceful forms at the bow and the stern.

related by blood. Some of these houses were one hundred and fifty yards long and twenty yards wide. Clan houses were frequently constructed in rows along the coast or island, their front doors looking out on the sea. The framework of the building was made of heavy logs and these in turn were covered with split cedar planks placed in either a vertical or a horizontal fashion. The planks were loosely fastened and could be easily taken down and moved to another location. Such homes as these accommodated a large number of people, and in a way resembled the modern apartment house. Within the clan house each family had its own particular area, the area being enclosed by partitions of cedar matting.

The artistry of these people was displayed not only in the **Crafts** construction of buildings, but also in decoration. Paintings in bright colours appeared on the front walls. Elaborately carved door posts stood on each side of the entrance.

These Indians rarely moved from place to place and thus

acquired many possessions. In their homes were dyed blankets, wooden masks, spoons, and bowls, chests and boxes of beautiful design. Wooden boxes, used for the storage of food and household articles, were extremely well made, many of them fitting together so perfectly that they could be used to boil water.

In making buildings and household effects, the Indians used hammers, chisels, drills, axes and adzes made from bone, antler, stone and shell. The cutting edges of such tools as the chisel and the adze (a type of chipping axe) were frequently made from jade found in the region of the Thompson River. Although today these tools may seem primitive, they were actually very effective in the hands of skilled craftsmen. Tools were also necessary in constructing dugout canoes of many sizes and shapes. Small hunting canoes were not more than fifteen feet in length but war canoes measured sixty-five feet from bow to stern and were capable of travelling hundreds of miles with crews of forty or more.

Social organization The social organization of the coastal Indians was so complicated and varied that it is difficult to understand. However, it appears there was a class or caste system which included nobles, commoners and slaves. Small groups of Indians, closely related by blood and often descendants of a single ancestor, made up the clans. A number of clans with similar customs made up the tribal group. Certain families held recognized authority and enjoyed the right to use crests, sing old songs and perform tribal ceremonies.

Potlach There was considerable rivalry among the local chiefs and nobles, particularly in displaying their wealth and prestige. One way in which this rivalry was expressed was the *potlach*, a social affair in which the host entertained his friends and neighbours. During the prolonged activities of dancing, singing and eating, the host gave away piles of presents to his honoured guests. Among such gifts were slaves, canoes, furs, blankets, oil and household articles. The more presents given away during the course of a potlach, the greater became the reputation of the host. Those who received gifts, however, were expected to hold potlachs of their own.

Totem poles, which form such a striking part of Indian **Totem poles**
artistry, are peculiar to the Pacific coast. It is not known whether
totem poles were carved before the coming of Europeans. It is
probable, however, that very few large totems existed before
traders brought knives, axes and other iron tools. Appreciating
the value of iron, Indian carvers proceeded to produce taller totem
poles, many of which reached astounding heights. It seems that
this was a natural development of the former activity of carving
elaborate door posts for the clan houses.

The strange figures of birds, animals and humans so skilfully
carved on the totem poles were often clan crests. Among the
figures were those of the raven, the eagle, the frog, the whale, the
fish and the bear. Carved representations of men's heads and
bodies, too, sometimes appear among the animals on the poles.
The figures on the totems cannot be read in the same way as
Egyptian hieroglyphics or sign writing. They simply represent
clan crests and may suggest a few well-known legends.

3

INDIANS OF THE PLAINS

On the central plains of North America, the natives owed their well-being to a high-shouldered, shaggy beast known as the bison or buffalo, the creature with "the hump like a camel and hair like a lion." The Plains Indians regulated their habits, tribal customs and even religious rites to conform to the ways of the buffalo.

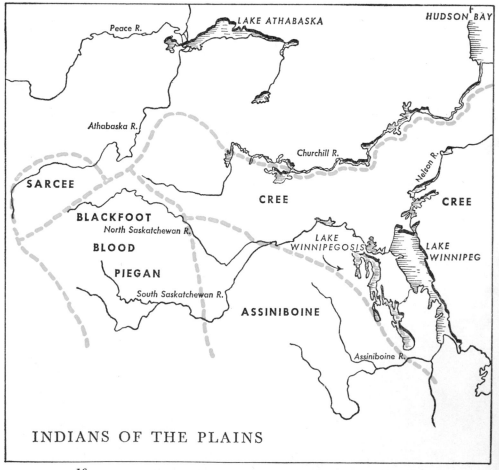

INDIANS OF THE PLAINS

The tribes of the prairies were the Sioux, Assiniboine, Cree, **Tribes** Gros Ventre, Piegan, Blood and Blackfoot. Although these Indians spoke at least four different languages, they lived, hunted and fought in very much the same manner. They were a strong, hardy people, somewhat taller than their coastal cousins, the warriors being unusually large and handsome.

The people of the plains had little difficulty in securing food. **Buffalo** They followed the buffalo which roamed in herds of millions up and down the Great Plains, those rolling grass-lands stretching from the north-west region of the continent down the eastward side of the Rocky Mountains and deep into present-day Texas. To the tribesmen, the buffalo was life itself; the meat was food; the hides made tents and clothing; rawhide, thickened by heating beneath a fire, made an arrowproof shield; stretched on willow wands, the hide formed a bullboat with which to cross rivers and lakes; buffalo hair was woven into ropes and used for ornaments; the sinews supplied thread and string and the horns were carved into headdresses and various ornaments. In addition, sinews could be used as bow strings, and the lining of the buffalo's stomach provided material for water bottles. Living off the huge animal, the Plains Indians were strong and healthy, while the swift movements of the hunt gave them agility and courage.

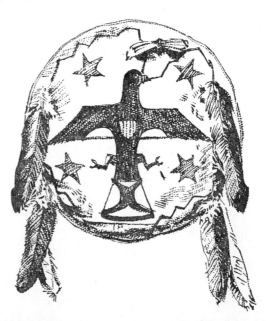

The shield formed a vital part of the fighting equipment used by the skilled and fearsome warriors of the Great Plains. This Sioux Indian shield is made from tough buffalo hide stretched over a strong but light wooden framework. Decorated with feathers and painted designs, many of the shields were extremely attractive in appearance. The symbols painted on the leather face of the shield were supposed to protect the warrior in battle.

Various methods were used in hunting the buffalo. Sometimes bands of Indians drove the animals into log enclosures or corrals where they became an easy prey to arrows and lances. At other times, the buffalo were killed by stampeding them over the edge of a sharp cliff. These hunts actually held considerable danger for the tribesmen. Terror-stricken animals sometimes broke out of the enclosures or turned away suddenly from the herd, charging directly at the Indians who were often trampled to death. In later times, when the prairie tribes obtained horses and rifles, the hunters formed running circles about a small herd and kept firing until all the beasts were killed.

Buffalo meat was practically the whole diet of the western tribes, although additional food was secured by hunting such other animals as deer, antelope, elk and rabbits. Among the vegetable products used were wild rice, lily bulbs, rose haws, roots and a variety of wild berries and cherries. These Indians were not an agricultural people, but a number of the tribes did grow a few vegetables, some maize and a little tobacco.

Pemmican To guard against the chance of buffalo being unobtainable during the winter months, the Plains Indians invented the greatest of all concentrated foods—pemmican. Pemmican was made from many animal meats but by far the best was buffalo meat. Dried by sun and wind or over a slow fire, the meat was pounded into a powder, sometimes flavoured with dried fruits and berries, mixed with melted buffalo fat, and then sealed in a hide bag with more fat. Packed in this manner, it lasted for years and took up a minimum of space. It could be eaten raw or cooked. It was a complete diet in itself.

Clothing Until traders brought blankets and cloth to the western plains, the tribesmen dressed in clothing made from animal skins. Expert tanners, the women knew how to create the variety of leathers needed to make shirts, loin cloths, leggings and dresses. Light, soft leathers were required for clothing, and tough sturdy leathers for moccasins. During the coldest weather men and women wrapped themselves in fur robes; in summer only the scantiest of clothing was worn.

For celebrations and ceremonies the Plains tribes used

costumes made from the best leathers, carefully tailored and ornamented with skill. Among the decorations worn were fur, human hair, shells and porcupine quills. However, when Europeans began to supply coloured glass beads, these gradually took the place of quills. Necklaces composed of shells, teeth, bones and claws formed an important part of ceremonial attire. There were also a number of ceremonial headdresses ornamented with antlers, buffalo horns and ermine skins. Large feathered headdresses were worn by only a few warriors. Most of the prairie tribesmen wore no head covering except in cold weather when they donned hats made of fur or bird skins.

Formerly, a way of telling a warrior's tribe was by his headdress. Each tribe had a distinct type of headgear, which varied from the eagle-feather war bonnet of the Dakota Sioux to the buckskin turban of the Iroquois. The most picturesque headdress was that of the Dakota Sioux. Each feather had a meaning. For instance, a feather with a red spot on the top announced the killing of an enemy; if the feather was cut off at the top it meant the enemy's throat had been cut; a split feather showed the warrior had been wounded in battle.

Indian homes on the plains were vastly different from those **Homes** of the Pacific shores. In the first place they were much smaller, and in the second place they were composed chiefly of hides. These prairie dwellings, known as *tipis,* were actually cone-shaped tents made from buffalo skins. Admirably suited to a wandering way of life, the tipis could be taken down quickly and moved to another location.

When erecting a tipi, the women stacked together a group of long wooden poles so that their bases formed a circle roughly eighteen feet in diameter. Then the poles were tied together near their tops to form a conical framework. When this was completed, the semi-circular tipi-cover was moved into position on the poles. The two ends of the cover were fastened together securely above the small doorway.

Fires burned inside the tipis and smoke found its way out through a hole in the top, but this arrangement alone was not sufficient to provide suitable ventilation. The Indians developed clever devices known as smoke-flaps—two triangular pieces of hide attached to the peak of the tipi—which created a draught effect. Each flap, supported by an exterior pole, could be moved to suit the direction of the wind. This operation, of course, prevented wind currents from blowing smoke back inside the tipi.

The Plains Indians had few possessions. This was perfectly natural, for the people of the plains, ever following the buffalo herds, could not transport heavy loads of household effects from

The Plains Indians led a wandering existence in pursuit of the buffalo herds that roamed the prairies. To move their possessions from one place to another, the tribesmen used the *travois*, a conveyance that has been described as a "waggon without wheels." Wooden poles formed the framework of the travois and frequently served a double purpose, since they were also used as tipi poles. Several crossbars of wood or rawhide supported the load. Here, a Blackfoot woman rides a horse drawing a typical travois. Note the high-backed saddle on which she is seated. The men, who scouted ahead during travel, scorned the saddle, preferring to ride their horses bareback.

one place to another. Their beds were simple affairs made of
hides or furs spread upon the ground. They had no benches or
chairs, but contented themselves with simple back rests which
were useful when sitting upon their beds. Some bowls and baskets
were used, but leather or fibre bags were most frequently employed
in the storage and transport of food and other possessions.

The horse, introduced into the Americas by the Spaniards,
eventually made its way in wild bands to the prairies where it
was caught and tamed by the Indians. The tribesmen quickly
accepted this animal as their chief means of transportation for
hunting, warfare and travel.

The early prairie tribes probably battled to a limited extent **Warfare**
among themselves, but once the warriors were equipped with
horses and later with firearms, warfare expanded in a surprising
fashion. The new method of movement permitted the tribesmen
to travel and raid further afield. One of the chief reasons for the
increase in conflict was the amount of horse-stealing that took
place. Warriors, realizing they could gain wealth and fame by
owning a herd of horses, risked their lives to secure the animals
from the camps of other tribes. A successful raid, however, often
invited a return attack.

The plainsmen were very skilful fighters and their activities
in hunting, travelling and horse-stealing kept them alert and agile.
They battled with bows, arrows, lances, clubs, knives and firearms.
War to them was almost a game to be played for sheer pleasure and
excitement. It is true that they scalped their fallen enemies, but
they were not as cruel as many of their eastern cousins. Their
torture of prisoners, for example, was far less frequent than that
of the savage Iroquois.

4

INDIANS OF THE EASTERN FORESTS

In the vast, forested regions that now comprise Ontario, Quebec and the Maritime provinces lived a large group of Indians who spoke different dialects of the Algonkian tongue. Since these natives were scattered across half the area of present-day Canada and played a large part in our history, it is important to note the hunting-grounds of each of the tribes.

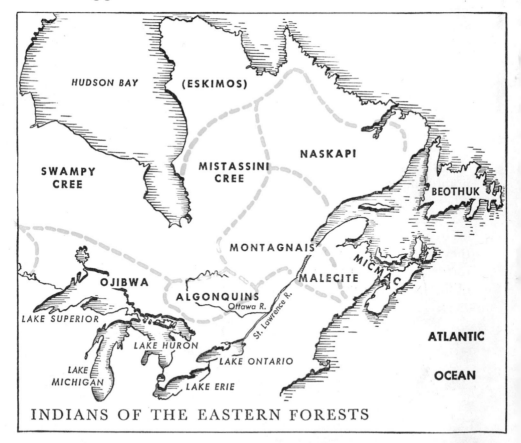

INDIANS OF THE EASTERN FORESTS

Far to the east in Newfoundland were the Beothuk, a tribe now extinct. The Micmac occupied what are now the Maritime provinces and a small portion of eastern Quebec. In a district overlapping western New Brunswick, eastern Quebec and a part of the state of Maine were the Malecite. Further west, in central Quebec, lived the Montagnais and the Naskapi. For some distance on each side of the Ottawa River the Algonquins made their homes. North of the Great Lakes and as far west as Lake of the Woods lived the Ojibwa or Chippewa. Then farther north and north-west, in an area stretching to the southern shores of Hudson Bay, were the Swampy Cree.

The Algonkian people were mainly wanderers who moved about hunting and fishing in their own districts, dependent for food and shelter upon the products of the forests, lakes and streams. In the northern sections this was particularly true, although farther south some tribes grew crops of maize, beans and squash.

The Algonkian people developed amazing skills in hunting and fishing and used many clever devices to deceive and capture their quarries. Moose, called with a small birch-bark horn, were caught while floundering in the deep snows of winter or killed while swimming across lakes. Snares made from thin strips of rawhide, fitted with running nooses and baited with meat, caught and strangled unwary animals. Traps, called deadfalls, triggered by an animal taking the bait, dropped logs weighted with stones to crush and kill the unsuspecting victim.

In fishing, these Indians were just as skilful. They used a wide range of fishing gear—nets, spears, traps, lines, hooks and harpoons. One of their most interesting practices was connected with night fishing, an operation that required a flaming torch and a long spear. The torch was placed at the front of the canoe to attract fish. Then, as the fish swam in the direction of the light, they were caught by Indian spears.

Like their prairie cousins, the eastern tribes dressed lightly in summer, but in winter donned leather clothing and fur robes. The Algonkian women were expert garment makers: they cut pieces of leather and sewed them together to fit the wearer. Tunics were an important feature of attire, men wearing them jacket-length, while women favoured knee-length garments. Indians of the northern regions often wore tunics with hoods like those of the Eskimos. Other items of clothing included leggings, moccasins, fur caps, breech-cloths and mitts. Some robes and garments were made from long narrow strips of rabbit fur woven into a light soft material. Although Algonkian costumes were well-made, they were not as attractive as prairie clothing; the eastern Indians seemed to have less interest in decoration.

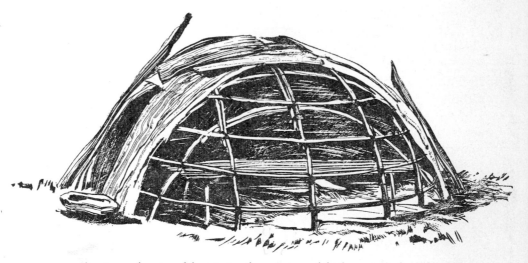

A cutaway drawing of the interior, the exterior and the framework of an Algonkian wigwam. Where the tipi was cone-shaped and made of hides, the wigwam was dome-shaped and covered with sheets of bark or reed matting. In order to keep the rather loose covering in position, it was necessary to place heavy poles against the outside walls of the wigwam. Note the long low structure inside the dwelling. Covered with fur robes or hides, it served as a bed.

Homes   The Algonkian people were roving hunters and needed shelters that could be taken down and easily transported from place to place. In consequence, they invented untidy-looking, dome-shaped structures known as *wigwams*. The framework of the Algonkian wigwam was composed of wooden poles, the butts of which were thrust into the earth. A number of materials supplied wigwam covers, among these, birch-bark sheets and reed mats being most commonly used. In the northern regions where reeds and bark were scarce, caribou skins were employed. When the Algonkian people moved camp, they left the wooden framework behind, taking with them only the wigwam covers. In the forests poles could be picked up anywhere.

Household articles were few in number. There was practically nothing in the way of furniture, for the Indians slept and ate on a floor normally composed of spruce boughs, over which were placed hides, furs, or reed mats. Around the fire were a few crude utensils in the form of bowls, spoons and cooking pots, many of which were made from birch-bark, but a few articles were made from wood, pottery or soft stone. Water could be heated in birch-bark containers by dropping in stones heated in the fire. The eastern Indians occasionally engaged in art work. Birch-bark articles were decorated by cutting away portions of the outer white bark to reveal the darker layers below. Baskets and boxes were often made more attractive by the addition of porcupine quills. Leather bags and garments were sometimes decorated with designs painted directly onto the materials; cradle boards used to carry babies were often painted in a similar manner. However, this large group of Indians did not rank high among the artists and craftsmen of the Americas.

Since rapid movement was important, the Algonkian Indians **Travel** developed some very interesting methods of transportation. Perhaps their most remarkable creation is the birch-bark canoe, a watercraft wonderfully suited to their way of life. Made from sheets of birch-bark fastened to a framework of wood, the canoe is graceful in appearance, swift in motion, and so light in weight that it is easily carried from one waterway to another. In addition, it draws very little water and so is useful in shallow streams. It is not surprising, then, that in later years traders and explorers adopted the canoe as their chief means of travel and transportation.

When the lakes and rivers were frozen over, the canoes were put away in caches. It was then that the Algonkian people took to their snowshoes, to move across the deep snows that blanketed the forests and the waterways. Snowshoes, light strips of wood webbed with animal sinews, supported the weight of the traveller

Some tribes of the eastern forests made maple syrup, using the basic method we have since copied. They tapped the maple trees, gathered the sap, and boiled it over fires. Above, we see Algonkian Indians engaged in this work. In the foreground is a tree into which a spike has been driven and the wooden pan into which the sap drips. An Indian is collecting sap from the pans, while the women in the background are "boiling down" the sap to reduce it to maple syrup.

even on the deepest snow. Varying in shape and design from tribe to tribe, snowshoes might be long and relatively narrow, or almost circular in shape.

Various tribes kept dogs, but these were seldom used as beasts of burden. It was the Indian women and children who carried the packs and pulled the *toboggans* during the winter journeys. (This custom of travel left the men free to watch for game or to repel unexpected enemy attacks.) The Indian toboggan was really a sleigh without runners, made from a few thin boards lashed together and turned up at the front end; it was light, strong and durable.

The Algonkians were divided into small bands that had little **Social organization** social organization. They had no laws, customs and ceremonials as elaborate as those of the coastal Indians. It is true that there were chiefs among them, but these men seemed to have possessed little actual authority. A chief secured the respect of his people through his own ability or achievements rather than through any tradition, law or custom. Decisions of importance seem to have been made by groups of older men who met in council whenever necessary.

The inhabitants of the eastern forests occasionally fought **Warfare** among themselves. These were not large-scale wars, but simple hit-and-run affairs in which a few people were killed and a few prisoners taken. Scalping was a common procedure, but the practice of torture varied from place to place. Some tribes killed their prisoners immediately after capture without engaging in torture, while others delighted in the use of the most horrible methods of producing pain. Most warriors employed such common weapons as bows, arrows, knives and tomahawks. In addition, some tribes fitted themselves with a crude, simple armour in the form of a breastplate created from pieces of wood tied together in a flexible manner.

5

THE PEOPLE OF THE LONG HOUSE

A number of powerful Indian tribes occupied much of present-day southern Ontario and the northern region of what is now the state of New York. They spoke dialects of a language quite different from that of the Algonkians. Three of these tribes **Tribes** lived in the southern Ontario region. The Hurons occupied a district stretching from Georgian Bay eastward to the St. Lawrence river. South and west of them were the Tobacco Indians, and still further south, near Lakes St. Clair and Erie, were the Neutral Indians.

The remaining tribes dwelt in the region lying directly to the

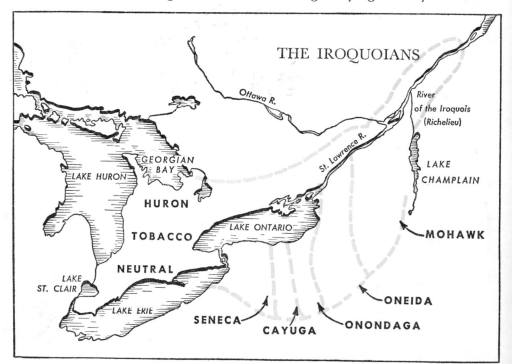

THE IROQUOIANS

Ottawa R.

River of the Iroquois (Richelieu)

St. Lawrence R.

GEORGIAN BAY

LAKE HURON

LAKE CHAMPLAIN

HURON

LAKE ONTARIO

TOBACCO

MOHAWK

NEUTRAL

LAKE ST. CLAIR

LAKE ERIE

SENECA

CAYUGA

ONONDAGA

ONEIDA

south of Lake Ontario and the St. Lawrence River. They were called the Seneca, the Cayuga, the Oneida, the Onondaga, the Mohawk and the Tuscarora. In appearance these Indians were little different from many of the dark-haired Europeans who first came to this country. Their skins had a slight brownish tinge, but lacked any oriental cast of feature. In strength, vigour and intelligence they ranked high among the early inhabitants of the Americas. They called themselves the *People of the Long House* and spoke the Iroquoian tongue.

The Iroquoian tribes seldom suffered from hunger. Their **Food** forests were rich in game and their fields plentiful with vegetables and grain. Hunters shot deer, bear, beaver, porcupine, squirrels, racoons, geese, ducks, turkeys and rabbits. The women collected wild blueberries, strawberries, raspberries, cranberries, cherries

and a variety of nuts. The maple tree provided syrup and sugar. In the fields surrounding their villages they grew crops of Indian corn, beans, squash, pumpkins and sometimes tobacco. Corn was a particularly valuable product, for the Iroquoians ate it as popcorn, or as corn-on-the-cob, or they ground it into flour for baking bread. Corn flour, too, was used as an ingredient of the thick soups which are still a favourite food of these people.

The Iroquoians were farmers settled in **Homes** definite districts who could afford to build large and comfortable homes. These dwellings were long structures housing a number of families, although none of the Iroquoian homes was of the great size and beauty of the Pacific shore clan houses.

Various Indian groups used stone adzes for carving and shaping wood and for squaring timbers. Although these tools are crude by today's standards, they were very effective in the hands of a skilled Indian craftsman. This Iroquois adze consists of a stone head attached to a wooden handle by means of leather thongs. When the North American Indians were able to secure metal knives and axes from Europeans, they were no longer satisfied with their own primitive stone tools.

When the Iroquoians constructed a house, they erected a sturdy framework of wooden poles, and then proceeded to cover this with sheets of cedar- or elm-bark held in position by cords or ropes.   Inside was a wide space or corridor where fires were kept burning and cooking was done.   On both sides of this open space were rows of compartments, each of which was occupied by a single family.   Low platforms within the compartments served as couches by day and as beds by night.   On a shelf placed some distance above the platforms, the families kept their personal belongings.

To the Indians, such conditions seemed reasonably comfortable, although a modern family would find the conditions almost

A scene in a typical Iroquoian village. The woman standing in the foreground wears traditional costume, composed of a full buckskin dress and long leggings.   In the background, men are building a lodge while women work with corn which has been recently harvested.   One woman grinds corn into coarse flour by pounding it in a large wooden container.   Another woman pours corn into an earthenware bowl in preparation for cooking.   Note the size of the two lodges.

The blow-gun, an odd weapon, was fired by blowing slender, wooden darts from a straight tube whose inner diameter was about half an inch. The Iroquois blow-gun shown above was reasonably accurate over distances up to 100 feet. It had, however, neither the range nor the striking power of the ordinary bow and arrow. Compared with the long blow-guns employed by the Indians of South America, the Iroquois weapon was really very small.

unbearable. Smoke hung in slow-moving swirls, unpleasant odours filled the air, cold draughts swept through the cracks in the bark sheets, flea-bitten dogs wandered in and out, children shouted and screamed and women quarrelled.

Most of the villages possessed a public building known as a Long House that served as a meeting place and a community centre. It was here that the Iroquoians held council meetings, enjoyed celebrations and performed tribal ceremonies. It was from the use of this building that they named themselves *The People of the Long House.*

Their means of transportation and travel were similar to those **Travel** of the Algonkians. Snowshoes, packs and toboggans were all employed as was the canoe. Birch-bark, however, was so scarce in many of the districts that canoes made of this material were often purchased from the Algonkians. Much travelling was done for the purpose of trading with distant tribes of Indians. Agricultural products were often exchanged for furs, canoes, flints, tobacco, medicines and various other requirements.

As warriors, the Iroquoians were among the best in history, for they fought with a ferocity and a bravery that has rarely been equalled. While on war journeys, they travelled quickly and quietly over long distances, living only on corn carried in leather sacks. They fought mainly with bow and arrow and with sturdy wooden clubs; they faced death without fear and torture without flinching.

Their larger settlements were almost fortresses in themselves, **Fortified** being protected by high, log stockades, sometimes thirty feet in **villages** height. Inside and near the tops of these wooden walls were placed platforms on which the defenders could stand and fire arrows or hurl stones at attacking forces. A supply of water was always kept on hand in case the fortifications should be set on fire during an attack.

Social organization

The intelligence and imagination of the Iroquoian people is clearly demonstrated by the methods of government they developed for themselves. The tribes organized themselves into large groupings or confederacies. By the time Europeans appeared in North America, there were probably three such confederacies: the Huron Confederacy, the Neutral Confederacy and the League of the Iroquois. The third group became the most powerful and in the end destroyed the other two.

League of the Iroquois

The League of the Iroquois, formed about 1570 by the Indian prophet, Deganawida, and the great Mohawk chief, Hiawatha, included the Mohawk, the Cayuga and the Oneida. When the Onondaga and the Seneca joined, the League was known as the *Five Nations*. Then later, in 1720, the Tuscarora came in to make up the *Six Nations*.

The chief aims of the League were to extend its power, protect its members and prevent inter-tribal warfare. There were

Since the region south of Lake Ontario had few birch trees, the Iroquoian people bought birch-bark canoes from the Algonkian tribes. Sometimes, the Iroquoians were forced to construct their watercraft from elm-bark. The elm-bark canoe shown above was heavy, slow, clumsy and not particularly safe. It was difficult to construct, rotted quickly, and was easily split by rocks. Thus, it is understandable why the Iroquoians were always eager to buy birch-bark canoes from the northern Indians.

really three levels of government within the League, each level having its own ruling body.   In order of importance, there was the Central League Council, then the various tribal councils and finally a great many clan councils.   By way of a rough comparison, we might say that these had some resemblance to our federal, provincial and local governments.   Each of the tribes in the confederacy sent a certain number of chiefs or *sachems* to sit on the Council which dealt with vital League matters.   This central government had the right to establish laws, protect the rights of citizens, punish criminals, take away the rights of citizenship, and declare war and make peace.   The tribal councils settled disputes within the tribe and the clan councils ruled on clan responsibilities and duties.

Many of the chiefs who sat on the Council were wise and clever men who spoke well and carried out the affairs of government in a skilful and satisfactory manner.   There is much to admire in the government of the League, because it guarded the safety and the happiness of the whole people in many of the ways that our government does today.   In addition, it must be remembered that few, if any, Indians in North America at that time were capable of creating a system of inter-tribal government.

It has been suggested by some historians that the practices established by the League of the Iroquois actually provided examples of government later adopted by the United States of America.

6

THE ESKIMOS

The Eskimos live in regions extending all the way from northern Siberia to Greenland. It is unlikely that more than a fifth of their number have ever made their homes on this continent.

Most of them depend upon the animal life of the sea for food and live along the Arctic coasts where sea mammals and fish are plentiful. When they temporarily leave these regions, it is for the purpose of hunting such land animals as caribou and musk-ox, or for fresh-water fishing.

Groups The Eskimos who live in northern Canada may be divided into four regional groups: the Mackenzie Eskimos near the mouth of the Mackenzie River, the Copper Eskimos near the mouth of the Coppermine River, the Central Eskimos of Baffin Island, Southampton Island and the middle mainland coast, and the Labrador Eskimos of northern Quebec and Labrador. These groups display differences in habits and traditions, but basically they share a common way of life.

Appearance The people are short, sturdy and remarkably strong. Their round faces, framed by straight, thick black hair, feature rather flat noses and high cheek bones. The colour of their skin varies from region to region, ranging all the way from a deep yellowish-brown to a light tan, and some Eskimos have skin colourings very little different from those of European people. In spite of the hardships and handicaps imposed by a harsh climate, they are hard-working, cheerful and kind to their children.

Food Their food is almost wholly meat: caribou, seal, walrus, bear, fish, ducks, geese and ptarmigan, which they eat raw only when forced to do so by difficult travel conditions. Meat constantly simmers in a rectangular stone pot suspended over a seal-oil lamp in the home, and since water is added periodically to the pot, it is possible to have soup or meat at nearly any time of day. During the summer months much of the cooking is done outside and at such times driftwood, small twigs, dried moss and other materials provide fuel.

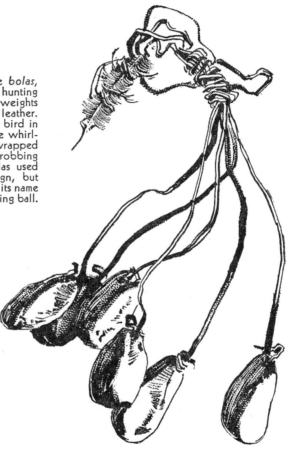

This odd weapon, known as the *bolas*, was used by the Eskimos when hunting birds. It consisted of several weights tied together by narrow strips of leather. The hunter threw the bolas at a bird in flight (or on the ground), and the whirling strips of weighted leather wrapped themselves round the prey, thus robbing it of the power to fly. The bolas used in Argentina is similar in design, but larger in size. The weapon gets its name from the Spanish word *bola* meaning ball.

With the coming of warm weather, the Eskimos store their heavy winter gear in stone caches and, moving inland, enjoy an easier living during the long days of the northern summer. They stalk caribou, catch fish, search for birds' eggs, hunt ducks, and pick various berries. Eskimos hunt along the ocean during the summer months, using the *kayak* and the harpoon to secure the seal and walrus and even the whale.

Hunting and fishing

During the winter, the Eskimos make their homes on the
coast or even far out on the thick ice of the Arctic Ocean. Fishing
and hunting continue but under different circumstances. Fish
are caught through holes in the ice by means of hook and line.
Seals are harpooned at their breathing holes in the ice or shot by
bow and arrow (and by rifle) as they lie basking in the sun.

Clothing Eskimo women are unusually skilled in designing and making
clothing cleverly adapted for use in Arctic conditions. Clothing
is painstakingly cut and fitted to the body of the wearer, since
warmth, lightness, durability and flexibility are desirable features.
Furs make an ideal material for Arctic clothing. Caribou and
seal skins are most frequently employed, but use is made of such
other furs as fox, polar bear, rabbit and wolverine. The women
take pleasure in creating attractive designs with furs of varying
hues. The average costume is a hooded tunic, fur trousers, sealskin boots and mitts. In order to provide warmth during severe
weather, two suits are often worn, one over the other. Although
Eskimo winter clothing may appear bulky, it is actually light,
warm and flexible. During the nineteenth century, European
explorers were to discover that none of their own garments could
compare with those of the Eskimo for comfort and protection.

Homes The type of winter house used by the Eskimos varies with the
region. In districts where driftwood is available, the people construct homes partially sunk into the earth, often dug into a sloping
bank. Floors and walls are made of flat stones while roofs are
built of wooden poles covered with skins and sod. It is in the
Central Eskimo region that the well-known, round snow-house
is commonly used. Some of these dome-like structures, built of
snow-blocks, are fitted with additions serving as storm porches,
store rooms, dog shelters and entrance corridors. It should be
noted that the term *igloo* simply means "house" to the Eskimo—
any kind of house—and does not apply solely to the snow-house.

The summer shelters of the Eskimos are usually leather tents
made of sealskin or caribou hide. The hides are often scraped
so thin that light makes its way through as it does in a modern
canvas tent. It is actually much easier for many of the Eskimos to
secure a skin covering for the tent than to find the wooden poles

which support it. Made from driftwood or large bones, the tent poles are carefully preserved and carried from one camping place to another.

Igloos actually contain more household articles than did most **Household** early Indian homes. On a low platform are spread fur robes and **articles** sleeping bags. Over the seal-oil lamp hangs a rack for drying clothes, and not far away from the lamp lie soapstone bowls, wooden dishes, ladles, knives and cooking forks. There is usually a collection of numerous other articles including wooden snow-shovels, skin water pails, leather bags, baskets, feather whisks, birdskin towels, wooden sun-goggles and bone beaters for knocking snow from clothing.

Eskimo men and women are skilled craftsmen, tools being among the most important articles found in the home. In a wooden box or leather bag a man keeps his collection of tools— knives, scrapers, picks, hammers, adzes and bow-drills. Among a woman's tools are awls (pointed instruments for punching holes in leather), needles, scrapers and the *ulu*, a semi-circular knife that has many uses in the preparation of furs and hides.

In winter, transportation and travel is almost entirely by **Travel** means of dog sleds, large sturdy affairs, some of which exceed fifteen feet in length. The sled is composed of two long wooden runners connected together by a series of stout crossbars. Given a good sled with iced runners, a well-trained dog team can pull a half-ton load at a rate of about seven miles an hour. These half-savage dogs possess incredible endurance, travelling for days on only a little frozen fish for nourishment and sleeping outdoors in a snowbank that forms around them as they lie resting.

In summer, the Eskimos travel inland on foot carrying their tents, household articles and hunting equipment. In this work they are assisted by dogs, fitted with two small packs, one on either side of the animal. Travel may also be done by means of the *umiak* and the *kayak*.

The umiak is a broad open boat, strong and large enough to carry thirty people, their equipment and their dogs. It is constructed by stretching a large covering of skins over a stout framework of wood. Unlike the canoe, the umiak is rowed by means of broad-bladed oars, and a person sitting at the stern steers the boat with a paddle. The umiak is often referred to as being a "woman's boat," because the women play the major part in the loading and operation of the craft.

Eskimos cover a kayak. This is a task normally undertaken during the warm months of spring. The men construct the light framework of the watercraft with care to ensure that the kayak will be strong, yet light and flexible. Women prepare the sealskin covering by scraping the skins clean, washing them, and then sewing them together with a double waterproof seam. In the illustration, the cover is being drawn over the bottom of the kayak. After this operation is completed, the skins will be sewn together underneath, thus completely enclosing the hull, except for the small round cockpit.

The kayak, basically a hunting or fishing canoe, is used by the men. It is a long, slender structure, one of the most gracefully-designed watercraft ever conceived by man. Pointed sharply at both ends, the wooden framework is completely covered with sealskin except for a "manhole," a round opening in the deck circled by a wooden rim constructed to fit the owner. Pushing his legs through the hole, the Eskimo seats himself on the bottom of the kayak, pulls the lower edges of his jacket over the wooden rim, picks up his double-bladed paddle and is off. Eskimo hunters are exceedingly skilful in the use of these craft, some of them being able to capsize the kayak and themselves into the water and come up on the other side. Even after this difficult operation, no water finds its way into the interior of the canoe.

The artistic efforts of the Eskimos are mainly confined to the **Crafts** carving of figures in ivory or stone. Possessed of patience, skill and keen powers of observation, their artists create carvings of a charming simplicity and beauty representing men, women, children and animals. In the western Arctic, where wood is relatively plentiful, Eskimo craftsmen design and carve wooden masks displaying unusually fine patterns and colour variations. It is only in recent years that we have begun to appreciate the remarkably creative talents possessed by these people of the northern coasts.

Today, many Eskimos are in close contact with trading posts **Modern life** or settlements and have moved away from the ancient ways of life. In their wooden cabins or caribou tents may be found rifles, outboard motors, lamps, sewing machines, musical instruments, radios, china dishes, metal cooking utensils and clothing of cotton or wool. Fewer Eskimos are now dependent upon hunting and fishing for a living. Some are employed by the Canadian government as construction workers on northern airfields or by industries established in the north. More and more of their children are attending schools. The younger people, in particular, are anxious to enjoy the benefits of the modern world.

TWO / *Early Expeditions to North America*

THE VOYAGES OF THE VIKINGS, ABOUT A.D. 1000

CHRISTOPHER COLUMBUS RE-DISCOVERS
NORTH AMERICA

SPANISH SETTLEMENTS IN NORTH AMERICA

JOHN CABOT EXPLORES THE EAST COAST, 1497

VERRAZANO ON THE EAST COAST, 1523

INTEREST OF EUROPE IN THE NEW WORLD

VOYAGES OF JACQUES CARTIER, 1534 TO 1541

CARTIER VISITS STADACONA AND HOCHELAGA

SIEUR DE ROBERVAL

7

EUROPEANS REACH NORTH AMERICA

It is one of the odd facts of history that large numbers of Asiatics could move to North America and settle and live there for thousands of years without Europeans being aware of them. The Europeans were not only ignorant of the Asiatic-Americans, but ignorant of the very land masses on which they lived.

It was probably the sea-roving Vikings of Norway who first **Eric the Red, 982** sailed across the North Atlantic to this continent. About the year A.D. 870, a number of these adventurous people had made their way to Iceland where they established an important settlement. One of the later settlers, Eric the Red, was forced into temporary exile after he had killed a man in a quarrel. During his exile, Eric the Red made a voyage westward (about A.D. 982) and eventually found himself off a rugged coast marked by mountains, fiords and grassy meadows. Delighted with the region, Eric called it *Greenland*. Within a few years he had established a Viking settlement on the western coast of the big island.

In the year 986, another Viking who lived in Iceland, **Bjarni, 986** Bjarni Herjulfson, decided to spend Christmas with his father in Greenland. During the voyage, he encountered a storm that blew him off his course, and he was later surprised to see before him a strange shore backed by a thick green forest. This, he realized, could not be Greenland; this was a land unknown to the Viking people.

Bjarni seems to have displayed remarkably little interest in the land, for without making a landing, he sailed north-eastward to Greenland. It is almost certain that the wooded region he left behind him was Labrador. Bjarni, then, may be the first European to have seen the continent of North America.

News of the unknown land to the west caused some interest in Greenland, and among those who listened to the tale was Leif Ericson, son of Eric the Red.

A Viking chieftain stands on the deck of his high-prowed longship.   He is dressed in a stout leather jacket, thick woollen stockings held by cross garters and a conical metal helmet decorated with wings.   The vessel itself is relatively small, perhaps seventy feet in length, and is fitted with a large square sail and banks of oars on each side.   It was in such ships that the Vikings sailed to Iceland, Greenland and North America.

About the year 1000, Leif, blown off his course while sailing between Norway and Greenland, made his well-known voyage along the eastern coast of North America, probably skirting the shores of what are now Labrador, Newfoundland and Nova Scotia.

It may even be that he reached a point as far south as Cape Cod in the present-day state of Massachusetts. According to one of the old Viking *sagas* or tales: "For a long time he (Leif) was tossed about upon the ocean and came upon lands of which he had previously no knowledge. There were self-sown wheat fields and vines growing there."

Although Leif Ericson was content with one voyage to North America, others followed his sea route to the west. Members of his own family and other Vikings attempted to found settlements on this continent, but these were short-lived affairs marked by Indian attacks and by quarrels among the Vikings themselves.

One of the sagas describes the adventures of a Viking expedi- **Karlsefni** tion led by Karlsefni who built cabins, made contact with the Indians and engaged in some trade. According to the tale the natives were pleased to exchange their furs for small bits of bright red cloth. It seems that business was progressing very well until:

a bull, which belonged to Karlsefni and his people, ran out from the woods, bellowing loudly. This so terrified the Skrellings (Indians), that they sped out to their canoes, and then rowed away to the southward along the coast. For three entire weeks nothing was seen of them. At the end of this time, however, a great multitude of Skrelling boats was discovered approaching from the south, as if a stream were pouring down, and all of their staves were waved in a direction contrary to the course of the sun, and the Skrellings were all uttering loud cries. Thereupon, Karlsefni and his men took red shields and displayed them. The Skrellings sprang from their boats, and they met them, and fought together. . . .

It now seemed clear to Karlsefni and his people, that although the country thereabouts was attractive, their life would be one of constant dread and turmoil by reason of the inhabitants of the country, "so they forthwith prepared to leave, and determined to return to their own country."

Viking dreams of colonizing the lands across the ocean were given up, and even the Greenland settlement mysteriously disappeared before the year 1400.

It was the search for sea routes to China and India which eventually brought Europeans back to North America. When the old trading routes between Europe and Asia were cut off by the unfriendly Turks after 1453, Europeans sought new ways of reaching the Orient. Portuguese navigators concentrated on the discovery of a sea route around Africa and on to India. This ambitious plan was almost accomplished when, in 1492, **Christopher Columbus, 1492** Christopher Columbus, an Italian in the service of Spain, sailed westward across the Atlantic in search of India and China, and landed on San Salvador Island in the West Indies.

Columbus misunderstood the true meaning of his discovery, for he believed the island he visited lay off the coast of Asia. On February 15, 1493, he wrote an enthusiastic letter to a friend at the Spanish court. The letter began as follows:

> As I know that you will have pleasure from the great victory which our Lord hath given me in my voyage, I write you this by which you shall know that in thirty-three days I passed over to the Indies with the fleet which the most illustrious King and Queen, our Lords, gave me; where I found very many islands peopled with inhabitants beyond number. And of them all I have taken possession for their Highnesses, with proclamation and the royal standard displayed.

It is evident that Columbus was very much impressed by the islands and that he thought them of worth to Spain. In the same letter he states:

> This is a land to be desired,—and once seen, never to be relinquished,—in which, in a place most suitable and best for its proximity to the gold mines and for traffic with the mainland both on this side (Europe) and with that yonder belonging to the Great Can (China), I took possession of a large town which I named the city of Navidad. And I have made fortification there . . . and I have left therein men enough, with arms and artillery and provisions for more than a year.

Spanish settlement Within an amazingly brief span of years, Spaniards were settled in various parts of the West Indies, along the Gulf of Mexico and around the shores of the Caribbean Sea. Fleets of high-towered galleons carried a stream of gold and silver from the New World to the homeland of Spain. The favoured position of the newcomers, however, was not long to remain unchallenged. Other European nations were stirring; other peoples were becoming interested in the lands across the Atlantic.

It is possible that between the time of the Vikings and that European fishermen of Christopher Columbus other Europeans may have reached the coast of North America, but records of such voyages are obscure. There are suggestions here and there in various historical documents that French and English fishermen may have been fishing off Newfoundland fifty years before Columbus crossed the Atlantic. We know that English west-country fishermen and traders out of Bristol were visiting Iceland in the fourteenth century. It is possible that some of them, and perhaps fishermen from Brittany, found the Grand Banks off Newfoundland after being blown off course en route to Iceland. The Banks are only a few fathoms beneath the surface of the sea, and to this day are one of the world's greatest fishing grounds. It would not be surprising if these fishermen kept news of this rich find to themselves, and quietly voyaged across the Atlantic each year to make their hauls for codfish.

It has been suggested, too, that a Danish seaman, John Scolp John Scolp reached the eastern mainland of Canada as early as 1472. But if such a voyage took place, it had little effect upon either Europe or North America.

8

THE ENGLISH AND FRENCH
RE-DISCOVER NORTH AMERICA

**Voyage of
John Cabot,
1497**   Five years after the first voyage of Christopher Columbus,
King Henry VII of England sent an expedition westward across
the Atlantic.   In command was an Italian navigator, Giovanni
Caboto, better known as John Cabot.   In his letter patent granting
permission for the voyage the King wrote:

> . . . Be it knowen that we have given and granted, and by these
> presents do give and grant for us and our heires, to our welbeloved
> John Cabot citizen of Venice, to Lewis, Sebastian and Santius, sonnes of
> the sayd John, and to the heires of them, and every of them, and their
> deputies full and free authority, leave and power to saile to all parts,
> countreys, and seas of the East, of the West, and of the North . . . to
> seeke out, discover and finde whatsoever isles, countreys, regions or
> provinces of the heathen and infidels whatsoever they be, and in what
> part of the world soever they be, which before this time have bene
> unknowen to all Christians: we have granted to them . . . and have
> given them licence to set up our banners and ensigns in every village,
> towne, castle, isle or maine land of them newly found . . .

Cabot sailed in a tiny vessel, the *Matthew* of Bristol, to the
eastern coast of North America, but had no opportunity to capture
cities, towns or castles.   It is probable that he touched on the
shores of Newfoundland, Cape Breton Island, and perhaps Labrador.   On a second voyage the following year, he skirted the coast
from Labrador to a point which may have been as far south as
present-day Virginia or the Carolinas.

Cabot, like Columbus, believed himself to be in some
unknown part of Asia, but he could not find the legendary wealth
of the Orient.   For this reason his voyages were a disappointment
to his sponsors, the English merchants of Bristol.   However, the
explorations of John Cabot became important in later years, for
they formed the basis of England's claim to territory in North
America.

John Cabot approaches the coast of what is now Cape Breton Island. A typical 15th century vessel, the *Matthew* was known as a "round ship" because it was very broad from side to side and very short from bow to stern. Relatively small by today's standards, the *Matthew* probably weighed no more than eighty tons. Note the very large area of canvas contained in the square sail of the main mast.

Following the two voyages of Cabot and the publicity given to his reports of the fisheries, there was a surprising amount of activity along the eastern coast of the new-found continent. English, French, Basque and Portuguese fishing vessels made their way to the Grand Banks and explorers examined the shore lines. In 1500 and 1501 a Portuguese nobleman, Gaspar Corte Reale, explored parts of Newfoundland and Labrador. Between 1504 and 1509 several French ships carried out further explorations.

In 1523, a more important French expedition, led by an Italian navigator, Giovanni da Verrazano, crossed the Atlantic and touched on the North American coast near present-day Virginia. Turning northward, he followed the coast to Newfoundland. A member of the expedition, describing the coastline wrote:

Voyage of Verrazano, 1523

And sayling forwards, wee founde certaine small Rivers and armes of the Sea, that enter at certaine creekes, washing the shore on both sides as the coast lyeth. And beyonde this wee sawe the open Countrie rising in height above the sandie shore, with many fayre fieldes and plaines, full of mightie great woods, some verie thicke and some thinne, replenished with divers sortes of trees, as pleasant and delectable to beholde as is possible to imagine . . . And the lande is full of many beastes, as Stags, Deare, and Hares, and likewise of Lakes and pooles of Fresh water, with great plentie of foules, conveint for all kinds of pleasant game . . .

After giving the name Nova Francia or *New France* to the eastern shores, Verrazano sailed back to Europe. This voyage caused much interest in France, but the nation was at war and so for the next ten years could spare no money for ventures to the New World.

In the meantime, two more expeditions, one English and the other Spanish, examined the gulfs and bays of eastern Canada.

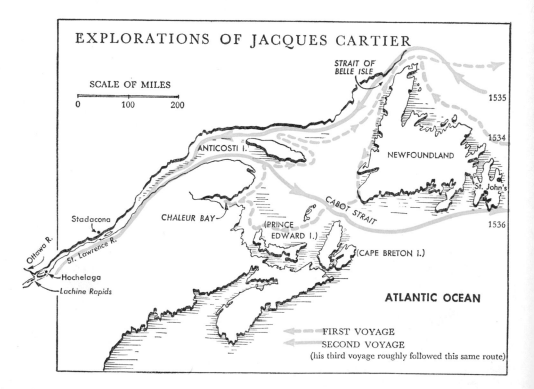

EXPLORATIONS OF JACQUES CARTIER

England, France, Spain and Portugal had all shown a commercial interest in the north-eastern coastal waters of the continent, but none had as yet penetrated inland or established permanent colonies in the huge region of the north. It was just a matter of time, however, until one of these nations should make the attempt.

The French king, Francis I, seeking a passage to the fabled East through this western land barrier, actually took the first important step in this direction with the three voyages of Jacques Cartier. During the first of these, in 1534, the famous mariner, making his way through the ice-floes of the Strait of Belle Isle, explored the shores of the Gulf of St. Lawrence, chanced upon the shores of a fair land (Prince Edward Island) and found a passage (the St. Lawrence River) leading westward. But it was late in the season and he left a close examination of this waterway until the following year.

Cartier's first voyage, 1534

Sent out again to North America in 1535 to find the water route to India and China, Cartier put in at a tiny bay near Anticosti Island on August 10. That day being the Feast of St. Lawrence, Cartier named the waters *Baye Sainct Laurens*. In later years the name St. Lawrence was applied freely to the gulf and the river itself.

Cartier's second voyage, 1535

Cartier sailed upriver, noting sadly that it was fresh water, and came upon the Indian village of Stadacona (near present-day Quebec City), and a second village, Hochelaga (near present-day Montreal). While at Hochelaga, he climbed a steep hill which he named *Le Mont Royal*. From its crest he looked in admiration over the sweeping countryside. He described the scene in these words:

> Towards the north there is a range of mountains, running east and west, and another range to the south. Between these ranges lies the finest land it is possible to see, being arable, level and flat. And in the midst of the flat region one saw the river (St. Lawrence) extending beyond the spot where we left our long-boats. At that point there is the most violent rapid it is possible to see (the Lachine Rapids), which we were unable to pass. And as far as the eye can reach, one sees that river, large, wide and broad, which came from the south-west and flowed near three fine conical mountains, which we estimated to

be fifteen leagues away. And it was told us and made clear by signs by our three local Indian guides, that there were three more such rapids in the river, like the one where lay our long-boats; but through lack of an interpreter, we could not make out what the distance was from one to another. Then they explained to us by signs that after passing these rapids, one could navigate along that river for more than three moons. . . .

The Indians told Cartier that another river (the Ottawa) led to a series of fresh-water seas, the largest of which was the farthest west "many moons journey"—and the Indians did not know if "there were ever man heard of that found out the end thereof." Cartier thought that this distant sea might lead to the Western Sea and thus to China

The French were hearing for the first time of the Great Lakes.

Cartier was doubly disappointed that he had found neither a salt-water route to the East nor wealthy Indian kingdoms in the valley of the St. Lawrence, but he was shrewd enough to realize that here was a land that should be possessed, a land worthy of French settlement. After a miserable winter spent near Stadacona, Cartier returned to France where he gave glowing accounts of the regions he had visited.

Cartier's third voyage, 1541 Five years later, in 1541, Cartier took part in a third expedition, this time as captain-general and master pilot under the command of one of the king's favourites, Jean Francois de la Roque, Sieur de Roberval. The aim of the venture was to establish a permanent French colony from which explorers would be sent out to find a way to the East and also to search for rich Indian kingdoms. In the beginning Cartier held high hopes for this endeavour, but as time went by he became discouraged. Roberval was slow in organizing the expedition and in the collection of supplies; few people except prisoners from the jails could be persuaded to cross the ocean as settlers.

Eventually, Cartier sailed from France, hoping that Roberval would follow in a few weeks' time with more ships and men. But the commander did not follow, and Cartier was forced to spend another difficult winter near Stadacona. He and his men were

During the winter of 1535-36, Cartier's men at Stadacona suffered terribly from scurvy. By the middle of April more than twenty-five had died, and at least forty of the survivors were seriously ill. Fearing that the Indians might attack if they discovered that the French company was so weak, Cartier ordered the dead to be buried secretly in the snow during the hours of darkness.

short of supplies and equipment; some of the party died of scurvy. In the spring of 1542 Cartier was only too pleased to set sail for home. At Newfoundland he met Roberval with a party of settlers bound for the big river, but Cartier would not turn back with the newcomers. During the night he slipped from the harbour (St. John's), and steered eastward toward France.

Roberval pushed up the St. Lawrence and took over the small fort erected by Cartier's men, but he, too, was anxious to sail for France after a long, cold North American winter.

Although Cartier's explorations did not lead to settlement, **Results of Cartier's efforts** they gave France a very sound claim to the land lying in the valley of the St. Lawrence, a claim which in future years was to become

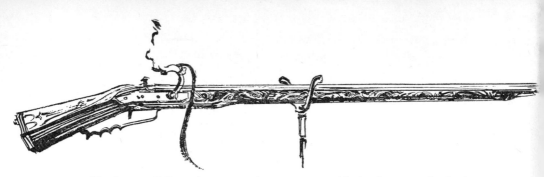

This firearm of Cartier's time was known as a matchlock. It was really the first improvement in handguns since their invention in the fourteenth century. The earlier weapons had consisted merely of a tube closed at one end and secured to a straight piece of wood that served as a stock. The first hand guns were loaded through the open end with gunpowder and lead balls and fired by touching a burning wick or "slow match" to the powder. The matchlock was much more mechanically reliable and accurate than the weapons which preceded it.

extremely valuable. More importantly, Cartier's explorations of the Gulf of St. Lawrence and his careful charting of its waters drew French fishing vessels westward into the gulf to ply the new and valuable fishing grounds he had discovered. (Cartier had, for example, taken careful note of the in-shore fishing of the Micmac Indians living in what is now New Brunswick.) The French fisheries thus increased their area and, in so doing, moved in towards the mainland where they were to come in closer contact with Indians eager to exchange fur pelts for the axes, knives and other iron tools of Europe.

SUMMARY—SECTION II

In the ninth and tenth centuries, the restless, adventurous Norsemen or Vikings sailed away from their homes in northern Europe to raid and occupy parts of the coasts of Europe. Some of them sailed out into the north Atlantic and settled in Iceland. Still others moved further westward to land in Greenland.

About the year 1000, a Viking ship, blown off course on its passage to Greenland, found yet another land in the west — the continent we call North America.

In later years, ships set out from Greenland carrying Vikings to this westernmost land, but no permanent settlements were established, and by 1400 even the Greenland colony had mysteriously vanished.

About this same time, 1400, the invention of a reliable compass and the astrolabe made a long ocean voyage a practical operation.

Able at last to set a sailing course and plot their position at sea, Portuguese navigators began to chart their way down the west coast of Africa.

In 1453, the Turks captured the port of Constantinople and began to tax the Eastern gold, jewels, silks, rugs and spices destined for the palaces, castles and market-places of Europe. Accustomed for centuries to selling these luxury goods, the merchants of Europe were outraged at the taxes which increased the prices of their merchandise. They wished there was some other route by which they could bring in the riches of India, Cathay, and the East Indies.

After 1453, Portuguese mariners pushed on further down the coast of Africa. By 1488, after much voyaging, they rounded the southernmost tip of Africa. The rich lands of the East must lie just a little further on. Another seaman, Christopher Columbus, heard about those long difficult sea journeys. However, many of the stories he had heard and read suggested that the world was round, and he began to believe that if this was so, he could reach the fabled East by a shorter route—westward across the Atlantic. Thus, the merchants of Europe would have direct and less expensive contact with the storehouses of the East.

Columbus did not find the Indies he sought but he did find the New World. Spanish settlers quickly followed his western route and made their homes in the islands of the Caribbean Sea and around its shores.

It was the news of Cabot's voyage of 1497 that startled Europe and made it aware of a whole new land in the west. From this time on, various English, French and Spanish expeditions cruised up and down the Atlantic coast of North America, and European fishermen worked the Grand Banks off Newfoundland. However, it was not until the voyages of Jacques Cartier between 1534 and 1542 that a European country became interested in the northern regions of America. Cartier was sent to find a passage through to Asia. He never found it, and French attempts to settle and then explore westward came to nothing. France lost interest while England at this time had no interest in westward exploration. North America was ignored by Europeans except for the fishermen who sailed off Newfoundland and sometimes came to the mainland for fresh water. But Cartier had shown the way to new fishing grounds in the western waters of the Gulf of St. Lawrence, and more and more French fishermen began to sail beyond Newfoundland to try their luck in the offshore fisheries.

THREE / *The Beginnings of New France*

THE BEGINNINGS OF THE FUR TRADE

CHAMPLAIN ON THE ST. LAWRENCE, 1603

FOUNDING OF PORT ROYAL, 1605

THE ORDER OF GOOD CHEER

FOUNDING OF QUEBEC, 1608

CHAMPLAIN'S JOURNEYS OF EXPLORATION

CHAMPLAIN AND THE IROQUOIS

EARLY RÉCOLLET AND JESUIT MISSIONARIES

LOUIS HÉBERT

THE COMPANY OF NEW FRANCE, 1627

A SCOTTISH SETTLEMENT IN ACADIA, 1628

QUEBEC SURRENDERS TO THE ENGLISH, 1629

QUEBEC RETURNED TO THE FRENCH, 1632

MAISONNEUVE FOUNDS MONTREAL, 1642

DESTRUCTION OF THE HURON MISSIONS, 1648

ADAM DOLLARD AT THE LONG SAULT
ON THE OTTAWA, 1660

9

THE FRENCH IN ACADIA

Discouraged by the hardships of the north, the French looked southward in the Americas to the regions claimed by the Portuguese and the Spanish. It was dangerous to compete for settlement in these lands, but the French were determined to secure a place in the New World. In 1555, an unsuccessful attempt was made to form a colony in Brazil, and in 1564, a settlement established in Florida was wiped out by the Spaniards. It was not until the opening years of the seventeenth century that French endeavours showed some signs of success.

Although the French crown made no attempt to establish **Fur trade** another colony on the St. Lawrence until nearly sixty years after Cartier's voyages, the French had not forgotten this part of the world. Fishermen continued to sail the Grand Banks and those from St. Malo, Rouen and La Rochelle were buying a few furs from the Indians of the lower St. Lawrence valley. The chief trading place was at Tadoussac, where the Saguenay River joins the St. Lawrence. Here, where codfishers, whalers and walrus hunters met to process and pack their catches and refill their water casks, they met Algonkian Indians who were more than willing to trade their fur cloaks for brightly-coloured European clothing and such items as combs and beads, but in particular for iron tools.

During the latter half of the sixteenth century this casual fur **Beaver** trading changed into a serious business enterprise financed by **hats** groups of merchants in France. At first, fashion decreed the use of fur as trimmings for cloaks and gowns but when a way was found to utilize the soft hairs of beaver pelt to make felting for hats, the handsome beaver hat immediately became an essential part of a wealthy man's costume. The tremendous demand in

Europe for such hats turned the trade in furs into a major business. French merchants began to band together to secure a trade monopoly, that is, the sole right to engage in fur trading. As it happened, the French crown was willing to grant trading rights if a company of fur merchants applying for a monopoly agreed to take settlers out to North America and also agreed to maintain their settlements.

The race for the fur monopoly began towards the end of the century, and for the next two hundred years the history of Canada is mainly the history of the trade in beaver pelts.

In 1600 a vain attempt was made to found a permanent colony and fur post at Tadoussac. After one winter the survivors returned to France.

Samuel de Champlain, 1603

Three years later another expedition, sent out by the same fur company, sailed to the St. Lawrence to explore the river and obtain furs. The ships visited Tadoussac and pushed upriver to where the villages of Stadacona and Hochelaga had once stood. Apart from a valuable cargo of furs, this journey is important for only one reason. It gave one Frenchman his first view of a region he was to know so well in later years. His name was Samuel de Champlain. It is evident that he was impressed by what he saw, for in his journal he wrote:

We came to anchor at Quebec which is a narrow part of the said river of Canada, some three hundred paces broad. At these narrows on the north side is a very high mountain, which slopes down on both sides; all the rest is a level and beautiful country where there is good land covered with trees such as oaks, cedars, birches, fir-trees and aspens and also wild fruit-bearing trees and vines . . .

Samuel de Champlain had been trained first as a soldier and later as a seaman. He had fought for France, sailed to the West Indies in the service of Spain, and written a book concerning his travels. This book won the author some fame and he was given the title "Royal Geographer" by the king of France.

De Monts, 1604

Champlain soon found himself a member of yet another expedition bound for Canada. This enterprise, begun in 1604, was under the command of a tall, striking Frenchman, Pierre du Guast, Sieur de Monts, a nobleman with a new plan for French colonization which would locate settlers on the Atlantic shores of North America rather than in the valley of the St. Lawrence. By doing this, De Monts believed that he could avoid cold winters and hostile Indians. On the coast bordering the south shore of the St. Lawrence was a land known to the French as "La Cadie", and later as *Acadia*. It may be that this term was developed from an Indian word, "aquoddie", that referred to a sea fish, the pollock.

It was Acadia, then, that De Monts chose for his new experiment in settlement. Along with him went 120 workers and a small band of noblemen. Among the latter group were Jean de Biencourt de Poutrincourt and Samuel de Champlain.

After crossing the Atlantic, De Monts' two ships turned into the Bay of Fundy and proceeded north-eastward to what is now Annapolis Basin, a charming place that offers an excellent harbour. However, they decided not to establish themselves there, but on Saint Croix island on the other side of the Bay of Fundy. Perhaps they believed that they could defend a small island against attack more easily than a section of the mainland. At any rate, St. Croix proved a poor choice: it was exposed to harsh winds that blew from the north-west. In spite of the shelter offered by sturdy buildings, the company suffered severely during the cold months. Nearly half the men died of scurvy before the winter dragged away.

It was clear to members of the company that the island would not do as a permanent place of settlement. In June, 1605, De Monts, Champlain and a few others set off in a ship to find a better location. Leaving the Bay of Fundy, they steered southward along the coast of what are now the New England states. Although the party sailed below the shores of Cape Cod, they found no spot that suited them. Returning to St. Croix, they decided that the settlement should be moved to Annapolis Basin, the place that had so pleased them the previous year.

The *Habitation* at Port Royal was built by De Monts in 1605. Small buildings were grouped tightly about a rectangular courtyard whose dimensions were about sixty-four feet by fifty-two feet. A well was sunk in the centre of this open space. The heavy beams and planks used in construction were all laboriously hewn or sawn by hand. All hardware, too, was created by craftsmen of the French company. Massive chimneys, built of local stone, were lined with brick made from clay dug from a nearby pit. The *Habitation* was destroyed by the English in 1613. That was not the end of its history, however, for it was re-built in 1938 on the original site by the Canadian government. Port Royal stands today as one of the most interesting historical sites in Canada.

Founding of Port Royal, 1605

Here, Port Royal was constructed—a compact settlement protected by a high palisade and cannon resting on raising platforms. Buildings stood side by side around the sides of a rectangular courtyard: the bakery, the kitchen, the dining hall, the trading

V. MOULD

room, the storeroom, the blacksmith shop, the sleeping quarters for the gentlemen and a large dormitory upstairs for the common men of the company.

Fortunately, the first winter was mild and the effects of scurvy not so severe, but twelve persons did die of the disease before the snows disappeared. It seems strange that these Frenchmen knew nothing of the spruce-bark remedy which Jacques Cartier had used at Stadacona.

The following autumn Champlain and Poutrincourt made a second voyage southward past Cape Cod, but their voyage brought no important results. On his return to Port Royal, Champlain faced his third and last Acadian winter, a prospect which caused him some concern. Finally, he founded a new club, *L'Ordre du* **Order of** *Bon Temps* (The Order of Good Cheer), to keep up the spirits **Good Cheer** of the gentlemen and improve their winter diet. Champlain's plan was to have each member in turn act as chief steward, taking responsibility for the meals of the day. The idea was successful from the beginning, and the gentlemen entered into the spirit of the occasion with pleasure and enthusiasm. As their turns came round, they spent their time searching for delicacies to add to the bounty of the dining hall. There was, of course, considerable competition among the members of the Order, for it was considered a disgrace to arrange a poor meal.

Each day, in an elaborate ceremony, a colourful procession moved from the kitchen to the dining hall. At the head of the line marched the chief steward carrying his staff of office and wearing the collar of the Order. Close behind him came the others bearing platters and bowls that sent delicious odours floating about the hall. The members sat down to dinners that sometimes rivalled the famous meals of Paris.

Marc Lescarbot, a French lawyer, poet and historian, who spent some time at Port Royal, described the dinners in these words:

> . . . I have already said that we had an abundance of game, such as ducks, bustards, grey and white geese, partridge, larks and other birds; moreover, moose, caribou, beaver, otter, bear, rabbits, wild-cats, nibachés (raccoon) and other animals such as the savages caught, whereof we made dishes well worth those of the cook-shop in the *Rue aux Ours,* and far more; for all our meats none is so tender as moose-meat (whereof we made excellent pasties) and nothing so delicate as the beaver's tail. Yea, sometimes we had a half-dozen sturgeon at once, which the savages brought us, part of which we bought, and allowed them to sell the remainder publicly and barter it for bread, of which our men had abundance. As for the ordinary rations brought from France, they were distributed equally to great and small alike . . .

In the writings of Lescarbot we also find reference to the attendance of Indians at the meals of the Order:

> . . . At these proceedings we always had twenty or thirty savages, men, women, girls and children, who looked on at our manner of

service. Bread was given them gratis, as one would to the poor. But as for the Sagamos Membertou, and other chiefs, who came from time to time, they sat at the table eating and drinking like ourselves. And we were glad to see them, while on the contrary, their absence saddened us . . .

The festivities accomplished more than Champlain had dared to hope when he first suggested the plan, for the men became healthier and happier than ever before. In his journal Champlain wrote: "This (the Order), all found useful for their health, and more advantageous than all the medicines that could have been used."

The Order of Good Cheer was invented to keep the gentlemen of Port Royal in good health and spirits. The members vied with each other in the preparation of lavish dinners, probably served on pewter plates and bowls. The ceremony and humour accompanying these dinners relieved the monotony of life in the wilderness. Some of the gentlemen of this time wore long shoulder-length hair, trimmed moustaches and chin whiskers. Others preferred short hair and full, square beards.

The future of Port Royal appeared bright. Frenchmen were learning to cope with the cold Canadian winters. Indians were eager to exchange their furs for trading goods. Unknown to the men at Port Royal, however, things were not going well for them in France. Merchants there were complaining about the high price of beaver skins, while other would-be traders were demanding rights in Acadia. Such men were jealous of De Monts' success, and worked against him at every opportunity. So vigorous were the complaints and demands that the king eventually decided to cancel the charter granting sole trading rights to De Monts.

French leave Port Royal, 1607

In the spring of 1607 the news of the King's decision crossed the Atlantic in the form of a letter commanding the French to abandon Port Royal and return to France. The news, of course, was a severe shock to the men who had worked so hard to establish a settlement and trading post. However, there was nothing to do but obey and return. Sadly they packed their belongings, loaded their furs and sailed for France.

Port Royal revived, 1610

This was by no means the last of Port Royal: in 1610, the little settlement was re-established by De Poutrincourt and his son, Charles de Biencourt. But Port Royal was not to remain in peace; three years later an English expedition raided and looted the settlement. Biencourt and a few companions fled and took up a wandering life among the Indians. When Poutrincourt died in 1615, he left his Acadian lands and rights to his son, and later when Biencourt died, he left his lands and rights to his friend, Charles La Tour.

Charles La Tour

Charles La Tour built a fort and trading post at Cape Sable on the southern tip of Nova Scotia. He was in fact, if not in title, the ruler of Acadia, and controlled the only French stronghold in the whole region. Thus, a few Frenchmen clung stubbornly to the eastern coast of Canada.

Port Royal and the Order of Good Cheer still exist today. On the site of the old fort stands an exact replica of the original buildings. If you visit it, a guide will show you the kitchen, the dining hall, the room where Champlain slept, the high palisade and the little cannon resting on sturdy platforms. Here is one of the places in Canada where you can feel history in the air about you. Listen and you hear the laughter of French gentlemen from the dining hall, the shout of sentries at the gate, the tramp of marching feet and the murmur of priestly prayers.

The Order of Good Cheer, the oldest social club in North America, has also been revived, thanks to the government of Nova Scotia. In order to qualify for membership, a person is required to spend at least seven days in Nova Scotia. The Order now has several hundred thousand members and its leading official, the Grand Master, is the Governor General of Canada.

10

THE FOUNDING OF QUEBEC

Although De Monts had suffered the loss of his charter, his settlement at Port Royal and much of his personal fortune, he was still interested in the New World. So persuasive was he at court that the king signed another charter granting trading rights for the period of one year. With his remaining money and funds borrowed from merchants, De Monts outfitted an expedition of three vessels. In command of these he placed his friend, Samuel de Champlain.

Founding of Quebec, 1608

In the late spring of 1608, Champlain crossed the Atlantic, sailed up the St. Lawrence, and again approached that place where the river narrowed, the place where once had stood the Indian village of Stadacona. After passing the Isle of Orleans, he came in sight of the towering cliff that casts a shadow on the St. Lawrence. Champlain wrote in his journal:

. . . From the island of Orlean to Quebec is one league, and I arrived there on July 3. On arrival I looked about for a place suitable for our settlement, but could find none better suited than the point of Quebec, so called by the natives . . .

Knowing that he must have comfortable shelter and strong defence for his company, Champlain ordered an immediate start on construction. During the bustling activity which followed, the ring of axes, the pounding of hammers and the hum of saws carried through the forest and over the waters of the river. The men erected three-storey buildings. At the second floor level, connecting galleries made communication between buildings simple and increased the potentialities of defence. The whole structure was surrounded by a high wall and a moat fifteen feet wide and six feet deep. Champlain's *Habitation* was strong enough to withstand the shock of Indian assault.

Although the weather was pleasant and building progress

Indians arrive at Champlain's *Habitation*, built at Quebec in 1608. Protection was afforded by a moat and an outer stockade fitted with cannon. Champlain's personal apartment was placed on the lower floor of the front building overlooking the wharf. Directly above him on the second floor were the quarters of the workmen. On the roof of this same structure were erected a flagpole and a small sundial. Champlain's garden can be seen at the lower left of the illustration. The tall tower in the background served as a pigeon house.

very satisfactory, the first days at Quebec were darkened by a serious plot that might have brought tragedy to the company. The leader of the conspiracy, Jean Duval, planned to murder Champlain and take control of the settlement. By good fortune, however, the conspiracy was uncovered before Duval could put his plans into action. Punishment was swift; the rebel leader was executed before the eyes of his fellows. His severed head was stuck on the end of a pike and displayed to remind them that treachery against Champlain was a hazardous business.

With the threat of mutiny gone, life at Quebec settled into a peaceful pattern. Champlain, delighted with the glories of the fall season, walked through the crimson forests and travelled the river for short distances. A natural sportsman, he enjoyed hunting the plentiful game in the region.

Winter hardships
The sharp, bright days of autumn gave way to falling leaves, cold winds, swirling snow and an icebound river. Before the final freeze-up, some of the company returned to France with bales of furs, leaving Champlain with only twenty-eight companions. During the winter months history repeated itself—half the men died of scurvy and other illnesses. Only fourteen men were alive when the snows melted and the great river ran free again, but fresh food worked wonders and by June they had regained their strength and their spirits.

The arrival of a vessel from France in the spring of 1609 brought news that was scarcely encouraging. De Monts' monopoly was coming to an end. At any time now, other Frenchmen might appear on the St. Lawrence to try their luck in a promising business.

Rival groups of Indians
Champlain was but a short time at Quebec when he realized that his settlement was located between the lands of warring Indian groups. Indeed, it is possible that he suspected this condition before he established the settlement. Jealousies, quarrels and power struggles were as common in North America as in Europe. North of the St. Lawrence were the Algonquins and Hurons. In the vicinity of Quebec roamed wandering bands of poor Montagnais. South of the river was the League of the Iroquois composed of five tribes welded together into a single nation. The tribes of the League were the fiercest, the strongest and the most intelligent Indians in North America. Not content to live in flimsy wigwams, they erected sturdy lodges protected by palisades; not content to rely for food on hunting and fishing, they cultivated crops of grain and vegetables in their own fields.

Rich and powerful as they were, the Iroquois desired to possess more land and to dominate other tribes. It was only natural that they should be the enemies of their kinsmen, the Hurons, and of the Algonquins and the Montagnais.

The Iroquois had little contact with Quebec and the Frenchmen there. Perhaps that is why Champlain underestimated their strength and their intelligence. It was the tribesmen living north of the St. Lawrence who brought their furs to the settlement and who became friendly with the white men.

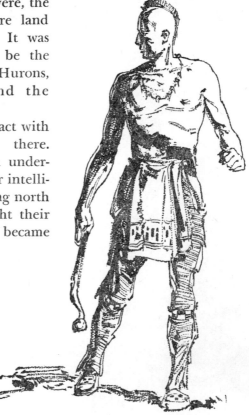

An Iroquois warrior, dressed for the mild weather of spring or early summer, wearing leather leggings, a breech clout, a small kilt and moccasins. During cooler weather his costume would include a warm buckskin shirt. Note that his head is shaven except for a thick ridge of hair across the centre of the crown, a style favoured by a number of Iroquois braves. In his hand he carries a sturdy warclub with a heavy wooden knob at its tip.

At some time or other Champlain must have promised help Champlain's journey of 1609 to the Indians who came to trade at his post. At any rate, word spread through the forests and up the rivers that the French were willing to fight the Iroquois. As a result, in the spring of 1609, a large band of Hurons, Algonquins and Montagnais gathered at Quebec to trade furs and secure French assistance for a raid on the Iroquois. It may be imagined that Champlain was rather startled by this swift development, but he managed to hide his feelings. He really had little choice in the matter, for unless he supported his customers, he ran the risk of losing his trade. Then, too, travelling with a war party gave him an opportunity to explore a new region.

In June, Champlain left Quebec with twelve of his own men and an impressive group of Hurons, Algonquins and Montagnais. The party travelled southwest along the St. Lawrence to where a tributary, the River of the Iroquois (the Richelieu), emptied its waters into the mighty stream. Here the expedition turned and proceeded due south into Iroquois country.

Some distance up the Richelieu, the expedition came upon a waterfall that proved to be an impossible barrier for the French boat. Champlain was annoyed by this unexpected difficulty, for he had been told that the boat would easily pass along the Richelieu to a large lake lying in the south. He was tempted to leave the Indians and return to Quebec, but after a conference, agreed to go on. When he had sent ten of his men back to the St. Lawrence, Champlain and two white companions embarked in Indian canoes and set off once more.

A French musketeer of Champlain's time wearing knee breeches, a short coat and a broad-brimmed hat. His weapon is a musket or arquebus, either being classed as a matchlock. In the illustration the man carries in his left hand a long fuse or match, which is burning. When prepared to fire, he places the match in a lock or clamp attached to the musket. When the trigger is pulled, the clamp shoots forward, plunging the burning match into a shallow pan of gunpowder. The resulting explosion shot a metal ball with great force from the barrel of the weapon. During the act of firing, the musketeer steadies his gun atop a forked rod or rest while the stock is held firmly against his chest.

The early confidence of the war party began to fade as they penetrated deeply into Iroquois territory. As time went by, more and more warriors dropped behind, only to disappear into the forest. The Iroquois reputation for ferocity and savagery was playing upon their fears.

Eventually, the fleet of canoes left the Richelieu and moved out onto the broad surface of a stretch of water, later to become known as Lake Champlain. To the Frenchmen, the lake appeared enormous and beautiful, marked as it was by rugged islands. By the end of July, the voyagers had travelled down the entire length of the lake and had reached the entrance to a second lake (Lake George).

Here, on a warm summer evening, they unexpectedly came upon a solid group of Iroquois canoes. It was too late to retreat, for almost at the same moment the enemy caught sight of the invaders. However, there was to be no battle that day; night was falling and neither party relished a clash on the water. Withdrawing to shore, the Iroquois made camp and began a noisy war dance round blazing camp fires. For most of the night their howls and screams carried across the still waters.

Unwilling to risk a landing, the French and their Indian allies spent the night on the lake, their canoes tied together in bunches. When daylight came, the invaders stirred into quick action. The three Frenchmen put on their metal breastplates and checked their muskets, those clumsy, heavy-stocked arquebuses that were the hand guns of the day. Under Champlain's plan of attack, the Frenchmen remained hidden as the canoes approached shore. Then as the party disembarked, the Indians advanced first, shielding the Europeans from view.

The Iroquois were not slow to meet the challenge. On they came, perhaps two hundred of them, laughing and shouting in supreme confidence. Uneasy at the advance of the enemy, the northern Indians moved aside to reveal the surprise they had in store. There was a shocked silence, a sudden halt, as the Iroquois warriors for the first time laid their eyes on a white man. Champlain himself described the event in these words:

> When I saw them make a move to draw their bows upon us, I took aim with my arquebus and shot straight at one of the three chiefs, and with this shot two fell to the ground and one of their companions

Battle with the Iroquois, 1609

was wounded, who died thereof a little later. I had put four balls into my arquebus. As soon as our people saw this shot so favourable for them, they began to shout so loudly that one could not have heard it thunder, and meanwhile the arrows flew thick on both sides. The Iroquois were much astonished that two men should have been killed so quickly, although they were provided with shields made of cotton thread woven together with wood, which were proof against arrows. This frightened them greatly.

Many Indians would have fled from the battle at the first thunderous roar of the arquebus, but not the Iroquois. They continued to loose a stream of arrows and uttered screams of defiance. Just as they were regaining confidence, however, a second Frenchman stepped forward and fired. This time there was real terror in the ranks of the enemy. One white god they were willing to face, but two of the weird beings were more than they could understand. In panic they fled through the forest.

Springing into swift action, the northern Indians set off in a terrible pursuit, taking prisoners, scalping and killing. That night in a wild celebration, the victors tortured one of their prisoners, using the cruelest possible methods of creating pain. When Champlain could no longer stand the barbarous scene, he sent a musket ball through the young brave's heart.

11

TRADE, TRAVEL AND
INDIAN WARFARE

Indian stories of lands and waters to the west of Quebec continued to interest Champlain. He was particularly intrigued by the descriptions of the vast lakes that spread like seas among the hills and forests. He believed that for the glory of France and for the greater prosperity of the fur trade these areas must be explored and claimed for the crown. Perhaps he would also find a way to the Western Sea and thus to the riches of the East.

In the beginning the friendly Indians themselves stood as a barrier to the westward expansion of the French. Hurons and Algonquins who lived near Lake Huron and along the Ottawa River were opposed to the French travelling beyond a rough stretch of water in the St. Lawrence now known as the Lachine

With his canoe balanced on hands and shoulders, this Indian could move rapidly across a portage. The term portage is derived from a French word *porter* meaning "to carry." It refers to the Indian system of carrying canoes and equipment around rapids in a river or from one body of water to another. The birch-bark canoe was so light that Indians could make long portages of up to twenty-five or thirty miles in length.

Rapids. The tribesmen possibly did not wish the French to have direct contact with other groups of Indians.

Trade at Grand Sault

As time went by, considerable trading took place each spring in the vicinity of Grand Sault (the Lachine Rapids) in addition to that done at Quebec itself. When Champlain's company lost the fur monopoly in 1609, independent French traders made their way to this new bartering place. Some of the newcomers were dishonest in their dealings and many included brandy among their trade goods. This strong liquor, which the Indians called "fire-water", became a curse to the natives and a source of trouble to the traders. Drunken, quarrelsome Indians, mad with brandy, became a sight that was all too common.

Champlain, having little control over the traders, became alarmed. He could see that the French were losing friends without whose help little in the way of exploration could be accomplished. Unless different steps were taken, France would make little headway in the New World. The solution to the problem, he decided, lay in the strict control of trade, in providing missionaries for the Indians and in attempting vigorous exploration to the west.

In 1612, Champlain returned to France to plead for these changes, and his efforts were partly successful, for he was given trading rights in the lands west of Quebec. His duties required him to trade in a friendly way with the Indians, to seek precious minerals (gold, silver and copper were hoped for), and to find the Western Sea.

Nicolas Vignau

While still in Paris, Champlain talked with a young Frenchman, Nicolas Vignau, whom he had sent up the Ottawa to spend a winter with the Algonquins. Vignau now told a vivid story of an adventurous journey through the wilds of North America to a great salt sea lying in the north. There on those cold, grim shores, Vignau said, was the wreck of an English ship. Champlain scarcely believed the tale, and yet its details agreed with those of another story, an English story concerning a navigator, Henry Hudson, who had lost his life on a vast bay somewhere in the north.

On his return to Quebec in the following spring, Champlain took Vignau with him and set out to find this northern sea. Excited by the prospect, the French leader believed he might be on the verge of a great discovery. Perhaps the mysterious sea lying beyond the forests was the true passage to China and the East Indies.

With an Indian guide, Vignau and three other Frenchmen, Champlain paddled up the Ottawa River. It was not an easy journey, for they had to contend with rapids, currents and jagged rocks. In addition to these dangers, there hung over them the constant threat of wandering bands of Iroquois warriors. _{Champlain's}

Champlain's journey of 1613

Through twelve warm days they paddled, made tiresome portages and fought off clouds of mosquitoes. Eventually they made their way to Allumette Lake (near the modern town of Pembroke, Ont.), where there was an Indian village. It was here that Champlain learned a disturbing truth from the Indians: Vignau had never travelled further than Allumette Lake and had never seen the shores of a great salt sea. These facts the Indians knew, for Vignau had spent his time with them in the village. Angry with the young Frenchman for denying the truth of their statements, the Indians were quite prepared to kill the frightened Vignau. Champlain, too, was furious at being duped by his imaginative countryman, but he had no intention of permitting Vignau's death. Of Vignau's final fate we know very little. Perhaps he was expelled from the French settlement; perhaps he disappeared into the forests.

Although disappointed in the result of the journey, Champlain was pleased with the country through which he passed. He claimed the land in the name of the French king:

And before I left, I built a cross of white cedar, bearing the arms of France, which I set up in a prominent place on the shores of the lake (Lower Allumette) and begged the Indians to preserve it, as well as those they would find along the trails by which we had come. They promised me to do this, and that I should find these things again when I came back to their country.

During one portage on the Ottawa, Champlain lost his astrolabe, an instrument he used to calculate latitude. Oddly

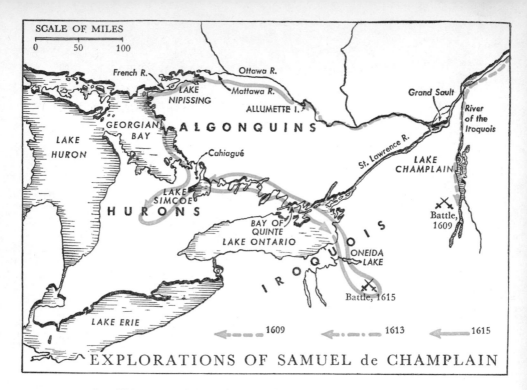

SCALE OF MILES
0   50   100

French R.   Ottawa R.
LAKE
NIPISSING   Mattawa R.
Grand Sault
ALLUMETTE I.
River
of the
Iroquois
GEORGIAN   A L G O N Q U I N S
BAY
LAKE
HURON   Cahiagué   St. Lawrence R.   LAKE
CHAMPLAIN
LAKE
SIMCOE
H U R O N S
Battle,
1609
BAY OF
QUINTE
LAKE ONTARIO   I R O Q U O I S
ONEIDA
LAKE
Battle, 1615
LAKE ERIE
1609   1613   1615

EXPLORATIONS OF SAMUEL de CHAMPLAIN

enough, 254 years later, it was found on a farm in Renfrew
County, Ontario.

Champlain spent 1614 in France where he continued to plead
with government officials for more settlers, more arms, more
supplies and priests to work among the Indians. His appeals were
so effective that a royal charter authorized a new company to
promote French affairs in North America. The new organization
agreed to pay Champlain a salary for administering its business
at Quebec, and, in addition, promised to settle six families each
spring on the shores of the St. Lawrence. The company was to
enjoy an eleven-year trading monopoly in French lands from
Gaspé westward. Champlain also received permission to have
four Récollet friars sent out as missionaries to spread the gospel
among the Indians.

Champlain's journey of 1615-1616 It was, therefore, a pleased and enthusiastic Champlain who
returned to Quebec in 1615. Among the problems awaiting his
attention was a new threat posed by the Iroquois nation. Friendly
Indians informed Champlain that their canoes bringing furs to
Quebec were no longer safe from Iroquois attack. So desperate

was the situation, they said, that unless strong action were taken, trade would be entirely cut off. They assured Champlain that if he would lead the way southward, a band of at least 2,500 warriors would be willing to fight.

Champlain agreed to the plan on the condition that the French were allowed to explore westward from Quebec. In consequence, large groups of Hurons and Algonquins gathered at Grand Sault in preparation for the invasion of the Iroquois country. Champlain, however, was unable to leave Quebec as soon as he had expected, and his impatient allies were left waiting on the river. Tired of inaction and fearful that disaster had befallen the French, the Indians broke camp and set off for home.

Eventually, Champlain and several Frenchmen left Quebec, travelling in two large canoes. One of the men, Etienne Brûlé, an interpreter, had already spent a winter among the northern Indians. Finding no war party at Grand Sault, Champlain turned into the mouth of the Ottawa River and moved north-westward over its waters. Passing Allumette Lake, the party paddled along a river leading west (the Mattawa, a branch of the Ottawa). It was a slow, hard journey filled with the labour of portages and the dangers of rushing white water. After weeks of travel they crossed a lake (Nipissing) and entered another river (the French) that in time led them to a vast expanse of water (Georgian Bay).

Following the eastern margin of the bay, the travellers paddled southward to Huronia, where, in an area stretching from Georgian Bay to Lake Simcoe, lived some 20,000 Hurons, scattered about in more than thirty villages. Moving across country, Champlain came to a large settlement, Cahiagué (which stood near the present Ontario town of Orillia). Here Champlain found the Hurons in a great state of excitement, eager for war against the Iroquois.

In the war councils it was decided that a powerful force should be sent against the Onondagas, an Iroquoian tribe living to the south of Lake Ontario. To further chances of success, Etienne Brûlé was sent south into what is now Pennsylvania to seek the help of the friendly Carantouans.

When plans were completed, the main war party started southward (through the Kawartha Lakes district) to a bay (Quinté) on Lake Ontario. Then, skirting the eastern end of Lake Ontario, they reached the southern shore where the canoes were beached and hidden from sight. Moving inland, the warriors marched in the direction of Lake Oneida, close to which stood an important stronghold of the Onondagas.

In 1615, Champlain tried to storm a fortified Onondaga village. The attack failed because his Indian allies refused to obey his commands. Ignoring the protective shield that had been constructed, they rushed forward into the open only to meet the deadly fire of the defenders. In the background can be seen the high siege tower from which the French directed their musket fire.

When Champlain finally came upon the Indian stronghold, **Battle with the Iroquois, 1615** he was startled by its evident strength. This was no simple little village, but a solid fort well-protected by high palisades. To the French leader the military problem was little different from that presented by the siege of a European castle. His plan was to push a wooden tower up against the palisade wall so that the French on top of the tower could fire musket balls inside the fortress. When the enemy had been terrorized by the musket fire, his Indians could then advance under cover of wide, heavy shields in an effort to set the fort afire.

But when the attack began, all became confusion as the Indians refused to obey orders. After several hours, the Hurons became disheartened and began to talk of retreat. Weakened as he was by a leg wound, Champlain was still ready for another assault, but he could not rally his braves. They bundled the French leader into a large basket, swung him onto the back of a husky Huron and set off at a quick pace in the direction of Lake Ontario.

In the meantime Etienne Brûlé and the friendly Carantouans were approaching the scene of battle, but they arrived too late— two days after the Huron defeat.

When the retreating Hurons arrived at Lake Ontario, they refused men and canoes to take Champlain back to Quebec, fearful that Iroquois pursuers might overtake the party before it could reach home. In any case French muskets would be useful in beating off any pursuers.

Champlain was disturbed at the thought of spending a winter **A winter in Huronia** in Huronia, for there was so much to be done at Quebec. However, as time went by, he realized that here was an excellent opportunity to study Indian life. He spent his visit in observation and enquiry, making careful notes of all that he saw and learned.

All through the winter the Hurons lived in constant fear that the Iroquois might strike in revenge, but no war parties made their appearance. By spring the Indians, regaining some confidence, agreed that Champlain should return to Quebec, and when the rivers ran free again, the French leader journeyed back to his *Habitation*.

Champlain's travels of 1615 and 1616 gave him a much greater knowledge of the region west of Quebec, but he remained unsatisfied. This is evident from his own writings:

> The experience that I have long had in the exploration and discovery of these lands has always had the effect of increasing my courage in seeking, as far as was in my power, the means of accomplishing my purpose to acquire perfect knowledge of certain things which others have doubted . . . For a long time I have been presenting to my Lords of the Council certain proposals and advice, which were always well received; but France has been so embroiled, the last few years, that what is chiefly sought is peace; and there is no money to spend (on exploration) . . . the toil and fatigue are great, but nothing is to be had without toil . . . my task will be to prepare the way for those who, after me, shall desire to engage in this enterprise.

12

SLOW GROWTH AT QUEBEC

As the years passed, the settlement at Quebec showed little growth. There was only a handful of people. The Company was more interested in profits than in its promises of settlement. The original galleried *Habitation* still stood below the cliff, and a scattering of small houses huddled about its palisades. Down by the river were some rickety wharves and a few shabby storehouses. On the cliff-top was a small fort, built by Champlain. When the yellow sun of late afternoon glinted on the river and lighted up the forests, Quebec held a certain charm, but it normally appeared drab and impoverished.

In 1615, near the spot where Jacques Cartier's fort once **Récollet friars** stood, Récollet friars had erected a log building that lay in the shadow of its own stockade. It was here that Fathers Joseph le Caron, Jean d'Olbeau, Denis Jamay and Brother Pacificus du Plessis established their headquarters. It was from here that these devoted men made their daring expeditions into the Indian country. Jean d'Olbeau, who chose the Montagnais as his flock, made an early journey into the north with these people. Joseph le Caron was already among the Hurons when Champlain made his tour of exploration in 1615.

There were some poor ragged clearings about Quebec and a **Arrival of** few crops were growing, but no one devoted himself vigorously **Louis Hébert, 1617** to agriculture—that is, no one did until the coming of Louis Hébert and his family in 1617.

Louis Hébert, an apothecary, had owned a prosperous business in Paris, but the call of North America rang strong in his heart. He had spent a brief interval in the short-lived settlement of Port Royal and it was there that he gained a love for the New World. So strong was this affection that Louis Hébert was easily persuaded by Champlain to bring his family to Quebec. The Héberts came to build a permanent home on the St. Lawrence.

Like Samuel de Champlain, Louis Hébert believed that Quebec could be more than a trading centre; it was a fertile region that could support a large population of colonists.

Louis Hébert was the first farmer in New France.   On the height overlooking early Quebec, he and his family cut down trees and removed stones from the cleared land. They planted wheat and other grains.   Other Frenchmen were slow to follow the Hébert example.   By the time Quebec was captured by the English in 1629, there were only five settlers farming in the area, and among them they had not cleared more than twenty acres of ground.

Louis Hébert built his home on the level ground that caps the great rock of Quebec. Here he erected a rough building and began clearing land on the ten acres granted to him. He cleared, ploughed and seeded his first field the year he arrived. In later years he grew wheat, oats, vegetables and small fruits. Doubtless he had an herb garden that gave him the materials necessary to prepare the drugs and medicines he prescribed for his fellow colonists. Hébert was the first of the French settlers to live by the produce of the soil. He and his family were so industrious that in a short time they possessed a substantial stone house surrounded by well-tilled fields of grain.

On warm evenings, Champlain sometimes walked slowly up the winding pathway to visit his good friends, the Héberts. It was pleasant to talk with the members of this happy family; it was pleasant to look down from the rock on the flat, silvery surface of the St. Lawrence. In all likelihood, Champlain and Hébert chatted and dreamed of the time when the river valley would be patched with farms, webbed with roads, and dotted with towns.

In addition to his farming duties, Louis Hébert was kept busy acting as druggist and doctor in the little settlement. His unselfish devotion to these tasks won him the love and the respect of the people. In the beginning, he received little payment for his services, but in time they were officially recognized. In 1626 he was granted additional land and given the title of Sieur d'Epinay. Thus, Hébert won a degree of prosperity and was admitted to the lesser nobility of France. In time, too, the Hébert daughters married and found homes of their own not too far from the original homestead.

For years, Champlain led rather a lonely life in Canada, for his young wife Hélène had remained in France. His bride had been but twelve years of age when the marriage took place. Probably Champlain believed that Quebec was too isolated and too rough a place for a young girl accustomed to a life of wealth and comfort in France.

In 1620, however, when Madame de Champlain was twenty-two years of age, she came out to join her husband. Her arrival caused nothing less than a sensation in the colony, for Champlain's wife was an attractive woman dressed in the height of Paris fashion. She and the four young ladies who came with her seemed

Madame de Champlain

almost unworldly figures in their gay dresses, tiny shoes and sweeping hats.

Champlain had grown accustomed to the rough conditions at Quebec, but the state of the *Habitation* was undoubtedly a shock to his young wife and her ladies. They were, after all, scarcely prepared for leaking roofs, rattling windows and uneven floors. The young mistress of Quebec could not help feeling depressed by the primitive conditions. Recognizing that the women were disturbed by their new surroundings, Champlain put carpenters to work on repairs, but the buildings still lacked cheerfulness and comfort. The first winter was a dreary one for Madame Champlain; there was little to do and few people to whom she could talk. When the deep snows came and the silent, frosty nights closed in, she felt as confined as if she had been a captive. At times she grew so lonely that she climbed the rugged trail to the crest of the great rock and pushed on to the home of the Héberts.

The people of Quebec and the Indians who came there grew to admire the lonely young woman, but they realized that she was not happy on the St. Lawrence. When she went back to France with Champlain in 1624, they knew she never would be back again to the *Habitation* on the river. It is unfortunate that we know so little concerning this young woman. Champlain, who wrote so painstakingly of many things, makes little mention of his wife or of her activities. Perhaps the more than thirty years difference in their ages created a situation which was not altogether happy. However that may be, the man who struggled so valiantly to establish a thriving colony was destined to live a lonely existence without the companionship of a wife.

Arrival of Jesuit fathers, 1625   The Récollet friars who had established themselves near Quebec found that they had neither enough members nor money to do satisfactory work in the settlement, at the various trading posts along the St. Lawrence and also among the Indian tribes. After some hesitation, they sought the assistance of the powerful religious order known as the *Society of Jesus* which was already beginning to show some interest in North America. The Récollets hesitated to issue this invitation because they realized that the vigorous Jesuits would soon dominate religious matters within the colony. They knew, too, that the Jesuits were feared and distrusted by many French people themselves. In parts of Europe the Jesuits were thought to have interfered unduly with the rights of citizens and with the authority of governments.

Despite their fears, the Récollets realized that the Society of Jesus was perhaps the only Roman Catholic organization of that time with sufficient wealth, staff, energy and courage to convert the Indians of New France. The Jesuits were known to be men who braved death itself in their efforts to bring the story of Jesus to savage peoples in South America, Ethiopia, Russia and other distant parts of the world.

Thus, in June, 1625, three Jesuit fathers disembarked from a French ship anchored before Quebec. These priests were Enemond Massé, Charles Lalemant and Jean de Brébeuf—men whose names were to become famous in the history of New France.

The three Jesuits remained with the Récollet friars for a short period, but before long they had established a headquarters of their own with buildings and an open space for gardens. Father Jean de Brébeuf, a tall athletic young man, soon made his way to the Huron country, where, with several companions, he began his missionary work. It was a difficult life, full of discouragements, loneliness and hardship. The canoe journeys in particular were sore trials, for they entailed hours of paddling, hours of carrying packs over the portages with only a little food at the end of a hard day to sustain the traveller. In addition to these conditions, Father Brébeuf faced the unpleasant realization that the Indians had little desire to receive the white man's God.

So began the work of the "Black Robes" in New France. Aside from their missionary efforts in the interior in 1635, the fathers founded the famous Jesuit College at Quebec. This college, originally begun as an elementary school for boys, expanded its courses until it could provide the same senior studies as those offered in colleges in France. Among the many boys who

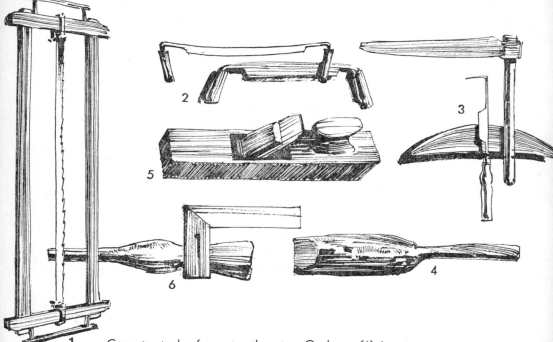

Carpentry tools of seventeenth-century Quebec. (1) is a two-man saw employed in cutting logs into planks. Draw knives (2) were sometimes used in making shingles. (3) frow knives and (4) frow clubs were also used to split shingles from blocks of wood. (5) is a plane and (6) a mitre square. Most of these tools, in modern form, are still employed by carpenters.

received their education in the Quebec college was Louis Joliet who in later years was to explore the Mississippi River.

Company of One Hundred Associates, 1627

While the Jesuits were establishing themselves in New France, other important events were taking place in the colony. By 1620, the monopoly of the company of 1614 had been cancelled to give other merchants a chance to enjoy the profits of the fur trade. The commission to trade changed hands several times, and on each occasion the members of the new companies failed to keep the promise to bring out settlers and finance their early years at Quebec. In 1627, the French government organized the *Company of One Hundred Associates* or the *Company of New France,* a wealthier and more powerful association than any of its predecessors. The Company was to people the colony at the rate of from 200 to 300 French Roman Catholics each year and assist them in making a start. It was also required to establish three priests in each settlement and maintain them or give them cleared land with which to maintain themselves. The Company was to fortify the colony and guard its trade routes. In return for these services, the Company was given full control of and complete trading rights in all of New France.

At the time, these developments appeared very encouraging to Champlain. Events, however, soon proved that the Company of New France had promised more than it could achieve. Only a fur trade of great volume could provide the profits necessary to support hundreds of people in the wilderness. Such trade and profits, of course, did not exist in those early days, and the Company was never able to settle the number of people promised.

To Champlain, who had hoped for so much, the results were bitterly disappointing.

look on page 14

13

THE LAST DAYS OF CHAMPLAIN

The French had been left comparatively undisturbed by other nations to trade and settle in North America. In the meantime the Spanish were expanding in the West Indies, in Mexico, in Central America and in various parts of South America. The English were founding scattered settlements along the Atlantic seaboard, but well south of the Gulf of St. Lawrence.

Sir William Alexander

Conditions changed for the French, however, when a small Scottish settlement appeared on the north-eastern coast of the continent. This new venture was established by a Scottish nobleman, Sir William Alexander, who in 1621 received a land grant from James I, King of England and Scotland. This was no small gift, for it included most of the region now occupied by the provinces of Nova Scotia and New Brunswick. The fact that the French claimed this land as Acadia did not in the least disturb King James or Sir William Alexander.

Baronets of Nova Scotia

Determined to found settlements in the land he called *Nova Scotia* (New Scotland), Sir William looked around for men and money to achieve his purpose. A shrewd business man, he devised a clever scheme. He organized the *Order of the Baronets of Nova Scotia,* and then he proceeded to inform the Scots that they could become members of his Order by payment of a comparatively large fee. Membership in the Order would give holders an hereditary title and a large estate in Nova Scotia. Even such honours as these, however, did not tempt the thrifty Scots to give up their money. Only when the price was reduced, were a few memberships sold.

Scots at Port Royal, 1628

In 1628, a group of Scottish settlers occupied Port Royal, the site of the early French settlement. Further along the Nova Scotian coast to the south at Cape Sable was a small French fort and trading post commanded by Charles de la Tour. To this fiery Frenchman, the Scottish settlers were mere intruders who had

86

no right to live on French territory. He very much regretted that he did not have the forces to drive them from the region.

The situation in Nova Scotia was not nearly as serious for the French as the one which developed shortly afterwards on the St. Lawrence.

By 1627, France and England were at war. The conflicts in Europe soon spread to the high seas and to scattered settlements in various parts of the globe. To the English it became clear that the enemy could be weakened by striking at his sea routes and by attacking the French colony in America.

English threaten New France

In 1628, a private fleet of three English ships under the command of David Kirke crossed the Atlantic, entered the St. Lawrence River and dropped anchor at Tadoussac. From here, Kirke sent a message to Champlain, demanding the surrender of Quebec. Although he was in no position to make a strong defence, Champlain boldly refused to give up his settlement. As a result, Kirke decided to capture all supply ships sailing from France to the colony and starve Quebec into surrender.

Eventually, four French vessels carrying 400 settlers, stores, building materials and cattle appeared on the river. Kirke promptly engaged the enemy ships in a gun battle which lasted for hours. Although hundreds of shots were fired, it seems that very little damage was done to either side. In the end, the French, handicapped by all their settlers, were forced to surrender. Pleased with this easy victory, Kirke sent his prisoners to France and returned in triumph to England with his captured vessels.

These heavy losses, quite naturally, were a severe blow to the Company of New France and to the colony at Quebec. Champlain had been counting heavily on the settlers, supplies and equipment aboard the captured vessels. Now he faced winter without the food and the materials he so desperately required. It was a grim prospect indeed.

The men in the settlement were poor hunters and fishermen; the Indians sold them food only at the highest prices. Champlain, nevertheless, was not the man to give up even under these circum-

stances.   He made his people search for food in the forest, and
during the course of the winter he sent them in small groups to
live with the Indians.   For a time, there were not more than sixteen persons left at Quebec.   There were occasions when Champlain even considered the possibility of marching southward to
capture food stores from the Iroquois, but this desperate plan was
never acted upon.

Because of food shortages, small groups of Frenchmen often spent the winter months
living with the Indians.   The dirt, the smells, the smoke and the noise and the confusion of the lodges proved most unpleasant to men accustomed to the more comfortable and orderly quarters at Quebec.   The two men seen here are talking over the
problems of living in a cold, draughty Indian lodge.

Somehow or other, the colonists managed to survive the cold months, and with the coming of spring they waited anxiously for the arrival of vessels from France. Weeks passed by without the sight of sails on the river, but on July 17, 1629, three ships dropped anchor before Quebec.

Champlain watched them grimly, for these were not French supply vessels: these were English ships with business-like cannon pointing toward shore.

The English captains, Lewis and Thomas Kirke, promptly sent a messenger into Quebec, requesting its immediate surrender. In a courageous reply, Champlain stated that any attempt to take the settlement would be met by French gun-fire. He added, however, that he desired fifteen days to consider the proposal of surrender. By delaying surrender for two weeks, there was always a chance that help might arrive from France or that some news of peace might be received. Impatient to finish their task, the Kirkes refused to listen to any plan but immediate surrender. Faced by overwhelming odds, Champlain had no choice but to give in, for he had neither the defenders nor the armaments to repel his enemies.

The following day, troops came ashore, and as drums rolled, the English flag was raised over Quebec.

When the ceremonies of surrender had been completed, the French were treated in a courteous manner, even though it was made clear they were prisoners of war. Thirty Frenchmen who expressed a desire to remain at Quebec were allowed to do so, while Champlain and the remainder were taken down river to Tadoussac.

Meanwhile, the English commander, David Kirke, travelled to Quebec to study the situation. Anxious to make as much profit as possible from his venture, he carried on an active fur trade with the Indians for some weeks. Kirke knew for certain what Champlain only suspected—that England and France had actually been at peace when Quebec was taken. Kirke realized that his victory might be protested by the French government and feared that even his king might not support the military action against Quebec.

New France returned to French, 1632 Towards the middle of September Kirke sailed for England, taking Champlain and his other prisoners. On arriving there, most of the French hurried on to France, but Champlain remained in London to begin his fight for the return of Quebec, and for several weeks he held many conferences with the French ambassador. Later, in Paris, he talked with members of the Company of New France, with the king and with his prime minister. Champlain urged them all to demand the return of New France and an end to the Scots settlement in Acadia. The demand was made and agreement reached, but the details of agreement took months of negotiation. It was the spring of 1632 before the exchange of the colony became official and orders were sent to the Port Royal colonists to return home.

With these matters cleared away, rapid plans were made to re-occupy and re-build Quebec. One of these plans was that the missionary work in the colony was to become the responsibility of the Jesuits alone. So it was that in April, 1632, three Jesuits led by Father Paul Le Jeune set sail for the St. Lawrence. Arriving at Quebec, they were shocked by the appearance of the settlement. One of the priests wrote:

Of that poor settlement — nothing is now to be seen but the ruins of its bare walls. The English dislodged, we again entered our little home. The only furniture we found there were two wooden tables, such as they were; the doors, windows, sashes, all broken and carried away, and everything going to ruin. It is still worse in the house of the Récollet Fathers . . .

The fathers were delighted the following spring when Champlain arrived with three ships carrying over 200 colonists and a few additional priests. Among these was Jean de Brébeuf who shouted with joy at being back in Quebec.

Samuel de Champlain, now titled Governor of New France, was getting on in years but was still a vigorous man. In token of

This Jesuit house at Sillery, just outside Quebec, was built by Father Le Jeune in 1637. Still standing today, it is probably the oldest house in Canada. Built of massive stone walls, the structure has gable ends covered with clapboard and shingles. In the beginning, the Jesuit fathers used the building as an Indian mission.

his thankfulness for the return of his beloved colony, he erected on the great rock of Quebec a small chapel named *Notre Dame de la Recouvrance,* "Our Lady of the Recovery."

At this time a Jesuit priest reported to France:

The wise conduct and prudence of Monsieur de Champlain, Governor of Kebec and the River St. Lawrence, who honours us with his good will, has caused our words and preaching to be well received; and the Chapel which he had erected near the fort, in honour of our Lady, has furnished excellent facilities to the French to receive the Sacraments of the Church frequently. The fort has seemed like a well-ordered Academy; Monsieur de Champlain has someone read at his table, in the morning from some good historian, and in the evening from the lives of the Saints. He has the Angelus sounded at the beginning, in the middle and at the end of the day, according to the custom of the Church.

Still filled with the dream of expanding French power, Champlain made plans for new posts and settlements along the St. Lawrence and in the region of the Great Lakes. His former Indian allies returned to Quebec with canoe loads of glossy furs. Conditions appeared very promising.

Death of Champlain, 1635

Champlain, however, had little time left to make his dream a reality. During the autumn of 1635 he suffered a severe stroke from which he never recovered. He died on Christmas Day of that year. All the honours that the poor little colony could afford were bestowed upon the dead Governor. On the funeral day a procession of soldiers, settlers and priests made its way through the snow to Champlain's last resting place. Father Le Jeune wrote in his own words: "I was charged with the funeral oration, and I did not lack material."

A memorial chapel was erected over the grave, but was later destroyed by fire. With the passing of years the spot was forgotten. Somewhere today under the busy streets of modern Quebec City lie the remains of the Father of New France.

Samuel de Champlain was a great man in many respects. He was much more than a leader, for he combined the talents of explorer, navigator, sailor, geographer, soldier, administrator, journalist and diplomat. He possessed a charming manner which at times delighted everyone from royal courtiers to Huron chieftains. Little interested in personal wealth and advancement, he devoted his career unselfishly to the establishment of French power in the valley of the St. Lawrence.

Although at the time of his death, New France may have seemed small and relatively unimportant, the colony was destined to grow and prosper.

14

THE FOUNDING OF MONTREAL

Under cover of darkness on the night of June 15, 1636, a French vessel slid into the harbour at Quebec, dropped anchor and came to rest. So quiet was the arrival that the residents of the settlement slept on undisturbed.

In the morning a dignified figure in a dark cloak came ashore, accompanied by a few officers in brilliant uniforms. This was Charles Jacques Huault de Montmagny, the next Governor of New France. Unlike Samuel de Champlain, Montmagny was a fussy, well-dressed man who took great pleasure in pomp and ceremony. Under his leadership Quebec was to witness many parades, ceremonies, religious processions and entertainments.

Governor Montmagny, 1636

At the beginning of the seventeenth century, French furniture was rather stiff and box-like in appearance. Chair backs were straight and of shoulder height as shown by the chair at the left. But as the century went on, furniture took on a delicate shape, displaying finer lines and curves, as is the case with the chair to the right, made about 1680. In the centre is a Louis XIII "lowboy" of about 1650, the ancestor of the modern dressing-table.

Quebec had changed somewhat since its earlier days. The warehouses of the Company of New France and some shabby dwellings stood by the river, but the newer and more important buildings were now atop the cliff. There was Champlain's fort, the governor's residence and a church. Among the houses was the Hébert homestead where Madame Hébert, now a widow, still lived on. Two miles away, standing within a wooden stockade near the St. Charles River, was *Notre Dame des Anges,* Our Lady of the Angels, headquarters of the Jesuits. It was from here that Father le Jeune and his fellow priests directed their missionary work and journeyed into the wilderness. By this time Father le Jeune had some knowledge of the Algonkian tongue and Father Brébeuf could speak the Iroquoian dialect of the Hurons.

Jesuit Relations

The Jesuit fathers wrote vivid descriptions of their travels and of Indian life in special records known as the *Relations.* Many of these records were published and widely circulated in France where they were eagerly read by churchmen and others. The *Relations* aroused tremendous interest in the achievements of the Church in the New World with the happy result that French priests and even nuns volunteered for missionary work among the Indians. In 1639, three Sisters of the Ursuline Order and three Augustinian nuns arrived in Quebec to teach the Indian converts and to labour in a hospital founded in the previous year.

Another result of this same Christian fervour was the founding in France of the *Society of Our Lady of Montreal,* a group of forty-five people, some of whom were very wealthy and influential. The Society's chief aim was to establish a settlement and mission station on Montreal Island. This was considered a dangerous venture, for the island lay much closer to the Iroquois country than Quebec. It was therefore vitally important to select a dependable person who could act as governor and military commander of the proposed settlement. Chosen for this important

Sieur de Maisonneuve

position was a distinguished French soldier, Paul de Chomedy, Sieur de Maisonneuve.

By another piece of good fortune the Society made contact

with a courageous young woman, Jeanne Mance, who felt a stronge desire to devote her life to the service of God in New France. She volunteered to found and maintain a hospital in the new settlement. Her application was accepted, and funds were donated for the erection of a hospital.

In 1641 Maisonneuve and Jeanne Mance, together with forty workers and soldiers, sailed to Quebec. Unfortunately, it was so late in the season when they arrived that plans for making a start on the settlement had to be postponed until the following spring. Some people at Quebec tried to persuade Maisonneuve that his project was a foolhardy one, for the Iroquois would surely wipe out any post set up on Montreal Island. Even the governor at Quebec suggested that Maisonneuve should consider choosing another site that lay closer to Quebec. Maisonneuve smiled and replied:

> What you suggest would be good if I had been sent here to deliberate and choose, but as the Society that sends me have determined upon my going to Montreal, my honour, as you will doubtless agree, requires me to begin a settlement there, even if every tree in that island were to be changed into an Iroquois.

True to his word, in May of 1642, Maisonneuve took his little party to the island where about one hundred years before Jacques Cartier had visited Hochelaga. Shortly after landing, a small altar decorated with wild flowers was erected. There, a Jesuit priest, Father Vimont, said the first mass, and to the people who knelt before him he said:

Founding of Montreal, 1642

> You are a grain of mustard-seed that shall rise and grow till its branches overshadow the earth. You are few, but your work is the work of God. His smile is upon you and your children shall fill the land.

The new settlement, known as Ville Marie, soon included a fort protected by a palisade, a windmill and a few small houses. It was not long, of course, before the League of the Iroquois learned of this new French outpost on the St. Lawrence. From then on Ville Marie became a marked spot, a place considered fair game by the wandering Iroquois warparties. A constant watch, night and day, had to be kept at the fort to warn the settlers of lurking bands of enemy. Workmen went to the fields muskets in hand. Even the priests at times went about their duties with swords at their sides.

Maisonneuve oversees the construction of Fort Ville Marie at Montreal, on the site of the old Indian village of Hochelaga. During the seventeenth century, the forts in New France were constructed entirely of wood. Outer stockades were literally high fences of heavy logs, the bases of which were sunk into the ground. The tower or bastion shown above is fitted with slit-like loopholes, which enabled the French to fire on Indian attackers. Fort Ville Marie lay close to the lands of the Iroquois and was attacked many times.

Jeanne Mance   During the first attack, which took place a few minutes after the settlement was founded, several men were killed and a number wounded. The wounded were among the first patients cared for by the gentle Jeanne Mance. A Jesuit priest reported:

No sooner was the hospital finished than there appeared plenty of sick and wounded to fill it: every day the Iroquois by their massacres found new guests for it.

In the months and years that followed, Jeanne Mance had many other patients, some of them French and some of them Indian.

Despite the dangers and hardships, the settlement survived. It grew slowly, however, for its hazardous position on the fringe of the Iroquois country frightened away settlers and friendly Indians.

In 1653, eleven years after the establishment of Ville Marie, **Marguerite Bourgeoys** arrived a vigorous French nun who was to play a vital part in the educational development of New France. She was Marguerite Bourgeoys, a determined, tireless person who was particularly interested in providing schooling for the children of Ville Marie. Her work had a humble beginning, for her first pupils were taught in a stable loaned by Maisonneuve. Of this building, Marguerite Bourgeoys later wrote:

> Four years after my arrival, M. de Maisonneuve gave me a stone dwelling for those who would help in the school. This stable had been used as a cattle-shed and dove-cote. Above, and reached by an outside ladder, was a loft in which we slept. The building was cleaned, a chimney built and everything prepared for the children's comfort.

In time Marguerite Bourgeoys founded a famous order of teaching nuns known as the Congregation of the Sisters of Notre Dame. Later, these sisters formed schools and taught children in various parts of New France.

Maisonneuve proved to be a good governor and a skilful commander. His defence of the little settlement against the almost constant peril of Iroquois attacks was nothing less than miraculous. The story most frequently told of his personal bravery concerns an incident that took place a short distance outside the walls of the fort.

One spring morning, the now famous watchdog, *Pilotte*, **Iroquois attack repelled** raised a loud howl of warning as she dashed from the forest to the gate of the palisade. Realizing that Iroquois warriors must be nearby, Maisonneuve with thirty armed men made a bold sally from the fort in the direction of the woods. It was a dangerous move, but the French commander hoped he could outfight and surprise the enemy. He was scarcely prepared, however, to meet a warparty more than three times the size of his own group. Soon after the skirmish opened, three of the French lay dead in the snow, while others suffered minor wounds. Knowing that he could not defeat the Iroquois in the open, Maisonneuve ordered a retreat. Then, as his men retired toward the fort, Maisonneuve covered their withdrawal. With a pistol in each hand he confronted the eager Iroquois.

An Iroquois chief, anxious to capture the French commander, sprang forward. Maisonneuve swung a pistol upward and pulled the trigger. There was only a dull click as the weapon misfired. Then his second pistol moved upward, his finger tightened on the trigger and a loud report echoed across the clearing. The chief fell dead, his body making a dark patch in the white snow.

15

THE HURON MISSIONS

The work of the Jesuit fathers was widespread. At various times there were small missions in Chaleur Bay, Cape Breton Island, the mainland of Nova Scotia, the southern portions of what is now New Brunswick, along the St. Lawrence and as far north and west as Sault Ste. Marie. Although the early Jesuits entered into their work with courage and determination, they realized that theirs was a difficult and dangerous task. Father Briard wrote:

It remains to tell you that the conversion of this country to the Gospel and of these people to civilization, is not a small undertaking nor free from great difficulties; for in the first place, if we consider the country, it is only a forest, without other conveniences of life than those which will be brought from France, and what in time may be obtained from the soil after it has been cultivated.

Among the Jesuit missionary efforts none can be compared in scope with that of Huronia. The land of the Hurons, stretching from Georgian Bay to Lake Simcoe, was thickly populated. Indeed, it is probable that almost as many people were living in that area then as there are at the present time. In order to carry out their work efficiently, the Jesuits divided Huronia into a number of missionary districts, each cared for by two priests who lived in an Indian village. At such centres churches were built and services were held for the people. Not content to remain constantly at their stations, the fathers travelled about their districts, teaching, preaching and visiting the lodges of the tribesmen. By the spring of 1649, no fewer than eighteen priests were working among the Indians of Huronia and among those who lived immediately south of that region.

Some idea of the Jesuit method of teaching may be gained from the following passage written by one of the fathers:

About the month of December, the snow began to lie on the ground, and the savages settled down into the village. For, during the whole summer and autumn, they are for the most part either in their rural cabins, taking care of their crops, or on the lake fishing, or trading; which makes it not a little inconvenient to instruct them. The usual method we follow is this: We call together the people by the help of the Captain of the village, who assembles them all in our house as in Council, or perhaps by the sound of a bell. I use the surplice and the square cap, to give more majesty to my appearance. At the beginning we chant on our knees the *Pater Noster* (the Lord's Prayer) translated into Huron verse. Father Daniel, as its author, chants a couplet alone, and then we all chant it again; and those among the Hurons, principally the little ones, who already know it, take pleasure in chanting it with us. After that we question the young children and the girls, giving a little bead of glass or porcelain to those who deserve it. The parents are very glad to see their children answer well and carry off some little prize, of which they render themselves worthy by the care they take to come privately to get instruction. On our part, to arouse their emulation we have each lesson retraced by our two little French boys, who question each other, —which transports the savages with admiration.

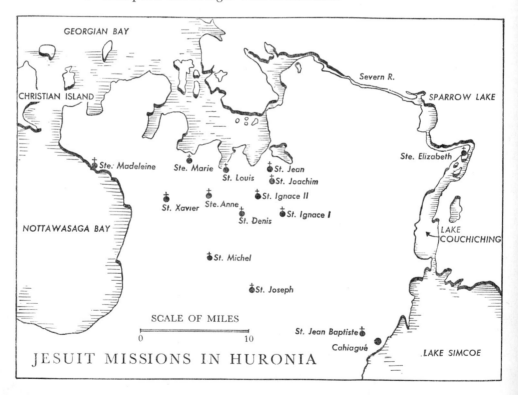

JESUIT MISSIONS IN HURONIA

In addition to the Jesuit priests there were other Frenchmen who served as servants, labourers and soldiers. The Jesuits tried to make their mission stations as self-supporting as possible. To this end they cultivated gardens and kept a few chickens, pigs and cattle. In the beginning, accommodation for the fathers was very crude, but as the years went by, their buildings and fortifications became more substantial.

Near the present location of the town of Midland, Ontario, **Sainte Marie** the headquarters of all the missions in Huronia was established. This famous station, known as Sainte Marie, received a special grant of money from the French government and in consequence the Jesuits were able to build a large, well-equipped station. Instead of the ordinary wooden palisade commonly used for defence, Sainte Marie boasted a fort with stone foundations and sturdy bastions from which muskets could be fired. Within the fortifications were a number of wooden buildings which included a home for the priests, a chapel, a small house for retreat, and quarters for the servants. Outside the main fortifications, but protected by a palisade of stakes, was an area containing the burial ground and accommodation for visiting Indians. Sainte Marie was so well protected that the Iroquois had good cause to give it a wide berth.

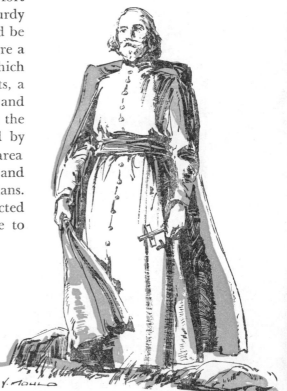

A Jesuit missionary dressed in the costume that became so familiar in New France. The Jesuits were not an ancient monastic order. Founded as the Company of Jesus in 1543 by a Spanish knight, Ignatius Loyola, the order was run efficiently along military lines with Loyola as its first "general." In addition to its fine work in New France, the Company of Jesus proved brilliantly successful in both India and China.

Several times a year the Jesuit priests of the scattered Huron missions gathered together at Sainte Marie to confer with one another and to relax from the rigours of their work. To those who lived among the Indians a short stay at the headquarters was a delightful experience. Although the mission at Sainte Marie was by no means luxurious, it was much more comfortable than any of the smaller missions. It was pleasant at such times to chat with other priests and to forget for a time the hardships, the dangers, the dirt, the smoke and smells of the Indian villages.

Once back at their own missions the Jesuits faced the difficult and often dangerous task of converting the Indians. The tribesmen were so accustomed to gambling, drinking, quarrelling, torturing and even eating the flesh of their enemies that they found it hard to change their manner of living. The warriors could not understand why they should not hunt on Sundays and why they should not have three or four wives. Considerable trouble, too, was encountered with medicine men who claimed powers of healing the sick and talking with the spirits. When the priests described these claims as foolish superstitions, the medicine men were angered, for they feared losing their authority among the people. One enraged medicine man attacked a priest, grasped him by the legs and dragged the Jesuit through a camp fire.

On various occasions Indians threw stones at mission chapels, burned buildings and assaulted the priests. Despite these dangers, the Jesuits persisted in their quiet, determined manner, winning more and more converts with the passing years. It is quite possible that if they had been permitted to continue, these missionaries might have entirely changed the life of the Hurons.

The proud warriors to the south had never forgotten the attacks which had been led by the French commander, Samuel de Champlain. Always dangerous enemies, the Iroquois became even more threatening after they were able to secure muskets from Dutch traders in the Atlantic settlements. With new weapons in their hands, they became bolder in their raids on the Hurons, the Algonquins, the Montagnais and the French.

During all seasons of the year wandering bands of Iroquois Iroquois danger haunted the valley of the St. Lawrence, ready to pounce upon Indians or French transporting furs and trade goods. These enemy operations were so successful that by 1647 the fur trade with Quebec had been cut to a mere trickle. As a result, the following spring the Hurons sent 250 warriors to protect the canoes carrying furs to Quebec. This action provided a fine measure of protection for the furs, but some of the Huron missions and villages were left unguarded.

On a warm July morning in 1648, Father Daniel was conducting mass in the chapel at St. Joseph, one of the most southerly of the Huron missions. The quiet murmur of the priest's voice was suddenly broken by alarmed cries of "The Iroquois! The Iroquois!"

Running from the chapel, Father Daniel urged all the villagers who could do so to escape through the back gate in the palisade. Some fled into the forest, but there was no escape for the old, the ill, and the Huron women with small children. In the meantime, the shrieking Iroquois were battering at the main entrance.

Although Father Daniel had ample opportunity to flee from the mission, he chose to stay and face the attackers. As he returned to the chapel, the terrified Hurons followed, shaking and muttering with fear. Once inside the chapel, Father Daniel spoke words of comfort and quickly proceeded to baptize the Indians. With no time for individual baptisms, he simply dipped his handkerchief in water and flung the drops over his trembling flock.

When the gate in the palisade was breached, the Iroquois warriors poured in with a fierce rush, and set fire to the Huron lodges. Since the moment of tragedy had arrived, Father Daniel stepped from the chapel door alone to confront the Iroquois. In his dark robe he presented a striking figure, quiet and unafraid. There was a moment of awed stillness and then the roar of a Death of Father Daniel, 1648 musket. Father Daniel fell dead. Rushing forward, the Iroquois cut open his body, dipped their hands in his blood and rubbed it on their faces. But even this ferocious treatment was not enough for the warriors, for seizing his battered body, they carried it into the chapel and flung it down before the altar. Moments afterward the building was set on fire.

Sometime later, the Iroquois, leaving a desolate ruin, moved away with a pathetic line of captives.

A fearful winter passed in the Huron villages, but no further attacks were launched by the enemy. In the spring of 1649, however, tragedy struck again. On March 16, the French at Sainte Marie saw a column of dark smoke rising above the trees of the forest. It was not a comforting sight, for the smoke rose from a point three miles to the south where stood the little mission of St. Louis, the mission at which were stationed Father Brébeuf and Father Lalemant. Presently, several wounded Huron hurried into Sainte Marie and blurted out the shocking news; the stations at St. Louis and St. Ignace were destroyed; the Iroquois were advancing on the headquarters of the Huron missions.

Death of Fathers Brébeuf and Lalemant, 1649

The French at Sainte Marie, however, did not know the full horror of events taking place to the south. Fathers Brébeuf and Lalemant had been stripped of their clothes and marched six miles to the gutted mission at St. Ignace. Here began the tortures that led to the deaths of the two heroic priests. About one o'clock in the afternoon the sturdy Brébeuf was tied to a stake in preparation for the ordeal. By three o'clock he was dead. The gentle, delicate Lalemant, forced to witness the brutal scene, suffered agonies as he watched the slow, awful death of his companion. It was six o'clock when Father Lalemant's frail body was tied to the stake. His frightful agony dragged on through the evening, through the dark night and well past daylight the following morning.

It seems incredible that even the ferocious Iroquois could have inflicted such calculated suffering. During the long hours of torture they lopped off hands, burned out eyes, cut away strips of flesh, tore out hair and hung red-hot tomahawks about the necks of the priests. Father Brébeuf died bravely. His heart was taken from his body, cooked over a fire and eaten by the excited warriors who thus hoped to acquire something of his courage and his endurance.

After the death of Lalemant, two hundred of the Iroquois braves pushed on in the direction of Sainte Marie. If they expected another easy victory, they were doomed to disappointment, for the Hurons rallied to the defence of the fort. The advancing Iroquois were driven back as far as St. Louis, but after gaining reinforcements, they defeated the Hurons in a stiff battle.

Hopes for the safety of Sainte Marie grew dim. Priests doubled their time for prayer; watchers stood stubbornly at the bastions. Then came the unexpected miracle which undoubtedly saved the lives of the defenders. The Iroquois suddenly seemed terrorized by the thought that they were in the centre of a hostile land, in the midst of a people angered by attack. On March 19 they retreated hurriedly, taking with them captives loaded down with spoils. Before leaving, the Iroquois tied a number of Hurons to stakes inside bark lodges still standing at St. Ignace. Then in a grim farewell gesture they set the buildings afire. The screams of the dying Indians rang eerily across the forest, as the enemy started southward.

The spirit of Huronia was broken by these events. After burning their own villages, groups of Indians made their way to Sainte Marie, seeking the protection of the Jesuit fathers. During the spring and summer months of 1649, literally hundreds of the tribesmen were baptised by the priests.

Regretfully, it was decided that Sainte Marie must be abandoned, for it was now too exposed to the Iroquois threat. The feelings of the priests are well expressed in the words of one of them:

Sainte Marie abandoned, 1649

But on each of us lay the necessity of bidding farewell to that old home of Sainte Marie,—to its structures, which, though plain, seemed in the eyes of the poor savages, master works of art; and to its cultivated lands, which were promising an abundant harvest.

In July, 1649, a company of Jesuits and Hurons abandoned Fort Ste Marie to the Iroquois and sought refuge on Christian Island in Georgian Bay. All the grain and food stocks, together with furniture, farm implements and cattle were placed on rafts, and poled, paddled and sailed across the bay to the new site on the island. Before leaving, the priests performed the sad duty of setting fire to their beloved mission buildings. For the next 150 years all traces of civilization virtually disappeared from Huronia, leaving the region in a primitive state. During the nineteenth century, British settlers in Simcoe County were amazed when ploughing to turn up old Indian and Jesuit relics.

Mission at Christian Island, 1649
Some thought was given to establishing a new fort and mission on Manitoulin Island, but this site was given up in favour of Isle St. Joseph (Christian Island) in Georgian Bay. A new mission, Ste. Marie II, was founded on the island, but after a year of hardship, the Jesuits agreed that this was not a suitable location.

By the spring of 1650 there seemed no other choice than to leave Huronia and return to Quebec with those Hurons who desired protection. It was a painful decision for the Jesuits who had worked, suffered and died to maintain their scattered missions.

Not all the Hurons took part in the canoe journey to Quebec, for groups of them travelled far to the west and the south-west.

V. MOULD.

Some actually reached the prairies and the valley of the Mississippi River. Numbers of them were killed by western warriors, but others were fortunate enough to secure safety with friendly tribes.

Huronia, the heart of the French fur trade and the cradle of Indian Christendom, was deserted. Only the charred and decaying ruins of once populous Indian villages were left to remind future generations of a short but important period in Canadian history.

Among the precious objects which reached Quebec with the Jesuits and the Hurons were two small boxes bearing the bones of Father Brébeuf and Father Lalemant.

Iroquois successes

Back in Huronia, the Iroquois moved in and took over the rich beaver lands. In the next ten years they endangered the very life of New France. They raided up and down the St. Lawrence. They killed the governor of Three Rivers and fifteen of his men. They prowled around Montreal. They ambushed Algonquin fur canoes coming down the Ottawa and carried off the pelts to their lodges. Supplies of furs, the life-blood of New France, were slowly but surely being cut off by the savage Iroquois. New France was being slowly strangled.

16

ADAM DOLLARD AT THE LONG SAULT

Iroquois
threat of 1660
In the spring of 1660, Montreal learned that the Iroquois planned an overwhelming attack on the settlement. Hundreds of the enemy warriors had spent the winter on the upper reaches of the Ottawa River, and hundreds more were moving northward down the Richelieu. The situation seemed beyond hope.

Dollard's plan,
1660
A young French army officer, Adam Dollard, Sieur des Ormeaux, living in Montreal suggested to Governor Maisonneuve that the best method of preventing the fall of Montreal was to go and attack the Iroquois before they could reach the settlement. He believed it was possible to destroy bands of the enemy as they moved south on the waters of the Ottawa River. At first this seemed a foolhardy plan to Maisonneuve, but in the end he gave his approval to the venture. Perhaps Dollard was right; bold tactics might prove to be the only means of salvation.

Dollard succeeded in persuading sixteen other Frenchmen to join his company. It was a very young group of men, most of them in their early teens, who made their wills, attended a service in the little stone church and said good-bye to their friends.

Long Sault
Rapids
Leaving Montreal, they paddled up the St. Lawrence to the mouth of the Ottawa, entered this river, and pushed on to the Long Sault. It was May 1, 1660, when they stepped ashore near the bouncing, frothing rapids. Not far back from the river they were pleased to find an old Indian stockade in a partially-ruined condition. This was no strong fort, but merely a rough enclosure that would provide some protection against attack. Had Dollard and his companions known what events lay ahead, they would have set about at once to strengthen these meagre defences. Instead, they camped in the open near the river and set up a watch for the Iroquois.

Adam Dollard posts his men along the river's edge in preparation for an expected assault by the Iroquois. His little party of Frenchmen, although extremely courageous, had little experience of Indian warfare. It seems that Dollard himself had been in New France only eighteen months before setting out on this dangerous mission. The tale of a few Frenchmen besieged by a large warparty of Iroquois is one of the most colourful stories in our history.

They were still settling themselves at the Long Sault when to **Indian allies** their surprise they were joined by a group of forty Hurons and four Algonquins led by two chiefs. These tribesmen, hearing in Montreal of the French expedition up the Ottawa, had themselves decided to offer their assistance. The addition of forty-four warriors was greatly encouraging to the group of seventeen Frenchmen.

After several days of waiting, guards posted on the river reported that two Iroquois canoes were coming downstream.

Dollard hid his men among the trees at a spot where he judged the enemy would land. Dollard's guess proved correct, for two birch-bark canoes bearing five Iroquois turned toward shore in front of the breathless watchers. The canoes touched land, the Iroquois leaped ashore, a volley of musket shots broke the stillness and four warriors dropped dead. By some strange chance, however, the fifth Iroquois, escaping unharmed, hurried back to warn a party of tribesmen who were following close behind. The river was soon alive with enemy canoes. It just took one glance to convince Dollard that this was no small warparty but one composed of at least 200 warriors. Unhesitatingly, he ordered his men to retire from the shore and take shelter in the old stockade.

Iroquois attack With supreme confidence the Iroquois landed and, without stopping to organize themselves, launched a brisk attack. This hasty advance, however, encountered such hot musket fire that it wavered and broke as warriors fell wounded and dying. Their chiefs soon saw that only a well-organized attack would defeat the defenders of the little fort. Withdrawing their forces beyond musket range, the attackers held a quick council of war.

After much excited talk, a small group of the Iroquois was sent forward to parley with the French. Without thinking of the consequences, Dollard's men fired, killing several of the messengers.

Angered by their losses and smarting at the failure of the first attack, the Iroquois settled down to a siege of the French position. First they began the construction of their own fort a short distance away in the shelter of the forest. This lull in the fighting was of advantage to Dollard and gave him an excellent opportunity to strengthen his own defences. His men hastily cut limbs from overhanging trees, strengthened the walls and closed gaps in the defences with earth and stones. As they worked, they could see the Iroquois breaking up the French and Huron canoes along the shore. This was a sobering sight to the defenders; their most important means of escape was now gone.

When the Iroquois had completed work on their own fort, they launched a second attack, a powerful assault aimed at all sides of the French position. Screaming in frenzy, the braves burst into the open, completely ignoring the danger of musket-fire. On they came, some of them carrying armfuls of fuel in the form of birch-bark from the smashed canoes. Throwing this against the wall, they tried to start a fire. But the French and their Indian allies kept pouring a deadly spray of musket-shots into the ranks of the attackers. The warriors fell in heaps.

An Iroquoian drum and drumstick. To the paced, rhythmic beat of these drums were held the war dances that lasted for hours. As the dancing progressed, the the warriors worked themselves into an emotional state of tremendous excitement.

Unable to fire the stockade, the Iroquois suddenly broke and retired in confusion. Two more attacks met the same fate. Disheartened and puzzled by the rock-like defence of the stockade, the attackers held another council of war. Deciding that a larger force was needed to win victory, they sent messengers to obtain reinforcements.

For five long days, the Iroquois kept a constant watch on the **The siege** French position. They fired their muskets at intervals to give the impression that an assault might be launched at any time.

In an effort to win the Hurons away from the French, the Iroquois shouted messages from the shelter of the trees. They told how hundreds and thousands of enemy attackers would soon be on the scene. They described the awful fate of the defenders when the last big assault was made. They begged the Hurons to leave the French while still there was time. At first these taunts and invitations had little effect, but as the hours dragged by, the Hurons became uneasy. One by one they climbed the palisade and dashed across the little clearing to join the enemy. Eventually only one Huron, Chief Anahotaka, and the four Algonquins remained. The cowardly Hurons lived to record what happened to the little garrison.

No one within the stockade now believed there was any hope of defeating the Iroquois or of escaping from the siege. Only death stood ahead. Dollard's sole comfort lay in the thought that by putting up a desperate defence and by killing Iroquois warriors he might lessen the threat that hung over the settlement at Montreal. In the meantime, he and his men suffered terribly from thirst, hunger and lack of sleep.

On the fifth day of waiting, loud shouts and whoops announced the coming of Iroquois reinforcements, more than 500 of them. Adam Dollard, leaning wearily against the palisade, watched the noisy landing. If the defenders had been out-numbered before, the situation was now infinitely worse, for almost seven hundred Iroquois were pitted against seventeen Frenchmen and a few Indians.

A fresh attack involving the new warriors was not long in coming as the Iroquois, in crowded masses, suddenly converged on the little stockade. But even this massive assault fell back before the brisk fire of the French marksmen. So unnerved were the attackers by this unexpected show of power, that there was open talk of abandoning the fight. Bolder fighters among the Iroquois, however, shamed their less courageous brothers and whipped up a fresh fighting passion.

When the next attack came, it was so furious and so over-whelming that Dollard's little garrison could not cope with the surging masses. An unforeseen accident, too, led to the sudden collapse of the French defences. As a last desperate measure Dollard had prepared a crude hand-bomb of bullets and gunpowder to hurl over the wall and into the tightly-packed ranks of the attackers.   At the last moment, however, he failed to put enough force into the throw, and the bomb, hitting the top of the palisade, rebounded among the defenders.   As it exploded with a thunderous roar several of the French were killed and others wounded.

During the uproar caused by the explosion the attackers pressed close to the palisade and began firing through holes in the wall.   Moments later, screaming warriors were clambering over the palisade and dropping inside.   Like painted devils, they went into swift action with tomahawks and scalping knives.   Adam Dollard was among the first to suffer death.   After the quick, deadly skirmish only four badly-wounded French remained alive. The Iroquois killed three of these right where they lay.   What became of the last Frenchman still remains a mystery.   Perhaps he died elsewhere of wounds.   Perhaps he met a horrible end by Iroquois torture. *Death of Dollard and his companions*

Adam Dollard and his men did not die in vain.   Their defence of the poor little fort destroyed Iroquois confidence.   If a handful of Frenchmen could fight like this in a tumble-down stockade, what could a larger garrison do behind strong defences? With this troublesome question in mind, the Iroquois returned home without attacking Montreal.

Dollard and his men had really saved more than Montreal. They had given New France a little time in which to strengthen itself against the next Iroquois assault.   They had also given the fur canoes coming down the Ottawa a better chance to arrive at Montreal unharmed.   Dollard and his men had checked the slow tide of Iroquois invasion.   It was now up to the government of France to turn that tide back and sweep it clear of the western fur routes, because without the fur trade New France would die. *Results of the Long Sault stand*

SUMMARY—SECTION III

Jacques Cartier and the Sieur de Roberval returned to France in 1542 and 1543, neither of them having been able to establish a permanent French colony.   Samuel de Champlain first saw the St.

Lawrence river in 1603. Much happened in the sixty years between the departure of Cartier and the arrival of Champlain.

Sixteenth-century Europeans ate a great deal of fish and little meat. Cabot's news of the New World fishing spread up and down the coastline of western Europe. Fishermen from England, Holland, Belgium, France, northern Spain and Portugal were at work at least forty years before Cartier's arrival, harvesting the waters around Newfoundland, searching in particular for the codfish, "the beef of the ocean."

From time to time, fishermen came to the mainland to refill their water casks. They met Indians and exchanged knives, lengths of rope and spare clothing for furs (probably muskrat, otter, fox and some beaver). These were taken back to Europe as interesting souvenirs. However, in France, a demand was growing for fur trimmings for cloaks and gowns. As early as 1544, French fishermen appear to have set up a whale fishery and fur-trading post at Tadoussac, at the junction of the Saguenay and St. Lawrence rivers.

In the latter part of the sixteenth century, the process of making fur hats was discovered and such hats became tremendously popular in Europe, beaver hats in particular. It was due to this accident of history that France became interested in North America as something more than a staging-post on the way to the East. It was the French who carried home the first pelts of fur. It was the French who first made their way into the continent in search of better and more numerous furs. The search led companies of fur-traders to Tadoussac, to the Acadian shore and then up the St. Lawrence beyond Tadoussac to the rock of Quebec, where the first European settlement was successfully begun and maintained by Samuel de Champlain. The search, destined to go on for a further hundred and fifty years, led Frenchmen beyond Quebec to the Ottawa river and up into the Huron country. The search for furs also involved the French in Indian wars and brought them up against the savage power of the mighty League of the Iroquois.

Champlain was the first to explore a way to the north and west of Quebec, looking for furs and a water route to the Western Sea. But before his searchings began, he found himself involved in helping his Huron allies stop the Iroquois raiding the canoes bringing furs down to Quebec. Champlain and his men fought and defeated the Iroquois. Thereafter, the Iroquois remembered the French as being allies of the

Hurons. For the next 150 years, the Iroquois were the sworn enemies of New France.

The French colony grew very slowly. The various companies of merchants permitted by the French crown to trade for furs did not keep their promises to bring out numbers of settlers and help them to start farming and lumbering. However, members of the Récollet Order, and later the Society of Jesus, came out to New France to convert the Indians. The Jesuits wrote to France of their experiences and inspired others to come and work in the colony. Priests volunteered to serve as missionaries. Nuns came to work as nursing sisters. In 1642, Montreal was founded as a settlement and mission station. But still there were few settlers in all of New France.

The colony survived several dangers. In 1628, a Scots settlement, begun at Port Royal in Acadia, threatened to take away some of the fur trade. In 1629, when France and England were at war, the free-booting Kirke brothers forced Quebec to surrender, and Champlain was taken prisoner. However, Champlain returned in 1633 to reoccupy Quebec and the Scots settlement in Acadia was withdrawn. In 1648 and 1649, the Iroquois wiped out the Huron missions and drove the remnants of the Huron nation north and west of the Great Lakes. For the next ten years the Iroquois raided the fur canoes coming down the Ottawa river to Montreal and Quebec from the north country, until they were halted for a while in 1660, when Adam Dollard and his brave companions inflicted heavy casualties on the Iroquois during a battle on the Ottawa River.

FOUR / *The English Colonies in North America*

THE "GREEN" AND THE "DRY" FISHERIES

NEWFOUNDLAND

HUMPHREY GILBERT AND WALTER RALEIGH

FOUNDING OF JAMESTOWN, VIRGINIA, 1607

CAPTAIN JOHN SMITH

TOBACCO PLANTATIONS IN VIRGINIA

SETTLEMENT IN THE BERMUDA ISLANDS

THE PILGRIM FATHERS SETTLE AT PLYMOUTH, 1620

THE FIRST THANKSGIVING DAY

THE NEW ENGLAND COLONIES

HENRY HUDSON EXPLORES THE HUDSON RIVER, 1609

THE DUTCH ESTABLISH THE NEW NETHERLANDS, 1623

THE PATROON SYSTEM

PETER STUYVESANT SURRENDERS NEW AMSTERDAM
TO THE ENGLISH, 1664

ENGLISH ROMAN CATHOLICS FOUND MARYLAND, 1634

WILLIAM PENN ESTABLISHES PHILADELPHIA, 1681

ENGLISH COLONIES IN THE WEST INDIES

17

NEWFOUNDLAND

It is possible that a few French and English vessels fished off the north-eastern shores of the continent before the time of John Cabot's first voyage to North America. However, French, English, Spanish and Portuguese vessels were making annual voyages to the fishing grounds soon after the time of Cabot.

A letter, written by a fisherman in 1578, includes this description of the sea life in the waters off Newfoundland:

As touching the kindes of Fish beside Cod, there are Herrings, Salmons, Thornebacke, Plase, or rather wee should call them Flounders, Dog Fish, and another most excellent of taste called by us Cat, Oisters and Muskles; in which I have found pearles above 40 in one Muskle, and generally all have some, great or small. I heard of a Portugall that found one woorth 300 duckets: There are also other kindes of Shel-fish, as limpets, cockles, wilkes, lobsters and crabs; also a fish like a Smelt which commeth on shore, and another that hath the like propertie, called a Squid: these be the fishes, which (when I please to be merry with my old companions) I say doe come on shore when I commaund them . . .

In the early days, all the fishermen cured and preserved their fish by packing them in salt. This was known as the "green fishery." But because salt was none too plentiful in England and expensive to import from Spain and Portugal, English fishermen developed a new curing method known as the "dry fishery." In this operation the fish were split open, flattened, lightly salted and dried in the sun. The method of "dry" curing required a minimum of salt and preserved the fish so well that they kept better than "green" cod and packed more closely.

The practice of the "dry fishery," of course, forced the English to go ashore on the island of Newfoundland. Accommodation for the crews had to be built as well as the staging on which the cod were processed and dried as they were unloaded from the boats. In the early days the crews fished in the spring and summer months and then returned to Europe in the fall. During the fishing season they found it convenient to use the sheltered coves of Newfoundland as harbours where they erected crude buildings on the shores. Here they cured their fish, made repairs and stored their gear for the winter months.

A "ketch" of the late seventeenth century. This was one of the smaller types of vessels employed in fishing along the Atlantic coast and in the Gulf of St. Lawrence. Small "dories", very much like those of today, were also used with these sailing craft. The term "ketch" is derived from an early English word "cache", which was applied to cargo boats. A seventeenth-century description states: "Ketches being short and round built, be verie apt to turn up and downe and useful to goe to and fro almost with any wind."

As more and more of the coastline was taken up with small wharves, shacks and "flakes" or drying racks, it became necessary to provide some sort of property protection.   There was always the chance that Indians or other fishermen arriving early in the spring might help themselves to the stores and gear.   As a safeguard, then, the fishermen adopted the practice of leaving men in Newfoundland to guard property and to occupy land.   Just when these caretakers were replaced by permanent residents with wives and children is not known.

There may have been permanent settlers at St. John's when, **Humphrey Gilbert, 1583** in 1583, Sir Humphrey Gilbert arrived in Newfoundland on his way to the mainland to establish colonies.   A record of Gilbert's voyage indicates that there were houses, paths and gardens along the margins of the harbour.   Other documents suggest that settlers were on the island well before this time.

When Sir Humphrey Gilbert proclaimed the sovereignty of Queen Elizabeth in the harbour of St. John's, he was ignoring the fact that during the sixteenth century, Spain claimed Newfoundland together with the rest of North America, although she allowed English, French and Portuguese fishermen to share the offshore fisheries.   However, in 1585, an English fleet under Sir Bernard Drake attacked the Spanish Newfoundland fishing fleet and damaged it so badly that in later years, fewer and fewer Spanish fishermen were seen in Newfoundland waters.

Gradually, more and more tiny English settlements appeared in the bays and coves along the eastern coastline.   They came into existence because of the fishing industry and were not officially-sponsored colonies, as were the later English colonies on the mainland.   It is true that several deliberate attempts at settlement were made by Englishmen in the early 1600's, but these proved to be failures.

One great handicap faced by those desiring to colonize New- **Settlement discouraged** foundland was the hostility of the fishing interests.   The wealthy English merchants who controlled most of the fishing operations viewed settlement as a threat to their own prosperous enterprises. They had no desire to see farms attracting fishermen to the island, or growing settlements taking over the best harbours, or settlers who could fish for themselves.   In protests to the English government the merchants declared that settlement could only destroy a great fishing industry that was vitally important to the nation. They pointed out, too, that the soil and climate of Newfoundland was not suitable to agriculture.

The attitude of the merchant-fishermen led to a long, bitter struggle between those who wanted settlement and those who opposed it.   Permanent residents already established on the island resented the fishing monopoly held by the large companies and the arrogant manner of the crews who came yearly to the fishing grounds.   Numerous clashes developed between the residents and the employees of the companies.   Frequent outbreaks of violence led to property damage, to human injuries and to sudden deaths.

Word of these disorders reached England.   Unfortunately, the merchants had more influence in Parliament than the residents of Newfoundland, and the settlers were made to appear a lawless, rebellious group of people.   In 1634, therefore, very strict regulations were passed to control the English fisheries and settlements in Newfoundland.

"Fishing
Admirals"
The most troublesome of the new regulations concerned the appointment of officials who came to be known as the "Fishing Admirals."   By law, the commander of the first boat arriving each spring in a Newfoundland harbour was to have complete authority that year over the harbour and any settlement located near it.

Local government by the "Fishing Admirals" gave great power to the merchants and none at all to the permanent residents of the island.   In some districts, houses, wharves and equipment were destroyed in an effort to drive residents away.   One law forbade settlers to build houses or other buildings within six miles of the coast.   Some residents ignored the law and others settled themselves in little coves along isolated parts of the island. All of these events brought poverty and miserable living conditions to those struggling to maintain homes in Newfoundland.   The dangers of hunger, disease and the destruction of their property were continual threats to their well-being.   Early visitors to the

Arguments and disputes between the residents of Newfoundland and the summer fishermen were widespread. By an English regulation issued in 1663, masters of vessels were prohibited from carrying settlers to the island, and rules were issued to bring back every fisherman taken over. Under these conditions it is little wonder that the settlement of Newfoundland progressed slowly.

island were appalled by the crude homes and difficulties of these unfortunate people.

Perhaps the saddest chapter in Newfoundland history is that concerning the white settlers and the Indians. The natives, known as Beothuks, were a proud but peaceful people who, from the beginning, showed the friendliest of intentions towards Europeans. There is actually no record of these Indian tribesmen fighting against the whites unless they themselves were first attacked.

It may be that the first troubles between the Beothuks and Europeans arose when the Indians "borrowed" fishing gear from the properties of the settlers. This procedure, in the minds of the Indians, was a perfectly natural one, for they accepted it among themselves as a common practice. To the white men, on the other hand, the borrowing of gear was considered sufficient excuse to hunt down and kill Beothuks suspected of stealing.

Massacre of the Beothuk Indians As a result the natives withdrew from the region of the settlements, avoiding the settlers as much as possible. Nevertheless, the murder of Indians continued for two hundred years, until finally the last of the Beothuks was wiped out. What had begun as fitful raids to punish the Indians, gradually developed into an organized campaign that represents one of the most barbarous and savage events in history. Hunting Indians literally became a cold-blooded sport in which settlers engaged for their own enjoyment. This was particularly true in the northern part of Newfoundland where the settlers were of a particularly lawless, brutal type. Men talked freely of their Indian "kills" and marked notches in their gun stocks in order to keep an accurate account. One trapper boasted a total of ninety-nine men, women and children killed.

Numbers of the Beothuks lost their lives in raids on tiny camps, but several large scale massacres took place. On one occasion, a party of fishermen trapped a whole tribe of Beothuks on a narrow neck of land stretching out into the sea. After driving the terrified Indians to the tip of the peninsula, the fishermen coolly shot them down one by one. When the carnage was over, about four hundred men, women and children lay in still heaps along the water's edge.

The killings in Newfoundland went on until 1823 when the few remaining Indians were either killed or captured. Six years later, in a hospital at St. John's, died the last of the Beothuks, an Indian girl named Shanadithi. A proud and peaceful people had been completely wiped out.

From 1585 to 1713, the English and French were fishing rivals in Newfoundland waters.   The English tended to gather in the south-eastern part of the island.   The French spread along the southern shore (and eventually to the mainland) and by 1662 dominated the whole southern shore from the garrisoned base of Placentia.   By 1700, repeated French raids on the English fisheries led to the building of Fort William at St. John's, and the establishment of a permanent English garrison.

In 1699, the right of English fishermen to go ashore on any part of Newfoundland and to exercise authority through their "admirals" was for the first time passed into law by Parliament. Settlers were still harassed by the merchant-fishermen and ignored by Parliament.   Newfoundland continued to be a fishing-station and a place where young seamen were trained, young seamen who later took their places in the Royal Navy.

18

VIRGINIA

During the long reign of Queen Elizabeth I, 1558 to 1603, English trade expanded rapidly, bringing new wealth to the nation from Europe, North Africa, the Mediterranean region, West Africa and from the Orient. English ships sailed the seven seas, making new discoveries and claiming new lands. It was inevitable that English traders should clash with those of other nations. In the New World, England tried to trade with the Spanish colonies but was continually repulsed by the Spaniards. The Spanish government was determined to shut other nations out of its colonies and deny them the gold and silver of Mexico and South America.

English and Spanish rivalry

At first, the English resorted to piracy. Such daring seamen as John Hawkins raided Spanish settlements in the Caribbean Sea and the Gulf of Mexico. Hawkins' pupil, Francis Drake, plundered Spanish treasure ships and ports along the west coast of South America. However, this was not enough for Queen Elizabeth who was interested in all she could learn about America —its people and products and its vast riches. The Queen was very interested in securing land in North America.

Humphrey Gilbert claims Newfoundland, 1583

An Englishman, Humphrey Gilbert, seems to have been among the first to suggest to his queen that colonies should be established in America. In 1578 Gilbert obtained royal permission to "search, find out and view such remote, heathen and barbarous lands, countries and territories not actually possessed of any Christian prince or people." The Queen provided a ship of her own, the *Falcon,* and a captain. Gilbert made several unfruitful voyages. He explored the south-western shores of Newfoundland, but never reached the North American continent. On his last voyage, while returning to England from Newfoundland waters, his ship, the *Squirrel,* and its crew, was lost during a storm.

124

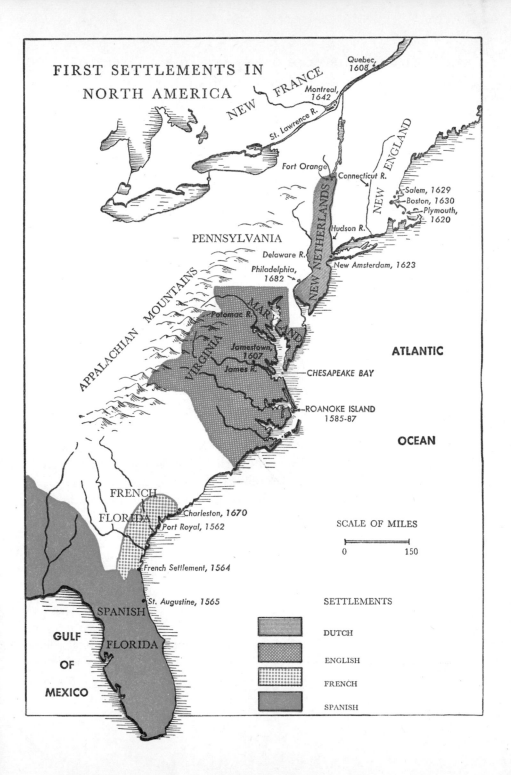

FIRST SETTLEMENTS IN
NORTH AMERICA

NEW FRANCE

Quebec, 1608

Montreal, 1642

St. Lawrence R.

NEW ENGLAND

Fort Orange

Connecticut R.

Salem, 1629
Boston, 1630
Plymouth, 1620

PENNSYLVANIA

Delaware R.

Hudson R.

NEW NETHERLANDS

Philadelphia, 1682

New Amsterdam, 1623

APPALACHIAN MOUNTAINS

MARYLAND

Potomac R.

VIRGINIA

Jamestown, 1607

James R.

ATLANTIC

CHESAPEAKE BAY

ROANOKE ISLAND
1585-87

OCEAN

FRENCH

FLORIDA

Charleston, 1670

Port Royal, 1562

SCALE OF MILES

0   150

French Settlement, 1564

St. Augustine, 1565

SPANISH

GULF

FLORIDA

OF

MEXICO

SETTLEMENTS

DUTCH

ENGLISH

FRENCH

SPANISH

Walter Raleigh and Virginia

Walter Raleigh, half-brother to Gilbert, believed that English colonies should be established in North America, even in those regions claimed by Spain. He was pleased, therefore, in 1584, when he received royal authority for such an undertaking. Raleigh dispatched two vessels, one of them again a Queen's ship, which made a landing at an offshore island (Roanoke). Here the commander of the expedition claimed the surrounding region and named it *Virginia* in honour of Queen Elizabeth.

Settlement on Roanoke Island, 1585

The following spring, a group of settlers was sent out to establish a colony on Roanoke Island. After one lonely, miserable winter these people returned to England. An attempt to settle on the mainland was made in 1587, but the sailors refused to carry the colonists beyond Roanoke Island. Then, because there was war in Europe, no English vessels returned to the island until 1590. When the ships finally reached the spot of settlement, the crews found nothing but a deserted ruin. What tragedy struck this unfortunate colony still remains a mystery. Perhaps it was wiped out by the Indians or by the Spanish.

New English trading companies, 1606

No further colonization was undertaken until 1606 when two English companies were formed to trade in North America. One of these, known as the *London Company,* was composed largely of London merchants. The other, the *Plymouth Company,* was made up of traders in the ports of Plymouth, Bristol and Exeter. The two companies were given the right to settle and trade in North America under certain conditions. Each company was to control a territory fifty miles north and south of its first settlement, a hundred miles out to sea and one hundred miles inland. Neither company was to found a colony within one hundred miles of the other. As it happened, the Plymouth Company made an unsuccessful attempt to settle in what is now the state of Maine in 1607-08.

In December, 1606, the London Company sent out three vessels, the *Susan Constant,* the *Godspeed* and the *Discovery* which arrived in Chesapeake Bay in May, 1607. Of the 120 colonists who had crowded aboard the ships, sixteen died during the voyage.

The ships sailed into the mouth of a river flowing into Chesapeake Bay. Here the weary people were delighted with the region they saw about them. One of them described the land in these words:

Wheresoever we landed upon the River, wee saw the goodliest Woods as Beech, Oke, Cedar, Cypresse and Wal-nuts, Sassafras, and Vines in abundance, which hang in great clusters on many Trees unknowne; and all grounds bespread with many sweet and delicate flowres of divers colours and kindes. There are also many fruites as Strawberries, Mulberries, and Fruites unknowne. There are many branches of this River, which runne flowing through the Woods with great plentie of fish of all kindes; as for Sturgeon, all the World cannot be compared to it. There is also great stores of Deere, both Red and Fallow. There are Beares, Foxes, Otters, Bevers, Muskats, and wild beasts unknowne.

Members of the expedition had been instructed to select a site in Virginia that was located on an island in a navigable river. Despite such instructions they chose to remain on a swampy peninsula near the mouth of a river they called the James in

Founding of Jamestown, 1607

There were means of illumination other than candles in pioneer days.   One of the earliest consisted of burning pine knots cut from the pitch pine. The burning knots were used by both Indians and white settlers in many colonies. Outdoors, the knots were burned in an iron frame called the "cresset", two types of which are shown. There were various designs, but they had in common a spike or pole thrust into the ground or attached firmly to some support. Rushes gathered in marshes, when dipped in tallow or grease, made a splendid light and thus were also much used.

honour of their king, James I. On this defensible peninsula was established the settlement, Jamestown. As soon as possible, a fort, a church, a storehouse and a few rude shelters were constructed.

Shortly after the ships returned to England, the colonists, their food supplies dwindling, began to suffer from disease and from Indian attacks. Due to the swampy nature of the land, mosquitoes became a worrisome pest, spreading malaria fever among the people.

Captain John Smith When the commander of Jamestown tried to save the food supplies by issuing short rations, he was put out of office by the colonists. Then a remarkable man, Captain John Smith, a soldier of fortune who had fought in many European wars, became the leader of the colony. He possessed all the courage and energy necessary to meet the crisis.

His first task was to put all the settlers to work seeking additional food supplies. It was not easy to develop a working spirit because among the settlers were some "gentlemen" who were either too lazy or too proud to exert themselves. By forceful measures, however, Captain Smith eliminated most of the idleness in Jamestown. To relieve the famine in the settlement, Smith and his followers roved through the region buying oysters, fish, meat and wild fowl from the Indians. Although he secured considerable food in this manner, it was never quite enough to satisfy the hunger of the settlement.

Misery and death The death toll taken by disease and starvation was appalling. After the first winter in Virginia only thirty-eight of the colonists were left alive. As time dragged on, their condition showed little improvement. Despite supplies from England, of the 900 people who landed in the settlement during the first three years only 150 survived in 1610.

In 1610 Virginia acquired a governor and Captain John Smith returned to England.

The Spanish, of course, were alarmed at having an English colony in a region they claimed as their own. Accordingly, Virginia was considered a serious threat to Spain's trade and growth in the New World. A Spanish ambassador of the time said, "such a bad project should be uprooted now, while it can be done so easily." Several Spanish expeditions were sent against Jamestown, but these accomplished little.

As the years passed, conditions slowly improved. More settlers arrived, more homes were built, livestock was imported and two forts were erected on the James River. Local Indians who had proved troublesome from time to time were attacked and brought under control.

In 1612, one of the settlers, John Rolfe, began the cultivation **Tobacco** of tobacco. He utilized good quality plants brought in from the **planting** West Indies rather than the harsh tobacco grown by the Indians. To his great pleasure the plants thrived through the warm summer days. But in the beginning not even he realized that here

An early Virginian settler cultivates his tobacco plants with a heavy crude hoe. After John Rolfe had begun the cultivation of tobacco, this product became of prime importance to the colony. The increasing popularity of smoking in England and in other parts of Europe opened a rich, large market for the tobacco planters of Virginia. In time, great plantations worked by negro slaves made their appearance on land once covered by thick forests.

was the agricultural product which the colony needed. Tobacco could be grown readily and every pound produced could be sold in England. An American historian has written:

> The managers of the London Company discovered that there were certain products peculiar to the New World which might be raised and exported with great profit. Chief among these native products was the plant called tobacco, the use of which had already become fashionable in Spain, England and France. This, then, became the leading staple of the colony (Virginia), and was even used for money. So entirely did the settlers give themselves to the cultivation of the famous weed that the very streets of Jamestown were ploughed up and planted with it.

In a few years' time tobacco became an important crop, a crop so vital that it laid the foundations of the future prosperity of Virginia.

Wives for the colonists   There were few women among the first settlers, but as the colony grew, several ship-loads of unmarried girls were sent out. This plan brought an enthusiastic response from the bachelors who made hasty proposals to the young ladies. It has sometimes been suggested that the men bought their new wives. This is wholly untrue. The men did not buy their wives, but they did pay for their transportation across the Atlantic. The cost of an ocean passage was 120 pounds of tobacco.

Over the years a number of large tobacco plantations were established. These were owned by company officials and by wealthy men who agreed to bring colonists to Virginia. The land on these estates was worked by tenants holding small sections. A new supply of field labour opened with the introduction of **The first negro slaves**   negro slavery. In 1619, a Dutch ship called at Jamestown and sold a cargo of twenty slaves. Some of these were purchased by tobacco planters who were only too pleased to pay a good price for sturdy workers. This was actually the beginning of slavery in the English colonies of North America. This cruel practice did not grow rapidly in the beginning, but before 170 years were to pass, Virginia contained thousands of negro slaves.

The growth of tobacco plantations resulted in the seizure of land that the Indians considered their property. This action so angered the tribesmen that they launched a sudden attack on the outlying areas, killing three or four hundred persons.   By way of revenge, the settlers countered with a stern campaign during which most of the Indians along the James and York rivers were wiped out.

The days of starvation, fear and mass death by disease were now left behind. By 1632, the population of Virginia had increased to 5,000 people scattered about in some twenty settlements. Tobacco exports to England continued to bring increasing prosperity to the colony.

Increasing prosperity

In the seventeenth century, young women were sent out from England to become the brides of Englishmen in Virginia.   The ships in which they travelled were extemely cramped and very uncomfortable.   In rough weather these craft rocked and pitched in an alarming manner.   Note the short hair and the rather elaborate dresses worn by the women.   Some dresses of the period bore peculiar affairs, known as hip-rolls, worn just below the waist, which gave a full appearance to the costume.

Jamestown almost disappeared after 1699 when the capital of Virginia was moved to Williamsburg, a new town located some five miles away. There is, therefore, no modern town or city on the site of old Jamestown. There is, however, a splendid reconstruction of the original settlement complete with palisade, storehouse, chapel and a few crude huts. Outside the palisade stands a replica of the little glass factory where colonists produced the first glass in North America. On the James River, about one hundred yards from the palisade, are life-size reproductions of the three small vessels which came to Jamestown in 1607.

A discussion of early Virginia would not be complete without mention of the Bermuda Islands, since the settling of Virginia led quite accidentally to the colonization of these islands.

Bermuda Islands   The Bermudas, lying six hundred miles east of North America, first came to the attention of the English through a shipwreck suffered in 1609. In that year the flagship of Admiral Sir George Somers was sailing from England to Jamestown when a storm at sea was encountered. Blown from its course, the ship went aground upon the coast of Bermuda.

On his return to England, Sir George gave glowing accounts of the islands and suggested that they were quite suitable for colonization. As a result a Bermuda or Somers Islands Company was founded in 1612. Settlers were sent to the islands and from the beginning the colony enjoyed success. The colonists were spared the dangers and hardships suffered by the early settlers of Virginia. By the year 1625, there were two or three thousand persons on the islands and they were producing more tobacco than Virginia.

In later years, when the English colonies on the mainland expanded and became prosperous, the agriculture and trade of the Bermudas became less important. The islands, however, did gain new value as a base for naval ships.

19

THE PILGRIM FATHERS

When the English first began to settle permanently in Religious unrest in England North America (1607), there was no true religious freedom in England. The official form of worship was that offered by the Church of England, the church all subjects were expected to attend. Three groups of English people were dissatisfied with these conditions. The *Roman Catholics* wished to worship in accordance with the beliefs and practices of their own faith. The *Puritans* accepted the beliefs of the Church of England, but disagreed with much of its ritual and ceremony. They wished, as they said, to "purify" the Church. The *Separatists* on the other hand were a group who desired to "separate" from the Church of England in order to form congregations of their own.

The Separatists were considered a troublesome, dangerous The Separatists in Holland group and were harshly treated by the English government. In order to escape persecution, numbers of them went to Holland in the hope that there they could worship as they pleased. Although they did gain religious freedom, there were other conditions that caused dissatisfaction and unhappiness. It was most difficult for Englishmen, working in a country whose language was not their native tongue, to gain a comfortable living. However, their children were rapidly acquiring the customs and language of the Dutch, and young English people were marrying young Dutch people. It became clear, then, that in the course of time this little English community would be completely absorbed by the country of its adoption.

Separatist leaders began to discuss the possibility of emigrating to North America where they could establish a settlement, worship as they chose and still remain Englishmen. Eventually, permission was granted for the founding of a colony. King James of England, who disliked the Separatists, did not give open approval to the plan, but agreed to "wink at their departure." Perhaps he was happy to see them go.

Preparations for the journey were quickly made. John Carver was named governor of the new colony, stores were purchased and two ships chartered for the voyage. The Separatists in Holland returned to England as the first step in the venture. William Bradford, a member of the proposed expedition and later a governor of the colonists, wrote in his *History of Plymouth Plantation*:

> So they left that goodly & pleasante citie (Leyden, Holland) which had been their resting place for near 12 years; but they knew they were *pilgrimes,* & looked not much on those things, but lifted up their eyes to ye heavens, their dearest countrie, and quieted their spirits.

The *Mayflower*, 1620   Eventually all was ready for the departure from England. One vessel, the *Speedwell*, proved unseaworthy, and so the company of 102 Pilgrims departed in the other ship, the *Mayflower*. The date was September 16, 1620. They were on their way to the coastline north of Virginia, a region explored in 1614 by Captain John Smith. He described his explorations in his *Description of New England*. The term he used is still given to this area of North America.

The Pilgrims   It is commonly supposed that the Pilgrims were Puritans; that they were a humble, quiet people; that they dressed soberly and that they were uninterested in worldly things. None of these remarks is completely true. The great majority of the Pilgrims were Separatists and a few were Puritans. Far from being a humble, quiet people, they were proud, bold, courageous and argumentative. They enjoyed the simple pleasures of the time, ate well, drank alcoholic beverages and liked colourful clothing. Only on Sundays did they dress in sober costumes. However, of the company which faced the Atlantic crossing, a number were "strangers" who did not belong to the Separatists or Puritans. Among these were members of the Church of England who had joined the expedition because they were interested in going to North America, some indentured servants and some hired sailors. Among these "strangers" was a short, red-haired man, Captain

Miles Standish, an experienced soldier, who was to become an important figure in the future settlement.

On November 21, 1620, the *Mayflower* anchored off Cape Cod, near the site of the present city of Provincetown, Massachusetts. The Pilgrims had no authority to settle in this region, but nonetheless they decided to do so. There is some evidence to suggest that they never intended to go to Virginia as their charter had instructed. Perhaps they deliberately avoided Virginia because they knew the settlers there to be members of the Church of England.

Mayflower Compact

The dignified Old Ship Meeting House in Hingham, Massachusetts, was a form of building quite common in New England during the seventeenth century. Town meetings as well as religious services were held in such quarters. The term "meeting house" was created by the Puritans because they so disliked the word "church". After coming to North America, they decided that their services would be held in a building unlike the churches they had known in England. The name "Old Ship", as applied to this particular meeting house, arose from the appearance of the interior which resembled an upturned ship.

Due to rebellious feelings among some members of the company, the Pilgrim leaders decided that a written agreement of their government should be signed before a landing was made. This agreement, known as the *Mayflower Compact,* is now considered to be one of the most important documents in United States history. By the *Compact* signed in the cabin of the *Mayflower,* the Pilgrims agreed to remain loyal to the English king, and to make whatever laws were needful for the "general good of the colony." They also re-affirmed that John Carver should be their first governor.

Plymouth Settlement, 1620   While the *Mayflower* rode at anchor off the tip of Cape Cod, scouting parties were sent to examine the shores of Massachusetts Bay, and a harbour, named after Plymouth, was chosen as the most suitable site for the new colony. It was actually more than six weeks after first sighting land that the whole company had the opportunity of standing on shore. Whether any of the company in landing actually stepped on the famous boulder now called Plymouth Rock is not known. However, Plymouth settlement arose on the land lying behind the location of the famous rock.

It was now the last week in December and weather conditions were anything but pleasant. Some of the settlers lived in rude shelters, while others remained aboard the *Mayflower.* The cold, damp weather and the lack of warm shelter resulted in difficult living conditions.

Winter hardships   During the remaining months of winter and early spring, the colonists suffered unbelievable hardships and tragedy. Disease struck with such force that at times there were daily deaths in the settlement. Whole families were wiped out. Bradford describes the plight of the people in these words:

But that which was most sadd and lamentable was, that in 2. or 3. moneths time halfe of their company dyed, espetialy in Jan: and February, being the depth of winter and wanting homes and other comforts; being infected with the scurvie and other diseases . . .; so as ther dyed some times 2. or 3. of a day, in the aforesaid time; that of 100 and odd persons, scarce 50. remained. And of these in the time of most distres, ther was but 6. or 7. sound persons . . .

In the beginning, no Indians were seen in the neighbourhood, **Indian contacts** but as time went by, an occasional tribesman or small group was observed. Fearful of sudden attack, the colonists elected Miles Standish as their Captain-General in charge of defence. Several cannon were brought ashore and plans were made for action in time of danger. The first really important contact with the Indians, however, required no battle for survival. An Indian simply walked into the settlement, smiled broadly and said, "Welcome!" If this native had flown in on wings, the colonists could not have been more startled. This rather amusing encounter was a vital one, for it brought lasting benefits to Plymouth. It led to a meeting with a second English-speaking Indian, Squanto, and eventually with Chief Massasoit who lived some forty miles from the settlement. By a remarkable piece of good fortune, Governor Carver was able to make a treaty with the chief, a peace treaty that was not to be broken for more than half a century.

On April 5, 1621, as the *Mayflower* sailed for England, the

The New England colonists frequently built homes in the form of "salt-box houses", so named because they resembled a salt container of the time. The house illustrated below was built in 1686. Compare its design with that of the French house on page 166. In New England, houses were often built around a giant central chimney that contained two or more fireplaces. Wood was in plentiful supply, and was commonly used in the construction of homes. Windows were small because glass was scarce and expensive. Some of the early homes were provided with secret passages to lofts or cellars as an escape route during Indian attacks. These narrow passages were sometimes fitted into the structure of the chimney.

The Pilgrims enjoy a Thanksgiving Dinner. During this period plates and bowls were usually made of wood. Dinner plates, known as "trenchers", were often turned over after the main course and the dessert eaten on the reverse side. Puritan thrift, too, sometimes required that more than one person should eat from a single plate. Forks were practically unknown and knives were often of the pocket variety. Spoons, the primary table implement, were sometimes improvised from hollow gourds in imitation of the Indian practice. Children, having no place at the table with their elders, were expected to sit or stand separately. The homes seen in the background represent "second" dwellings built by the colonists. These structures were considerably more substantial and comfortable than the first crude affairs erected on arrival in North America. One essential feature of even the smallest house was a massive field stone fireplace, which was used for cooking and heating.

colonists watched her departure sadly, and their sadness was further increased a week later when Governor Carver died. A new leader, William Bradford, was elected. He was an energetic, intelligent, courageous young man and was to govern Plymouth for more than thirty years.

The Indian, Squanto, who enjoyed living at Plymouth, was an invaluable member of the community. The colonists discovered that he spoke their own language because he had spent several years in England, a result of being carried off across the Atlantic by an English explorer. Squanto's knowledge of hunting,

V. MOULD

fishing and Indian methods of agriculture undoubtedly saved the colony from total starvation. It is recorded that he:

directed them how to set their corn, where to take their fish and to procure their other commodities, and was also their pilot to bring them to unknown places for their profit and never left them till he died.

The first crop harvested by the colonists was not as bountiful as they had hoped, but it did increase their food supplies. There were other things to be thankful for as well: trade in beaver skins had begun; there was no illness in the settlement and seven houses and four dormitories had been erected. In view of all these blessings, the Pilgrims decided to hold a festival to give thanks to God for their survival. By way of preparation, men were sent out hunting in the forest and an invitation to the festival was extended to Massasoit and his followers. When the time came, the chief arrived in the company of ninety hungry tribesmen. This was to be no mere Thanksgiving dinner as we know it today, but a three-day celebration complete with a military review, games of skill and songs and prayers. Despite the many guests there was no lack of food; the company feasted on venison, wild geese, wild ducks, clams, fish, corn bread, watercress, leeks, plums, berries and wine made from wild grapes.

Growth in trade and settlement

Trading posts and small settlements were soon established in the districts around Plymouth. Nevertheless the colony grew slowly. Even after ten years there were but 300 people living there. However, conditions improved bit by bit, and by 1642, twenty-two years after the founding of Plymouth, the town boasted 3,000 citizens. By this time, too, they had many neighbours.

Along the New England coast, a Puritan group, known as the Massachusetts Bay Company, founded several settlements among which were Salem (1629) and Boston (1630). In succeeding years settlements of thousands of people came into being to form the New England colonies of Massachusetts, New Hampshire, Rhode Island, and Connecticut (and at a much later date, Vermont and Maine).

Trade, farming, Industry

Due to the rock-strewn, hilly nature of the New England region, farming was carried on only with great difficulty. Lacking thick layers of rich soil and level stretches of ground, colonists were just able to grow food sufficient to meet their own needs. They had no crop of Virginian tobacco to bring steady profits into the northern colonies. Many of the people living immediately on the coast turned to fishing as a means of supporting themselves. Indeed some of them managed to combine the occupations of farming and fishing.

The ample supply of good timber close to the ocean helped to make shipbuilding an industry of importance. This activity began as early as 1631 when the governor of Connecticut built a small vessel known as the *Blessing of the Bay*. In time small shipyards arose at the mouths of nearly every navigable river running down to the sea through timber country. In these yards the neighbourhood farmers, fishermen and trappers worked in the off-season building vessels. New England built hundreds of ships for which there was a ready sale in the colonies and in England. But the New Englanders did not sell all their vessels. They used many of them to transport their prime export—fish—to the other colonies, to the West Indies and Europe in exchange for tobacco, fruits, sugar, rum, furniture, cloth, linen and other household items.

A representative group of table utensils, made largely of wood, of the type used in New England during the seventeenth century.   The two large articles are drinking vessels, on the left being, (1) a "noggin", which was passed from person to person at the table, and (2) a staved "tankard".   In the background is (3) a wooden sugar bowl, and in the foreground are two spoons, one (4) of wood, and the other (5) made from a nut with handle attached.   A dipper (6) is formed from a dried gourd. Item (7) is a wooden salt cellar.   Most utensils were left in their natural state, free of paint or varnish.   The grain of the wood, usually maple, provided a rich, beautiful appearance.

Thus, because there was little manufacturing and little ready cash in New England, families were forced to trade for most of their own daily needs.   Life under such conditions developed an independent people, resourceful, shrewd and thrifty.   These were the people who first became known as *Yankees* (a word of **Yankees** unknown origin, but meaning a person born or living in New England).   In time, they became vigorous traders and merchants. In time, they were to play an important part in the formation of the United States of America.

20

THE NEW NETHERLANDS

During the seventeenth century, the Netherlands (Holland) became an important trading nation, sending ships on long voyages to Africa, Ceylon, India, Java and the East Indies. The Dutch East India Company owned and controlled most of these roving vessels. Since the ships were forced to sail around Africa in order to reach India, the Company was interested in discovering a shorter and more direct sea route and, in 1609, employed an English seaman, Henry Hudson, to search for a north-west passage to the Orient.

Hudson's voyage, 1609
Henry Hudson set out across the Atlantic in a ship named the *Half-Moon*. After sighting Newfoundland, the explorer sailed southward along the coast to a point somewhere below Virginia. Then returning northward, he continued sailing until he came to what is now New York harbour. Finding there the wide mouth of a river (the Hudson), and thinking that this might be the sea passage he sought, he made his way upstream, until he reached the spot where the city of Albany now stands. By this time, the salt water of the channel had turned to fresh, and Hudson realized that the waterway could not be a sea route to the East.

Hudson's voyage was a disappointment to the Dutch even though the explorer explained that valuable furs could be obtained by trading with the Indians along the upper reaches of the Hudson. Most of the Dutch were unimpressed, but a few traders appreciated the possibilities of the region and conducted trading operations with the Iroquois. In 1614, the New Netherlands Company was formed and given trading rights. A rapid expansion of the fur trade and exploration quickly followed.

Settlements in New Netherlands
The first Dutch colonists were sent out to North America in 1623. Most of them settled on what are now Manhattan Island and Staten Island, but a few pushed on up the Hudson to Fort Orange near the site of present-day Albany. New Amsterdam was

the name given to the Manhattan Island settlement. No one at the time, of course, realized that part of the City of New York, would eventually rise on this location. Purchasing the island was a simple matter: it was secured from the Indians in exchange for trade goods worth no more than twenty-four dollars. The cost amounted to about one-sixth of a cent per acre. Today Manhattan is one of the most valuable pieces of real estate on the globe and twenty-four dollars would not buy one square foot of sidewalk.

Defence was always one of the first considerations in the founding of a new colony. The Dutch built a strong fort at New Amsterdam and stationed a warship nearby. There was always the chance that the Spanish, the English or the Indians might launch a surprise attack.

In 1635, Fort Amsterdam replaced the earlier Fort Manhattan, built by a Dutch trading company in 1613. The buildings, storehouses and soldiers' quarters were designed in much the same fashion as other structures in New Amsterdam. Notice that the buildings are completely surrounded by a stout wall, and are protected by cannon. During the day, Dutch troops carried out military drill on the green in front of the fort.

One interesting place in modern New York City derives its name from early New Amsterdam. The centre of the great financial district of New York is Wall Street, named after a defensive wall that once stood across the lower end of Manhattan Island.

Patroon system Since the future of the region called the New Netherlands seemed promising, the Dutch began a large-scale settlement of the Hudson Valley. Their plan of colonization was known as the *patroon system,* a system composed of wealthy landowners and poor tenant farmers.

The landowners or *patroons* were granted estates along the Hudson, each holding extending sixteen miles along the waterfront and stretching as far back from the river as the owner wished. Important privileges were granted to the patroons; their agreements stated that they were to "possess and enjoy all the lands lying within the aforesaid limits, together with the fruits, rights, minerals, rivers and fountains thereof." A patroon receiving a land grant agreed to pay transport from Holland of his tenants, equip and stock their farms and provide a schoolmaster and a clergyman.

In return for these privileges, the tenants agreed to work the patroon's land for ten years, sell their own produce to the patroon, bring grain to the patroon's mill and pay for the grinding, and bring all land disputes before the patroon's court. In addition, certain restrictions were placed upon the freedom of the tenant. He could not leave the service of the patroon without consent: he could not fish or hunt on the patroon's estate and he could not weave cloth, being forced to buy material imported from Holland.

Under such circumstances as these the patroons became wealthy and powerful men enjoying the rights of landowners, rulers and judges. Tenants were in no position to contradict the will of the patroons or challenge their authority. The negro slaves who worked on the estates had even fewer rights than the tenants.

As the land on both sides of the Hudson was taken up, more estates were established on nearby rivers. The spread of settlement caused such alarm among some of the Indians that they became restless and hostile. At times they launched attacks. However, trade in Iroquois furs was unaffected and continued to flourish.

In 1647, the New Netherlands acquired a new governor in the person of Peter Stuyvesant, a man hot-tempered and stubborn but at the same time honest and fearless. Having lost one leg in European warfare, Peter Stuyvesant limped about on an artificial limb, carved out of a block of solid wood and bound with silver. He was known among the colonists as "Old Silverleg."

Peter Stuyvesant's temper and determination landed him in trouble from time to time. In the beginning he ruled the colony in a very dictatorial manner, but was eventually forced to adopt more democratic methods. He was made to accept an elected "Council of Nine Men" to assist him in the management of the colony.

In spite of his faults, Stuyvesant proved to be a good governor. He took energetic measures to improve conditions in the town of New Amsterdam. Regulations were passed to control crime, rowdiness, the sale of liquor and the breaking of the Sabbath. The town, as a result, took on a new appearance of orderliness and industry. By 1656, the population was 1,000 people, many of whom were negro slaves.

The New Netherlands prospered, but threats of English interference were causing considerable alarm. Nearby English colonies were closing in about the Dutch land and numerous quarrels were arising over boundary lines. There were attempts on both sides to seize borderline districts.

This tense situation came to a climax in 1664 when King Charles II of England granted his brother, the Duke of York, all the land from the Connecticut River to Delaware Bay. Charles was quite aware that the New Netherlands occupied part of this region, but that made little difference to him. He believed the whole eastern coastline of America belonged to England, because John Cabot had claimed it in 1497.

In 1664, an English fleet appeared before New Amsterdam and demanded its surrender. Hot-tempered Peter Stuyvesant was furious with this enemy action. He replied to the English com-

mander stating that he had "nothing to answer."   One history of
New Amsterdam describes Stuyvesant's actions as follows:

Thus having thrown his gauntlet, the brave Peter stuck a pair
of horse-pistols in his belt, girded an immense powder-horn on his
side, thrust his sound leg into a Hessian boot, and clapping his fierce
little war-hat on top of his head, paraded up and down in front of his
house, determined to defend his beloved city to the last.

A street scene in New Amsterdam, a settlement that once stood in the lower part of
what is now New York City.   Note the costumes and the windmill in the background.   Homes were constructed in the Dutch fashion with high ornamental
gables.   Much of the brick used in building was actually transported in ships
across the Atlantic.

Unfortunately for the governor, the Dutch colonists did not share his fighting spirit. They saw little gain in battling a well-disciplined and well-armed English fleet. New Amsterdam surrendered after making suitable terms with the enemy, whereby the Dutch were guaranteed life, liberty, religious freedom and a share in government. New Netherlands surrendered to the English, 1664

When the English took control of the New Netherlands, the area became the Colony of New York, and New Amsterdam became "His Majesty's town of New York."

Discouraged by this turn of events, Peter Stuyvesant sailed to Holland, but a love of North America ran strong in his blood. After a short time he returned to New York where he spent the rest of his life on the farm he called his "great bouwery," an area occupied by today's Bowery district of New York City.

In later years the Dutch and the English settled down in peace to develop what later became the wealthy and vital State of New York.

21

MARYLAND

Fourteen years after the Pilgrim Fathers crossed the Atlantic, a company of Roman Catholics left England in search of freedom of worship. At this time, English Roman Catholics were as much subject to religious pressure as were such Protestant sects as the Separatists, the Puritans and the Quakers. The Church of England was the established Church, the national Church, and all subjects were required to attend Anglican services. Those who did not ran the risk of being arrested and fined.

Founding of Maryland, 1634

The Roman Catholic move to North America was initiated by Lord Baltimore, an English nobleman. Lord Baltimore received from King Charles 1 the ownership of land which the king himself named Maryland in honour of his own Queen. Thus, in the spring of 1634, a company of about 300 persons landed on the north bank of the Potomac River, a location some distance north of Jamestown, Virginia. Approximately twenty of the new-arrivals were Catholic gentlemen while the rest were mainly labourers of whom some were Protestant.

Lord Baltimore was extremely generous in the administration of his colony, allowing considerable political and religious freedom to the colonists. All Christians were permitted to worship in accordance with their own beliefs and faiths. This freedom was confirmed by a law passed in 1649, stating that no man professing belief in Jesus Christ should be "in any ways troubled molested or discountenanced for or in respect to his or her religion nor in the free exercise thereof." In no other English colony, except in the later one of Pennsylvania, was such liberty extended to the people.

Agriculture

From its earliest days Maryland was an agricultural colony. The land was divided up into large estates held by a few wealthy men who brought out colonists to work for them. Some of these

148

great estates lying along the rivers and on Chesapeake Bay varied in size from 2,000 to 5,000 acres. Each estate paid a yearly rent to Lord Baltimore. As in Virginia, tobacco became the most important crop. The culture of tobacco gained a vital place in Maryland's economy and there was little in the way of industry. There were no towns of any consequence. Roads were few and most travel and transportation depended upon the river and the coastal waters.

In seventeenth-century North America the water well was normally located in the yard not far from the house. Water was raised from the well by means of a "well-sweep" connected to a rope and an oak bucket. The sweep itself was a long pole, often of birch, placed on a wooden support. Being balanced nicely on its support, the sweep drew up a pail of water when a light pull was given to the rope. In later years, the colonists employed improved lifts in the form of the windlass.

The colony prospered with the passage of time. The wealthy tobacco planters built large homes staffed by negro slaves and equipped with fine furniture. Among the many furnishings of these plantation homes were silverware, table linens, pictures, mirrors, brass fixtures, chinaware, tapestries and musical instruments. These homes were in sharp contrast to the crude slave quarters and the shabby homes of the labourers and small farmers.

Boundary disputes   From time to time the colony became involved in boundary disputes with Virginia and also with Pennsylvania which was founded towards the end of the seventeenth century. One of the most interesting disputes was that of 1682 concerning the proper boundary between Maryland and Pennsylvania. This problem was eventually solved by a land survey made by two noted English surveyors, Mason and Dixon, who were engaged to establish a boundary agreeable to both colonies. Mason and Dixon surveyed a line from the north-eastern part of Maryland westward for a distance of 300 miles. In later years the Mason-Dixon line was to signify much more than a boundary between two English colonies. Events were to make this line the division between the free and the slave states of the United States.

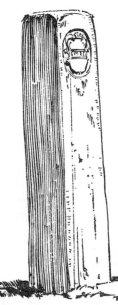

The colony of Maryland remained a proprietary colony under Lord Baltimore's descendants until the time of the American Revolution in 1776.

One of the original stone boundary markers placed between the colonies of Maryland and Pennsylvania. The marker bore on one side the crest of Pennsylvania, and on the other the crest of George Calvert, who was created Lord Baltimore.

22

PENNSYLVANIA

While Virginia, Maryland, New York and the New England colonies were expanding, yet another English colony was established on the east coast of North America.

Among the Protestant sects of England were the Friends, or **Quakers** Quakers, a sober, gentle, devout people who held ideas considered odd and even disloyal by the members of other religious groups. The Quakers, believing that all men are born free and equal in the sight of God, would not use titles of respect, nor would they take off their hats to anyone—not even the king. They would not give testimony under oath in a court of justice; they would not pay taxes to support any form of public worship, and unwilling to kill, they would not engage in military service. In view of these attitudes the Quakers were in unending conflict with the government and with the Church of England. Indeed, the Quakers became a persecuted group both in England and the colonies.

Fortunately, the Quakers acquired a strong champion in the **William Penn** person of a well-educated, wealthy gentleman named William Penn. A Quaker himself, Penn was anxious to secure land in North America where members of his sect could found a colony of their own, a place where they could live by themselves in peace.

As it happened, the spendthrift English king, Charles II, owed Penn's family the sum of £16,000. Sensing an opportunity in this situation, William Penn suggested that the king give him land in America by way of repaying the loan. Charles was only too pleased to agree; such land would cost the royal pocket nothing at all. Thus, Penn received a large grant of land fronting the **Penn's** Delaware river. The king himself named the area *Pennsylvania*, **Woodland** "Penn's Woodland," in reference to the beautiful forests of that region.

An advance party was sent out in 1681, and William Penn followed the next year with a company of approximately one hundred English Quakers. These settlers began the establishment of Philadelphia, "the city of Brotherly Love." Penn had given careful thought to the planning of the settlement, and Philadelphia became the best-designed city in colonial America. Its streets were made so straight and wide that they have required little alteration since. Many of the fine brick houses built are still standing, and the many parks laid out in early days can still be seen.

William Penn had no desire to administer his colony for the benefit of Quakers alone. He hoped that other people, dissatisfied with life in Europe, might find a haven of freedom

Among the various European groups who settled in Pennsylvania were many people from the lands along the river Rhine and from Switzerland, all of whom became known as the Pennsylvania Dutch or Pennsylvania Germans. They brought with them a unique and colourful culture, which survives in part to this day. One interesting feature of their way of life was the use of the outdoor bake-ovens (a practice also common in Quebec). Ovens of stone or brick were erected near the kitchen door and used for baking bread, pies, cakes, cookies, and also for drying fruits. Ovens were generally large enough to allow the baking of a dozen loaves of bread at one time.

in his colony.   The plan of government he promoted, therefore, was based upon two vital principles: the people were given liberty to make their own laws and the people had to give strict obedience to their laws.

From this idea of government came a number of practices that were to have important effects in later years; all colonists enjoyed the right to worship as they chose; all resident tax-payers were given the right to vote in elections; the members of any religious denomination could become members of the legislative assembly; the death penalty was to be inflicted only for the crimes of murder and treason; prisons were to be places of reform rather than places of punishment.

These ideals were remarkable for their time; they showed an interest in the rights of all citizens and offered religious freedom to all denominations.   Such rights and freedoms, of course, did not exist in England or the Europe of that period and thousands of people came to Pennsylvania from England, Wales, Ireland and various European countries.

Wisely, William Penn made early contact with the local **Indian relations** Indians, and after several meetings concluded a peace treaty in 1682.   According to the traditional story of this event, Penn met representatives of the Indians below the branches of a huge elm tree, and it was there that the details of the treaty were agreed upon.   A monument marking its site still stands in modern Philadelphia.   Another relic of the event is a wampum belt which acted as the Indian record of the treaty.   Made from coloured beads, the belt contains two figures standing side by side, holding hands, thus signifying peace and friendship.   Remarkably enough, the wampum belt is still preserved.

As long as the Quakers held control of Pennsylvania, the white colonists and the Indians lived at peace.

Philadelphia, growing rapidly, soon boasted a tannery, a **Growth of** sawmill, a flourmill and a brick kiln.   Trade was begun with the **Philadelphia** other mainland colonies.   Pennsylvania grain and beef also found a market in England and the West Indies.   A school was established and a printing press put into operation.   Long before the days of the American Revolution, Philadelphia was to become the largest and perhaps the most important city in the English colonies of North America.

William Penn himself was not a permanent resident of his colony. He lived there for several years, but he spent much of his

Candles were the chief means of illumination in pioneer days. During the spring and fall, large numbers of candles were made from the suet or fat of sheep and cattle. Long wicks of hemp-tow or cotton twine cut into proper lengths were looped around a stick and then dipped into a large kettle of melted tallow. The wicks were withdrawn, allowed to cool, and dipped again. The process continued until a sufficient thickness of tallow had built up on the wicks. Between dippings, the candles often hung from sticks resting on the backs of kitchen chairs. The nursery rhyme, "Jack be nimble. Jack be quick. Jack jump over the candle stick," sprang from this old process of candle-making.

time in England, where he managed his colonial interests and encouraged the growth of settlement.   His expenditures in Pennsylvania, however, became so burdensome that he was forced to borrow money.   This development, along with other misfortunes, actually placed him in debtors' prison for a time.   His financial situation became so desperate that he was arranging the sale of his North American rights at the time of his death.

Pennsylvania was to become not only a prosperous colony, but one which in later years was to gain special historical importance. It was in Pennsylvania that United States independence was to be declared, in Pennsylvania that the Constitution of the United States was to be framed and in Pennsylvania that the first United States government was to meet.

23

THE WEST INDIES

Extending in a curved chain of islands from Florida to within a few miles of Venezuela in South America lies the great archipelago known as the West Indies. These islands were named by Christopher Columbus who believed they lay off the west coast of India. They and their waters represent the Spanish Main of history and romance.

Island groups There are really three groups of islands within the archipelago: the Bahamas, which stretch south-eastward from Florida, the Greater Antilles, consisting of Cuba, St. Dominigue (the modern Haiti), Hispaniola, Jamaica and Puerto Rico, and the Lesser Antilles which begin east of Puerto Rico and stretch southward toward South America.

Indians When the Spanish first came to the Indies, the islands were occupied by Indians who may have migrated there from South America. They were of two groups: the Arawak people who inhabited the Bahamas and the Greater Antilles, and the Carib people who lived in the Lesser Antilles. Although the two groups appear to have lived in a similar manner, there were various differences in custom and tradition. It seems that the Caribs were cannibals and that the Arawaks were skilled farmers. There are some indications that natives of the West Indies had some communication with Indians living in Mexico and Florida.

Inhaling tobacco smoke through tubes was an established practice among the West Indians. The smoking tube itself was named "tobacco." In later years, however, the name was applied to the tobacco plant and to its cured leaves. The West Indies tobacco was of a milder quality than that grown by Indians on the mainland of North America and for this reason, tobacco plants from the islands were imported by the early planters of Virginia.

Spanish settlement In 1492, Columbus made his first landing on an island that he called San Salvador. San Salvador was probably the island of the

156

THE WEST INDIES, 1600-1700

ATLANTIC OCEAN

GULF OF MEXICO

FLORIDA

BAHAMA IS.
1612, ENG.

San Salvador I. (1492, Sp.)
(later Watling I., (Eng.))

Cuba (Sp.)

GREATER

Jamaica,
1655 (Eng.)

ANTILLES

St. Domingue (Fr.)
Hispaniola (Sp.)

Puerto
Rico (Sp.)

LESSER
ANTILLES

St. Christopher, 1625 (French)

St. Martin, 1648 (French)

St. Bartholomew, 1648 (French)

Antigua, 1688 (English)

Monserrat, 1632 (English)

Guadeloupe, 1635 (French)

Dominica, 1640 (French)

Martinique, 1635 (French)

Barbados, 1625 (English)

Grenada, 1650 (French)

Tobago, 1632 (Dutch)

Trinidad (Sp.) —

SCALE OF MILES
0   500

SOUTH AMERICA

Bahamas group now known as Watling. During the next fifty years Spanish settlements were made on all the larger islands and many of the smaller ones. In the course of Spanish occupation, thousands of Indians were killed and thousands more forced into slavery.

For a time gold mining was profitable, but farming became the prime industry and plantation owners used Indian slave labour to produce cotton, sugar and raise cattle. When the slave population rapidly decreased, the Spanish were forced to bring in negroes from Africa.

The Spanish were soon challenged in the West Indies by English, French and Dutch freebooters who quickly became aware of the opportunities to be gained. So daring and effective were these sea-rovers that the Spanish had to provide armed protection for galleons sailing between Spain and the colonies. During the latter half of the sixteenth century such English seamen as John

European rivalry

Hawkins and Francis Drake captured many Spanish vessels and raided settlements.

Raids by the freebooters, the decline of mining and the loss of Indian slaves gradually made the West Indies less attractive to the Spanish, who tended to settle in what is now Mexico, and Central and South America.

English settlements As Spain's interest and power in the West Indies waned, a magnificent opportunity to move in was given to other European powers. English action began on the Lesser Antilles in 1623, just sixteen years after the founding of Jamestown, when a settlement was formed on a small island named St. Christopher. In the same year, a second colony was begun in the Barbados. Several years later, additional settlements appeared on Antigua and Monserrat. By 1639, there were 20,000 English settlers in the West Indies at a time when there were only 7,000 in Virginia.

In later years other important settlements were established in the Lesser Antilles and in Jamaica, captured from the Spanish in 1655.

English settlers were particularly interested in the development of agriculture. Plantations were soon producing excellent crops of cotton and tobacco. It was sugar cane, first planted about 1650, that eventually became the most important product. Negro slaves, of course, formed the greater part of the labour force on the big plantations. So constant was the demand for slaves that during most of the eighteenth century 5,000 negroes were brought each year to Jamaica alone.

English planters built fine homes and made themselves as comfortable as possible in the hot climate. An early description of life on the plantations states:

"The Gentlemen's Houses are generally built low, of one Storey, consisting of five or six handsome Apartments, beautifully lined and floored with mahogany, which looks exceeding gay; they have generally a Piazza to which you ascend by several Steps, and serves as a Screen against the Heat. The Negroes have nothing but a Parcel of poor miserable Huts built of Reeds, any of which can scarce contain upwards of two or three."

Since English colonial trade was strictly regulated and duties imposed on many goods, smuggling became a profitable trade for adventurous seamen. The illustration shows smugglers loading their cargo from a beach in the West Indies. Their ship rides at anchor in deep water some distance out from the shore.

Despite Spanish opposition, the English, French and Dutch managed to establish themselves in scattered parts of the West Indies.

Trade gradually developed with the colonies of North America. New France traded with French colonies on the islands. Furs, lumber, fish and grain were sent south from New France while sugar and rum were shipped north from the West Indies. Similarly, the English mainland colonies traded furs, lumber, fish, wheat, beef and tobacco for slaves, fruits, sugar and rum, much of the fruit, sugar and rum being taken to England and exchanged for such manufactured goods as hardware, cloth, furniture, linen and wines.

At first, the English colonies in the West Indies grew rapidly, producing and exporting more goods than the mainland colonies. In time, however, the latter were to outstrip the former in population and production, and the West Indies trade eventually became of lesser importance.

SUMMARY—SECTION IV

The Newfoundland fisheries may have been known to a few European fishermen before Cabot's voyage of 1497 gave so much publicity to the Grand Banks. However, by the end of the sixteenth century, English seamen-settlers were living in coves and bays along the rocky edges of south-eastern Newfoundland. French fishermen, living all along the south shore of the island, often attacked the English fishing fleets in attempts to destroy them. The Spanish Newfoundland Fleet was driven out of the island waters by the English who now settled down to a battle for power with the French in Newfoundland.

Between 1607 and 1670, the English and Dutch managed to found colonies on the mainland of North America. France, still looking for a western route to Asia, was already establishing herself in the St. Lawrence region. Spain, settled in the New World since 1493, and now possessing land and riches, fought off attempts to enter and occupy her territories. Thus, Englishmen, Frenchmen, Spaniards and Dutchmen began to explore and colonize the Atlantic coast of North America, but it was England who came off best in the struggle for possession. Her colonists settled all along the seaboard of the continent and also in those West Indies islands ignored by Spain. The Dutch, who first explored the Hudson as a way to China, placed settlers up and down that river, but were eventually conquered by the English.

The mainland English colonies were founded for various reasons. Some of the colonists who left England wanted freedom to hold their own land and earn a better living. Others crossed the Atlantic in search of freedom to worship God in their own manner. In addition, most of the colonists were eager to find a land where they could live and govern themselves free from the rule of kings.

Many of the colonies experienced starvation and disease in their early years. But they persevered and in time became self-supporting, healthy prosperous communities, engaged in agriculture, lumbering and ship-building. They traded freely with each other, with the sugar plantations of the West Indies and with the merchants of England. Their success was destined to be a serious threat to the French in Quebec, Acadia and Newfoundland.

FIVE / *Growth in New France*

BISHOP LAVAL AND THE GOVERNORS OF NEW FRANCE

NEW FRANCE BECOMES A ROYAL COLONY, 1663

DE TRACY HUMBLES THE IROQUOIS, 1666

INTENDANT JEAN TALON

THE SEIGNEURIAL SYSTEM

LIFE IN NEW FRANCE

EXPLORATIONS OF RADISSON AND GROSEILLIERS

FOUNDING OF THE HUDSON'S BAY COMPANY, 1670

COUNT FRONTENAC ARRIVES AT QUEBEC, 1672

FRONTENAC MAKES PEACE WITH THE IROQUOIS

JOLIET AND MARQUETTE EXPLORE THE
MISSISSIPPI RIVER, 1673

LA SALLE ON THE MISSISSIPPI, 1682

EXPANSION OF THE FUR TRADE

FRONTENAC RECALLED TO FRANCE, 1682

THE IROQUOIS CLOSE IN ON NEW FRANCE

GOVERNOR LA BARRE AND THE IROQUOIS

GOVERNOR DENONVILLE AND THE IROQUOIS

THE VENGEANCE OF THE IROQUOIS—LACHINE, 1689

FRONTENAC IS ORDERED BACK TO NEW FRANCE, 1689

24

BISHOP LAVAL

The appointment of François de Laval de Montmorency as Arrival of Laval, 1659 Vicar-Apostolic of New France was a pleasing event for the colonists. When he arrived at Quebec on a June day in 1659, he was greeted by the ringing of bells, the firing of cannon and the cheering of citizens.

Laval was an unusual man who combined the devoutness of a monk, the gentleness of a nurse, the dignity of a nobleman and the determination of a soldier. At times he was so humble he cared for sick Indians; at other times he was so haughty he defied the highest French officials.

In New France all authority belonged to the governor. This was an unfortunate circumstance because a series of power quarrels developed between Laval and the governor. Laval and Governor d'Argenson were both forceful, determined men, each of whom considered himself the supreme colonial authority. They often fought over matters that now seem unimportant. For example, Laval was annoyed because soldiers would not take off their hats and kneel before him during a state ceremony. D'Argenson, on the other hand, was angry because he could not sit where he wished in church.

The next governor, d'Avaugour, had little interest in pomp and ceremony, and thus had no reason to disagree with Laval over such matters. However, they did quarrel over a much more serious affair.

Quite rightly, Laval was deeply concerned for the welfare Liquor trade with the Indians of the Indians, particularly those to whom French traders were supplying brandy in exchange for furs. The effect of spirits upon the tribesmen was frightening to witness. Drunken braves, mad with liquor, ran wild, killing and maiming their fellows. An

early French writer who spent some time in New France describes
the terror of the Indian women on such occasions:

> The women remove from the cabins the weapons on which the
> men can lay hands—muskets, axes, spears, bows and arrows, even
> knives, everything which might inflict deadly wounds. . . . Then they
> clear off to the woods with the children and hide.

Another account states:

> This drink destroys all these unfortunate people; men, women,
> and even boys and girls. Each of them eats and drinks as he or she
> desires. They become intoxicated very quickly and are then maddened.
> They run about naked, and with various weapons chase people day
> and night. They run unchecked through the streets of Quebec.

In an attempt to stop the flow of liquor to the Indians, Laval
announced that he would excommunicate any Frenchman who
dared to place brandy among his trade goods. Since excommuni-
cation meant being forbidden the services of the Roman Catholic
Church and becoming a complete outcast, the traders began to
be much more cautious in their dealings. The governor agreed
to support this campaign by enacting a stern law that decreed the
death penalty for supplying liquor to the Indians.

Although d'Avaugour had passed this harsh law, he found
it difficult to sentence his countrymen to death. When, in 1661,
two men were actually executed and a third one flogged, there was
a loud protest from the citizens of the colony. Deciding that he
could not please everyone, the governor withdrew the death
penalty. This action was naturally a cause for celebration among
the traders. In the months which followed, the Indians continued
to get drunk and cause terror in their own villages.

Angered by the unexpected turn of events, Laval returned to
France to protest against the conduct of the governor and the
fur traders. As it happened, Laval had great influence with the
government, and was able to stop the trade in liquor. D'Avaugour
was recalled and Laval was permitted to name the next governor.

**French, English
and Dutch
rivalries**

On his voyage homeward, d'Avaugour wrote a report on New
France containing a number of suggestions for the French government to note and act upon. He began his report by stating his

In sight of their own stockaded village, drunken Indians battle viciously in the snow. The liquor trade caused incredible suffering, terror and even death among the people of many tribes. On occasion, crafty tribesmen pretended drunkenness in order to commit crimes, knowing full well that the blame would be placed on the traders who provided brandy.

belief that New France held a great future, but he feared the English and the Dutch who were establishing colonies along the Atlantic coast of North America. In order to meet the English and Dutch threat he proposed that two great forts be built at Quebec, one on each side of the St. Lawrence. He suggested, too, that he be permitted to lead military expeditions against the English and Dutch colonies. It would be an easy matter, he thought, to take over the enemy settlements and place them under French governors. If the French government had acted upon this bold advice, the history of the North American continent might have developed along very different lines. But instead of the French, it was the English who went into action. It was the English who took over the New Netherlands and it was the

English who secured the trade and military alliance of the Iroquois.

New France as a royal colony, 1663 With Laval and others urging changes in the government of New France, it was not long before important improvements were made. In 1663, the control of the colony was taken away from the Company of New France and placed directly under the French crown. New France thus became a royal colony. Under the new arrangement, New France was to be governed by a Council consisting of the governor, Laval and five councillors. Two years later, in 1665, a third important official, the *Intendant,* was added to the Council. The position of intendant was an important post; the man who occupied this position ranked with Laval and the governor.

This house, no longer in existence, was one of the earliest in Quebec City. Like most of the early French colonial buildings, it was built of wood. Wooden homes, crowded closely together, were a constant fire hazard in Quebec. In the year 1682, a disastrous fire actually burned most of the Lower Town to the ground.

The fur monopoly now passed from the Company of New France to the people of the colony.   Henceforth, the most influential persons in the colony became interested in securing furs from the Indians.   In the years to come, governors, their officials and various individuals were to engage in the fur trade and the evils of brandy-trading were to return despite continued efforts by Laval to stop the sale of liquor to the Indians.

Having been given the right to name the next governor of New France, Laval selected an old friend, De Mézy, a dignified old soldier.   While sailing in the same ship across the Atlantic, the two men made plans for the governing of the colony.   But in the following months even these two friends were destined to fight bitterly over the appointment of members to the Council. The disagreement was to end only with the death of the governor in 1665.

Laval was anxious to have young men trained in New France **Education** for religious duties.   To accomplish this aim, he established the *Grand Seminaire,* a seminary for the education of priests and the *Petit Seminaire,* a school for boys.   These were supported mainly by religious taxes or *tithes* paid by the settlers of the colony.   The tithes, which were compulsory, amounted to one twenty-sixth of the harvests of grain grown on the farms.   Laval himself was so devoted to this project that he gave up his own private income for its support.

25

WAR AGAINST THE IROQUOIS

In addition to the settlements in the valley of the St. Lawrence, France now had colonies in Guiana (South America) and in the West Indies. In charge of all these colonies was placed an experienced soldier Alexandre de Prouville, Sieur de Tracy, who was given the title Lieutenant-General of the French dominions.

Arrival of de Tracy, 1665 In 1664, de Tracy left France with troops and a small fleet of ships to inspect the colonies. After lengthy visits in Guiana and in the West Indies, he eventually arrived at Quebec in the summer of 1665. Following a rousing welcome, the Lieutenant-General marched up Mountain Street to the church where Laval waited to receive him.

De Tracy carried news that gave great encouragement to the colonists. The government of France was taking fresh interest in the colony. More settlers would find homes in New France; young women would arrive as wives for unmarried men; strong defences would be built and the Iroquois would be crushed into submission. As proof of the government's military intentions, de Tracy had brought with him a body of regular soldiers who had distinguished themselves in the wars against the Turks. The *Carignan-Salières* regiment, composed of more than 1,100 officers and men, disembarked at Quebec. It was a stirring sight as they marched through the streets with bands playing and flags flying. Here was military protection completely unknown in the days of Champlain.

The first move against the Iroquois was the construction of three forts on the Richelieu River. The locations were carefully chosen: this was the waterway that the Indians used to attack the heart of New France.

De Courcelle invades Iroquois territory, 1665 Eager to start action against the Iroquois, the new governor, Daniel de Rémy, Sieur de Courcelle, urged immediate attack. De Tracy and some of his officers, however, preferred to make more careful preparations before invading the Indian lands. In spite of de Tracy's advice, Courcelle gathered together about 500 volunteers from Quebec, Three Rivers and Montreal. In midwinter they set off to attack the Mohawks.

It was a foolhardy expedition. The winter weather was bitter and the men had to travel on foot with heavy packs on their backs. Being w i t h o u t proper winter clothing, many of the marchers suffered from frozen hands and feet. The expedition pushed on to what is now the city of Schenectady in the state of New York, and during all this rugged march saw no signs of the Iroquois. Courcelle was surprised to meet Englishmen who informed him that his troops were invading the territory of an English colony. Moreover, the English said, he would not meet the Iroquois because they were away from their villages.

An officer of the Carignan-Salières Regiment wearing a uniform composed of a brown coat, grey stockings, a white belt and a wide-brimmed black hat. Soldiers of this famous regiment had gained much battle experience in Europe before coming to North America. Following their military campaigns in New France, a number of the officers and men requested their discharge and remained as settlers in the colony.

Seeing no value in advancing farther, the governor turned back toward New France. The return trip was even more desperate than the outgoing one. Food supplies ran low. The French were poor hunters, and killed little game. Before the

Two Mohawk warriors watch from a height of land as their villages burn in the valley below. De Tracy had been prepared to retire, unaware of the existence of one large, fortified village, Andaraque, but he came across an old Algonquin woman who had once been a Mohawk prisoner. With pistol in hand, she led the French through the forest to this impressive fort. After the destruction of this and other forts, there was widespread famine throughout the Mohawk land.

little army had stumbled back to Quebec, sixty men had died from starvation and hardship.

Although the march into the Iroquois region had failed, it so alarmed the Mohawks that they tried to make peace with the French. To this end, they sent a group of tribesmen to Quebec. One of these warriors made the error of boasting that he himself had murdered a Frenchman. In anger, de Tracy seized the brave and had him hanged before the eyes of his fellow tribesmen. This stern action seems to have prevented the two groups from coming to any peace agreement.

De Tracy attacks the Iroquois, 1666   In the fall of 1666, de Tracy decided that the time had come for a strong blow against the Iroquois. It was a season suited to attack; the weather was pleasant, and the enemy crops stood ripe and golden in the fields. Leaving Quebec with a flotilla of flat-bottomed boats, de Tracy and 1200 men moved up the St. Lawrence and Richelieu rivers and down the length of Lake Champlain to Lake George.

Leaving the boats behind, the French column began a one hundred mile march through forests aflame with autumn colours. During crisp, fall days they followed woodland trails, climbed ridges and forded swift, cold streams. At one point de Tracy escaped drowning only through the quick action of a Huron guide.

The invaders' intention was to attack and destroy Mohawk villages. However, there were to be no surprise attacks, for Iroquois scouts kept watchful eyes on the advancing column.

When de Tracy eventually reached Mohawk territory, he discovered deserted villages. No warwhoops sounded in the forests, no arrows hissed through the air. The great wooden lodges stood still and silent, with the grey ashes of dead fires scattered about the earthen floors. Even in the largest and best-protected of all the villages there was no Mohawk garrison.

The last of the strongholds, Andaraque, had three rectangular palisades, thirty feet in height and fitted with sturdy bastions which commanded the whole length of the walls. This was unlike **Destruction** any other Iroquois fortress, and the French concluded that Dutch **of Mohawk villages** soldiers had helped in the construction of the fortifications. So strong were these defences that had the Mohawks remained, the French might well have been unable to take the villages.

As it was, de Tracy's men simply broke through the main gateway and passed into the centre of the stronghold. Here the French were amazed at the design and the size of the lodges, some of which were 120 feet in length. In underground cellars they found great stores of dried meat, dried fish and corn meal.

When the French set the buildings afire, the dry wood burst into flames, which soaring aloft, could be seen for miles. It was not a pleasant sight for the Indian scouts who watched from the distant hills.

By November, 1666, de Tracy was back at Quebec reporting the results of his expedition.

The Mohawks managed to survive the winter even though their villages lay in ruins. By now, they, along with the other Iroquois tribes, were prepared to "bury the hatchet" with the French. The Iroquois were still busy fighting their southern neighbours, the Andastes Indians, for access to the furs of the Ohio and Mississippi valleys and were not at this time prepared to do battle with the French as well.

Indian peace, 1667   In July, 1667, representatives of the League met at Quebec and made peace with the French. For the next twenty years the French and the Iroquois were to remain on peaceful if not friendly terms.

That same summer, in the month of August, de Tracy sailed for France. In a farewell ceremony, colonists paid tribute to the determined old warrior who had rid them of the Iroquois peril.

26

MONSIEUR JEAN TALON

Traditionally, the government of the provinces of France was managed by a governor, a great nobleman who represented the king on ceremonial occasions, and an *intendant*, a trained official who represented the king's government and attended to the administration of law, tax-collection and the control of business. In time, it was the intendant who acquired power and control in each province.

Jean Talon, the first intendant of New France, was already familiar with the duties of his office, having been intendant of the French frontier province of Hainault for ten years. Talon was a clever, able, energetic person who had great patience even for the smallest of details. He came to New France determined to make it a busy, flourishing, agricultural society resembling that of rural France.

In the instructions given him, Talon was required to administer public funds, encourage the clearing and cultivation of land and promote the establishment of industries. He was to create a series of populous town and village communities that would form a sturdy, self-supporting colony.

Talon arrived at Quebec in September of 1665. One of his first actions was to gather information about conditions in the colony. In doing this he was not content just to read reports, but visited settlements and homes asking countless questions. He learned that the state of the colony was not as promising as he had hoped. His enquiries revealed that in New France there were about 3,000 settlers of whom 2,000 were men and boys. Quebec itself had but 547 citizens. The shortage of professional people and skilled tradesmen was alarming; in the colony there were but four lawyers, four doctors, twenty shoemakers, eleven bakers and seven butchers.

His first task then was to find people to settle on the land. Since the French government was unwilling to send more than a

Arrival of
Talon, 1665

In the days before matches were commonly used, it was often difficult to rekindle a fire. The simplest way was to get some hot coals from a neighbour's fireplace. The metal fire-scoop shown above was used to carry coals from one house to another.

few hundred people at long intervals, Talon appealed to the Carignan-Salières regiment to settle in New France. Governor Courcelle and the colonel of the regiment objected to the breakup of this military force, but the appeal to the soldiers was successful. A number of land grants and tenant farms were given to officers and men, particularly in the area of the Richelieu, the Iroquois invasion route, where nearly 400 soldiers took up residence.

Talon next recruited settlers from western France, in particular from Normandy, by offers of free passage and the provision of land on easy terms.

The "King's daughters" The need to provide wives for all the settlers was always a problem. Most people settling in the colony were men without families. Talon wanted settlers to be married and raising large families. There was no objection to Frenchmen marrying young Indian women. Indeed, this practice was encouraged by Talon and the council. Other wives were found by bringing unmarried women out to the colony from France. Every effort was made to select these women with care so that lazy, weak or unsuitable persons were not placed among the immigrants. Every year fine young women, orphan girls and daughters of poor families, known as "filles du roi," "the King's daughters," arrived in the colony and rapidly found husbands among the numerous bachelors. The following statement was made concerning the arrival of one group of women:

At the end of a fortnight not one was left. I am told that the plumpest were taken first, because it was thought that, being less active, they would more likely keep at home, and that they could resist the winter cold better.

Intendant Jean Talon watches the construction of an *habitant* home. Note his splendid costume with knee length coat and deep cuffs. He wears a fashionable French *periwig*, made up of long curly masses of hair falling to the shoulders. Talon brought out from France carpenters, masons and blacksmiths, who taught the *habitants* to construct homes, furniture, wagons, sleighs, hinges, locks and tools.

Thus, by bringing people from France, Talon helped to increase the population of New France.

As a further encouragement to marriage and the raising of large families, the Council gave wedding presents and allowed tax reductions. **Assistance for young couples** A young settler who married before he was twenty years of age was given a money gift on his wedding day. In addition, he was freed of tax payments until he became twenty-five years of age. Such young men soon discovered that if they had large families they could expect to receive further gifts from the Council. For example, a settler who had ten children was paid a yearly amount of 300 livres (roughly $300), and a settler with twelve children was paid 400 livres (about $400).

It is interesting to note that in the English colonies of North America settlement was proceeding under a different plan. Many of the English settlers brought their wives and children with them when they came. Such colonists, too, were forced to survive without gifts of money and without special consideration from the English government.

Talon's success   Talon's plan of settlement was expensive, but it was successful, for new land was cleared and the population increased in an encouraging manner. It is estimated that between 1665 and 1672, some 2,000 state-aided immigrants reached New France and that the birth-rate was adding almost 1,000 persons a year to the population.

If Jean Talon were living in Canada today he might well be a millionaire, because he had all the ability and drive of a top-ranking business man. His alert mind was continually occupied with plans to enlarge the productive capacity of New France. An account of his activities appears in the Jesuit *Relations*:

> . . . He was so successful (in seeking means for rendering the country prosperous) that fisheries of all kinds are in operation, the rivers being very rich in fish, such as salmon, brill, perch, sturgeon . . .
>
> Of similar nature is the seal-fishery, which furnishes the whole country with oil, and yields a great surplus that is sent to France and to the Antilles . . . he is directing a careful search for mines, which appear to be numerous: he is causing the felling of all kinds of timber, which is found everywhere in Canada . . . he is also giving his attention to wood suitable for ship-building, trial of which has been made in this country by the building of a bark which is found very serviceable, and of a large vessel which is all ready to be launched. . .

Farming   To increase the volume and the value of farm products, Talon encouraged the colonists to grow hemp which could be manufactured into cord, rope and coarse cloth. Another farm product, flax, made it possible to produce linen.

Such domestic animals as horses, cows, sheep and pigs were imported in larger numbers than ever before. Talon set up a model farm on his estate near Quebec, and there he raised blood horses. Many of these eventually found their way to various

This baker of New France uses a brick oven built over a stone fire box. Suspended above him are wooden spatulas for sliding bread in and out of the oven. Behind him is the kneading trough where dough is prepared. King Louis XIV imposed a great number of annoying laws on the people of the colony. Among these were several connected with the baking business. Bakers were ordered to make dark brown bread, although there was no demand for it, because the king believed it to be twice as nourishing as white bread.

farms throughout the colony. The increase in sheep, of course, meant that wool came into plentiful supply, and spinning and weaving became vital operations. In a letter written to the king, Talon boasted that he could dress completely in the clothing of New France.

Talon's dream of trading ships sailing out from the colony **Trade abroad** became a reality. Vessels sailed to the West Indies with cargoes of timber, fish, furs, peas and corn. From there they crossed the Atlantic to France with loads of sugar and rum and returned to New France with a great variety of goods.

But even all these improvements were not enough to satisfy Jean Talon. He cherished a great dream of a New France stretching westwards from the valley of the St. Lawrence. He thought that the French and Dutch should combine forces to weaken the power of England in North America. He considered, too, the possibility of claiming lands far to the north and west of Quebec. He encouraged the westward march of the fur trade and the exploration of the regions beyond and below the Great Lakes in the hope of discovering the copper and other mines reputed to be in these areas.

In 1668, Talon returned to France and gave a full report of conditions in the colony. In the spring of 1670 he was back at Quebec again to found new settlements and build more ships to trade with the West Indies and France.

Fur trade Talon now became actively interested in the fur trade. Attracted by the profits to be made, he invested money in several trading voyages and made a handsome profit out of these ventures. Talon even had the Council lift the ban on the sale of liquor to the Indians on the condition that they were not allowed to get drunk.

Talon also advised the French government to allow him to have two forts built, one on each side of the eastern end of Lake Ontario, in order to trade with the Iroquois who were trapping to the north of the lake. The intendant felt sure that the Iroquois would then sell their furs to the French instead of taking them down to the English at Albany. This was clever reasoning. Talon knew very well that it was the beaver pelts shipped to France and sold there that paid the salaries of the officials of New France, that paid for the import of French goods and provided the money with which to establish lumber companies, equip new fishing fleets and settle people on the lands of New France. But Talon's advice was refused. A few years yet were to pass before the western forts were built. A few years yet were to pass before greater quantities of fur came down the western waterways to Montreal and Quebec.

27

LIFE IN NEW FRANCE

The settlement of New France was almost a repetition of Feudal system of Europe an ancient European manner of land-owning known as the *feudal system*. Under this system, large tracts of land were granted by a king or emperor to his noblemen, who in turn granted pieces of their land to lesser nobles, who in their turn granted still smaller portions of their land to others and so on right down to the workers of the fields themselves, the peasants. In return for these land grants, each landowner or vassal owed loyalty to his immediate superior or lord and was often required to follow him in military service.

In the course of many centuries, the military service given Seigneurial system in New France to the lord changed to payments of a simple kind. For example, every small landholder paid his lord, or *seigneur,* an annual rent, in money and in produce. It was this new form of feudal system, known as the *seigneurial system,* that was transferred from France to the banks of the St. Lawrence.

Jean Talon promoted this system by granting many more seigneuries than had existed before his time. Among these were a number of important land grants made to officers of the Carignan-Salières regiment, who agreed to settle soldiers on their new lands. Some of the villages which later appeared were named in honour of these officers—St. Ours, Verchères, Soulanger, Varennes, Contrecoeur, Berthier and Saurel (Sorel), and so on.

In New France the seigneur's obligations to his formal The Seigneur superior, the king, were few. He was, of course, required to render loyalty to his sovereign from whom all land was held. But his most important duties were to live on his seigneury, divide it into farms, settle it and ensure that each year crops were harvested and cattle raised.

179

A bird's-eye view of a seigneurial settlement in New France. The Manor-house (1) owned by the *seigneur* was, as a rule, very little better in construction than those of the more successful *habitants*. It was comfortable rather than imposing, being made of rough-hewn timbers, or more commonly, of stone. In this particular case the seigneur's mill (2) is a windmill, but water mills, too, were used in many places. If the wind was slack, the habitants often had to wait days for the grain to be ground. The early parish church (3) was a simple structure. A parish usually covered the same area as the seigneury, although this was not always so, for in the case of the larger seigneuries there might be several parishes.

Note how the houses and the road hug the river's bank, and how the properties extend far back from narrow frontages. Note, too, that the farms vary greatly in width. In the beginning, the seigneurs often granted from 1,000 to 2,000 feet of land along the river. Although not drawn to exact scale in the illustration, such a grant is represented by (4) the house and farm. When a habitant died, by French law, his property was evenly divided among his sons. This, of course, resulted in (5) several farms being crowded into the space once occupied by one, thus making very narrow plots.

Habitant homes were steep-roofed structures designed to shed the snows of winter. A lean-to behind or at the side of the house often served as a store-house, and nearby was (6) a barn and stable, normally constructed of wood.

Most homes had (7) an outdoor bake-oven and (8) a root cellar half-buried in the ground and banked with earth or sod. Around the collection of buildings ran a fence of some kind or other—wood, rail or piled stones, and somewhere in the plot lay (9) the habitant's garden. For the sake of convenience, a cattle pasture (10) was kept not too far from the stable. Wild hay was abundant, and the habitants frequently made stacks of it along the river or (11) on the edges of marshes. Some properties (12, for example) were cleared of forest more than others.

A new seigneur was faced with such problems as clearing land, settling families on small holdings, finding a parish-priest or *curé* for his people, erecting a flour mill, opening roads and building a manor-house for himself. Settlers were given long, narrow strips of land, each with a small frontage on the river. Such an arrangement, of course, placed all the farm houses close together on the bank of the river and thus created a village.

F. D.—7

For a few years after the establishment of the seigneury, the owner had little or no income from his lands. No money was **The habitant** paid when the tenant or *habitant* (the word simply means resident) first occupied his farm, and normally the habitant was not required to pay rents until he had had a chance to clear land and harvest crops.

When once established, the habitant was expected to pay *cens et rentes,* annual rents in money and produce due every St. Martin's Day (November 11). Because there was little money in use outside the larger settlements, the habitant often paid the *cens* in the form of a very small sum of money and the *rentes* was paid with grain or poultry. The annual day of payment frequently became a holiday occasion during which the habitants and their families gathered at the manor-house. While the seigneur entertained his guests with food and wine, the chickens brought in part payment of rent raised loud cacklings in the yard. In addition to the rents, the seigneur also received *lods et ventes,* fees due when a farm changed hands other than by direct inheritance.

A third source of income, the *droit de banalité,* was based upon charges made for the seigneur's provision of such necessary services as the wine-press, the bake-oven and the flour-mill. The sturdy stone mill with its imported machinery was one of the most important buildings on any seigneury. Because the mill was a very expensive piece of construction, the government of the colony sometimes paid part if its cost. The mill was sometimes put to a use other than grain grinding; being built of stone, it served in emergency as a place of refuge during Indian attacks. Actually, the mill was extremely important, for the habitant had to bring his grain there to be ground into flour. He could build and use his own wine-press and bake-oven if it pleased him to do so. For the use of his mill, the seigneur usually collected one-fourteenth of all grain brought for grinding.

Another privilege enjoyed by the seigneur was the *corvée,* a form of labour provided by the habitant. It was understood that each tenant gave one day's work in the ploughing season, one at seeding time and one at harvest time. In addition to these customary duties, the habitant at times assisted in building a manor-house, a church, a mill, a road or a bridge.

Although the people of New France had neither an easy nor a comfortable life, they undoubtedly were happier and much better off than the French peasants of the time who owed their seigneurs many more and much heavier services. The farms on the St. Lawrence valley produced good crops, the forests were alive with game and the streams abounded in fish. Habitants could build their own homes and barns, make their own clothes, cut their own fuel and raise their own cattle and horses. The habitants wore plain garments spun from the wool of their sheep and woven into cloth. Knitted woollen caps and brightly-coloured sashes were popular dress items. Furs could be had cheaply and made excellent winter coats. Even the children had beaver coats. Both young and old smoked the rank *tabac* grown and cured in the seigneuries. So common was pipe smoking that distance was measured in terms of how far a person could walk while smoking one pipeful of tobacco—about three-quarters of a mile.

During the first few years on a new farm the people lived in crude cabins. But after the land had been cleared and crops were growing, they erected substantial one-storey houses of timber or stone with steep roofs to shed the snow. Even then there were no glass windows, but merely sheets of oiled paper to let in some light. The main doorway of the house led directly into a huge kitchen, the most important room in the house. Here was the centre point of family life, serving also as a living-room, a recreation room, a workroom and often as a bedroom. At one end of the kitchen stood a huge fireplace, large enough to burn the heaviest logs. There were no chairs; just a few benches placed here and there. In the kitchen were served great meals of rich pea soup, home-baked bread and smoked fish and game. On long winter evenings this room served as a snug haven for the household until it was time for the children to go to bed in the small rooms leading off from the kitchen, or in the still smaller rooms in the attic.

Seigneurial mills, built of stone, were generally erected near a river bank to catch the breezes. Mills tended to be clumsy, inefficient affairs. However, constructed in a solid fashion and fitted with small windows, they could be used as forts when occasion demanded. Habitants took their grain to the seigneurial mill where it was ground into a coarse meal, vastly inferior to modern flour. The bakers of Quebec often complained that the meal was unfit for use.

In the evenings the habitant smoked his *tabac,* and his wife, and perhaps his daughters, worked at the spinning wheel or the loom. When friends or relatives dropped in for a visit, there would be much singing of folk songs and telling of stories over glasses of wine, or perhaps a little brandy. Many of these stories were ancient French tales, such as the one concerning the ghostly priest who went on murmuring prayers long after he was dead. There were Canadian legends as well . . . of phantom *voyageurs* who paddled their canoes through the skies above the forest, and of a White Witch who led unsuspecting Frenchmen into the hands of the Iroquois. Weird tales were told of demons, devils, ghosts and other terrifying creatures that were half men and half wolves. It is not surprising then that many a child was unable to sleep after a lively evening of songs and stories.

Somewhere in the little collection of homes making up a village stood the shop of the blacksmith, and in its own way the smithy was as important to the people as the flour mill. In exchange for labour on his land, the blacksmith beat out on his anvil a number of necessary articles—hinges, bolts, window-fasteners, tools, plough-shares and horseshoes. On occasion he painstakingly created religious devices and ornaments.

In the towns of Montreal and Quebec people of wealth and Town life in New France position led gay lives patterned somewhat upon the gaieties of the French court. Manners were gracious, hospitality was lavish and social events were numerous. The upper classes entertained themselves card playing, dancing, skating, boating, horse-racing, riding, sleighing and shooting. The daughters of wealthy families were inclined to amuse themselves in rather useless household activities or in looking about for future husbands. Both mothers and daughters were intensely fond of dressing in elaborate and expensive costumes. A French visitor to New France noted that:

The Gentlemen that have a Charge of children, especially Daughters, are oblig'd to be good Husbands, in order to bear the Expence of the magnificent Cloaths with which they are set off; for Pride, Vanity and Luxury, reign as much in New France as in Old France. In my opinion 'twould do well if the King would order Commodities to be rated at a reasonable price and prohibit the selling of Gold and Silver Brocades, Fringes and Ribbands, as well as Points of rich Laces.

These happy pictures of life in New France are not the whole story of these times.

The easy wealth of the fur trade was stealing men away from the seigneuries along the river and from the stores and workshops of Quebec and Montreal. Even a few seigneurs, themselves owners of poor, unproductive acres, deserted their land to captain the fur brigades that voyaged to the north and the west of the colony. The Council was unable to keep the fur trade under control and it gradually absorbed a heavy proportion of the able-bodied men of New France. Talon's plans for a series of populous town and village communities forming a sturdy self-supporting colony did not come to pass as well as he had hoped. New France continued to depend on the beaver for its livelihood.

28

RADISSON AND GROSEILLIERS

Interest in the lands to the west had begun in the days of Champlain and continued to stir French curiosity. It slowly became clear that up in these regions were friendly Indians and a very promising trade in pelts, heavier than any previously encountered. The French slowly learned the geography of the Great Lakes basin.

About 1623, well before the death of Champlain, Etienne Brûlé had paddled his way across northern Lake Huron to the entrance of another great lake (Superior). In 1634, another young Frenchman, Jean Nicolet, entered yet another lake (Michigan), made his way to Green Bay, and travelled some distance up an unknown river (the Fox). Then, in 1641, a Jesuit priest, Father Isaac Jogues, travelled to the region of Sault Ste. Marie to preach to the Chippewa, and while there gained important information about the enormous extent of Lake Superior. The riddle of the mighty lakes was slowly being solved. All of these travels proved to be a prelude to other explorations that were to have far-reaching effects upon the French fur trade and also upon the English fur trade after 1685.

Between 1654 and 1660, two young Frenchmen, Pierre Esprit Radisson and his brother-in-law Médard Chouart, Sieur des Groseilliers, made several journeys in the lands bordering Lakes Michigan and Superior. Unfortunately, the historical record of these events is quite confusing and depends largely upon the colourful, but imaginative journals of Radisson. Some of the events and dates mentioned do not agree with scattered references found in the writings of the Jesuits. It seems likely, however, that the two daring adventurers took their canoe and trading goods the entire length of Lake Michigan. It is possible that they also struck southward into the upper reaches of what the Chippewa Indians called the *Messipi River,* the forked river: this was

187

probably the "Big Water" reported to Nicolet by Indians, but he thought he was hearing about the Western Sea. They certainly made contact with various Indian tribes living around Lake Superior and found everywhere an eagerness to trade. The tribesmen, it seems, were particularly interested in securing French firearms. Some of the Indians they encountered, such as the Ottawas and Hurons, were tribesmen who had fled from their former homes to escape the rage of the Iroquois.

New fur regions   Radisson and Groseilliers were pleased to learn that a promising fur trade lay open to the French, but they could see various difficulties in its operation. If the Indians feared to take their furs past the Iroquois to Quebec, it would be necessary for the French to carry their goods all the way to the Indians. Such business, they decided, would be too costly and time-consuming.

Early French trade goods were very much in demand among the Indians. In the centre are two brass kettles, (1) a very large one and a tiny one having a diameter of no more than two inches. Brass kettles were greatly desired by the tribesmen because they were less breakable than the native clay pots. Other articles illustrated include: (2) an iron axe, (3) a silver-plated *gorget* or breast ornament, (4) chisel and knife blades, (5) a copper pipe for smoking tobacco, (6) an iron gouge, and (7) copper arrowheads.

In the course of their wanderings Radisson and Groseilliers heard many tales of a vast salt water sea lying far to the north of the Great Lakes. In time they came to believe that such a sea actually existed. They even debated between themselves upon the possibility of French ships sailing into these salt waters which must lie much closer to the rich fur country of the north-west than Quebec or Montreal. Thus was born the magnificent dream that in time was to have such a profound effect upon the development of Canada.

Setting aside, for the moment, all thought of seeking the northern sea, the two adventurers returned to Quebec in 1660 with a fleet of sixty canoes riding low with the weight of furs. In his journal Radisson described their arrival: *The return to Quebec, 1660*

> We came to Quebec, where we are saluted with the thundring of the guns and batteryes of the fort, and of the 3 shipps that weare there at anchor; which had gone back to France without castors (beaver pelts) if we had not come.

Radisson and Groseilliers were treated as heroes in the settlement. They had saved the season's trade. They had reopened the old Ottawa fur route. However, when they sought the governor's permission to make an expedition north, they met considerable difficulty. Governor d'Argenson agreed that they might make the journey provided he were to receive half of all profits made in the fur trade. He further required that two of his men should accompany the expedition. Angered by this demand, which they considered outrageous, Radisson and Groseilliers refused to make any such agreement. In his turn the governor then gave express orders that the two men should not depart on another journey.

Fortunately, in the summer of 1661 a group of Indians from the region of Sault Ste. Marie arrived at Three Rivers where Radisson and Groseilliers were living and urged them to return west with them as soon as they traded their furs. Regretfully, the Frenchmen refused the invitation, but a short time after the Indians' departure they impulsively decided to go. Stealing secretly out of Three Rivers at night, they took to their canoes and caught up with the Indian party near Montreal.

They were gone for two years.

**Northward and
westward
again**

After surviving several Iroquois attacks along the Ottawa River, they made their way over to Georgian Bay, past Sault Ste. Marie and on along the south shore of Lake Superior. Before winter had set in, Radisson and Groseilliers had constructed a log fort on Chequamegon Bay near the western end of the lake where they cached their supplies of kettles, hatchets, knives, needles, combs and mirrors. Indians of the Ottawa, Cree and Sioux tribes brought furs to the fort and showed their eagerness to continue trading with the French. Radisson and Groseilliers later travelled north of the lake and met the Crees, from whom they bought beaver pelts richer and heavier than any they had yet seen.

According to Radisson, he and Groseilliers, with a group of Indians, made yet another long, difficult journey northward through the wilderness until finally:

"we came to the seaside, where we finde an old howse all demollished and battered with boullets."

It is very difficult to accept the full truth of this statement. First, the description of the journey is very vague and brief; second, it does not seem possible that Radisson and Groseilliers in all their various wanderings had sufficient time to make such an extended trip.

**"Sea of the
North"**

It is quite possible, nevertheless, that Indians may have guided the Frenchmen to Lake Winnipeg, or even to some river leading into Hudson Bay or James Bay. The tale of actually reaching salt water was probably created by the wild fancies and wishes in Radisson's mind. Whether or not they reached the "sea of the north" is not significant. The important fact remains that Radisson and Groseilliers were now certain that trade could be carried on directly from Hudson Bay. They maintained that if forts were built on Hudson and James Bay, the Indians would carry their fur down the rivers to the posts.

Radisson and Groseilliers rather half expected that the governor of New France would forgive their illegal trading expedition, especially since they were returning to Quebec with over 300 canoe loads of furs. Unfortunately, the governor was not in a forgiving mood. When the two adventurers arrived that summer, they were arrested and fined, and their furs were seized. When matters were finally settled, Radisson and Grosseilliers were allowed to keep no more than seven per cent. of the value of the furs.

The two traders were greatly angered by the treatment of the governor. Groseilliers hurried off to France in an effort to lay complaints before the king. Officials at the royal court, however, paid little attention to the angry bushranger from New France. This was a costly mistake on the part of the French government, for it was eventually to bring a strong rival nation into the fur trade.

In 1665, by a remarkable piece of good fortune, Radisson and Groseilliers met a noted English seaman and merchant, Sir George Carteret. Having taken a liking to the two Frenchmen, Sir George listened intently to their tales of adventure and to their ideas of trading in Hudson Bay. Then, convinced that they were telling the truth, he took them off to England where in 1665 he presented them to King Charles II.

Radisson and Groseilliers in England, 1665

The vivid accounts of travelling and trading in the North American wilds told by Radisson and Groseilliers soon captured the attention of Prince Rupert, a cousin of the King. The keen mind of this dashing cavalry officer grasped the importance of this new trade plan being put forth by the visiting Frenchmen. Seeing an opportunity to increase English power and to make large profits, Prince Rupert persuaded friends to finance an expedition to the Bay. They called themselves "the Gentlemen Adventurers of Hudson's Bay."

In June, 1668, Radisson in a ship named the *Eaglet* and Groseilliers in a second ship, the *Nonsuch,* set sail for the northern shores of America. The ocean crossing went well, but near the mouth of Hudson Strait the *Eaglet* received such a hard pounding during a storm that a serious leak developed and the ship was forced to return to England. The *Nonsuch* sailed on alone, finally reaching the mouth of a river (named for Prince Rupert) on the eastern shore of James Bay.

After constructing Fort Charles, a rough stone fort and a

Radisson and Groseilliers discuss their fur trading plans with Prince Rupert.
Notice the furniture in the room.   This type of oak refectory table with crude melon-
bulb legs and heavy stretchers about the lower legs was one of the first draw-top
tables ever made.   The chair shown is an English panel-back of the period.

protective stockade, Groseilliers and his English companions
settled down for an uncomfortable winter. No one in the party,
of course, dreamed that their crude shelter was to be the first
post in a great chain of trading posts that was eventually to spread
across the northern lands of the continent. Groseilliers was soon
able to establish contact with the northern Indians, and trade
began. By the time ice was breaking up in the spring and the
wild geese were winging northward, the *Nonsuch* was loaded
with furs.

The return of the *Nonsuch* in 1669 caused tremendous
excitement at the English court. Here was proof that "Mr.
Radishes and Mr. Gooseberry" knew what they were talking about.

Here were furs and profits that exceeded the hopes of the men who had financed the expedition.

Prince Rupert and his associates eagerly urged King Charles to grant them a charter allowing them the right to establish a company for continued trade. This request was readily granted by the monarch, who, in 1670, placed his signature upon a royal charter composed of five large sheets of parchment. The imposing charter outlined the privileges, the rights and the duties of the new company which was to be known as "The Governor and Company of Adventurers of England trading into Hudson's Bay." Founding of Hudson's Bay Company, 1670

Through this simple action, the King gave to his "dear and entirely beloved cousin, Prince Rupert," and his associates the "sole trade and commerce" in the regions whose waters emptied into Hudson Bay. Neither Charles nor the men of the new company had any idea of how vast a region had been placed under their care as "absolute Lordes and Proprietors." Actually, Prince Rupert and his friends were granted all the land now occupied by northern Quebec, northern Ontario, Manitoba and Saskatchewan, the southern half of Alberta and the southeast portion of the North West Territories. Besides granting the right of trade in furs and fish, the Company was given a monopoly of the gold, silver, gems and precious stones found in all of what the charter called "Rupert's Land." The original reason for granting the charter was to command the members of the Company to find a north-west passage to the East. The Merchant Adventurers never took this order seriously. They were too interested in the riches of the fur trade.

It was a strange trick of fate that caused two French adventurers to help found a great English enterprise—"The Hudson's Bay Company."

29

COUNT FRONTENAC

In 1672, two years after the founding of the Hudson's Bay Company, New France was given a vigorous, new governor, one who was to have a profound effect upon the colony.

Arrival of Frontenac, 1672 On the day of his arrival, the citizens of Quebec gathered at the dockside to catch a first glimpse of their new leader. When the time for landing came, twenty guardsmen in brilliant new uniforms marched smartly down the gangplank. Then came the governor, Louis de Buade, Comte de Palluau et de Frontenac, a striking figure, magnificently dressed in a wide-sweeping hat and a soft grey coat. A long, well-curled wig falling to his shoulders framed a face that was both strong and showed signs of a quick temper. From the plume on top of his hat to the tips of his fashionable shoes, he looked a commander of men. The citizens were no doubt impressed by what they saw.

The new governor was a French courtier and soldier who had gained his experience of war on the battlegrounds of Europe. He had grown up and lived most of his life in the French court. Like any other courtier who wasted money, Count Frontenac was heavily in debt. The post of governor of New France was not a position he would have chosen for himself; the salary was small and New France a long way from the comforts, amusements and pleasures of the king's court. But his debts gave him little choice in the matter. After all, he considered, a salary was better than nothing, and he would be the most important man in the colony.

It is true that Frontenac had many weaknesses; he was proud, vain, stubborn, impatient and careless of how he obtained and spent money. On the other hand, he possessed qualities that must be admired. He was above all a man of courage and daring, who was frightened of nothing—not even the Iroquois. He fought off the English assault on Quebec, humbled the Iroquois and led the way into the heart of the North American continent in search of furs.

194

In spite of his arrogance, Frontenac had a genius for handling people—all kinds of people from habitants to high officials. His pride did not prevent him from being charming to anybody and everybody in an effort to seek information and discover what they were thinking and talking about. Before making any changes in government, Frontenac travelled through the settlements, noting their condition, and inspecting trading posts. He also examined the duties of colonial officials. He finally came to the conclusion that government by Council was not in the best interests of New France. Somewhat impulsively he established an old French form of government known as the *Three Estates*, consisting of three groups of men representing the nobility, the Church and the common people. In his haste to complete this change, the governor neglected to notify the authorities in France. When news of Frontenac's decision reached them, dispatches were sent at once stating that the habitants of New France were to have no part in colonial government.

Frontenac quickly gave his attention to the matter of the Iroquois. It was vital to the safety and well-being of New France that the Iroquois should be kept under control and prevented from raiding the Algonkian tribes who were allies and commercial partners of the French. Although the Iroquois were not an immediate threat, there were increasing signs that conflict was approaching. In order to strengthen the French position, Frontenac decided to build a fort at Cataraqui, a small bay at the eastern end of Lake Ontario. The circumstances under which this fort was constructed were very unusual and perhaps even humorous in a grim sort of way.

The governor sent a bold young man, Robert Cavelier de la Salle, to the Jesuits living among the Iroquois, telling the priests to invite the chiefs of the Five Nations to travel north for a council with the new French leader. Annoyed by this demand, the Iroquois replied that the French governor could travel to the Iroquois lands and hold council there. Frontenac's second message indicated how well he had come to understand the Indians. The message stated that "It is for the father to tell the

Count Frontenac travels through the Thousand Islands area of the upper St. Lawrence. It was a difficult journey from Montreal, due to dangerous rapids and toilsome portages. But eventually, the magnificent flotilla, with pennants fluttering, reached Lake Ontario. There were one hundred canoes arranged in four squadrons, together with several flat-bottomed boats, brightly painted in red and blue. The total number of the company was about 400.

children where to hold council." He would, Frontenac said, meet the Iroquois chiefs at Cataraqui.

Determined to overawe the Iroquois with the power of France, the governor made careful preparations for the meeting of 1673. With a group of men, provisions, barges, boats and canoes, Frontenac set out from Quebec and arrived at the mouth of the Cataraqui river.

The Iroquois waiting on the shoreline were startled by the size of the flotilla which made its way toward land. On it came, canoes loaded with woodsmen, barges heaped with supplies, boats bearing Frontenac and his officers resplendent in gleaming breastplates and bright uniforms, and a rearguard of French troops crowded into canoes. After a quick landing, the French set up

tents and raised a great white flag bearing the golden lilies of
France. These preparations were hardly completed before woodsmen and carpenters started the construction of the new fort. The
Iroquois watched and listened as axes rang and saws rasped in
the shadows of the forest.

Five days later, Frontenac, wearing his plumed hat and Cataraqui council, 1673
carrying a sword in his hand, seated himself in a beautifully-
carved chair before the sixty Iroquois delegates. Although the
Indians appeared cool and unexcited, they were uneasy at the
swift work taking place about them. Frontenac, through his
interpreter, the Sieur le Moyne, addressed them in this manner:

I have a fire lighted for you to smoke by and for me to talk to
you. You have done well, my children, to obey the command of your
father. Take courage; you will hear his word, which is full of peace
and tenderness. Do not think that I have come for war. My mind is
full of peace and she walks by my side.

Such words pleased the Iroquois; here was a man who talked
like a chief—a man who could use flowery words such as were

employed in their own councils. So impressed were they, that they forgave Frontenac for addressing them as "children." For the next four days the discussions went on and on, long speeches being made by Frontenac and the visiting chiefs.

All this time the French craftsmen were erecting Fort Cataraqui with astonishing speed. The inner buildings, the stockade, the gun platforms and the deep moat appeared as if by magic. To the watching Indians this was a miracle, which only served to indicate still further that the French were a people who held frightening powers.

The Cataraqui council was a triumph for Count Frontenac.

Peace agreement with Iroquois Before the discussions were over, the Iroquois chiefs had agreed to live in peace with the French, and they had promised not to interfere with the fur trade of other tribes. Carrying presents given to them by Frontenac, the Iroquois embarked in their canoes and headed homeward. Memories of the council lingered long in their minds. Almost every year thereafter Frontenac journeyed to this new post to trade with the Iroquois, who, as long as their war with the Andastes continued, appeared to be willing to trade with the French at Cataraqui instead of the English at Albany.

This peaceful settlement with the Iroquois made it possible for the French to proceed with greater plans for the expansion of the fur trade. Even before the arrival of Frontenac it was evident that French activities would spread westward. The prospects of profitable trading in the upper Great Lakes region had caught the imaginations of Frenchmen.

It was becoming clear that the seigneuries along the St. Lawrence and the little industries established by Talon would never produce anything other than the necessities of life. They failed to produce a surplus of goods for export. The only colonial surplus was furs. It was this prospect of easy riches that lured many a young habitant into the woods where he traded in furs with or without the consent of the Council.

Coureurs de bois These daring adventurers, who came to be known as the *coureurs de bois* (the rangers of the forest), took naturally to life in the wilds. They became skilled woodsmen, trappers, hunters, fighters and scouts who often equalled the Indians in skill and also in their cruelty and savagery. They angered the Council by defying the laws forbidding hunting or trading outside of the colony without permission. They angered the Montreal fur merchants who watched fewer and fewer Indians coming down the St. Lawrence to trade pelts. As the coureurs de bois captured more and more trade, the Montrealers were forced to employ them as their representatives to secure furs and smuggle them into the colony. The Council made several unsuccessful attempts to cut down the growing number of coureurs de bois. By 1681, the Council decided to issue no more than twenty-five official *congés*, or trade licenses, in any one year. Only these licence-holders would be permitted to journey up country and trade in the Indian villages. But this law, too, was ignored. There was too much money to be made in the trade of the forest, and the younger habitants continued to slip away into the western woods.

A *coureur de bois* dressed in buckskin leggings, coat and fur cap. The weapon he carries is known as a snapchance musket, one of the earlier types of flintlock. These muskets were a great improvement on the firearm used in Champlain's time in that they did not require the long burning fuse or match, but manufactured their own spark by means of a flint. The *coureurs de bois* adopted many Indian habits and customs. They dressed like Indians and smeared their faces with grease and paint as protection against mosquitoes and black flies.

Some of the coureurs de bois made their way to the region of Lake Superior and Lake Michigan where they established trading operations.   How many of them went westward and what regions they explored we do not know, for men trading without permission are not apt to write of their explorations.   By 1680, when the population of New France was about 10,000, it seems that there were some 500 or 600 of them paddling the streams and roaming the forests.

Growth of English colonies   So it was that the hopes of New France centred almost wholly upon the fur trade.   In the meantime, the English colonies in North America were establishing solid settlements along the Atlantic coast and their sailing ships were engaged in a prosperous trade—fish from Newfoundland—sugar and molasses from the West Indies—manufactured goods from England.   Ocean-going trade such as this had little interest for the Frenchmen whose eyes were blinded by the glitter of profits in the fur trade.   In the end, this decision was to prove a costly error.

30

THE EMPIRE OF THE MISSISSIPPI

During their respective terms of office, Count Frontenac and intendant Talon took a keen interest in any activity which might extend French trade and influence in North America. The exploration of new territory, in particular, was an operation they encouraged.

By 1672, the French knew that it was possible to sail from Quebec to Lake Michigan by following the St. Lawrence and the lower lakes, providing that a portage were made around Niagara Falls. This route, surprisingly enough, was rather a late discovery, for early travellers had gone westward by the Ottawa River-Georgian Bay route.

In the promotion of exploration, Frontenac and Talon had the co-operation of two young Frenchmen named Louis Joliet and La Salle. La Salle, whom we mentioned in the last chapter, was a fur trader of great ambition, energy and intelligence. Unlike most traders of the time, La Salle became interested in the lands below Lakes Ontario and Erie. It seemed to him that the whole country lying south of these waters was rich fur country. Indian tales of a large river (the Ohio) aroused his curiosity and led him to make journeys southwest of Lake Erie.

Louis Joliet, a former student of the Jesuit College at Quebec with a talent for mathematics and surveying, had been sent by Talon to the upper regions of Lake Michigan where traders were actively engaged in promoting the fur business. While moving about among the Indians, Joliet heard tales of a great river, the "Mississippi," which the Indians said flowed southward to a wide sea.

When word of this legendary river reached Quebec, Talon, in search of mineral wealth and new land, decided that an expedition should be sent to investigate the waterway. There was some hope that this river might lead to the Pacific, but it was also realized that the river might empty into the Gulf of Mexico. At any rate the river was worth investigating.

La Salle was to have lead the exploring party, but at this time he was more interested in the Great Lakes area. As second choice, Louis Joliet was selected to go in search of the big river. Father Jacques Marquette, a Jesuit missionary stationed at St. Ignace at the mouth of Lake Michigan, was named as a travelling companion for Joliet.

Joliet and Marquette, 1673 In the summer of 1673 the two men made their way southward over the waters (of Lake Michigan to Green Bay on the north-west shore. From there they paddled up the Fox River for some distance, finally reaching an Indian village. On June 10, they portaged their canoes over a height of land and set them in another river (the Wisconsin). Joliet later wrote in his journal:

. . . thus we left the waters flowing to Quebeq, four or five hundred leagues from here, to float on those that would thenceforward take us through strange lands. . . .

The Mississippi A week later, they paddled out of the mouth of the Wisconsin and drifted onto the surface of the Mississippi. As they moved southward, Joliet and Marquette marvelled at the beauty of the forests and prairies and the abundance of birds and wild animals. On the whole, the Indians they encountered were both helpful and friendly. A band of wandering Illinois tribesmen, recognizing Marquette as a Black Robe, were kind enough to present the travellers with a peace-pipe. This was a more valuable gift than Joliet first realized, for in the following days it was to serve as a passport through the Indian lands. The Frenchmen, when meeting strange tribesmen, had merely to hold up the peace-pipe as a sign of friendship and they were welcomed.

As the voyage continued, they passed the mouths of other large rivers (the Missouri and Ohio). The fact that their general direction of travel continued to be southward proved a disappointment to Joliet, for he had hoped the big river would swing westward toward the Pacific. They now saw tropical country with lush undergrowth—and clouds of mosquitoes.

Marquette and Joliet make camp after a day's travel during their famous voyage down the Mississippi River. Travelling in two canoes, the adventurers were accompanied by five other men. On the journey southward they encountered such interesting Indian tribes as the Miamis, Mascoutins, Wild Rice and Kickapoos. On the whole, they were treated in a very friendly fashion by the tribesmen, on one occasion being entertained to a feast of seven courses that included Indian corn, fish, roasted dog and buffalo meat.

Pushing onward to the mouth of another river (the Arkansas), **The Arkansas** the Frenchmen stopped to seek information from local Indians. Here the tribesmen informed Joliet that he was but a few days' journey from the sea. It would be foolish, however, they said, to proceed further, because hostile Indians with Spanish guns controlled the region between them and the sea. Taking this advice seriously, Joliet and Marquette decided that no useful purpose would be gained by paddling further south. In his journal Marquette wrote:

Monsieur Joliet and I held a council, to deliberate upon what we should do,—whether we should push on, or remain content with

the discovery we had made.   After attentively considering that we
were not far from the Gulf of Mexico, the basin of which is at a
latitude of 31 degrees 60 minutes, while we were at 33 degrees
40 minutes, we judged that we could not be more than 2 or 3 days'
journey from it; and that beyond a doubt, the Mississippi River dis-
charges into the Florida or Mexican Gulf . . . We further considered
that we exposed ourselves to the risk of losing the results of this
voyage, of which we could give no information if we proceeded to
fling ourselves into the hands of the Spaniards who, without doubt,
would at least have detained us as captives.

Return journey   Turning northward, the travellers faced a long, hard journey
during which they fought a constant battle with the strong
currents of the big river.   On the return route they took a short
cut up the Illinois River and portaged to the southern end of
Lake Michigan, an area where the city of Chicago now stands.

After reaching Green Bay, the two men spent the winter
there.   In the spring Joliet headed eastward toward Quebec,
probably by the Great Lakes route.

On reaching Quebec, Joliet reported his discoveries to
Frontenac who showed considerable excitement at the prospect
of adding new regions to the French empire in America.   What
a vast stretch of territory it would be—stretching from the St.
Lawrence to the Gulf of Mexico!   What made the thought even
more enticing was that good waterways would provide transportation through the whole length of the area.

La Salle   In following years, the travels and trading activities of the
Sieur de la Salle were to strengthen France's claim to the Mississippi valley.   He has been described by some historians as a
romantic dreamer, who searched continuously for a water route
to China.   (The seigneury granted to him on Montreal Island at
the head of the rapids was mockingly called "La Chine" (China)
by his servants.)   But other historians picture him as a shrewd
merchant, who planned to establish the most profitable fur trade
on the continent.   For example, he went all the way to the French
court to secure possession of Fort Cataraqui and the surrounding
lands as a settlement, and then he promptly monopolized the

French share of the Lake Ontario fur trade. John Brebner, a Canadian historian, writes:

> Actually there is abundant evidence that La Salle (the son of a rich merchant of Rouen) was primarily a fur trader who hoped to revolutionize the business by large-scale methods.

We do know La Salle was constantly planning to increase his own trade, and at a later date, to expand France's power in the New World. It was his misfortune, however, to lack the money, the supplies, the men and the power to carry his plans to success. The cost of his trading activities was always so high that he was perpetually in debt.

It is unfortunate that the record of his earlier travels in the **La Salle's early travels** region of the Great Lakes is rather obscure. Perhaps he preferred not to advertise his business trips. However, his writings confirm his discovery of the Niagara river and the Ohio river. He may not have actually been the first to see them but he is the first to record their discovery. By 1676, he had built a fur post on the Niagara river.

In 1674, Louis Joliet returned to Quebec from his voyage **Plans for trade and empire** down the Mississippi with news of passing through a vast area peopled by tribes with an abundance of furs. La Salle immediately saw a chance to extend his trading activities whilst discovering a new route into the heart of the continent. He decided that French forts should be built at the mouth of the Mississippi to guard the trading posts and settlements he would establish in the interior. He felt that unless some such measure were taken the English or Spanish would certainly move into the centre of the continent by crossing the Appalachian mountains or exploring up the Mississippi.

In 1678, La Salle gained royal approval for his plan to locate the mouth of the Mississippi at his own expense. He was given a monopoly of trade in buffalo hides, but was forbidden to engage in trading with tribes who came to Montreal. Returning to New France, he built a post at the southern tip of Lake Michigan, a second one on the Illinois River and yet another on the Mississippi below the Ohio. His scheme of transporting furs included the use of sailing ships on the Great Lakes and the Mississippi, but this plan received a setback in 1679. In that year, La Salle's ship, the *Griffon,* built near Niagara Falls, was lost on a return journey from Lake Michigan. The loss of the ship and its cargo of furs was so costly a blow that he had to give up his plan to build a fleet of ships.

After three years of fur trading, La Salle decided to start off on the voyage he had promised to make—the long voyage down the Mississippi to its mouth. In January, 1682, La Salle, his Récollet friar Father Membré and the one-armed Henry Tonty gathered at the lower end of Lake Michigan with a party of twenty-one Frenchmen and thirty-one Indians. Despite bitter winter weather, the party crossed the short distance overland (the Chicago portage) to the Illinois River and began to move along **La Salle on the** its course. Early in February they reached the main stream of the **Mississippi,** **1682** Mississippi. It had not been an easy journey thus far, for it had been necessary to drag the canoes for many miles along the frozen waterway.

They travelled swiftly southward, enjoying the warmer weather and the appearance of the country. La Salle noted the rich soil, the buffalo herds and the thick forests edging up to the banks of the river. Without serious trouble, they eventually **La Salle claims** reached the open waters of the Gulf of Mexico. Before returning, **Louisiana for** La Salle raised a wooden cross bearing the arms of France and in **France, 1682** a short ceremony claimed for Louis XIV all the lands and waters of the entire Mississippi basin. He named the land Louisiana in honour of the monarch. La Salle's arrival at the mouth of the big river was a fitting climax to the long series of explorations which had opened up the St. Lawrence River, the Great Lakes region and the broad valley of the Mississippi. The French had established where it was that the Mississippi reached salt water.

So far the French had been able to penetrate well south without coming into conflict with the Spanish. This achievement was only possible because the Spanish had been content to settle in Mexico and Florida without taking possession of the land lying between these two regions.   If France were to hold her claim to the Mississippi region, however, she had to do more than raise a wooden cross and declare her ownership.   Already English and Dutch traders were crossing the Appalachian mountains and were moving westward.   Spanish priests and Spanish adventurers were roving the southern interior of North America.

Aware of this situation, La Salle went to France to seek support for the establishment of a French colony in Louisiana. The actual presence of Frenchmen in a settled community, La Salle believed, would strengthen the French claim to the valley of the Mississippi, where he would build an empire based on furs and also on farming, lumbering and mining.

With royal approval for this second venture, La Salle left France in 1684 with a small group of ships bearing a company of settlers.   The little fleet made the Atlantic voyage, crossed the Gulf of Mexico and touched land at Matagorda Bay, several hundred miles west of the Mississippi.   Here the wreck of the vessel carrying stores and equipment forced La Salle to build a fort and set up his little colony.

It is not known whether La Salle deliberately chose this location or if he did so after missing the mouth of the Mississippi. Perhaps he planned to attack some of the Spanish settlements and thus desired to be closer to Mexico than the mouth of the Mississippi.   Whatever his reasoning, Matagorda Bay proved a poor spot for a settlement.   In a short time, the unhappy settlers were suffering from loneliness and lack of food.   La Salle made several journeys of exploration into the surrounding territory.   One of these was to the southwest in search of rich mining areas belonging to the Spanish, but this was a disappointing affair.   He made no contact with the Spanish and found no mines.

By 1687, the little colony was in such pitiful condition that **Death of** La Salle started off northward with a small group to find aid for **La Salle, 1687** the colonists.   He must have hoped to reach the French posts in the Illinois valley.   As the journey went on, the men became tired, discouraged and bitter, grumbling continually at a fate which had placed them in such a plight.   Tragedy brought a swift climax to

EXPLORATION OF THE MISSISSIPPI

Route of Marquette and Joliet 1673

Route of La Salle 1682

SCALE OF MILES

0   250   500

the situation when several men mutinied and shot their leader. La Salle's body, stripped of clothing, was left where it lay.

A few survivors of the party actually made their way to New France where they told the sad story of the Matagorda Bay colony. They were very careful, however, to avoid any reference to La Salle's murder. But in time even this came to be known.

In the meantime Indians attacked the remaining settlers, killing some and capturing the remainder.

La Salle's efforts to establish a settlement failed, but eventu- **Settlements in** ally led to some very important developments. In 1699 the **Louisiana** French returned to the Gulf of Mexico and founded settlements in Louisiana (one of which is still called New Orleans) near the mouth of the Mississippi. French fur traders from the Great Lakes area pushed down into the southern and south-western regions and established trade with Indian tribes. Because these traders were liberal with their presents and because they carried superior trading goods, they had no difficulty in outbuying Spanish traders who roamed the same regions.

The French, in fact, did very well in the southern trade until years later when large groups of English traders and frontiersmen began to invade the valley of the Mississippi.

31

FRONTENAC RECALLED

While it is true that Frontenac's attentions to the Iroquois insured peace for New France, it is also true that his stubbornness and pride involved him in continual quarrels with the other colonial authorities. These disagreements were so severe and so numerous that an endless stream of official complaints flowed out of Quebec and across to France.

Frontenac's quarrels Frontenac argued with the governor of Montreal in support of the coureurs de bois. He engaged in bitter dispute with the new intendant, Jacques Duchesneau, who continually tried to prevent the up country fur trading and accused Frontenac of taking a personal interest in the profits of the trade. Although Frontenac and Laval never quarrelled openly, Frontenac knew the latter's strong views against brandy-trading and knew that he was complaining about it in letters to the French court. Frontenac hit back—at the Jesuit priests themselves, claiming that they were not teaching the French language to the Indians. In spite of many protests put forward by individual Jesuits, Frontenac insisted that the fur traders had every right to barter brandy with the Indians. In reply one Jesuit priest remarked that, "If brandy were forbidden among the Indians, we could have thousands of converts to report."

The charges and counter-charges flew back and forth, and of course, over to France. For five years Frontenac and intendant Duchesneau wrangled bitterly over the fur trade and over the threatening presence of the English on Hudson Bay about whom Frontenac seemed to be quite indifferent. Then to make matters worse, Bishop Laval began to side with Duchesneau. As a result, the people of the colony were split into two sections— one supporting the governor's party and the other the intendant's party.

210

Farm implements used by the habitants were generally crude in design and relatively inefficient in use. This is a late seventeenth-century plough with a single handle and iron-sheathed double blades. Fields under cultivation were ploughed but once a year, much waste land being left between the furrows. Fertilization of the soil was very rare and crop rotation was almost unknown. Oddly enough, the habitants so loved horses that they often kept two or three, even though there was never sufficient work for the animals.

By 1682, the king of France had become so discouraged by the unsettled condition of the colony that he commanded both governor and intendant to return to France. In a dispatch to Frontenac the monarch wrote:

Frontenac recalled to France, 1682

I am writing to you this letter that you are to return to my court on the first ship which will leave Quebec for France.

After the governor and the intendant had left the colony, New France became uneasy. People were still bickering among themselves but there were unpleasant rumours about the Iroquois. Stories kept coming to Quebec that the Iroquois were no longer fighting the Andastes. Reports said that the Andastes were now busy attacking the Virginia frontier settlements and that the Iroquois were coming north again on the warpath.

The reports were quite true. The Iroquois were coming. They wanted the western fur trade and were preparing to wipe

New Iroquois threat

out the French as competitors.   By 1681, they had crushed the
Illinois tribesmen.   By 1682, they were attacking the Algonquin
tribes.

The new governor, Le Febvre de la Barre, was not the man
to take charge at such a critical time.   A conceited, greedy, blundering person, he made serious mistakes from the very start.
Taking a dislike to La Salle, he made light of the explorer's
achievements and accused La Salle of misusing his trading
privileges.   La Barre actually seized Fort Frontenac (Fort
Cataraqui, renamed Fort Frontenac by La Salle) and also took
over La Salle's fur posts in the Illinois country.   Then La Barre
himself proceeded to engage in the fur trade with the help of
various merchants. It soon became apparent, too, that the Iroquois
had far less respect for the new governor than they had held for
Count Frontenac.   In a bold move, they attacked and captured
French canoes carrying trade goods to Lake Michigan, and
attacked Fort St. Louis, the fur post on the Illinois river.

Frightened by the Iroquois hostility, La Barre appealed to
France for more troops. A small group of about 150 soldiers was
dispatched to Quebec, but it was not a disciplined fighting force,
and the men did not bring clothing and food supplies.

In an effort to impress the Iroquois, La Barre met the chiefs in
a council at Fort Frontenac.   His blustering, nervous manner,
however, did not have the effect he had hoped.   During the long
discussion one chief remarked, "I am not asleep.   My eyes are
open; and by the sun which gives me light I see a great captain
who talks like a man in a dream."   La Barre, himself, left the
council a very worried person.

The people of New France and the Indians of the friendly
tribes soon lost confidence in the governor, and when this became
known in France, La Barre was commanded to leave Quebec.

Playing card money Before we leave the story of La Barre, we might take note of
one interesting event that took place during his term of office.
The intendant of the time, Jacques de Meulles, discovered that
he had not sufficient money on hand to pay the wages of the
soldiers in the colony.   The regular annual shipment of French

coins had not yet arrived. As a result, the ingenious intendant had money made from playing cards. A whole card represented a certain sum of money, while half-cards and quarter-cards represented lesser sums. These remarkable bits of paper served as real money until the shipment of coins was received. But, when in later years money still remained scarce, the government, the soldiers and habitants continued to use the card money. They found it much more convenient than the old system of trade and barter. This odd money continued in use for years in New France and indeed in the English colonies as well. In time, of course, money came to be printed on proper paper and the use of cards was discontinued. So it was that paper money was introduced into North America.

Jacques René de Brisay, Marquis de Denonville, who succeeded La Barre in 1685, was a soldier of some experience and a man intensely loyal to his king. Denonville, realizing that the Iroquois were his greatest problem, made ambitious plans to keep them under control. He secured more troops from France, fortified Montreal and built a new fort at Detroit. This he planned as the beginning of a long string of forts stretching from Quebec to the mouth of the Mississippi. In addition, he ordered every man in the colony over the age of fourteen to provide himself with arms. He sent an order to Henry Tonty and the other commanders at the up country posts to muster such forces as they could and join him on the western edge of the Seneca country. Denonville then collected a strong force of soldiers, coureurs de bois and friendly Indians and moved south and west into Iroquois country, by way of Fort Frontenac and Niagara. He was joined by Tonty, du Lhut and a force of coureurs de bois and Indian allies at Niagara. There was little contact with the Seneca themselves. They fled before the coming of the invaders. When the French, tired and short of supplies, withdrew, they left many villages in ruins and numerous burnt-out corn fields. Destruction of Iroquois villages. Denonville had not crushed the Seneca but he had prevented the Iroquois from breaking the French hold on the western fur trade.

F. D.—8

Even this hard blow hurled at the League of the Iroquois failed to cow the spirits of the warriors. It simply made it more certain than ever that the Seneca and the other tribes of the League would strike back at the French with fury and with bitterness.

The Iroquois began to harass the outlying settlements, cutting down men working in the fields and burning habitant homes.

Lachine Massacre, 1689

The full force of their revenge came in August, 1689. During an evening of thunder, lightning and driving rain, 1500 Iroquois warriors crept close to the little French settlement of Lachine, just up river from Montreal. The next morning, in the grey

Iroquois warriors raid the little settlement of Lachine near Montreal. It is estimated that about 1,500 Indians took part in the assault. Although a group of French troops were camped within three miles of the settlement, they provided no protection for the helpless victims of the attack. The French officer in command had gone to Montreal to attend a reception for Governor Denonville. Without their commander, the French troops made no move until it was too late. When they finally reached Lachine, they found the dead lying in the streets, but the houses were largely intact. Indian attempts to fire the village had been hampered by a fall of rain.

light of a dawn thunderstorm, the habitants were terrified to see naked, painted braves running down the streets. War whoops rose above the rumble of thunder. Then followed a scene of horror unequalled in the history of New France. Men, women, children and babies were set upon by the screeching Iroquois who cut them down with knife and tomahawk. A few captives were hurriedly tied to stakes and tortured to death. When the grim slaughter was complete, the war party moved off with more than a hundred terror-stricken prisoners. Of this attack the Canadian historian, George Wrong, has this to say:

> It was the direst tragedy that had happened to the French; and the savages carried out their work with vengeful shouts that Denonville had betrayed them, and they now retorted in kind, "Onontio, you deceived us, and now we have deceived you."

Full of confidence after the success of their attack, the Iroquois roamed the countryside around Montreal for several weeks, killing habitants in their fields, slaughtering cattle, and burning crops, barns and homes.

In October of 1689, New France received the news that England and France were at war. This meant that with the active help of the English behind them, the Iroquois would now wage total war on the colony. The king, disappointed at Denonville's failure to crush the Iroquois, but ignorant of the number of troops really required to accomplish this task, recalled his governor. In desperation he turned to the aging Count Frontenac, a proven leader and a man who claimed to understand the Iroquois. "I send you back to Canada," the king said, "where I expect you will serve me as well as you did before. I ask for nothing more."

England and France at war

SUMMARY—SECTION V

In 1663, a new French king, Louis XIV, took charge of the affairs of New France. He ordered the appointment of a Council in New France to act on his behalf and in accordance with his instructions. Louis XIV was determined that New France would be turned into a

smaller France of farmers and manufacturers.   There was to be little
if any fur trading.

New France soon felt the force of these changes.   A settlement
was planted on Newfoundland, and protected by a garrison of soldiers.
A royal regiment was sent out to tame the Iroquois.   The king next
despatched families of settlers, young unmarried women, large supplies of food and farm equipment.   He also sent out a succession of
governors to lead the colony towards peace, plenty and prosperity.

By 1670, the Iroquois had been punished and frightened into
peaceful activities.   The steady flow of French settlers was directed by
Intendant Jean Talon to the lands bordering the St. Lawrence River, to
the fisheries in the Gulf of St. Lawrence and to the growing industries of
lumbering, ship building and manufacturing in the towns and villages
of the St. Lawrence Valley.   The colonists were discouraged from
engaging in the fur trade, and estates or seigneuries were established
where habitants were settled to till the soil and raise cattle.

In spite of all these French efforts, progress was slowed by the
fur trade.

In New France, as early as 1665, the fur trade expanded in an
amazing manner.   Now that Iroquois wars were no longer a barrier in
the west, and since Huronia had been destroyed, the fur traders had to
paddle far into the west and north to find pelts.   Radisson and
Groseilliers pioneered the way to Lakes Michigan and Superior.   They
were the first to suggest the use of Hudson Bay as a route to ship furs
out to Europe.   The French government would not listen to them, but
the English did—and founded the Hudson's Bay Company.   French
traders met western tribes of Chippewa, Sioux, Illinois and Cree for the
first time, and found these Indians greedy for iron kettles, axes, knives,
muskets, clothing, beads and brandy.   Eagerly, the tribesmen handed
over furs better than those ever supplied by the Hurons and the
Algonkians.   As in the past, the explorer and the priest were a part
of this westward movement, and thus trading-centres, supply posts
and mission centres were established in the regions to the west of
Lake Michigan and south of Lake Superior.

The Iroquois, busy fighting their southern neighbours, the
Andastes, left New France in peace.   When Count Frontenac arrived
in 1672, he persuaded the Iroquois to trade with the French and remain
on peaceful terms with the colony.

In 1682, the French Empire in North America reached its final boundaries. La Salle, travelling by land, found the mouth of the Mississippi. He returned again by sea and claimed the river valley and all the lands drained by the river on behalf of King Louis XIV. La Salle dreamed that the fortified waterways of the St. Lawrence, the Great Lakes and the Mississippi could shut off the English colonies from the western lands. He dreamed of a greater New France in Louisiana, an empire founded on furs and on farming, lumbering and mining. But his dreams were shattered by the Iroquois and the English.

By 1682, the Iroquois were no longer fighting with their Indian neighbours, and Frontenac was not there to pacify them. His many quarrels with the officials of New France caused his recall to France. The Iroquois were determined to take the western fur trade away from the French. They terrorized the Indian allies of New France and then began to close in on New France itself. Governor Denonville tried to stop them, but he did not have enough soldiers and supplies. In 1689, the Iroquois attacked the village of Lachine and came further east to raid the seigneuries around Montreal.

In 1689, France and England went to war. The Iroquois, now certain of support from the English colonies, began raiding along the St. Lawrence towards Quebec. Louis XIV sent Frontenac back across the Atlantic to save New France.

SIX

The Struggle for Power

GROWTH OF THE HUDSON'S BAY COMPANY

HENRY KELSEY REACHES THE PRAIRIES, 1690

COMPANY FORTS CAPTURED BY THE FRENCH

KING WILLIAM'S WAR, 1689-1697

MADELEINE DE VERCHÈRES

FRONTENAC ATTACKS THE IROQUOIS, 1696

PEACE, AND THE TREATY OF RYSWICK, 1697

NEW FRANCE KEEPS HUDSON'S BAY CO. POSTS AND ACADIA

DEATH OF FRONTENAC, 1698

QUEEN ANNE'S WAR, 1702-1713

BRITISH RECAPTURE PORT ROYAL, 1710

PEACE, AND THE TREATY OF UTRECHT, 1713

BRITAIN REGAINS HUDSON'S BAY CO. POSTS AND GAINS ACADIA

THE FRENCH BEGIN THE FORTRESS OF LOUISBOURG, 1713

KING GEORGE'S WAR, 1744-1748

NEW ENGLAND TROOPS CAPTURE LOUISBOURG, 1745

PEACE, AND THE TREATY OF AIX-LA-CHAPELLE, 1748

NEW FRANCE REGAINS LOUISBOURG

THE BRITISH FOUND HALIFAX, 1749

THE BRITISH EXPEL THE ACADIANS, 1755

LA VÉRENDRYE BUILDS WESTERN FUR POSTS, 1731-1744

HENDAY DISCOVERS THE ROCKY MOUNTAINS, 1754-1755

TROUBLE IN THE OHIO VALLEY

THE FRENCH DEFEAT GENERAL BRADDOCK'S ARMY, 1755

32

THE HUDSON'S BAY COMPANY

It had long been taken for granted by Englishmen that they English exploration in the North had an historic right to occupy land around Hudson Bay and freely engage in the fur trade. English exploration of the northern regions began in Elizabethan days when Martin Frobisher, looking for a north-west passage to China, made unsuccessful attempts in 1576 to penetrate the ice fields of the northern channels. By 1602, the English had found the strait that led into Hudson Bay, although it was not until 1610 that Henry Hudson sailed right through and down into the Bay. Englishmen continued to seek out a north-west sea route to the East. Thomas Button sought it along the western shores of the Bay in 1612. In 1616, William Baffin, searching further northward than any navigator for two hundred years after him, discovered the bay that now bears his name. In 1631, Luke Foxe and Thomas James tried to break through to the north by sailing to the west of Baffin Island, but they were turned back by ice.

All these voyages made it clear that a north-west passage did not lie through Hudson Strait or Hudson Bay and for many years discouraged any further attempts to find such a route.

In 1670, following the grant of the Hudson's Bay Company Beginning of English fur trade charter, a well-equipped expedition was sent out in two ships to the Bay. The traders, thanks to the influence of Radisson and Groseilliers, were better fitted out for commerce than on the voyage of 1668. They carried with them ample supplies of beads, but they also took along large numbers of muskets, pistols, hatchets and knives, items that would be of the greatest service to Indians hunting the beaver.

Construction of
forts on Hudson
Bay

In keeping with the plans of Radisson and Groseilliers, the men of the Company built forts, or factories as they were sometimes called, at the mouths of the rivers leading into Hudson and James Bays. By 1685, they had constructed Fort Nelson (later York Factory), Fort Severn, Fort Albany, and Fort Moose. There was also, of course, the original Fort Charles (known later as Rupert's House) on the Rupert river. Within a remarkably short time, the Indians of the north were making annual visits to these new stations. This was a very convenient arrangement for the Company. It meant that its traders did not make the long expensive canoe trips into the interior that the Montreal traders were forced to undertake. On the whole, the Company adopted a business-like and fair attitude toward its customers. No attempt was made to cheat or trick the tribesmen. In time, the Indians learned that they could place absolute faith in the Company, and thus, yearly flotillas of canoes continued to bring cargoes of furs down to the forts on the Bay.

The coat of arms adopted by the Hudson's Bay Company bears replicas of common northern animals—four beavers, two moose and a sitting fox. It is significant that the shield of the coat of arms contains no fewer than four beavers, indication enough that the Company was much aware of the busy animal that later became the emblem of Canada.

Beaver hats

The beaver skins of those early days were used to make fur hats, coats, capes and scarves, but the great majority of skins were brought to Europe for an entirely different purpose. They were imported to make men's felt hats, because beaver fur made the softest and best quality "felt." In order to make "felt", it was necessary to remove the thick mass of long, outer hairs from the beaver skin. The soft, silky, inner "beaver wool" thus obtained was treated and pressed into the sheets of felt that were shaped to make rich, handsome beaver hats.

The most highly-prized beaver skins were those that had been worn for a season by the Indians. Such skins were softer and greasier than hides stretched and cured in the ordinary way.

The longer and coarser hairs of the pelt were worn away by the action of wearing, leaving only the soft, short, downy hairs so much desired by hat-makers.

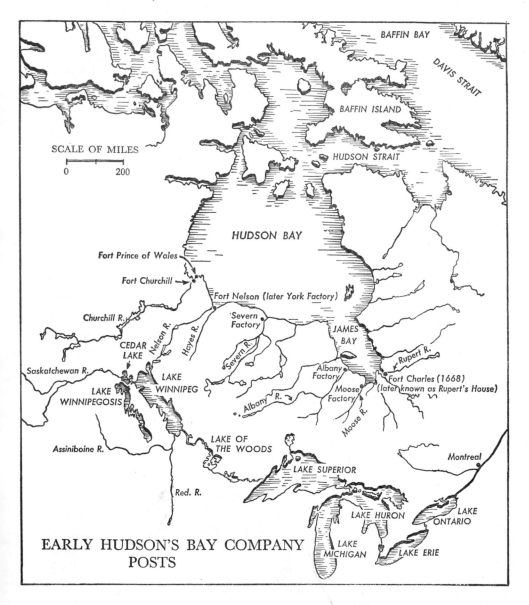

EARLY HUDSON'S BAY COMPANY POSTS

A continuous demand in Europe for beaver hats insured a steady market for good skins. Magnificent hats were made for wealthy gentlemen, and special designs were created for the headgear of army and navy officers.

Trade goods

In order to meet increasing Indian demands for various European goods, it became necessary for Company posts to stock a variety of merchandise. For example, in the year 1684, the post at York Factory imported the following trade goods:

300 guns	252 brass kettles
185 barrels of shot	20 pieces of "plaine Callico"
29½ dozen powder horns	2 gross of lace
2,000 hatchets	8 pieces of "Victory canvas"
3,000 jack-knives	350 yards of cloth
3,000 large "Rochbury" knives	390 blankets
2,000 small knives	445 coats (plus ninety-eight for boys)
15 gross tobacco pipes	2 dozen "plaine shoes"
5,000 lbs. roll tobacco	80 caps
247 hogsheads of leaf tobacco	10 lbs. vermilion paint
2 gross "sissers" (scissors)	3 gross of ivory combs

Money in the form of coins or notes had no part in the exchange of furs for trade goods, but some sort of standard value had to be established. Beaver skins, which were very common, came to be recognized as the standard by which other values were calculated. Thus, in the early days of the Company, an Indian could buy a gun for twelve beaver pelts, a hatchet or a pound of beads for one beaver pelt and a pound of shot for half a beaver pelt.

Explorations of Henry Kelsey

For the first twenty years of its existence, the Company took little interest in the interior. In 1689, however, the first inland journey was made by a young employee named Henry Kelsey, who was sent into the barren lands to the west of the Bay to look for customers among the northern tribes. Unlike most of the early English traders, Kelsey took naturally to life in the wilderness. "Little Giant" lived among the Indians, learned something of their language and in time gained an understanding of their ways. As it happened, his search for new customers was fruitless.

Northern Indians arrive at a seventeenth-century Hudson's Bay trading post. The early posts were mostly constructed of wood, and soon became very dilapidated in appearance. A governor of York Factory, on seeing it some years after its construction remarked, *"it is a heap of rotten old Houses without form or Strength—not half so Good as our Cowhouse was."* In later years, the Company built several permanent posts, many of them of stone construction. Note the trade goods—pots, iron kettles and powder horns. Contact with the trading posts introduced the Indians to a host of new and wonderful articles that greatly changed their lives. One result was that they tended to give up making their own weapons, tools and cooking utensils.

During a journey to the prairies in 1690, he spent two years in the valley of the Saskatchewan. He had been sent there to find the country of the Assiniboines, make them keep peace with the Crees, and invite them to come in greater numbers to the Bay.

Fortunately, Kelsey kept a journal in which he gives interesting descriptions of the country, the Indians and the animals. The introduction to his journal is written in very bad but amusing poetry. Part of the introduction reads:

> Then you have beast of severall kind
> The one a black a Buffilo great,
> Another is an outgrown bear wch is good meat
> His skin to gett I have used all ye ways I can
> He is man's food & he makes food of man
> His hide they (the Indians) would not me it preserve
> But said it was a god & they would Starve
> This plain affords nothing but Beast & grass
> And over it in three days we past
> getting unto ye woods on the other side
> It being about forty six miles wide
> This wood is poplar ridges with small ponds of water
> there is beavour in abundance but no Otter.

Kelsey's long journey cannot be mapped in detail (his report mentions few identifiable landmarks), but we have a general idea of his wanderings. Leaving York Factory, he went up the Nelson—or the Hayes River—to Lake Winnipeg, or perhaps Lake Winnipegosis, and then on to the Saskatchewan River, becoming the first European known to have seen it. Somewhere out on the great plains, he met the Assiniboine and spent the winter with them. He spent a summer and another winter wandering with Indians about the prairies and returned to York Factory in 1692.

Kelsey's journeyings caused a number of new tribes to visit York Factory, but his importance to history is that he was the first white man known to have seen the prairies, the great buffalo herds and any group of Plains Indians. Kelsey must have heard of mountain ranges to the west (the Rocky Mountains), and indeed, in his report, he speaks of a further tribe he tried so hard to find, the "mountain poets." But we hear nothing from him of the mountains themselves. They continued to lie in the far west, unknown to Europeans.

French capture
H.B.C. posts
To the French in the valley of the St. Lawrence the success of the English fur trade was an alarming development. The

Hudson's Bay Company trade token. One of the interesting practices of the Hudson's Bay Company was to issue "trade tokens" to Indians bartering furs at a post. The purpose of the tokens was to show a tribesman the value of his furs in relation to the goods he could select from the shelves of the trading store. Over the years, the Company employed various objects as tokens—musket balls, porcupine quills, ivory disks and numbered sticks such as that illustrated above. A whole token represented one "Made Beaver," meaning the skin of an adult, male beaver in prime condition. This was actually the unit of trade established by traders. In 1854, the Hudson's Bay Company began issuing special brass tokens to the value of 1, ½, ¼ and ⅛ "Made Beaver." However, in some posts, the earlier types of token continued in use for many decades after this date. In the Arctic, the Company now uses aluminum tokens based on Canadian money, the unit of trade being the Arctic white fox.

French claimed the northern land as their own, and they disliked losing trade to the English. From time to time, there were minor clashes between the rival traders, but no organized fighting occurred until 1686, when Governor Denonville sent a French expedition overland to attack the Company posts on James Bay. This was an amazing exploit, for the French travelled in winter, walking on snowshoes. The party, consisting of thirty soldiers and seventy bush rangers, was under the leadership of the Chevalier Pierre de Troyes, an officer of the famous Carigan-Salières Regiment. In three months they covered 600 miles by snowshoe and canoe.

The English, considering an overland attack impossible, were totally unprepared for the phantoms who appeared out of the south. Pierre le Moyne, Sieur d'Iberville, hero of the expedition, had no difficulty in capturing Forts Moose, Charles and Albany. During the next eleven years, James Bay and Hudson Bay were the scenes of many skirmishes on land and sea. There were victories and defeats on both sides. After 1697, the English held but a single fort, but they continued trading, determined not to be driven from the north.

Perhaps the most colourful event of the northern conflict took place in 1697, when d'Iberville, in his ship the *Pelican*, attacked three English vessels off York Factory. This strange battle lasted four hours.   A short history published by the Hudson's Bay Company describes the scene:

D'Iberville's *Pelican* was raked fore and aft but she resisted all attempts to board her. With startling suddenness the English man-of-war, *Hampshire,* ceased fire, lurched and sank, taking with her two hundred and ninety men.   Soon the *Hudson's Bay* surrendered with one hundred and ninety men.   The third ship, the *Dering,* escaped into the mouth of the Nelson River.

Although sadly weakened by the loss of forts, supplies, ships and men, the Company clung to the land and its claims of ownership.   It was not until 1713 that the Company regained undisputed control of the Bay.

33

THE LAST DAYS OF FRONTENAC

Count Frontenac received a tremendous welcome when he arrived at Quebec in October, 1689. The worried citizens of New France were more than delighted to have the tough old man back in their midst again. His arrival was none too soon. The year before, the French and English had begun a European war. In North America it was known as *King William's War*.

Governor Frontenac was faced with a number of difficult problems. The Iroquois, still a menace to the St. Lawrence seigneuries, were trying to cut off French trade with the western tribes. The English colonies along the Atlantic coast were also trade rivals. The future of New France was thus again threatened by an English-Iroquois alliance already many years old. It was English muskets, lead and powder and English knives and hatchets that the Iroquois used to slaughter the habitants of the St. Lawrence valley. In addition, the English in Hudson Bay were winning away much of the northern fur trade, and were also taking over more and more of the Newfoundland fisheries.

Frontenac's solution of the English problem was to defeat them in the eyes of the Indians. Frontenac and the government in Paris knew that as long as the English remained in North America, New France was in danger. It seemed, then, that the immediate course of action was to terrorize the English colonies and force them out of the fur trade. At a later date, they could be forced out of North America.

Frontenac ordered out raiding parties from Quebec, Montreal and Three Rivers with instructions to attack and destroy some of the New England settlements. Thus, Frontenac began the tragic frontier raiding of King William's War that brought so much suffering, horror and death. Both sides used their Indian allies

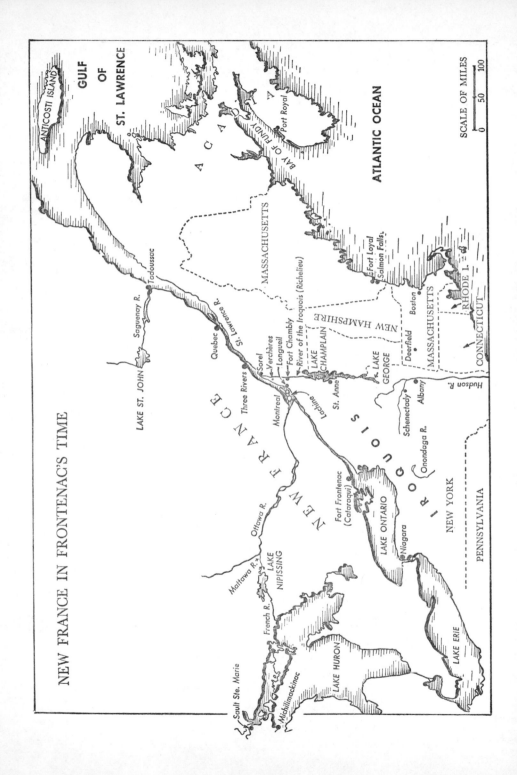

NEW FRANCE IN FRONTENAC'S TIME

A French garrison gun of the period 1650-1700. Guns of that time were made of either bronze or iron, although bronze was the preferred metal. The weapon above is placed upon a sloping wooden platform protected by a stone embrasure. Note how heavy a support the sides or "cheeks" of the carriage rest upon. Louis XIV of France is thought to have been the first monarch to organize artillery as a permanent part of his army and to establish gunnery schools.

in the conflict, so that at times the attacks were marked by incredible ferocity and savagery. In 1690, French and Indian war parties fell upon the settlements of Schenectady (in New York), Salmon Falls (in Massachusetts) and Fort Loyal (also in Massachusetts). It was the Lachine massacre all over again. Men, women and children were murdered, homes burned, and few prisoners taken.

The merciless quality of the frontier struggle may be judged by the fact that Frontenac offered rewards for enemy scalps and prisoners brought to Quebec. Professor George Wrong, a Canadian historian, writes:

He (Frontenac) offered a reward of ten écus for every scalp, Iroquois or English, and sometimes, perhaps, since French scalps were like English, he may have paid his treacherous allies for the scalps of murdered Frenchmen. He was more merciful in offering the high price of twenty écus for male and ten for female white prisoners brought in alive. After this it became more profitable for his allies to spare life; and invariably the French treated such captives kindly.

It should be said in all fairness that before the long border conflicts were at an end the English, too, were buying French scalps from the Iroquois.

The raids of 1690 restored French prestige with the Indians. That summer, the fur routes to the west were opened and alliances with the western Indians were confirmed. The raids also caused the English to attack Acadia and Quebec.

Phips captures Port Royal, 1690 The attacks on the English settlements roused a deep and lasting anger among the New England settlers. In Massachusetts in particular there was a loud demand for revenge. A small English fleet under the command of Sir William Phips, the governor of Massachusetts, hurried off to Acadia in 1690 where it attacked the French settlement at Port Royal. The almost defenceless citizens of the settlement were forced to stand and watch while the English sacked their church and looted their houses. Phips helped himself to the silverware, clothes and wigs of Port Royal's governor.

It was a shabby victory, but Phips became a hero in Boston. By August, 1690, he was off again to the northward with forty ships and 2,200 men. On October 16, Phips arrived at Quebec and promptly demanded its surrender. Over-confident of his power and lacking military training, he failed to see the difficulties of assaulting the fortress of Quebec.

Phips fails to capture Quebec Count Frontenac received a young messenger from Phips carrying the written order of surrender. Then, angered by the casual demand to surrender, the old man drew himself up haughtily and thundered:

I have no reply to make to your general other than from the mouths of my cannon and muskets. He must learn that it is not in this fashion that one summons a man such as I. Let him do the best he can on his side as I will do on mine.

The oldest church still standing in Canada. Erected in 1688, in the Lower Town of Quebec, the church was originally named *L'Enfant Jesus*. In 1690, to celebrate the repulse of Sir William Phipp's naval attack on Quebec, the church was renamed *Notre Dame de Victoire*, Our Lady of Victory. In 1711, to commemorate the defeat of yet another British naval attack, the church was again renamed, this time, *Notre Dame des Victoires*, Our Lady of Victories. The church was heavily damaged in 1759, as shown in the picture on page 316, but was rebuilt.

That evening Quebec received reinforcements from Montreal amounting to about 600 men—soldiers and coureurs de bois. The roar of welcome that greeted their arrival was not a pleasing sound to the British invaders.

Phips' guns opened fire on Quebec, and several land attacks were launched during the next few days, but these were beaten back by the accurate fire of French sharpshooters. At the end of seven days Sir William raised anchor and sailed for home.

The failure of the English attack on New France caused keen disappointment in Boston. In Quebec itself the citizens were relieved, but there was no lasting sense of security, for they expected the enemy to return with a larger fleet and more troops.

The fortifications at Quebec were strengthened and all garrisons along the St. Lawrence were kept on the alert for Indian attacks. Small bands of lurking Iroquois became such a menace that French settlers working their fields had to be protected by armed soldiers. During this uneasy period a number of heroic events stand out against a background of tragedy. Of these events, none is more moving than the gallant defence of a seigneury on the St. Lawrence River. What makes the tale even more startling is the fact that the commander of the fort was a young French girl—fourteen years of age.

Madeleine de Verchères, 1692 In October, 1692, the Seigneur de Verchères was absent on military duty in Quebec. His wife was visiting in Montreal. His daughter, Marie Madeleine, was left in charge of the family property, which was located on the south bank of the St. Lawrence, some twenty miles below Montreal.

One bright autumn morning, Madeleine and one of her father's friends stood on the wharf, probably discussing the need to take the marker buoys out of the river before the winter freeze-up. Behind them at some distance, a group of men worked steadily in the fields. Then, through the peaceful stillness of the morning came the sudden roar of a musket shot that sent echoes rolling across the river.

"Run, mademoiselle, run!" cried her companion. "It is the Iroquois!"

Iroquois attack Dashing back toward the manor house and the safety of its palisade, the two could see the agile forms of Indian warriors falling upon the workers in the fields. Bullets whistled about the two figures as they ran through the gateway of the palisade and swung the heavy door into position.

Although she realized that the situation was almost hopeless,

Madeleine did not lose her courage or her sense of responsibility. She shouted, "To arms! To arms!"

It was a pathetic little garrison which she held under her command—two soldiers, an old man of eighty, two servants, a few women and children, and her two brothers, aged ten and twelve. The able-bodied workers who might have added strength to the defence already lay dead in the fields. Her neighbours had also been killed, probably the night before.

The young commander was startled to find her two terror-stricken soldiers hiding in the armoury and making preparations to blow up the manor with gunpowder. In anger, she handed them muskets and ordered them to the palisade. Sheepishly, they marched off and took up positions at the walls.

With amazing skill Madeleine roused the courage and hopes **Siege at Verchères** of the group of men, women and children. While the women loaded guns, the men and the two boys rushed madly about, firing from all the loopholes in turn. To the Iroquois on the outside, the fort must have appeared full of well-trained troops.

Day after day this pretence was kept up by the weary little band inside the stockade. At night they slept fitfully in turns, while at intervals came a loud, clear sentry call, "All's well! All's well!"

The Iroquois were completely deceived by these activities, and in a council of war they decided that it would be too danger-ous to attack the fort.

Madeleine herself, weary and pale with exhaustion, moved about constantly, musket in hand. Scolding, encouraging, plead-ing and praying, she kept the defenders alert and at their positions.

During the dark hours of the eighth night, came a loud clear hail from the river.

"Who goes there?" shouted Madeleine.

"French," came the reply.

The girl commander's relief must have been enormous as she heard the welcome answer. Verchères had been saved.

Alone, Madeleine passed through the gateway in the stockade **Relief of the fort** and advanced to meet the rescuers. When she encountered

In mid-summer, Count Frontenac left Montreal on an expedition against the Iroquois with twenty-two hundred men, including some battalions of regulars, eight hundred Canadians and a large number of Indians. Their canoes and *bâteaux* were laden with cannon, mortars and rockets. On the Oswego River progress was slowed by the strong current, and eventually by a waterfall. Canoes, *bâteaux* and supplies had to be portaged up a narrow pathway nearby. Frontenac was borne aloft in his canoe by the Indians, who sang and shouted as they pushed on to the top of the slope.

Lieutenant de la Monerie on the pathway to the river, she saluted and said, "Sir, you are welcome. I surrender my arms to you." The officer, deeply moved by the slight girl, so weak and tired, yet so dignified, gave her a courtly bow and replied, "Mademoiselle, they are in good hands."

As the French soldiers entered the fort, their faces showed the amazement they felt, for in their minds they were asking themselves, "What miracle made it possible for a girl with feeble garrison to hold off the Iroquois for seven days?"

To men who knew fighting and understood the Iroquois, here was courage unequalled in the whole history of New France.

In 1696, Count Frontenac, then seventy-four years of age, Frontenac attacks the Iroquois, 1696 dealt a last hard blow at the Iroquois. Old as he was, the determined governor led a strong force of French and Indians across the eastern end of Lake Ontario and up the Onondaga River to the centre of the Iroquois lands.

During the rugged campaign which followed, the French and their allies destroyed the chief town of the Onondagas and an Oneida village. Crops were put to the torch. Although this expedition did not crush the League, it had a depressing effect on Iroquois confidence, already shaken by the losses of nine years of warfare with the French and their Indian allies.

This was the last main event in Frontenac's life. His final

days were beset by problems and worries. Government officials, traders and Jesuits had reason to fear and hate the domineering old man. He was accused of wasting money, of interfering in the affairs of others and of selling too many licences to the coureurs de bois. He was also accused of being too eager to spread French power to distant parts of North America instead of safeguarding New France. Even in the king's court Frontenac was losing favour, because these charges against him were so frequent and so severe.

Peace of Ryswick, 1697   In 1697, the *Peace of Ryswick* ended the conflict in Europe. The North American terms of the treaty favoured New France, which regained control of Acadia. In addition, New France was allowed to retain all the Hudson's Bay Company posts excepting the post on the Albany River. Thus, Frontenac's efforts to save the colony had not been wasted.

Death of Frontenac   A little more than a year later, Frontenac died after a few weeks' illness.

In the past, Frontenac may have been placed too high in the list of Canadian heroes. He was a man who possessed a few great strengths but many faults. He was a gracious, charming man, but he could also be a bloodthirsty savage, shouting, dancing and drinking around Indian campfires. He was a fighter who saved New France at a critical time in her growth, but he was also greedy and grasping, seemingly ready to fill his own pockets with profits from fur-trading. He was kind and helpful to his friends and associates, but he did not hesitate to lie about his enemies and exaggerate his own accomplishments. He was really not much better and not much worse than many men of his rank and position who lived at that time in France, in England and in North America.

34

A SECOND WAR IN NORTH AMERICA, 1702-1713

Peace between the French and the British did not last for long. By 1702, they were fighting again in Europe and in North America. The conflict was known in Europe as the *War of the Spanish Succession* and in North America as *Queen Anne's War*.

Queen Anne's War, 1702–1713

Scattered attacks burst like flames along the frontier and in Newfoundland where the French from Placentia sacked the port of St. John's. The settlers of New England, in particular, suffered from hit-and-run raids launched by the French and the Indians. The hapless people of these colonies remained in constant terror, not knowing when warwhoops might ring through the darkness.

Stung by a series of attacks and massacres and the terrible sight of the New England towns of Deerfield and Haverhill in ruins, the New Englanders once again determined to hit hard at the Acadian French. Once again the target was Port Royal.

Although Port Royal was considered the capital of Acadia, it was still a struggling, neglected settlement with a garrison of no more than 300 troops. By contrast, the New England city of Boston was a bustling, thriving centre where well-to-do merchants lived as comfortably as those in England.

Nevertheless, it was not until 1710 that any serious attempt was made to attack Acadia. That year, a strong force of colonials and British regulars sailed into the harbour at Port Royal. The invaders were at least six times as numerous as the defenders, and the French had no choice but to surrender. This was the last time that Port Royal changed hands. It was renamed Annapolis, in honour of the British queen, Anne, who came to the throne the year war broke out.

Capture of Port Royal, 1710

An English sixty-gun ship of about 1710. The great wooden battleships of the period were classified according to "rates." Thus, a ship with a hundred or more guns was of the "first rate." From this top level ships were classified downward by stages to the fifty- to sixty-gun ship, which was considered "fourth rate." Ships having less than fifty guns were too light to be rated. In 1703, a number of general changes in ship design were made by the Royal Navy. Decoration, which up to this date had been lavish and ornate, was greatly simplified. Figureheads, carved animals, birds, etc., that had decorated the bows of many ships were standardized to a crowned lion design for all but first rate ships. This regulation remained until 1773. The ship illustrated above has a small fourth mast (spritsail topmast) mounted at the front on the bowsprit. Cannon used on rated ships normally included thirty-two pound brass on the lower decks and lighter ones above.

Failure of the expedition against Quebec, 1711

A fleet sent against Quebec the following year had much less success. Seventy ships, carrying about 12,000 men, moved northward from Boston to the Gulf of St. Lawrence. Unfortunately for the British, the expedition had neither capable leaders nor skilled pilots to navigate the dangerous channels of the river.

Many of the soldiers and sailors were uneasy. They had been told harrowing tales of New France's climate and of ice conditions in the St. Lawrence. They pictured themselves starving or freezing to death or losing their ships in the crushing grip of the river ice.

As it happened, the fleet encountered heavy winds and dense fogs in the region of Anticosti Island. After the fleet commander lost his bearings, a brisk wind drove eight troop ships and two supply vessels on to the rocks of the north shore. Completely shaken by this event, the invaders decided that it was much too dangerous to proceed further upstream. They set sail for home even though a large number of ships and nearly 10,000 men still remained in the powerful force. Quebec had been saved by bad weather and by the enemy's ignorance and fear.

France and Britain brought Queen Anne's War to a close by **Treaty of Utrecht, 1713** the famous *Treaty of Utrecht*, 1713. The treaty greatly favoured Britain's position in North America. The French surrendered the forts and territories of the Hudson's Bay Company, Newfoundland and Acadia. In the case of the latter region, it meant that Britain was to have not only Acadia, but also a very large part of what is now New Brunswick, while France kept Cape Breton Island (then known as Ile Royale) and Ile St. Jean (Prince Edward Island). France's claims to the valley of the St. Lawrence and the Mississippi region were recognized by Great Britain. Her claim to control the Iroquois was refused. The Iroquois became British subjects.

Spain had been a French ally during the war, so Britain made peace terms with this nation by which the British gained new trading rights with the Spanish colonies. It was not long before the British were doing a thriving business in those southern colonies.

Following the Treaty of Utrecht, Britain had the most **Britain's rising power** powerful navy in the world and a goodly fleet of merchant ships. She had an ample supply of manufactured goods and men eager to carry on trade with the most distant markets. It is little wonder that in time Britain was to become known as a "nation of shopkeepers."

In both North and South America Britain's position was greatly improved. She maintained a profitable trade with Portuguese colonies in Brazil, with her own colonies along the Atlantic coast and with Spanish colonies in the West Indies, Mexico, Central America and South America.

Not only was business prospering, but the Atlantic colonies themselves were expanding. Villages became towns and towns became cities. Beautiful homes, schools, churches and public buildings began to appear in the shade of old elm trees. Farms and plantations spread across fertile valleys. Roads linked up settlements. The population grew so rapidly that it outpaced that of New France.

Britain was gradually taking up a leading position in the New World. The Dutch had been absorbed into the Atlantic settlements. The Spanish colonies were no longer as rich as they

About 1703, the whipstaff, a vertical lever for steering ships, was given up in favour of the steering apparatus shown above. This was actually a form of windlass, which, in time, led to the single wheel we know today. Navigation of the time depended largely upon an instrument known as the "Davis backstaff", which had been in use for more than one hundred years. It continued in use for almost another century, although made old-fashioned by the appearance in 1731 of a new and better instrument known as "Hadley's quadrant."

had been, for much of the great mineral wealth of their lands had been mined and shipped off to Spain. The French still claimed vast territories along the St. Lawrence and Mississippi rivers, but had neither the population nor the armed forces to hold them securely.

While the Treaty of Utrecht brought almost thirty years of peace to the French and British, the struggle for power would begin again. In North America, there were about 20,000 people in the French Empire—fishermen, farmers, fur traders and a few soldiers. It was not a rich or powerful empire. What wealth it had came from the fur trade. It faced a British Empire in North America composed of thirteen times as many people, an empire that was becoming rich and powerful by trading within itself and also with the West Indies and the colonies of Spain. New France remained short of men and supplies. British ships began to bring more people and supplies to the Atlantic colonies, to Acadia (now called Nova Scotia) and into Hudson Bay. After 1713, the British began to close in on the French fur trade. Sooner or later, the struggle for power would be resumed.

35

THE FOUNDING OF LOUISBOURG

After the Treaty of Utrecht, France set about strengthening her overseas empire. Now that Hudson Bay was again English, the old Lake Superior fur posts of Chequamegon and Kaministiquia were re-occupied. The establishments at Michilimackinac (at the head of Lakes Huron and Michigan), Fort Frontenac, and the newer posts of Niagara and Detroit were strengthened, while additional small forts were built in the Mississippi valley. The trading post at Niagara was particularly strengthened, and New Orleans was founded near the mouth of the Mississippi to guard the southern water entrance to the French Empire. Trade and settlement spread north from New Orleans to meet the trade and settlement coming south from the upriver posts.

Beginnings of Louisbourg, 1713 Then, in order to guard the northern water entrance to their empire, the French planned a great fortress on the south-eastern side of Ile Royale. It was named Louisbourg in honour of the king. The site chosen for the new stronghold was an excellent one; it was a peninsula with a fine harbour on one side and the ocean on the other. A swampy area lying at the base of the peninsula was an added protection in case of land attack. The vicinity was not suited to farming, but this was not important. Louisbourg would protect the St. Lawrence fisheries and New France. It would also be a naval base from which raiders could attack the British in Annapolis and in the New England colonies.

Before the winter of 1713 had really begun, about 140 people were settled on the site of the proposed town, some of them French fishermen, pleased to be moved away from their former homes in Newfoundland. Two years later, there were over 600

242

citizens.   Stores, barracks, public buildings, a church, a school and a hospital had all made an appearance.   Officers of rank, prosperous merchants and government officials lived in comfortable homes and were fashionably dressed.

By 1719, work began on the massive fortifications that were to make Louisbourg a fortress rivalling Quebec itself.   Using the best military engineers of the time, the work of construction took no less than twenty years, by which time the town was completely enclosed by stone walls fitted with bastions and protected by cannon.   The cost, even at that time, ran into millions of dollars. Louis XIV, complaining of the huge expenditures of money, remarked bitterly that he expected to look out of his palace windows one day and see the walls of Louisbourg rising above the horizon.

As the town expanded, Frenchmen were busily engaged in fishing out of Louisbourg and the nearby inlets which served as snug anchorages.   In time, hundreds of fishing boats, many of them built on the island, were working the coastal fisheries.   One result of this activity was the establishment of a number of small fishing villages along the shorelines in the region of the "Great Fortress."

Fishing was eventually of the greatest assistance to a surpris- **Louisbourg as a** ingly prosperous trade which centred around Louisbourg. Large **trading centre** vessels sailing to France with cargoes of fish returned with shipments of French manufactured goods.   These return cargoes, of course, were so large that the citizens of Louisbourg could not buy them all.   However, such extra goods were exchanged for the cargoes other vessels brought into Louisbourg harbour.   To Louisbourg came ships from New England with farm products, fish and building supplies, and ships arrived from Quebec with food supplies and from the French West Indies with rum, molasses and tobacco.   Thus, Louisbourg became a port in which a great variety of goods were exchanged.   French wines, laces and canvas sails found their way to New England.   Fish and timber were taken to the West Indies.   Rum, tobacco and molasses could find markets anywhere in North America.

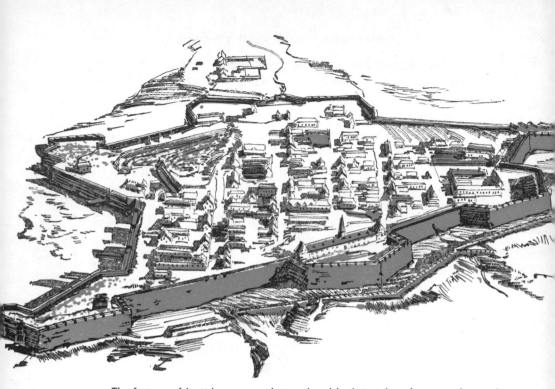

The fortress of Louisbourg was designed and built to take advantage of natural hillocks on its site. A number of large bastions (spade-shaped projections in the fortifications) were connected by long stretches of wall. In some places, further protection was afforded by ditches and outer walls. There were additional fortifications (not visible in the illustration), housing about seventy guns, located at strong points around the harbour. The enclosed town of Louisbourg was about half a mile long and a quarter of a mile wide. Six narrow streets ran east and west and nine others ran north and south. The long building with the spire, located in the centre of the lower wall, was the governor's residence, the Château St. Louis, which also contained barracks and a chapel.

It is interesting to note that the Acadian French living in the British territory of mainland Nova Scotia, came in their own little ships to Louisbourg, bringing their grain, fruits, vegetables and meats to trade on the quays.

As early as 1713, the French government hoped that the Acadians would move out of British territory and settle on Ile Royale, or perhaps elsewhere in New France. But the Acadians had been living for generations on their little farms, tilling their fields and sowing their crops. They had no desire to leave land that had been settled by their forefathers. They were not traders, adventurers or coureurs de bois; they were a simple people, without education and without great ambition. They preferred to stay in Acadia, living under the British flag, but keeping stubbornly to their own language and the Roman Catholic faith.

Louisbourg grew and prospered, but there were many quarrels and misunderstandings among its people. Priests complained that the citizens spent too much time in idleness, drinking, dancing and gambling. The careless conduct of the troops stationed in the town and the rude manners of French children were always being criticized.

In time, the French government spent less money on Louisbourg and lost interest in its military worth. Discipline among the troops weakened. Greedy officers made profits by selling wines and liquors. Reinforcements and replacements sent out from France were of inferior quality. Badly housed, badly fed and poorly paid, many soldiers found part-time jobs with merchants or fishermen. Military commanders appealing to France for supplies, equipment and arms, often found that their requests went unheeded. The French government was repeating the same old mistake of establishing a healthy settlement and then neglecting it.

However, the British troops stationed on the mainland at Annapolis (formerly Port Royal) fared little better than the French at Louisbourg. The British, too, were often short of the supplies and the equipment necessary to maintain an efficient military establishment. Britain, in fact, was making little attempt to strengthen or settle the Acadian lands she had won from France.

36

A THIRD WAR IN NORTH AMERICA, 1744-1748

On the north-east coast of the continent, the years following 1713 were uneasy ones. It was generally recognized by the French that the British controlled what is now the mainland of Nova Scotia. But, because a definite boundary line had not been drawn between British and French territory, there was an area of disputed land along what is now the New Brunswick-Nova Scotia border. Here, the French urged the Indians to attack any English traders or settlers who might work their way into the region. Of course, this led to ruthless raiding by both sides. The savagery of these frontier skirmishes was such that the colonies of Massachusetts and Connecticut paid as much as 350 English pounds for an Indian scalp.

An added source of friction was the presence of Louisbourg, a constant reminder to the Atlantic colonies that a French threat lay very close to British mainland territory and British fisheries. At times, Boston itself feared a naval attack by the ships from Louisbourg.

King George's War, 1744–1748 In 1744, thirty-one years after the signing of the Treaty of Utrecht, the French and British were once again at war in Europe. It was inevitable, of course, that the fighting should spread to the colonies. In Europe the conflict was known as the *War of the Austrian Succession* and in North America as *King George's War*.

The French struck first. An expedition from Louisbourg destroyed a small British fishing station in the strait of Canso. Prisoners captured during the raid were taken to Louisbourg, but because food supplies were low, they were handed back to the British in Boston. The released prisoners supplied authorities with the interesting information that Louisbourg faced a shortage of food, supplies, men and arms.

246

Leaders in the Atlantic colonies decided that their only safety lay in the capture of the fortress. They realized, however, that little help could be expected from the mother country, for Britain herself was fully occupied with battles of her own in Europe. It seemed, then, that the task of taking Louisbourg was up to the colonists themselves.

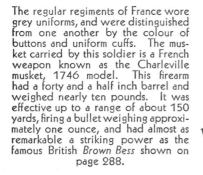

The regular regiments of France wore grey uniforms, and were distinguished from one another by the colour of buttons and uniform cuffs. The musket carried by this soldier is a French weapon known as the Charleville musket, 1746 model. This firearm had a forty and a half inch barrel and weighed nearly ten pounds. It was effective up to a range of about 150 yards, firing a bullet weighing approximately one ounce, and had almost as remarkable a striking power as the famous British *Brown Bess* shown on page 288.

They decided to attack Louisbourg early in the spring of **Capture of Louisbourg, 1745** before a fleet from France could bring aid to the fortress. Colonel William Pepperell, a Massachusetts merchant, was chosen as commander-in-chief of the expedition. He was not a professional soldier, but despite his lack of military training, Pepperell proved an intelligent and able commander. Men with beating drums hurried through the colonies in search of recruits for the coming campaign, and eventually three thousand men, mostly from New England, gathered to attack Louisbourg.

On March 24, 1745, a hundred ships sailed north out of Boston, being later joined by a small group of British warships. For several weeks the fleet was delayed by ice off Ile Royale, but

Colonel Pepperell's New England troops bombard Louisbourg from the abandoned French Royal Battery across the harbour from the fortress. In addition to its own defences, Louisbourg had strong supporting fortifications at two locations, one, the harbour, the other being the Royal Battery with its thirty-six guns. The Battery was abandoned by the French without contest on May 1. The following day, the English turned the guns on Louisbourg, creating considerable damage within the town.

by mid-April, the first men were landed on the coast near Louisbourg.

Shortly after coming ashore, a small party of colonists captured a shore battery of French guns and then turned these weapons on the town itself.   More cannon were dragged a distance of some three miles through woods and swamps to a hill, which lay within a few hundred yards of the French walls.   This back-breaking work was done at night when the French could not observe movement.   The colonists, slipping and falling, clambered over rocks and waded waist-deep in slimy water and mud.   It was a daring and surprising move.

With cannon firing on the town and ships blockading the harbour, there was little chance of the French escaping or receiving help from the outside.   Four merchant ships from France were captured and a French warship put out of action during a short sea battle.

In the meantime, the colonial forces were having their own troubles.   On one occasion more than 1,000 soldiers were ill with the fever.   To make matters worse, lurking bands of Indians proved an annoyance, because they attacked and captured small groups moving about near Louisbourg.

When the siege was two months old, Du Chambon, the French commander, sadly decided that there was no choice but to surrender.   There was no hope, he felt, of holding out successfully against such a strong ring of men and ships.   The ceremony of surrender took place on June 28, 1745. By agreement, the colonists were to take over the fortress, and the French troops were to be transported safely to France.

The victory at Louisbourg was all the more remarkable because neither Colonel Pepperell nor his men were professional fighting men; they were merely determined colonists, who had taken up arms to defend the New England colonies.   In later years, there were to be many more such examples of what men could do when they found a reason to fight.

The news of the victory caused great rejoicing along the Atlantic seaboard.   Some people were inclined to believe that

Heaven had intervened on their behalf. A poem appearing in a Boston publication contained these words:

> The Prince of Light rode in his burning car,
> To see the overtures of Peace and War
> Around the world, and bade his charioteer,
> Who marks the periods of each month and year,
> Rein in his steeds, and rest upon High Noon
> To view our Victory over Cape Britoon.

France, of course, was shocked that it only took a small army of amateurs to capture the great fortress. In an effort to gain a quick revenge, a large fleet of French warships and troopships was dispatched to retake Louisbourg and ravage the coasts of the Atlantic colonies. The expedition, however, was plagued by incredible misfortune in the form of bad weather, disease and faltering leadership. The fleet was scattered; ships were wrecked; men drowned or died of disease. Without accomplishing anything, the remnants of the expedition limped ingloriously back to France.

By 1747, it was becoming difficult for France to send men and supplies to New France. British naval forces were sailing the waters of the Gulf of St. Lawrence. Thus, feeble land attacks from New France down into the Atlantic colonies and upon Chignecto and Grand Pré in Nova Scotia were failures.

Treaty of Aix-la-Chapelle, 1748   King George's War came to an end with an agreement known as the *Treaty of Aix-la-Chapelle,* 1748. By its terms, both sides agreed to return places captured during the course of the conflict. This meant that the French returned the trading station of Madras, India, which had been captured from the British, who in turn handed back the fortress of Louisbourg.

In Europe, this may have appeared as a fair trade, but to the British colonists it seemed a ridiculous arrangement. They had sacrificed money, ships and men to capture Louisbourg, a victory of which they had been vastly proud. Now their efforts and their sacrifices were reduced to nothing. The French had been given back a fortress that would continue to threaten the colonies. The colonists believed that this was very much like handing a gun back to the enemy and inviting him to shoot. There was a good deal of grumbling and angry comment among the people of the Atlantic shore.

It was not really peace that had been declared. It was a state of truce before fighting broke out again. Each side prepared for the future in two different ways. The British built a garrison port in Nova Scotia to offset the menace of Louisbourg. The French, turning inland, strengthened their hold on the west and the fur trade.

37

THE FOUNDING OF HALIFAX

After Louisbourg had been handed back to the French in 1748 under the terms of the Treaty of Aix-la-Chapelle, British interest quickly centred on the mainland of Nova Scotia. Decisions were made to colonize the entire region and construct a military stronghold to counteract French power on Ile Royale.

It had long been the practice for English colonies to be established by trading companies or by groups of private citizens. In the case of Nova Scotia, however, the British Parliament agreed to found a colony through its own efforts and at its own expense.

At this time in Britain there was a large number of discharged soldiers and sailors, whom peace had thrown out of employment. To these men and to others, the government offered free passage to Nova Scotia, a land grant of fifty acres, food and supplies for one year and freedom from property taxation for a period of ten years. The amounts of land and special privileges held out to officers were even greater than those offered to ordinary citizens.

Founding of Halifax, 1749 In the early summer of 1749, a fleet of British transport ships crossed the Atlantic, carrying about 2,500 settlers. Among the hopeful company were ex-soldiers and ex-sailors, carpenters, masons, blacksmiths, upholsterers, butchers, shoemakers and a few lawyers, clerks and merchants. Some of the people were hardy determined folk, but many of them were ill-suited to face the hardships and the dangers of pioneer life in North America.

They landed on the shores of a magnificent harbour, well placed on the eastern shores of Nova Scotia—a spot known previously as Chebucto, an Indian word meaning "the great long harbour." The settlers quickly cleared the ground and began to erect buildings. G. G. Campbell, in his history of Nova Scotia, describes their activity:

Among the people were men of every class and occupation, from the young Governor down to the little serving girl and the negro slave; from the New England merchant, who was reaping handsome profits from the building boom, to the baker, the butcher, the tailor, the smith, who found themselves pressed into such uncongenial occupations as cutting, lifting and carrying trees, pulling stumps and building stockades.   Snobbish young officers in bright uniforms directed operations and soldiers worked side by side with civilians.   There was a schoolmaster without a school.   An Anglican clergyman, who had the ear of the Governor, was making plans for a stately church in the middle of the city.   The whole affair was something quite new in Acadia's long history, and Acadian workmen, going home to spend the winter, had strange tales to tell in their villages.

Part of the city of Halifax as it was in 1750.   Note the lamp-post in the foreground. Four hundred lanterns, ordered from Boston, were hung on posts eight feet high, and located at landing places and in dark streets or lanes.   Unfortunately, rowdy seamen took pleasure in smashing the lights with cudgels.   The church in the background is St. Paul's, which was opened in 1750.   Like most frame buildings erected in the Halifax of that time, it was constructed of pine and oak brought from Boston. Behind the church lay a large expanse of ground called the "parade," a square used for the assembly and drilling of troops.

The bustling new town was named Halifax in honour of Lord Halifax, President of the British Board of Trade and Plantations. Its young governor was the Honourable Edward Cornwallis, an energetic and capable military officer.

Many of the new colonists, becoming discouraged, complained bitterly of the crude houses, the muddy streets and a total lack of the comforts they had known in Britain. Numbers of them were so disappointed that they left Halifax as soon as they could find a ship to give them a passage.

However, the citizens of New England soon became interested in the new colony. Before the first snows had fallen, there were almost 1,000 New Englanders in Halifax. These shrewd, thrifty Yankees realized that the British Parliament was pouring large sums of money into the construction of the town and its fortifications. Such being the case, they thought, there was no good reason why New Englanders should not have some of the golden guineas being spent. Carpenters and masons came to help build homes; merchants came to open stores; fishermen came to work the fisheries; smugglers came to sell rum; adventurers came to hunt Indian scalps and a lone printer brought his press to establish a newspaper. All of these enterprising people, of course, brought a new spirit of industry and a new sense of life to the settlement of Halifax.

Elected assembly Misunderstandings did arise between British officials and the people who arrived from the New England colonies. Britain desired that Nova Scotia should be firmly ruled by appointed officials, while the New Englanders looked for a democratic form of government in which the people had some part. They were not a bit hesitant in saying that military officers and government officials were haughty and domineering. In time, the New Englanders gained so much influence that they persuaded the governor to rule with the aid of an elected assembly, which represented the interests of the people.

Throughout the early years of Halifax, the population increased rapidly. Money was freely spent and there was employment for all. But when the period of construction was over, many of the newcomers drifted away to seek their fortunes elsewhere. Those who remained were a hardy, determined people, willing to settle permanently in various parts of the colony.

Meanwhile, the French still remained a threat to the peaceful development of Nova Scotia. They still occupied border forts. From these bases, the French sallied forth on many occasions to incite the Micmac Indians to attack British settlers. This left the Acadian French in a particularly embarrassing situation.

On March 23, 1752, in this shop on Grafton Street, in Halifax, John Bushnell produced the first copy of the Halifax *Gazette*, Canada's first printed periodical. The *Gazette* is still published today. Bushnell had just been appointed King's Printer, and the *Gazette* began as a paper for the issuance of the proclamations and laws of Nova Scotia's governor. It also carried the latest local and foreign news, together with advertising. Printing, even after 300 years of development, was still slow and inefficient. Paper imported from England was hand-made from linen rags. To make such paper a little softer for use in the printing presses, it was dampened with water and placed under weights.

38

THE EXPULSION OF THE ACADIANS

Acadians   Many Acadians were willing to live in Nova Scotia under British rule as long as they were left undisturbed by the authorities of the colony. As it happened, they were permitted to keep their properties in Acadia, and those who moved north and west into French territory were allowed to take their possessions away with them. The majority remained where they were, along the coast of Fundy, tilling the soil as their fathers and grandfathers had done before them.

The Acadian French were a peaceful folk who enjoyed farming and dairying. They loved their ancestral land. Unlike their fellow colonists in the valley of the St. Lawrence, they took little interest in travelling, exploring or trading; their lives were centred around their churches, homes, fields, orchards and herds of cattle.

Evangeline   English stories and poems picture the Acadians as a thrifty, hardworking, God-fearing people, who lived in a land of beauty and plenty. One such piece of literature is Longfellow's *Evangeline,* a lovely and stirring poem, which begins:

In the Acadian land, on the shores of the Basin of Minas,
Distant, secluded, still, the little village of Grand Pré
Lay in a fruitful valley. Vast meadows stretched to the eastward,
Giving the village its name, and pasture to flocks without number.
Dikes, that the hands of the farmers had raised with labor incessant,
Shut out the turbulent tides but at stated seasons the flood-gates
Opened and welcomed the sea to wander at will o'er the meadows.

Evangeline is a moving poem, and gives a romantic picture of the region and its people. History reveals that the Acadians were an uneducated, rather simple people. They were content to live in their own little areas where their manner of life was without change and where the events of the world had little effect. They were quite unwilling to mix with British settlers. Above all, the Acadians were stubbornly determined to maintain their own customs, language and their Roman Catholic faith. Since Acadia had changed hands so many times, they probably thought that they would again live under the flag of France.

After 1713, when Acadia became British, several half-hearted attempts were made to make the Acadians swear allegiance to the British crown. These efforts proved unsuccessful, largely because the Acadians feared that at some future time they might be called upon to fight against their countrymen or against their Indian allies. On the other hand, the British authorities were worried that in time of war the Acadians would take up arms in support of the French and thereby threaten the security of Nova Scotia.

Acadians refuse oath of allegiance

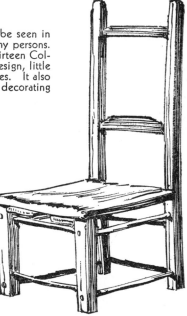

An Acadian chair. Softwood chairs like this were to be seen in all homes in Acadia and Quebec except those of wealthy persons. Unlike the colonial furniture of English settlers in the Thirteen Colonies, this furniture was noted for its plain, box-like design, little or no attempt being made to beautify it with curved lines. It also makes interesting comparison with the Louis XIV furniture decorating the well-to-do homes of Quebec.

Following the founding of Halifax in 1749, Governor Cornwallis adopted a much more serious attitude toward the French-speaking people of the region. He explained that the property rights of the Acadians would be respected and that there would be no interference with their customs, language or religion—but they must take the oath of allegiance to the British sovereign.

Probably, if the British had been satisfied to offer a limited form of citizenship, free of military service, the Acadians would have accepted it. However, such a settlement was not acceptable to the British because it did not remove the danger of an uprising in time of conflict.

The Acadians steadfastly refused to meet the demands of Governor Cornwallis.

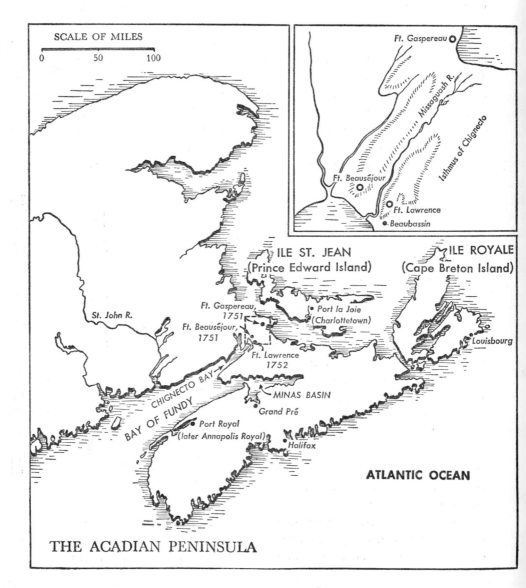

THE ACADIAN PENINSULA

There is good reason for believing that a French priest, Abbé **Abbé Le Loutre**
Le Loutre, played an important part in persuading many Acadians
to avoid the British oath of allegiance.   The abbé was a powerful
figure in the region.   He enjoyed the confidence of the Acadians
and the friendship of the Micmac Indians.   Totally unlike the
devoted, hard-working French priests of the time, Le Loutre seems
to have been a sinister, evil man who had great ambition and a
greed for power.   J. L. Rutledge, a noted Canadian historian,
says of him:

> He did not do God's will but his own.   He did not serve the
> Acadian people in wisdom or kindness or understanding.   He worked
> to make his dream of dominion come true at whatever cost.

Le Loutre did not hesitate to raise the Micmacs against the
British, and it was probably he who arranged the treacherous
ambush in which a British officer was murdered.   At any rate, the
abbé's actions caused alarm among the British and embarrassment
among the Acadians.

The Micmacs went on the warpath, attacking a marching
column of soldiers, a small fishing village and several military
outposts.   Their attacks became so bold that citizens were killed
on the outskirts of Halifax.

Gradually, Governor Cornwallis extended British military
control over the whole peninsula.   In the region lying at the
eastern end of the Bay of Fundy, not far from the present boundary
of New Brunswick, there remained a body of French troops, a
concentration of Micmacs and a few Acadian settlements.   To
this region, in 1750, the governor sent a force of British soldiers
with orders to drive off the French and their Indian allies.   There
was, however, no intention of disturbing the Acadian settlements.
As the British approached the little village of Beaubassin on
Cumberland Basin, they found the houses in flames.   The ruthless
Le Loutre had forced the Acadians to burn their own homes, and
he himself set fire to the village church.   Driving their herds
ahead of them, the poor bewildered Acadians crossed the Missisguash River into the territory held by the French.   In the period

which followed, the tiny Missisguash River became a hotly disputed line with the French in Fort Beauséjour on one side and the British in Fort Lawrence on the other.

Capture of Fort Beauséjour, 1755

Fort Beauséjour was considered a threat to the peace of Nova Scotia, and the British decided to mount a strong attack. In June, 1755, a force of 2,300 men moved up from the New England colonies and into the Bay of Fundy. After a siege of about two weeks, Beauséjour fell into the hands of the British colonials. Among the defenders of the fort were some 300 Acadians. By way of explanation, the French commander stated that the Acadians had been forced to take up arms in defence of the fort. But even this assurance did not affect the increasing distrust the British felt for the Acadians.

Shortly after the fall of the French fort, Cornwallis left for England, leaving Colonel Charles Lawrence as acting governor. Lawrence, a capable military officer, faced a difficult situation. He feared that if a strong French fleet should arrive off Halifax and the Acadians rose, he would not be able to hold Nova Scotia with the forces under his command. He suspected that the Acadians were giving military information to the French, and he knew they were sending food supplies to the fortress at Louisbourg.

After consulting with officials in the New England colonies, Colonel Lawrence finally decided that the only solution to the problem was to remove the Acadian people from Nova Scotia. He did not, however, inform the British government of his plans, but took the chance of obtaining later approval.

When the Acadians once again refused to take the oath, Lawrence took stern action. Speaking to a group of Acadian representatives whom he had called to Halifax, he gave them one more chance to take the full oath of allegiance, warning them that if they did not do so, "You are no longer subjects of the King of England but of the King of France. You will be treated as such and removed from the country."

For the last time, the Acadians refused to take the oath.

Expulsion of the Acadians, 1755

The trying work of deporting the Acadians began at Grand Pré on Minas Basin. There, on a pleasant summer day, the frightened French farmers sat in their little church as an English officer, Lieutenant-Colonel John Winslow, read the fatal words:

> Your lands and tenements and cattle and livestock of all kinds are forfeit to the crown with all your other effects, except money and household goods, and that you yourselves are to be removed from this province.   Through His Majesty's goodness I am directed to allow you the liberty of carrying with you your money and as many of your household goods as you can take without overloading the vessels you go in . . .

Shocked by the finality of these words, the Acadians could scarcely believe that the British were in earnest.   For years the British had not seriously forced the issue.   Could they really mean it this time?   Many of the frightened people concluded sadly that the time for treating with the British had passed and there would be no other opportunity to take the oath.   The last chance was gone.

The operation of expulsion was a slow and difficult process at Grand Pré and at the other villages in the western areas of Nova Scotia.   Since there were few ships at hand to move the whole Acadian population, many unfortunates were held as prisoners until such time as vessels arrived.   Every attempt was made to keep the Acadian families together, but in some instances fathers were separated from mothers and children.   Winslow, speaking of his work at Grand Pré, said, "This affair is more grievous to me than any service I was ever employed in."

Many of the Acadians gave themselves up to the British; some were taken forcibly from their homes; some took to the woods and fled into parts of New France.   Many of them saw their herds of cattle being rounded up by soldiers and their homes put to the torch.

When the long slow process of removal had been accomplished, about 6,000 Acadians had been shipped out of Nova Scotia and scattered in small groups throughout the length of the British colonies in North America.   Most of them were very unhappy in their new surroundings.   They found themselves

Acadian hardships

There was a long period of waiting following the order to expel the Acadians. These unfortunate people were divided into groups in preparation for the exile which awaited them. The younger and supposedly more dangerous men were promptly put aboard vessels sent from Boston. Due to a shortage of shipping, it actually took nearly five months to complete the process of expulsion. Note the costumes of the Acadian settlers. They are dressed in coarse, practical clothes bearing little resemblance to the stylish dress worn by the wealthier citizens of Quebec and France.

among people who spoke a different language and who, in most cases, held a different religion. In many places, the exiles were treated rudely and unkindly. The British hoped that the Acadians would soon forget their language and customs and take their places as members of the Atlantic colonies. This was not the case. Substantial numbers of the Acadians gradually made their way southward to New Orleans or northward to New France. Even in Quebec the Acadians were treated as poor relations who had no right to sympathy or aid.

It is very difficult to weigh the rights and the wrongs of this sad story. A simple, peace-loving people were caught in a gigantic struggle for power in North America. The French insisted that the Acadians be loyal to France, while the British insisted that the Acadians take a new allegiance to Britain. And because it was impossible to do both at the same time, the humble inhabitants of old Acadia were driven out of their homes. This is one episode in history in which neither the French nor the British can take any degree of pride.

39

FURS AND THE WESTERN SEA

While Britain was challenging French rule in Acadia, the lure of the fur trade was again leading the French further into the continent.

By 1713, the French had become acquainted with the Great Lakes country and the Mississippi valley. They then began to wonder what sort of country lay further to the west. Vague Indian stories of the western regions came to the trading posts. There were tales of the fierce Sioux warriors who lived beyond the land of the Chippewas, who held the westernmost end of the French fur trade. But the most persistent story was of a new race of Indians, sometimes white, sometimes bearded, who lived in magnificent cities beside a lake or sea.

The French had begun to hear about the Mandan Indians.

None of the descriptions was very clear or accurate. However, the French always discussed an Indian story that out beyond the Great Lakes was a river which flowed westward to the Pacific. Perhaps this was the way to the Western Sea. And, of course, they always hoped for the possibilities of more trade in this unknown west.

As early as 1716, the governor of New France suggested to the French government that a line of trading posts and forts should be constructed westward from the Great Lakes. He thought that by this means, fur trading and exploration could be conducted at the same time. Perhaps by such a plan Frenchmen might actually find their way to the Western Sea. Unfortunately, the government in Paris was not willing to finance such an ambitious scheme, and little was accomplished until the last great trader-explorer blazed a trail into the west. His name was Pierre Gaultier de Varennes, Sieur de la Vérendrye, a son of the governor of Three Rivers, Quebec.

264

La Vérendrye, a soldier at the age of twelve and a veteran of European wars by the time he was twenty-four, came back to New France in 1711 to join the family fur business, and by 1727, was in charge of a trading post on Lake Nipigon, which lies to the north of Lake Superior. While there, La Vérendrye talked constantly with the Indians who came to his post, and, in time, he became convinced that if he were given men and supplies he could reach the Western Sea by means of a river that the Indians said, "flowed toward the setting sun and into a lake: beyond this lake is a river which flows west, and at its mouth is a sea."

A beaver hat of the eighteenth century, of a style known as "continental." The most desirable beaver pelts for hat making were those secured during the winter months, when furs were thick and heavy. Pelts were at their best if they had been worn by the Indians for a year, during which time they acquired a glossy and rather greasy appearance. Since the habit of wearing beaver robes was a common custom among the northern Indians, the Hudson's Bay Company was in an excellent position to obtain these highly-valued skins.

His appeals for assistance were refused by the French government, but he was given trading rights in the territory west of the Great Lakes. In effect, he was told that he might go to the Western Sea, but in so doing he must pay his own expenses.

Using his own funds and money borrowed from Montreal merchants, La Vérendrye outfitted an expedition and set out in 1731. With him, he took about fifty men. Also in this company were his three sons and a nephew, La Jemeraye.

After reaching the end of Lake Superior, La Vérendrye was halted by a mutiny amongst some of his men and he had to send La Jemeraye ahead to the north and west by means of the Pigeon River. Near its mouth were nine miles of rapids so rough that the French had to carry all goods and supplies along the shores. In future years this place was to become famous as *Grand Portage* (the big portage). After this difficult passage, the explorers encountered forty-seven more portages before reaching a large lake (Rainy Lake).

Beginnings of western fur trade, 1732

During the winter of 1731, La Jemeraye built a post, Fort St. Pierre, on Rainy Lake, and in the summer of 1732, La Vérendrye travelled further north and west to build Fort St. Charles on Lake of the Woods. Here, La Vérendrye made a small clearing and planted wild rice to avoid famine in the cold months. That winter, the Cree Indians appeared and engaged in an eager trade for the goods the French had brought with them. It became clear to La Vérendrye that the Indians could be weaned away from the Hudson's Bay Company, providing the French established convenient posts for the use of the tribesmen.

In 1733, La Vérendrye wrote a letter to the governor of New France describing the progress he had made. Part of the letter reads:

> The savages being numerous, there is reason to expect that we shall get a large quantity of furs now going to the English at Hudson Bay. Provided there are Frenchmen on the road they travel, the savages will not go to the English, whom they do not like and even despise, saying that they are not men like the French and that they are afraid of them (the Indians), only allowing a few of their old men to enter the fort; the French they say are very different as they fear nothing and are kindly.

In 1734, a third post, Fort Maurepas, was built near the mouth of the Winnipeg River, close to the eastern shore of Lake Winnipeg.

Financial difficulties

As trade increased, canoes travelled back and forth between Montreal and these western posts, carrying furs to New France and returning with fresh loads of trade goods. Although business was good, the expenses of operating the posts and maintaining the long transportation route were very high. La Vérendrye often found himself in great financial difficulties because his Montreal associates were demanding greater profits, while the French government was urging more exploration. Tragedy, too, came to make La Vérendrye's burden even heavier, for his nephew died of hardship and overwork and his eldest son was killed by a war party of Sioux Indians.

Several times the explorer was forced to make the long canoe journey to Montreal to straighten out his tangled business affairs and report to the governor. The French government, knowing nothing of conditions in the west, continued to complain of the delay in exploration.

For three years, La Vérendrye developed trade at his posts and did not travel beyond them. However, he kept getting information about the west, confusing information, but he did learn that the "river to the sea" he had heard of at the Nipigon post went north-east, not west. It was the Nelson river, which led into Hudson's Bay Company territory. At the same time, he began to hear about another river, a larger river, going west, although it was reported as being at three different locations. However, what was reported as the River of the Mandans (the Missouri) seemed to him to be the actual river of the west. By 1738, he was ready to look for it.

On the evening of October 2, 1738, La Vérendrye reached **Mandan Indians** a point now occupied by the city of Portage La Prairie, Manitoba (a portage route of the Assiniboines on their way to Hudson Bay), and there on the banks of the Assiniboine River he built a fourth fort, Fort La Reine. Within two weeks, the fort had been constructed and La Vérendrye continued towards the Mandan country. When he got to a Mandan village, he found no white or bearded men. He found just another tribe of buffalo-robed Indians, some of whom had light skins and some of whom were even fair-haired. But their river seemed to run south-west and this meant it went into Spanish territory. He did not realize that it eventually swings south-east. As it happened, he returned disappointedly to Fort La Reine.

In April, 1739, after a gruelling journey back to Fort La **Journey of the** Reine, La Vérendrye sent off his son, the Chevalier, and a small **La Vérendrye brothers** party with instructions to explore a large river which, the Indians said, flowed into Lake Winnipeg. In a small lake (Cedar Lake) next to the northern end of the long lake, the young La Vérendrye found the mighty river we know as the Saskatchewan. Moving upstream, he travelled the waterway to the point where it forks and becomes the North Saskatchewan and the South Saskatchewan. The Cree Indians informed La Vérendrye that the Saskatchewan came from "very far, from a height of land where there were very lofty mountains and beyond the mountains was a great lake, the water of which was undrinkable." The Chevalier was hearing

A Mandan scout runs into the village with news of La Vérendrye's approach. The Mandans, a Siouan group, became relatively well-known to early explorers because these Indians were friendly and hospitable. Their impressive towns were fortified and often situated on a high hill overlooking a river. An agricultural tribe, they grew crops of corn, as did most Indians of the region. Early visitors tell of corn actually stretching for miles along the river banks. In the foreground is a chief wearing a horned headdress resembling the famous Sioux warbonnet. His long shirt is decorated with porcupine quills skilfully worked into the leather.

about the Rocky Mountains and the Pacific. The Saskatchewan (although he didn't know it) was the broad waterway to the fur riches of the north-west and the actual route to the Western Sea.

Another expedition was made into the south-west—beyond the land of the Mandans—this time by the Chevalier and François La Vérendrye. They were out on the plains from April, 1742, to July, 1743. During this adventuresome tour, they crossed prairies and bad lands, and on the first of January, 1743, finally came within sight of mountains on the western horizon. Although the La Vérendryes believed these to be the mountains of rumour on the edge of the Western Sea, it was probably the Black Hills of South Dakota at which they gazed.

By 1749, although unappreciative of all La Vérendrye's efforts, officials in New France decided that the Saskatchewan

To the early explorers of the west, the Mandan lodge must have presented a startling appearance. Only one other tribe, the Pawnees, possessed anything like it. The Mandan home had a heavy wooden framework, filled in with willow branches, and covered with grass, sod and earth. Roofs were strong enough to bear the weight of several persons, and the tribesmen enjoyed sitting on top of their lodges during warm, pleasant evenings. Each lodge was fitted with a vestibule, constructed of logs and placed on the east side. Note the circular bullboat which stands near the doorway of the lodge. This clumsy, skin watercraft served a double purpose, for on occasion it was placed over the smoke hole of the lodge during stormy weather.

river should be explored to its source. They felt "it is today the most convenient route by which to pursue the discovery of the Western Sea."

Although Pierre La Vérendrye was sixty-four years of age and weakened by his many winters in the north country, it was he who was chosen to lead the expedition to the Saskatchewan. Eagerly he prepared for the journey, but before he could look after the final details, he fell ill and died.

Importance of La Vérendrye's work Pierre's sons never reached the Western Sea. They were never given another chance. But the dramatic explorations of the Vérendrye family had proved that the continent of North America was much wider than anyone had imagined. Their efforts in the fur trade, too, pointed the way to a new and rich fur region in the north-west, which was to be exploited by both the English and the French. In the meantime, their work offered a strong challenge to the traders of the Hudson's Bay Company who had long been content to remain on Hudson and James Bay, and who now saw their trade being strangled by the French fur posts that dotted every important canoe route leading to the Bay.

40

HENDAY REACHES THE ROCKY MOUNTAINS

The Hudson's Bay Company knew that the French were building trading posts as far north and west as the entrance to the Saskatchewan river. However, it was not until five years after the death of La Vérendrye that a Company man went inland to investigate the gradual decline in the numbers of Indians coming down to the Bay. In 1754, the Company sent one of its servants, Anthony Henday, to persuade the western Indians to give up their trade at the French posts and resume the long journey to the Bay.

In June, 1754, Henday, in company with a group of Cree Indians, left York Factory and paddled up the Hayes River to the north of Lake Winnipeg and up the Saskatchewan River. His journey was marked by the usual hardships of early canoe travel—rapids, portages, mosquitoes, wet weather and scanty food supplies. Pushing westward along the mighty Saskatchewan, Henday reached a small cabin on the edge of the river near the present site of The Pas, Manitoba.

As Henday approached the river bank, two Frenchmen hurried to a small wharf to view the unexpected visitors. Their eyes opened wide with surprise when they realized the stranger was an Englishman. It was a dramatic moment. This was probably the first prairie meeting of French and English, and they were meeting on ground which each nation claimed as its own.

Astonished though they were, the Frenchmen greeted Henday courteously and entertained him for two days. On leaving the post, Henday presented his hosts with "two feet of tobacco" formed into a coil and looking very much like a piece of dark rope.

Henday and his Assiniboines pushed westward along the Saskatchewan. After two days' travel, they left the canoes and

Henday on the Saskatchewan, 1754

271

started across country on foot. The summer weather was unusually hot and dry, and the river's level had dropped to such a low point that canoe travel was difficult. The exact course of Henday's journeyings is not altogether clear, but it seems that he maintained a generally westward direction of travel. On that long trek he crossed what is now the Province of Saskatchewan and much of the Province of Alberta. At his farthest westward point the young explorer entered the foothills of the Rockies, becoming the first Englishman, probably the first European, to view these **Blackfoot** towering masses. Here he met the proud Blackfoot people who **Indians** rode horses and hunted the buffalo. Perhaps these were the "mountain poets" that Henry Kelsey had heard of in his prairie travels back in 1690.

Henday greatly admired the hunting skills and proud bearing of the Blackfoot. He attempted to persuade them to trade with

Before steel traps became available to them, Indians caught beaver by finding the low houses located near beaver dams. Having located a house, they blocked off the animals' underwater doorway by driving stakes down through the ice in front of the doorway. Then, piercing the roof with long poles fitted with chisel blades, they killed the beaver. Indians found their dogs most helpful in discovering whether or not beaver houses were inhabited.

the forts on Hudson Bay, but found they were not the least bit interested. They had no need, they said, for the trade goods of the English because all their requirements were supplied by their own lands and by their own people. They had horses to ride and buffalo to hunt. What, then, was the purpose of making the long and dangerous journey to the posts far away on Hudson Bay?

Henday and his Indian companions wintered with the hospitable Blackfoot. They did some trapping and fur trading. Then in the spring, after building canoes, they started homeward by way of the North Saskatchewan River. On June 20, 1755, they reached York Factory.

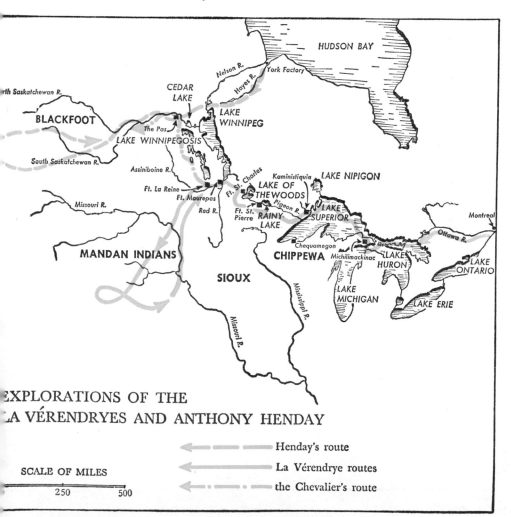

EXPLORATIONS OF THE LA VÉRENDRYES AND ANTHONY HENDAY

SCALE OF MILES

250   500

⟵ ⟵ ⟵   Henday's route
⟵ ⟵ ⟵   La Vérendrye routes
⟵ · ⟵ · ⟵   the Chevalier's route

Importance of Henday's work

Henday's explorations were most important, for they served to increase knowledge of the western regions. Henday was probably the first European to push west of the forks of the Saskatchewan, and was likely the first European to travel among the Blackfoot and other western tribes.

It would be pleasant to relate that the Hudson's Bay Company appreciated his efforts and rewarded him for his achievements. Unfortunately, like Henry Kelsey, Anthony Henday became a forgotten man—a man whose vital contribution to western exploration remained officially unrecognized. Fellow employees, perhaps jealous of Henday's success, mocked his discoveries in their reports to London. Then, too, Henday's colourful stories of Indian horsemen hunting buffalo were not believed by Company officials. A man who told such tall tales, they thought, could not be trusted to give accurate descriptions of territory he had explored.

Discouraged by this treatment, Henday resigned and left the service of his employers.

By good fortune, the Henday's journals were preserved by a sympathetic agent at York Factory. This agent, feeling that the explorer had been unjustly treated, said of him, "I knew this man; he was a bold and good servant."

The travels of Henday brought no immediate benefits to the Company's trade. Except for the Crees with whom he originally set out, and who were already Company customers, he had no success in persuading Indians to trade at the Bay. He found that the French had the loyalty and affection of the western Indians. Indeed the western Crees told him they would continue trading with the French. Band after band of Assiniboines told him the same story.

Obviously, the answer to the trade problem was for the Company to go into the interior and compete with the French. As it happened, the Company didn't have to go inland for quite awhile. The French Empire in North America was doomed to defeat. War was again flaring up in the east between the French and the British.

41

CONFLICT ON THE OHIO FRONTIER

By 1755, the French had made magnificent efforts in North America. They had explored the waterway of the St. Lawrence, the regions around the Great Lakes and the long length of the Mississippi valley. They had pushed westward onto the edge of the prairies and built fur posts on the lower reaches of the Saskatchewan River. They claimed vast regions of North America, but only held on to them by means of a few scattered settlements, forts and trading posts from Quebec to New Orleans and west and north to Lake Winnipeg.

This huge but expensive empire was the result of the fur trade.

The French demand for furs had been so persistent that the Indians killed off the beaver without any thought for the future. As the beaver were wiped out in the eastern regions, the French were forced to go farther and farther into the western lands. This led to a situation where a small population of about 60,000 people hung on to vast stretches of territory ranging from Cape Breton Island in the north-east to the Gulf of Mexico in the south-west and, of course, the lands north-west of Lake Superior.

The British, on the other hand, were in a much stronger position, for they were settled in the compact regions lying between the Atlantic Ocean and the Appalachian Mountains. There they were satisfied to remain until their colonies were well established, their agriculture flourishing and their trading operations in full swing. The population in these colonies grew steadily from year to year. One main reason for this growth was that unlike New France the English colonies welcomed settlers from other European countries.

By 1760, there were at least twenty Britishers for every Frenchman on the continent.

French achievement

British achievement

In New France, the very presence of the St. Lawrence River and the Great Lakes encouraged the French to travel. They took naturally to canoe travel and thought little of making long river voyages. Along the Atlantic coast, the British had no such excellent waterways to the interior, and travel tended to be slower and shorter. The absence of long rivers and broad lakes had another economic advantage in that it forced the British to build roads from settlement to settlement. Over these roads moved the slow, lumbering wagons which carried trade goods, food supplies and equipment. The roads opened up new districts for settlement and encouraged the clearing of additional farming land. Along these roads appeared numerous towns and villages, each with its own solid houses, churches and public buildings. Here lived a sturdy, determined people who loved their land and who were jealous of their rights as citizens. As land was gradually taken up along the coast, later colonists began to move inland toward the west. Year after year they made their way up through the river valleys until in time they reached the Appalachian mountains. This slow but determined movement led them to territory claimed by the French.

French territorial claims After Louisbourg was returned to France in 1748, the French became overconfident of their power in North America. In so doing, they re-stated their bold claim to all lands drained by the St. Lawrence and the Mississippi rivers. This, in effect, meant that the French were claiming ownership of the eastern half of Canada and most of what is now the United States, since the long tributaries of the Mississippi drain huge areas of land between the Great Lakes and the Gulf of Mexico and between the Rocky Mountains and the Appalachians.

It was the inward movement of British settlers, ready to dispute France's claims to the interior that brought on the last battles in the struggle for power in North America.

By 1750, it was the area lying to the south of the Great Lakes and in the Ohio River valley that became disputed territory, claimed by French and British alike. The Ohio territory, the

British said, was not French land but belonged to such well-established colonies as New York, Pennsylvania and Virginia.

There was no sign of trouble in the Ohio country until after Trouble in the Ohio valley the formation of the Ohio Company by a group of Virginians. Founded to explore and sell land to settlers who wanted to go to the Ohio valley country, the Company sent its first land scout over the mountains in 1750. When the French learned that the new company intended to establish a large English settlement on the upper Ohio, they themselves moved into the region and built several forts below Lake Erie.

Disturbed by this action, the governor of Virginia sent a warning letter to the French whom he considered intruders. Entrusted with the delivery of the message was a young surveyor from Virginia. A slim, young fellow who enjoyed travel and felt very much at home in the forests, his name was George Washington. No one at the time dreamed what an important man he was to become, or what a vital part he was to play in history.

Major Washington made the difficult and dangerous journey on foot through forests, over mountains and across rivers for a distance of about 300 miles. The message was delivered to the French, but their answer was a disturbing one. They made it very clear that they had no intention of withdrawing from the Ohio country. It became evident that if the Ohio Company were to establish a settlement, it would have to hold it by force of arms.

By way of preparation, then, the Virginians began to build a fort on the upper Ohio to the south of Lake Erie. But before the construction was finished, the French seized it, completed the erection of the fort and named it Fort Duquesne in honour of the governor of New France. Washington, with a band of Virginians, built another fort, named Fort Necessity, forty miles away, but it too was captured.

These French successes alarmed both the British colonies and Defeat of Braddock, 1755 the British government. In 1755, a British general was given a substantial body of troops and sent across the Atlantic to sweep the French out of the Ohio valley.

F. D.—10

In May, 1755, General Braddock marched overland from Virginia towards Fort Duquesne. With him were 1,550 British regulars and 450 Virginian militia men under Major Washington. It was a difficult journey. The regulars were unused to such rough conditions of travel and, furthermore, heavy cannon had to be dragged along on this long journey. Washington's knowledge of the country, of course, was of the greatest assistance to a general who was quite ignorant of wilderness travel.

Military field desk of a type used during General Braddock's campaign against the French. Portable desks were taken along on military expeditions and used by officers when preparing reports, dispatches, maps, or when attending to administrative matters. The desks were often elegantly styled in the mode of the period. Field desks of all kinds are, of course, still used during military operations.

Accustomed to the European method of fighting in the open with great masses of men, Braddock knew nothing of the cunning and savagery of North American forest warfare. He could not appreciate the necessity of fighting a swiftly-moving battle using the shelter of trees, hills and rocks. To him, this was a cowardly, impossible method of fighting, quite unfit for professional soldiers. His plan was simply to march on Fort Duquesne, batter it with cannon and, if necessary, capture it by an overwhelming assault.

In spite of warnings given by Washington, the General refused even to consider the possibility of being challenged before he reached the fort. Braddock had never seen Indians in action and therefore could not appreciate the dangers of sudden ambush.

Seven miles from Fort Duquesne the troops suddenly came face to face with a force of about 200 Frenchmen. Cannon-fire quickly scattered the French, but an unseen enemy poured a withering fire from the shelter of the forest. Braddock and his troops could hear shrill warwhoops, but they could see nothing of the Indians who were supporting the French.

Acting as he would on a European battlefield, Braddock kept his regulars in a compact mass. His men fought courageously even though hundreds of soldiers dropped before the fire of the French and the Indians. Bright red uniforms and the thickly-massed ranks made easy targets for the sharpshooters hidden among the trees. The Virginians, who understood this kind of fighting, took shelter and fought back in the same effective manner.

After two hours of cruel punishment, the British regulars broke ranks and fled from the battle scene. It was one thing to fight on an open battlefield with the enemy in full view, but quite another to stand up against Indians screened by the leaves of the forest. There was something frightening and uncanny in the swift, deadly flight of arrows shot from unseen bows. General Braddock, himself wounded, had no choice but to issue an order for retreat. After a short pursuit, the French were content to let the enemy escape.

It was one of the severest and most humiliating defeats in British military history. A body of skilled, professional soldiers had been whipped by a small group of French and Indian allies. The British losses were heavy; about two-thirds of the regulars were killed or wounded, and Braddock himself died shortly after the battle.

Thanks to the cool thinking and actions of Washington, the survivors and some military equipment were brought back to Virginia.

When the column of British troops advancing towards Fort Duquesne was attacked by the French and their Indian allies, General Braddock rode swiftly to the front ranks where the fighting was taking place. In the course of the battle, the general was forced to use several horses, since one by one they were shot from under him. Eventually, he was struck down by a bullet that lodged in his lung. During the retreat that followed, he was carried in a small wagon drawn by horses. He died when about forty miles from the scene of battle.

Results of British defeat The defeat of General Braddock had two important results. First, it aroused Great Britain to the realization that the defeat of the enemy in North America was to be no simple task. Second, it gave the French a renewed confidence in their own ability to hold the Ohio valley and other regions they claimed. During the next few years at least, this confidence was to seem well justified.

SUMMARY—SECTION VI

In 1688, fighting broke out in Europe between France and England. The following year, when Frontenac returned to New France, the conflict flared up in North America. Between 1689 and 1748, three wars, each spreading from Europe to North America, were fought in the forests of New France and the New England colonies, on the St. Lawrence River, in Acadia and on Hudson Bay. By 1748, New France had lost all claim to Newfoundland and Acadia, which in 1713 became Nova Scotia, a British colony. New France won the forts and territories of the Hudson's Bay Company and lost them again. By 1748, New France was left with her newly-built fortress of Louisbourg, the islands in the Gulf of St. Lawrence, Quebec and the lands around the Great Lakes and in the valley of the Mississippi. By 1755, Britain had established the fortress-port of Halifax in Nova Scotia and had expelled the Acadian French from the colony.

Defeated on the north-east coast of the continent, New France turned inland and explored a new fur route beyond the Great Lakes. La Vérendrye and his family pioneered a new canoe route onto the prairies, establishing trading posts that took away the bulk of the fur trade from the English posts on Hudson Bay. Sent out by the Company to change this situation, Anthony Henday failed to persuade the Indians to journey to the Bay, but he did travel far enough west to explore the western plains and see the Rocky Mountains.

By 1755, conflict had again broken out in the east. The last struggle for power began when the British colonists, moving steadily inland from the Atlantic coast, decided to cross the Appalachian Mountains and settle in the Ohio valley. New France and the British colonies alike laid claims to this region. When the French kept driving the colonists out and then defeated General Braddock's army near Fort Duquesne, in effect, another North American war had been started.

SEVEN

The Seven Years' War in North America, 1756-1763

MAJOR-GENERAL MONTCALM ARRIVES AT QUEBEC, 1756

MONTCALM CAPTURES FORT OSWEGO, 1756

MONTCALM TAKES FORT WILLIAM HENRY, 1757

MONTCALM DEFEATS GENERAL ABERCROMBIE AT FORT CARILLON, 1758

THE FALL OF LOUISBOURG, 1758

WEAKNESS AT QUEBEC

THE BRITISH ARRIVE AT QUEBEC, 1759

THE SIEGE AND THE BATTLE

NEW FRANCE SURRENDERS, 1760

THE TREATY OF PARIS, 1763

NEW FRANCE BECOMES BRITISH

PONTIAC'S REBELLION, 1763

THE PROCLAMATION OF 1763

GOVERNORS MURRAY AND CARLETON

THE QUEBEC ACT OF 1774

NOVA SCOTIA, 1755-1775

42

MAJOR-GENERAL MONTCALM

Although fighting had already started between the French and the British in North America, the *Seven Years' War* between France and Britain did not begin in Europe until 1756. Britain was poorly prepared for action at this time. Although her navy was experienced and up to strength, her army was badly-disciplined and she lacked capable generals. In addition, her government lacked a powerful leader.

The French were better prepared for war. Knowing that hard fighting would soon develop in North America, they quickly set about strengthening their defences. In the spring of 1756, **Arrival of Montcalm, 1756** Louis-Joseph, Marquis de Montcalm-Gozon, seigneur de Saint-Véran, arrived at Quebec, accompanied by two fine regiments, to take charge of the defence of New France and defeat the British. The forty-four-year-old Montcalm, a man of noble family, was a brave and efficient officer with considerable European experience. (He had been commissioned at the age of twelve and was an active soldier from the age of fifteen.) When appointed to command the forces of New France, he was given the rank of *maréchal de camp* (Major-General). Montcalm was welcomed to New France by its Governor General.

The Governor General of New France, Pierre de Rigaud, **Rivalry between Montcalm and Vaudreuil** Marquis de Vaudreuil-Cavagnal, a native of Quebec, was a vain, pompous, somewhat overbearing person. He was not pleased with Montcalm's appointment and often made difficulties for the new military commander. Montcalm had expected to have a fairly free hand in planning his campaigns against the British. Such an arrangement, however, was not possible. The governor was also the commander-in-chief. Already in command of militia troops, Vaudreuil insisted on being recognized as the senior military official, even though he had no experience of warfare or command. He continually interfered with Montcalm's planning.

Vaudreuil's attitude towards Montcalm was largely the result of pride and prejudice. The governor showed a marked dislike for persons of authority who came to the colony from France. Of course, Vaudreuil was not the only one to feel this way, for jealous bickerings and quarrels often occurred between the militia officers of New France and the professionals from the mother country. For that matter, French officials, whatever their position, were inclined to look down upon the "Canadians" as being inferior, boorish people, while the citizens of New France tended to think of the French as being pompous and proud. It was in fact, an awakening feeling of nationality, a pride in being Canadian, and a resentment of the many years of French neglect and French domination. This same resentment and jealousy was alive among the rank and file. It existed between the French regulars and the men of the colonial militia and handicapped Montcalm in his efforts to build a unified force with which to fight the enemy. But in spite of these difficulties, Montcalm won a series of important victories in his campaigns against the British.

Fort Oswego surrenders to Montcalm, 1756   In order to hold the northern end of the Ohio valley, Governor Vaudreuil decided that the British post, Fort Oswego, which lay on the south shore of Lake Ontario, had to be taken. In the summer of 1756, Montcalm spent many busy weeks preparing the attack. Working from dawn to midnight, he completed his plans and supervised the collection of men, provisions, ammunition, voyageurs and boats. His careful preparations were worth while; Fort Oswego surrendered after a three-day bombardment. Montcalm's men burned the fort and turned homeward with 1,700 prisoners and large stocks of captured materials. Before leaving the scene, Montcalm's Indian allies, to his great horror, butchered about one hundred of the unfortunate British captives. To the French commander this was a stain on the honour of

France, because the British troops had been guaranteed safe conduct from the fort. It was this incident in particular which caused Montcalm to distrust the tribes who supported France throughout the war.

Vaudreuil, when reporting to the French government on the capture of Fort Oswego, made it clear that it was his own brother and the Canadian militiamen who had been the real heroes of the engagement. This is largely true. Even Montcalm in his journal speaks warmly of the Canadian contribution to victory. But by 1757, governor and major-general were at odds with each other.

A second British outpost felt the weight of French power the following year, 1757, when Montcalm led an expedition against Fort William Henry which lay just south of Lake Champlain. With about 8,000 men, large stores and heavy cannon, Montcalm arrived before the British fort. Once the French guns were in position, they began a savage barrage that soon reduced the fort to ruins. Outnumbered and outgunned, the British could only surrender. Once again the Indians fell upon the British as they marched out of the fort. In the confusion that followed, Montcalm and some of his officers risked their own lives to prevent a massacre, but they could not restrain the excited braves. Hundreds of the British, some of them women and children, were injured or killed in this treacherous Indian assault. Of the 2,200 people who marched out of Fort William Henry, only 1,400 arrived safely at another British post, Fort Edward, eighteen miles farther south.

Montcalm destroyed Fort William Henry and retired to the peninsula that stands between Lakes Champlain and George. Here, the French strengthened the defences of Fort Carillon, later known as Ticonderoga.

Still determined to discredit Montcalm, Vaudreuil reported that the Indian massacre of the British had been the general's fault. Furthermore, he complained that Montcalm had not pushed on and taken Fort Edward while the opportunity presented itself.

Smarting at the sting of two defeats and at last reinforced with regular troops from Britain, the British determined to

Fort William Henry surrenders, 1757

French strengthen Fort Carillon (Ticonderoga)

capture Fort Carillon before invading the St. Lawrence valley. In the summer of 1758, an impressive army of 7,000 British regulars and 9,000 colonial troops led by General Abercrombie arrived before the French position. The British, completely outnumbering the French, should have had little difficulty in winning. However, General Abercrombie was an unimaginative, foolish old man. He bungled the battle from start to finish.

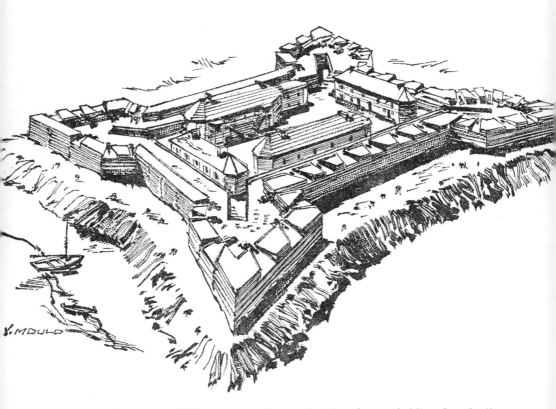

This is Fort William Henry. Compared with such strongholds as Fort Carillon (later called Ticonderoga) and Louisbourg, Fort William Henry was small and vulnerable. Its barracks and walls were only of log construction. It depended for defence on four heavily-armed bastions, located to permit artillery fire along the fronts of the outer walls when under close infantry attack. Compare Fort William Henry with the huge defence works of Louisbourg shown on page 244. Fort William Henry had a very short life. Constructed in 1755, it was unsuccessfully attacked in 1757 by Governor Vaudreuil. After its capture by General Montcalm, in August, 1757, French troops destroyed it by fire.

Montcalm had made hasty preparations to strengthen his defences. Dissatisfied with the ill-kept, crumbling condition of the stronghold, he prepared a strong defensive position on a ridge a little to the west of the fort. Here, on a height of land, he erected a barricade of logs nine feet high, in front of which all trees were cut down for a distance of about 500 feet. On both sides of this tangled mass were areas of marshy ground—soft, wet and treacherous.

British defeated at Fort Carillon, 1758

Behind this hastily-prepared position, Montcalm, with a force of about 3,500 men, waited the onrush of an enemy army almost five times larger.

General Abercrombie might have been wise to have put a ring of troops around the French and thus starved out the defenders. Had he done so, nothing could have saved Montcalm and his troops. As it was, Abercrombie made a costly, stupid blunder for which the British were to pay a high price in dead and wounded. Hoping to complete his task by means of one powerful thrust, the British general decided upon a frontal assault—straight into the mouths of the French guns and muskets.

From the British position not a Frenchman could be seen. They were well hidden by the crooked log rampart that snaked 500 yards across their front and into the thickets edging the marshes on either flank.

The British advanced with the men of the famous Black Watch Regiment in the lead, their bayonets fixed for the final rush. But when they struck the tangled mass of fallen trees, the even ranks dissolved into struggling masses of men, climbing, slipping, falling. Soldiers were pushed forward relentlessly by the pressure of those coming on behind. Many of them stumbled across the deadly *chevaux-de-frise,* which the French had scattered among the trees. These vicious wooden barriers, spiked with sharp metal points, pierced the bodies of those who fell upon them.

The scarlet uniforms of the British made excellent targets against the dark green of the forest. Grapeshot from French cannon and musket fire raked the floundering attackers. It was a desperate position for the British, because they could neither carry out a quick attack nor could they return an effective fire. Seeing that the action was hopeless, the disheartened troops fell back, leaving their dead, their dying and their wounded among the jumbled trees.

Undaunted by the failure of the first assault, the stubborn Abercrombie ordered his men into another similar attempt. This effort was so determined that a few Scottish Highlanders reached the log barricade and jumped over to land among the defenders. But even their magnificent courage was in vain. The Highlanders died on French bayonets.

Charge after charge was made. Each one failed.

One of the British regiments that fought at Ticonderoga was the 42nd Regiment of Foot, the Black Watch Regiment. A soldier of this regiment wore a scarlet tunic and plaid kilt, and carried the heavy broadsword known as a claymore. Since the kilt had no pockets, the soldier kept small personal items in a case called the *sporran*, which hung in front of the kilt. His gun is the famous *Brown Bess* flintlock, a weapon used by British infantry from about 1670 until well into the nineteenth century. Weighing about eleven pounds, it had a barrel length of forty-six inches. Fired at a range of 100 feet, it could send a one-ounce ball through several inches of wood.

As the warm summer night fell over the battlefield, the last attack faded away, leaving the British a disheartened, defeated force. Abercrombie judged he had lost 2,000 men, killed, wounded and missing—but most of them were dead. Montcalm's losses, while heavy enough, were much lighter—about 400 dead and wounded.

When Montcalm sent out scouts to see what the enemy was doing, they found that the British had hurriedly retreated. Supplies, provisions and equipment were scattered about in heaps, and in the marshes were empty boots that had stuck in the mud as terrified men ran away from the scene of battle.

The victory was Montcalm's. It is true that his success was partly due to the blundering of a British general, but it is equally true that he had achieved a miracle with small forces and hastily-prepared defences.

Three French victories in succcession — Oswego, William **French successes** Henry and Carillon — appeared to secure France's future in North America. But even while these events were taking place, across the Atlantic in Britain, William Pitt, the new British Secretary of State for War, had put the final touches to a master plan that was to shatter the French hold on North America.

43

THE FALL OF LOUISBOURG

William Pitt, British Secretary of War   In 1757, William Pitt, the new British Secretary of War, began working tirelessly at the task of creating a military force strong enough to defeat New France. He ignored the war in Europe and sought to humble France by winning her colonial possessions and taking over her colonial trade. Only a man of great energy and courage could have accomplished the work he did. Fearlessly, he dismissed incompetent senior officers and replaced them with young skilled commanders who had shown promise. He tightened up discipline in the army and navy. He improved arms and gathered ships, supplies and equipment. He studied maps of North America and investigated reports of the strengths of the various French forts and lines of communication. No detail was too small to escape his attention.

It soon became apparent to Pitt that the French naval stronghold of Louisbourg guarding the mouth of the St. Lawrence was the key that would unlock the gateway to New France. Louisbourg became his first objective.

As commander of the British force sent against Louisbourg, Pitt chose General Jeffrey Amherst. His three senior officers were Brigadiers Whitmore, Lawrence (the Lawrence who had played such an important part in the expulsion of the Acadians) and Wolfe, a young man of thirty-one who had shown unusual courage and intelligence in European warfare. Of all the officers Pitt sent to North America, it was James Wolfe who was to become the most famous. He was destined to catch Pitt's eye at Louisbourg and be given higher rank and an awful responsibility.

Louisbourg expedition, 1758   It was an impressive expedition which, in 1758, set sail for Louisbourg. Under General Amherst was an army of 12,000 men, while the fleet which transported the British force was manned by 14,000 sailors. On the other hand, the French at Louisbourg had not more than 3,000 regular troops, 1,000 militia, a few hundred Indians and a dozen naval vessels. However, although relatively small in numbers, the French were protected by stone walls, a good defensive position and an armament of 200 cannon. Furthermore, the commander, Augustin de Drucour, was a stout-hearted leader who had every intention of beating the British invaders.

On June 2, 1758, as a dense sea fog cleared away before the morning breeze, French lookouts at Louisbourg gasped in astonishment. There on the heaving surface of Gabarus Bay, in a great, sweeping semi-circle, lay more than a hundred British ships, riding at anchor. However, a high wind whipped the salt water into foam and blew for nearly a week with such force that General Amherst dared not attempt a landing. By June 8, the bad weather had subsided sufficiently to permit this dangerous move. There were just three suitable landing places, and these were spaced along the shore at a distance of one to four miles south and east of Louisbourg. It was in this area that the shrewd French commander had placed two-thirds of his garrison, supported by cannon.

In three separate groups, the British made their way in small boats over the choppy waves. Patiently, the French waited until the enemy were close inshore and then they let loose a barrage of musket balls and grape shot. James Wolfe, directing his brigade toward shore, was surprised by the sharp French fire. Waving his cane as a signal, he ordered his boats to draw away from the French position. But before the withdrawal could be completed, a small band of daring infantrymen dashed to the shore and took shelter among the rock and trees of a point of land. Realizing immediately that here was the proper place to make a landing, Wolfe ordered the whole brigade to head for this position.

The band of men that had landed were soon attacked, and in such a vigorous manner that the infantrymen found themselves in an extremely dangerous position — but not for long. Wading quickly to land, James Wolfe organized his brigade as it came ashore and with bayonets fixed the British charged the French.

Alarmed by the successful landing and the vigour of Wolfe's assault, the enemy hurriedly retreated, fearful of being cut off from the shelter of Louisbourg. Another British brigade further along the shore fought its way ashore and there, too, the French pulled back. A general retreat began along the whole French line until Drucour's men were within the protection of Louisbourg's guns.

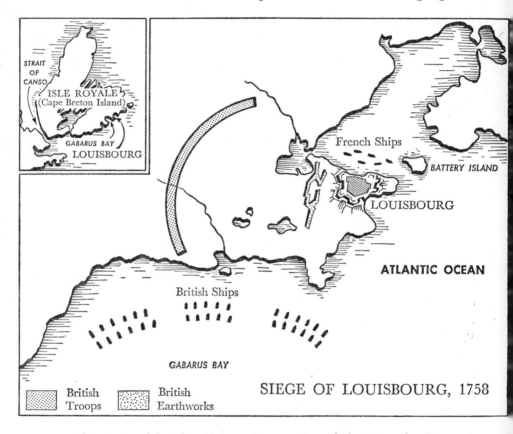

SIEGE OF LOUISBOURG, 1758

Content with a landing and a repulse of the French, General Amherst proceeded to camp his men in a sweeping two-mile crescent to the west of the fortress. In so doing, he encircled Louisbourg with men on land and ships at sea.

Amherst was a careful, methodical commander who had the patience to make every preparation before assaulting the enemy stronghold. The tedious work of unloading supplies and cannon continued day after day from dawn to dusk. It was no easy task to move heavy guns from ships to shore in rough water. This operation was so difficult that nearly one hundred small boats were smashed on the rocks, and a number of guns sank into the sea.

A crude road was built over the rugged ground from the British camp to a forward position where trenches were dug and breastworks were constructed. Brigadier Wolfe took an important part in establishing batteries of cannon in strong positions along the shore. This was hard, exhausting work for his men, who worked in teams of one hundred, dragging guns up hills and over rocks. Once in place, Wolfe's cannon were most effective against French shore batteries and against the French naval ships bottled up in the harbour.

In all this work the officers of the British army and the Royal navy worked in complete accord. Wolfe wrote:

> The Admiral and General have carried on the public service with great harmony, industry and union. The Admiral has given all, and even more than we could ask of him. He has furnished arms, and ammunition, pioneers, sappers, miners, gunners, carpenters and boats.

A relatively unimportant but very dramatic event took place on June 18, when the little French ship, the *Echo*, tried to escape from the harbour under cover of fog. When the fog unexpectedly lifted, the tiny vessel was pursued and forced to surrender. Much to the surprise of the British, Madame Drucour, wife of the French commander at Louisbourg, was found on board. This courageous woman had been trying to reach Quebec with her husband's dispatches. With all possible kindness Madame Drucour was returned by the British to Louisbourg. The gallantry of that time may be judged by the fact that a day or two later General Amherst complimented Madame Drucour on her courage and sent her a gift of pineapples. In return, the French governor forwarded to the British lines a handsome present of various wines. After this pleasant exchange of courtesies, the cannon took up their deep-throated roar.

Siege of Louisbourg

During the French colonial period, sugar was not sold in the modern granulated and lump forms, but in big blocks or loaves, which had to be broken up for table use. The special sugar scissors or cutters shown above were created for this purpose. These scissors had two sharp cutting heads that turned inward to cut off a particular quantity of a sugar loaf. For cooking purposes, sugar was crushed into a fine powder by using a mortar and pestle. It is interesting to note that Louisbourg was an important trading centre for sugar imported from the West Indies. Spices, too, were much used in flavouring and preserving foods. Some spices had to be ground before use in a spice grinder similar to the one illustrated above. The spice was placed in the wooden cup and the spiked grinder inserted and twisted round and round to pulverize the contents.

Two and a half weeks after the British landing, the French had lost all defensive positions outside the fort. By this time, French shore batteries had been silenced and the French fleet had been severely mauled. A daily barrage of ball and shell battered the stone walls of Louisbourg or fell crashing inside.

Drucour, knowing that he had no longer any hope of breaking the siege, still hung on grimly, determined to hold off the enemy as long as possible. He knew that if he kept the British occupied at Louisbourg they could not attack Quebec. He made every effort to delay the enemy. French sailors deliberately sank six of their own ships in the mouth of the harbour to block the entrance. Guns on board French naval vessels were used against the British entrenchments. Perhaps more troublesome than any of these tactics were the hit-and-run raids launched without warning on the British lines. But none of these desperate attempts was enough to loosen the tight British ring of ships and men that was slowly choking Louisbourg to death.

Conditions in the town The French position gradually became worse. In a dashing assault led by Wolfe, the British captured a hill within musket-shot of the enemy walls. Then, on June 21, a British shell struck the magazine of a French ship, causing a violent explosion and much damage in the town. The following day a British shell dropped through the roof of a barracks and started a fire that destroyed several wooden buildings. As the flames shot high in the air, the British poured cannon fire into the centre of the stricken fortress.

British shells fall on Louisbourg, striking a large building behind one of the main fort bastions, and also hitting the Governor's quarters, a chapel and a barracks. During the fire that followed, flames swept toward underground rooms where women, children and wounded soldiers had taken refuge.   Fearing death by burning or suffocation, women rushed out into the midst of cannon fire and fled screaming through the streets.

By June 25, Louisbourg was in a desperate plight. The place was crowded with soldiers who had no barracks and with sailors who had no ships. Only four French guns were able to reply to the enemy barrage. A Frenchman who was present in the fortress wrote in his diary:

> Not a house in the whole place but has felt the force of their cannonade. Between yesterday morning and seven o'clock tonight from a thousand to twelve hundred shells have fallen inside the town, while at least forty cannon have been firing incessantly as well.

All this time the British were making final preparations for an overwhelming attack on Louisbourg. Each officer knew his duty in the forthcoming operation. Assault troops stood by with their scaling ladders. With a thousand loaded cannon the fleet was ready to break into the harbour. It was a grim choice for the French—surrender or death.

General Amherst had not only prepared an assault, but had drawn up terms of surrender. If Drucour would give in, Amherst was prepared to have the French regular troops sent to England as prisoners of war and accept the unconditional surrender of Louisbourg, Ile Royale and Ile St. Jean.

It was eventually the townspeople of Louisbourg who forced **Surrender of** the issue. Fearful of a devastating bombardment and an over-**Louisbourg,** whelming attack, they were ready for surrender at any price. **1758** Sadly, Drucour accepted the duty he knew he could not avoid. In a formal ceremony on June 26, 1758, he and his men gave up their arms and became prisoners of war.

Then began the work of transporting the French troops and some civilians to Europe. Even in this peaceful operation, misfortune clung to the French, for hundreds of them lost their lives in storms and shipwrecks. Even after the gallant defenders of Louisbourg finally reached France, they were treated somewhat disdainfully. It was small thanks for the courage they had shown and the hardship they had endured in their defence of the prime outpost of the French empire.

France, of course, was shocked by the loss of Louisbourg.

With this fortress gone, the gateway to the St. Lawrence was wide open.

The news of the fall of Louisbourg caused many excited celebrations throughout the British colonies in America. In Boston, the citizens built a great bonfire, while in Philadelphia they shot off fireworks. At Halifax, in a noisy celebration that lasted for days, soldiers, sailors and townspeople consumed thousands of gallons of rum in honour of the victory.

44

WEAKNESS AT QUEBEC

By the 1750's, Quebec had a population of about 8,000 people. There is an interesting description of the fortress city, written by a Swedish scientist, Peter Kahn, who visited New France at this time:

. . . The mountain on which the town is built, rises still higher on the south side, and behind it begin great pastures; and the same mountain likewise extends a good way westward. The city is distinguished into the lower and upper. The lower lies on the river, eastward of the upper . . . The upper city lies . . . on a high hill and takes up five or six times the space of the lower, though it is not quite as populous. The mountain . . . reaches above the houses of the lower city, notwithstanding the latter are three or four stories high. There is only one easy way of getting to the upper city, and there part of the mountain has been blown up. This road is very steep . . . it is made winding and serpentine. However, they go up and down it in carriages, and in wagons. All other roads up the mountain are so steep, that it is difficult to climb to the top of them. Most of the merchants live in the lower city, where the houses are built very close together. The streets in it are narrow, very rugged, and almost always wet. There is likewise a church and a small market place. The upper city is inhabited by people of quality, by several persons belonging to different offices, by tradesmen and others. In this part are the chief buildings of the town.

It was to such a town that there came the startling news of the fall of Louisbourg. Its capture shocked the French even more than it elated the British, for now there was nothing to prevent the enemy from sailing up the St. Lawrence to Quebec itself.

Could Quebec be taken by the British? Despite his recent victories, Montcalm knew that he could not hope to hold Quebec in the face of siege by a powerful army and navy. Quebec was too much like a dying tree — firm on the surface, but soft and decayed within. The inner weakness of New France lay not in her people, but in its government, in the officials at Quebec who misused their power.

Governor Vaudreuil was extremely jealous of Montcalm's **Difficulties of defending Quebec** military record and ability. Their mutual dislike made it impossible to create an efficient, unified military force of regular troops and colonial militia, working harmoniously together. In addition, Montcalm was faced with problems of insufficient supply, equipment and defence works, largely because government money intended for such military needs often found its way into the pockets of dishonest officials. For example, the colonial militia were actually so badly-equipped that at times Montcalm was forced to outfit them from stores intended for the regular troops. It is not surprising, then, that he complained bitterly of the dishonesty he saw all about him. Speaking of some government officials, he said, "It seems as if they were all hastening to make their fortunes before the loss of the colony."

Undoubtedly, the greatest thief in New France was the **Bigot, the dishonest intendant** greedy, pleasure-loving intendant, François Bigot. The office of intendant was a vital one in New France. An incapable or dishonest intendant was in a position to strangle prosperity and seriously weaken the defence of the colony. This is exactly what Bigot did. Bigot was an industrious, shrewd and intelligent person, who might well have rivalled the achievements of an earlier intendant, Jean Talon. He chose, however, to debase his talents by the steady theft of public funds to finance his appetite for expensive living. In New France he found ample opportunity to steal and spend.

Bigot gathered about him a group of ruthless men to whom he sold positions of authority. These rogues kept false accounts, sold government supplies at unnecessarily high prices, pocketed the wages of non-existent soldiers and workmen (although these officials claimed they were real people), retained money for provisions which were never supplied, and accepted salaries for services which were never rendered. Crops of grain were bought from the habitants at low rates and were resold to the French government at high prices. Bigot and his gang approved contracts for high-priced transport vehicles, bad ammunition and poorly-

Intendant Bigot held frequent dinner parties for members of Quebec society. The intendant's palace was a large, rather ugly building, but was well suited to the gay, lavish life he loved. At his parties, Bigot offered his guests dancing, masquerades and gambling. Some of the guests lost large sums of money at the gaming tables. Note the costumes. This was a period of wigs for both men and women. Gentlemen's wigs were short, and sometimes tied at the back. Lace was very popular, even on male attire, where it was worn at the throat and at the wrists.

built fortifications, and then charged the contractors a fat fee for giving them the chance of government business.

Bigot himself shared the tremendous profits of all these activities and even built up "side-lines" of his own. One of them was a business venture in which he imported goods from France, stored them in a large warehouse, and later sold them to the government. His sales prices were always fantastically high.

Bigot even profited by gambling. In his luxurious palace, **Gambling at** where he often entertained, Bigot encouraged his guests to take **Quebec** part in games of chance. As a result, young noblemen, prosperous business men and gay army officers lost substantial sums of money. Montcalm, who was sometimes a guest of the intendant, was very much disturbed by what he saw. On one occasion, he wrote in his diary:

> The gambling has been so great and so much beyond the means of the players that I thought I was looking at fools, or rather people sick with a burning fever. . . . I left at one o'clock, annoyed at seeing so much play and gambling.

Montcalm was both enraged and sickened by Bigot's ruthless plundering of government money. To make matters worse, Vaudreuil seems to have deliberately shielded Bigot and his associates by writing reports that gave glowing accounts of the intendant's work. There is no reason to suppose that Vaudreuil was sharing these illegal profits. It seems he was prepared to support Bigot in order to spite Montcalm.

As the final clash between the French and British approached, Montcalm and Vaudreuil were still quarrelling bitterly about seniority. It may be that Vaudreuil was not entirely to blame, for Montcalm at times made some very cutting remarks about the governor. If both men had been more tactful and forgiving, it is possible that they might have patched up their differences.

Montcalm knew that the colony could not be successfully **Bougainville** defended unless more help was sent from France. Accordingly, **seeks military** **aid, 1758** he suggested that his aide-de-camp, Louis-Antoine de Bougainville, should be sent home to plead for military assistance. Vaudreuil agreed to this arrangement, but secretly wrote to France, stating that Bougainville could not be trusted.

Bougainville reached France in December, 1758, and there laid Montcalm's plans and requests before the government. Although a very young man, just twenty-nine years of age, he informed officials that Montcalm believed it necessary for the French to make an attack overland from New France on one of the British colonies, perhaps Virginia or the Carolinas. These colonies were known to be weakly defended. Such an attack would force the British to move troops southward instead of northward against Quebec. Bougainville also explained that Montcalm urgently required more troops—especially artillerymen and engineers—muskets, much ammunition, a train of artillery, food, and goods to buy the services of the Indians.

Montcalm disappointed   Although Bougainville argued long and persuasively, the French government would not agree to all the suggestions made by Montcalm. Authority to organize an expedition against the British colonies was refused, but certain aid to New France was approved. When it arrived, Montcalm was bitterly disappointed. Four French ships arrived at Quebec with 400 soldiers, forty gunners and a few engineers. The vessels also carried ammunition, arms and food supplies, but in what quantities we do not know. In all probability, there was only a little of each of the many items he needed so badly.

This French furniture of about 1750 is in the style of Louis XV. It represents the height of grandeur in design, having graceful, flowing and delicate lines. In front is a game table with a built-in backgammon board. Behind is a small settee known as a canape. Compare these beautiful furnishings with those shown on page 93. Notice how much more refined the products of this later period are.

Montcalm was told to wait for additional men and stores, and in the meantime to defend New France as best he could. There were several reasons why the French government feared to risk large forces in North America. In the first place, France was at war in Europe and had to maintain her own military strength. In the second place, the French government had lost confidence in the officials of New France. The king and his ministers were well aware of the quarrels, the bribery and the dishonesty that were destroying the vigour and the vitality of the colony.

Knowing the bitter feelings which existed between Vaudreuil and Montcalm, the French government would have been wise to have recalled at least one of them. This was not done. Vaudreuil was considered a valuable man because of his influence with the French colonists and the Indians. Montcalm had been successful in his military activities against the British and was, therefore, indispensable. Vaudreuil was ordered to give way to Montcalm on military matters, but his later actions suggest he paid little attention to his king's commands.

The whole period between the battle of Fort Carillon and the final struggle for Quebec was a period of intense discouragement for Montcalm. He was so disheartened and depressed that on one occasion he asked to be recalled to France. This request was refused at once. Who else had the skill to defend the colony? Tired of the continual bickering, trickery and treachery, Montcalm longed for home and family on the estate he loved so much. In his diary he wrote, "When shall I be at the château of Candiac, with my plantations, my grove of oak, my oil mill and my mulberry trees?" But he was an honourable man, determined to do his duty to the bitter end. As he remarked in his last letter to his wife, "I think I should have given up all my honours to be back with you, but the king must be obeyed. . ."

45

MAJOR-GENERAL WOLFE

William Pitt, the British Secretary of State for War, had planned a major campaign against the French for the year 1758. He had aimed three separate blows at New France—the capture of Louisbourg, the capture of Fort Duquesne, and the main operation, an advance up the Lake Champlain route and the occupation of Montreal. Only the first two attacks had been successful. General Abercrombie, marching for Montreal, had met disaster at Fort Carillon.

British plan of war for 1759 Pitt's plan for 1759 was again three blows at New France. General Amherst would advance on Montreal or Quebec by the Lake Champlain route—or down the St. Lawrence. Brigadier-General Prideaux would attack Fort Niagara, which stood at the spot where the Niagara River meets Lake Ontario, and the third attack, a sea-borne expedition against Quebec, was entrusted to the command of the newly-promoted Major-General James Wolfe, the young brigadier who had done such excellent work at Louisbourg.

James Wolfe Of the three proposed actions, the third was the most difficult, and for this reason it is surprising to learn that Wolfe was given the command. It is true he had shown daring and distinct promise, but he was young, just thirty-two years of age, and had always suffered from ill-health. In appearance, he looked anything but a commander. He was a tall, gangling man with red hair, a great hooked nose and a tiny chin. By temperament he was changeable. He could be fierce, stern and impatient; he could also be friendly, kind and understanding. However, there was no question at all about his courage, for on many occasions he had acted with perfect coolness under fire. His men respected and admired him. Above all, the great Pitt had faith in Wolfe's desire and ambition to be a successful commander.

Quebec expedition, 1759 Pitt had hoped to provide Wolfe with 12,000 troops, but in the end their total number was little more than 8,500. Nonetheless,

304

their quality was first rate—several battalions of regular troops, a small battalion of grenadiers (grenade throwers), three companies of the Royal Regiment of Artillery and six companies of American Rangers. There were no militia men and scarcely any Indians, and the regulars had experienced North American battle conditions. Above all, Wolfe's troops were led by a group of officers of whom it was said that "they were probably the finest body of British officers which has ever taken the field."

The British fleet assigned to escort Wolfe's men to New France was a powerful force of forty-nine Royal Navy warships, twenty-two of which were armed with fifty or more guns. In addition, there were over 120 transports and other vessels to carry troops, ammunition, guns and food stores. This sturdy array was manned by 13,000 sailors and marines under the command of Vice-Admiral Charles Saunders, an experienced and skilful naval officer.

The intention to attack Quebec was no secret to the French **French preparations** in Europe or at Quebec. A French dispatch received by Governor Vaudreuil told of Wolfe's preparations and the size of his military force. Montcalm, who had been at Montreal, rushed to Quebec to bolster its defences. He issued orders for the movement of his regulars from Montreal and Three Rivers to Quebec. Then he set to work to prepare the strongest defence possible. Batteries of guns were set up along the shores; fire ships were made ready; a bridge was constructed across the St. Charles River and two hulks were sunk at its mouth; navigation buoys were removed from the St. Lawrence, and trenches were dug along the north shore to the east of the city. In order to safeguard military supplies, supply ships carrying food and ammunition were sent fifty miles up-river. Thus, if the town of Quebec were to fall, the army could retreat to a main supply base.

It is not clear how many men Montcalm had under his **Montcalm's forces** command. Varying accounts have come down to us. It is probable, however, that his forces numbered between 14,000 and 15,000, including regulars, militia, volunteers, Indians and a few sailors. With amazing zeal, boys still in their teens and old men in their eighties hurried to Quebec, hoping to take some part in the coming events. There was, however, more enthusiasm than military skill among the militia and the volunteers. On the whole, it must be admitted that Moncalm's forces were neither as well-trained nor as well-disciplined as those under Wolfe's command.

The French expected the British fleet to encounter serious difficulty in navigating the treacherous channels of the St. Lawrence. Even French ships, after years of sailing the river, sometimes met disaster. Those who foretold British shipwrecks did not count on the skill of Captain James Cook and several other naval officers who patiently made soundings of the river's depths and drew up charts of its course. Their work was so excellent that not a single British ship was lost in the river passage up to Quebec. This was the same Captain James Cook who later made three notable voyages in the Pacific Ocean. During the third voyage he explored the long, rugged coastline of British Columbia. It is one of the strange coincidences of history that two famous Pacific explorers — Cook and Bougainville, Montcalm's subordinate—should both have been engaged at the same time and on opposite sides at the taking of Quebec.

British land before Quebec On June 27, 1759, Wolfe landed his troops on the south shore of the Ile d'Orleans, which lies just downriver and to the east of Quebec. With a small escort, he made his way quickly to the west end of the island to catch his first glimpse of Quebec. What he saw was not encouraging. The town itself was well protected by the towering cliffs on its southern flank. But even more serious were the long lines of trenches, breastworks, batteries, camps and strong points that stretched east for six miles along the north shore of the river—the Beauport shore—all the way from Quebec to the mouth of the Montmorency River. Wolfe was disappointed; he had planned on seizing this Beauport shore as the first step in his campaign against Quebec. As he stood examining the strong defences, he could only admire Montcalm's shrewd preparations.

The French made no move to prevent the British landings. However, they decided to strike the following evening. It was a desperate, dramatic action, aimed at causing confusion and destruction among the British vessels lying at anchor in the channel south of Ile d'Orleans.

After nightfall, Royal Navy seamen were startled to see seven burning ships bearing down on them, all of them wreathed in flames and riding in on the river's current. On they came with loaded guns exploding in the heat of the leaping, crackling flames.

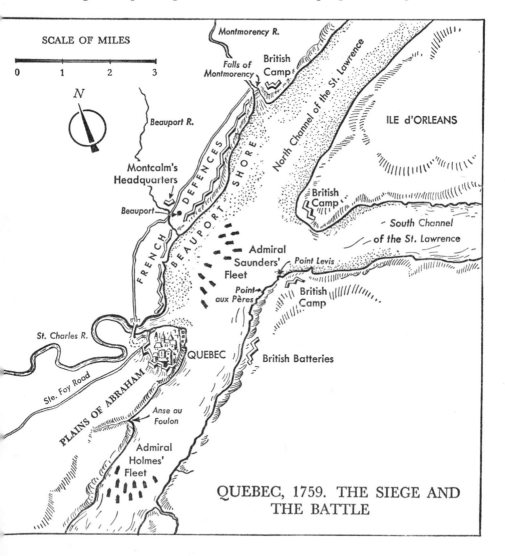

QUEBEC, 1759. THE SIEGE AND
THE BATTLE

The nearest British ships fired guns to warn the rest of the fleet, pulled up anchor or cut cables, and moved swiftly out of danger. Then, with admirable courage, sailors pushed out in small boats towards the fire-ships, threw grappling lines aboard and towed the blazing hulks toward shore.

Bombardment of Quebec

On the afternoon of June 30, a small British force occupied Point Levis on the south shore of the river. Two days later, the British seized Point aux Pères, directly opposite Quebec, and landed heavy siege guns under French fire. One week later, British troops made a landing on the north shore of the St. Lawrence just east of the Montmorency River. This move placed a substantial British force directly on the east flank of the long French line of defence.

Wolfe set up his headquarters in this habitant house at Montmorency. During the month of August, 1759, he lay dangerously ill in an upper bedroom. It was from here that he wrote his dispatches to William Pitt, the British war minister, and letters to his mother. On September 2, he wrote his last dispatch, in which he said at one point: *The obstacles we have met with in the operations are much greater than we had reason to expect or could forsee — not so much from the number of the enemy as from the natural strength of the country.*

On July 12, Wolfe gave the command that set the guns at Point aux Pères blazing against Quebec. At first, the shells fell short of the target, but as the gunners corrected their aim, the missiles struck within the Lower Town and high up on the crest of the cliffs. Shells crashed against stone walls and fell hissing through the roofs of buildings. A Frenchman, describing conditions within the town, wrote:

> The people all fled from their Homes and sought refuge upon the Ramparts, on the side next to the Country. When day appeared, and the Gate was opened, Women and Children were seen flying in crowds along the fields; and the damage done to the Town during the first night was very considerable.

This was just the first bitter taste of what British guns could do.

As more cannon were set up on Point Levis, the punishment suffered in Quebec was fairly heavy. The Lower Town and Upper Town were both raked so fiercely that 180 houses, the cathedral, a church and other buildings were destroyed.

Although the shelling frightened the citizens of Quebec, it seemed to have little other effect. Montcalm and his army stood unharmed in the long lines of defence that stretched eastward from Quebec to the Montmorency.

Wolfe knew that Quebec must be taken during the summer months; he had neither the provisions nor the equipment to fight through the bitter months of winter. It was one thing to **Battle of** batter Quebec with siege guns, but quite another to assault and **Montmorency** occupy the town. Wolfe considered several plans of attack, but attempted nothing until the end of July. The first important clash between the two opposing forces came on July 31, when a strong British force attacked a French strongpoint on the Beauport shore some distance west of the Montmorency River.

It was a humiliating defeat for Wolfe.

The boats could not get close enough to shore; soldiers waded in water to their waists; the first men ashore attacked the enemy positions without waiting for support; a withering fire of ball and

General Wolfe's batteries fire upon Quebec from positions about a mile away across the St. Lawrence River. The city was well within the range of the British guns, and when the citizens of Quebec saw the British artillery being moved into place, they begged the governor to allow them to organize an expedition to destroy the guns. A mixed group of about 1,500 Canadians and French regulars actually crossed the river, but retreated in confusion without making contact with the enemy. In the weeks that followed, the heavy siege guns caused much damage within the walls of Quebec. Note the long, massive "siege carriage" on the cannon.

shell poured from the French lines and then, to climax the situation, a violent rain-storm burst over the scene of battle. Wolfe ordered a retreat.

This engagement, known as the Battle of Montmorency, was a costly action. The British lost 210 men killed, 230 wounded, and accomplished nothing.

Defeat left Wolfe in a quandary. Quebec itself sat on a cliff. To the east, it was protected by the lengthy defence line. To the west, sharp banks ran along the river for miles. Where could he strike with any hope of success?

Wolfe's uncertainty For some time, Wolfe's senior officers had been restless and dissatisfied with his management of the campaign. They felt that

their commander was slow to make up his mind and that he had made a serious error in attacking the Beauport shore. They wished he would be more decisive and announce a clear-cut plan for the capture of Quebec. Many of the officers disliked the British destruction of French homes and farm crops throughout the countryside.

When, in the latter part of August, Wolfe asked his brigadiers for suggestions, they promptly offered a complete plan of attack. They argued that the whole British operation should be shifted west of Quebec where the river's shore had no strong defences and where the French supply lines from the west could be cut off. They reminded Wolfe that only small groups of British troops could be used against the Beauport shore, whereas the main strength of the army could be employed to strike at the north shore to the west of Quebec.

Wolfe accepted their arguments, but he seems to have been discouraged by the difficulties which lay ahead. He was conscious of his own errors in the campaign and perhaps he overestimated the defensive strength of the French. The poor condition of his health, too, undoubtedly added to his troubled state of mind.

46

THE PLAINS OF ABRAHAM

Wolfe and his brigadiers agreed that the main body of the British army would launch an offensive west of Quebec. But where?

Wolfe's decision

In early September, Wolfe and some of his senior officers made several brief trips of exploration above Quebec in the hope of discovering a place where troops and guns might be disembarked with a minimum of difficulty. A number of locations were suggested to Wolfe, but it seems that the final choice was his own. It was the *Anse au Foulon* on the north bank of the St. Lawrence, a mile and a half up river from Quebec, a place which is now known as Wolfe's Cove.

The Anse au Foulon strongly recommended itself to Wolfe. It was close to Quebec, it seemed to be weakly defended, and it offered a chance of reaching the heights above. Wolfe's chief engineer has described the spot:

> . . . it must be observed that the bank which runs along the shore is very steep and woody, and was thought so impracticable by the French themselves, that they had then only a single picket to defend it. This picket, which we supposed might be about 100 men, was encamped upon the bank near the top of a narrow path which runs up from the shore; this path was broke by the enemy themselves, and barricaded . . . but about 200 yards to the right there appeared to be a slope in the bank which was thought might answer the purpose.

It was to serve Wolfe's purpose very well indeed.

French fears

In the meantime, Montcalm was well aware of British activity west of Quebec, and it caused him some concern. For a few hours, a battalion of French troops was moved westward to a point near the Foulon, but was withdrawn on orders from Montcalm, who believed that Wolfe would strike directly at the Lower Town or at the middle section of the Beauport shore. Governor Vaudreuil seems to have worried more than Montcalm about the danger of an unexpected landing on the other side of his town, but he did not guess Wolfe's immediate intention.

312

The shore west of Quebec was partly defended. Small groups of men were scattered here and there for miles along the river, and a mobile striking force of about 1,000 men was kept ready for emergency use. The latter group was kept marching to and fro in order to keep an eye on the British ships which moved up and down the St. Lawrence. All troops and posts west of Quebec were under the command of Montcalm's aide, Bougainville.

Knowing that secrecy and surprise were essential to the success of his plan, Wolfe ordered a swift, silent, night landing at the Anse au Foulon. Troops were to be shipped a few miles above the proposed landing place. Then, under cover of darkness, the men were to drift silently back on the river's current in small boats. The boats of the main body of the British fleet were to row back and forth between the Beauport defences and the St. Charles river to divert the enemy's attention from the area west of the city. This demonstration was successful. It was carried out until four in the morning—the hour of landing at the Foulon. *Wolfe lands his forces at Anse au Foulon*

About 2.00 o'clock on the morning of September 13, 1759, the first "wave" of about 1,800 troops assembled in the ships' boats, cast off, and dropped down river. Half an hour later, sloops and other vessels followed with stores, ammunition, guns and the men of the second assault wave. In the meantime, still more men, the third wave, were being assembled on the south shore of the St. Lawrence directly across from the Foulon.

Shortly before reaching the landing spot, the first group of British boats is said to have been challenged from the shore by French sentries who called, "Qui vive?" (Who goes there?) A Scots officer responded, "La France et vive le Roi." (France. Long live the King.)

The British boats were permitted to pass without further investigation. It seems that the French had been expecting supply boats of their own to pass down river, and so mistook the British craft for their own. At any rate, the French did not require a password.

The first British boats grounded just to the east of the Foulon, and three companies of infantry made their way up the *Climbing the heights* steep embankment. It was a stiff climb of some 175 feet over ground covered with loose shale. Pulling themselves up with the aid of trees and shrubs, the men made their way upwards. As they approached the top, they encountered Frenchmen guarding the Foulon pathway.

Astonished by the sudden appearance of the enemy from out of the night, the French picket on the pathway began firing. But as more British troops scrambled upward, the small group of defenders was brushed aside, some being killed and others

Wolfe's troops prepare for their journey down river in small boats toward the *Anse au Foulon.* At a lantern signal from Wolfe's ship, the *Sutherland*, the craft moved out into the current, thus beginning the bold venture that was to end on the Plains of Abraham. The two large British men-of-war at the right are "seventy-fours", meaning they each carried seventy-four guns. Ship design had changed only in a minor way since the time of the vessel of 1710 shown on page 238. The spritsail topmast was no longer in use, and ships were classified not by rates but in accordance with the number of guns carried.

wounded. A few escaped, shooting as they went. As the alarm spread, a French battery to the west of the Foulon sent shells roaring in the direction of the British boats. Some damage was done.

After this short flurry of action, the landings progressed smoothly with little interruption. Wolfe himself was astonished by the rapidity with which his men made their way to the cliff top, where they formed ranks as if on parade.

In the meantime, Montcalm was at his headquarters on the Beauport shore. It was several hours before he and Vaudreuil were notified of Wolfe's position outside the city. This sudden turn of events must have been a tremendous shock to both men, who seem to have considered it impossible to make a large-scale landing in the Foulon area. They had been completely deceived by the boats from Admiral Saunders' ships rowing back and forth off the Beauport shore. Montcalm did the only thing possible—

abandoned his well-defended position on the Beauport shore and marched to meet the British beyond Quebec. One vital point worried Montcalm. How far west of the city were Bougainville and his men? Did Bougainville know of the British landings?

During the siege of Quebec British naval bombardment caused tremendous damage to the Lower Town.   Here is the church of *Notre Dame des Victoires* which we saw previously on page 231. This illustration is based upon a series of twelve outstanding drawings, made in 1759 by Richard Short, who was purser of H. M. S. *Prince Orange*, a naval vessel serving at the siege.   His drawings constitute the most accurate record we have of many buildings in the Quebec of that time.

On the Plains of Abraham

Wolfe, guessing that the French would soon attack, looked about for a suitable spot to face the enemy. He moved his men a short distance to the east of the Foulon path and lined up his battalions to face the walls of Quebec. The place he selected was a flat, open area generally known as the *Plains* or *Heights of Abraham,* named after an early river pilot, Abraham Martin, who had owned land in that vicinity. While the troops were being positioned, British sailors were hauling two light guns up the rugged path from the river.

By 9.30 in the morning, Montcalm's units were in place opposite the British. Cannon roared occasionally while roving French militia and Indians kept up a damaging fire of musket balls. Both sides lost men in these skirmishes.

The exact sizes of the two opposing armies is not too clear; various totals appear in historical records. However, it seems that the forces were roughly equal, there being about 4,500 men on each side. It was their quality that differed. Wolfe commanded steady, well-trained regulars. Perhaps one-third of Montcalm's men were ill-disciplined militiamen and untrained Indian allies.

At 10.00 a.m., Montcalm still did not know the whereabouts **Battle of the Plains of Abraham** of Bougainville, but he gave the order to advance. The regimental flags were unfurled, the drums rolled out the charge, and the French sent up a fierce cheer. They moved forward at a rapid trot. The straight and even ranks soon showed a ragged appearance, due to the militiamen who had been included among the regulars. These badly-trained and poorly-disciplined men fired when they liked and sometimes lay down on the ground to reload their muskets.

The two British guns hurled grapeshot at the advancing line, but Wolfe's men, perfectly disciplined, stood as motionless as statues. When the French were within forty yards, the British platoons, firing in succession, tore great gaps in the ranks of their attackers. Then, again at a range of thirty or perhaps twenty yards, they let loose one general volley that blasted apart the oncoming French. Shuddering down its entire length, the French battle line sagged and broke. One of Wolfe's officers, John Knox, described the scene:

> Hereupon they gave way, and fled in precipitation, so that by the time the cloud of smoke had vanished our men were again loaded, and, profiting by the advantage we had over them, pursued them almost to the gates of the town and the bridge over the little river (the St. Charles), redoubling our fire with great eagerness, making many officers and men prisoners.

Wolfe was in the thick of action, recklessly exposing himself **Death of Wolfe and Montcalm** to enemy fire. During the violent climax of the battle, he was leading a charge of the Louisbourg Grenadiers when he was fatally wounded, perhaps by a sniper's bullet. As he lay dying on the field of battle, he heard someone say:

"They run. See how they run."

"Who runs?" asked the dying man.

"The enemy, Sir."

Wolfe roused himself and said, "Go one of you, my lads, to Colonel Burton. Tell him to march Webb's regiment with all speed down to Charles's river to cut off the retreat of the fugitives from the bridge."

Turning on his side, he added, "Now, God be praised, I will die in peace."

Minutes after the fall of Wolfe, Montcalm, too, was hit—probably by grapeshot from one of the British guns. Suffering intensely from a wound in the stomach, he had to be held in his saddle by three soldiers as his horse carried him back into the city. He died at four o'clock the next morning, and was buried in a shell-hole in the floor of a chapel.

The encounter that ended French dominion in North America had lasted fifteen minutes.

47

THE END OF NEW FRANCE

The short meeting of British and French on top of the rock of Quebec was not quite the finish of French resistance. It was not even the end of the battle.

As the British pursued the beaten foe back towards the city, on the northeastern edge of the battlefield, some hundreds of Canadian militiamen stopped the onward rush of a Highland regiment and killed many of its members. It was only when American rangers came up in support of the Highlanders that the Canadians were driven back past Quebec and over the St. Charles River. However, the Canadians had given the French regulars time to escape back to the Beauport camp. Bougainville finally arrived after the battle was over. When menaced by two British battalions, he withdrew to the west. By the late afternoon, all fighting had ceased. But the French army had only been defeated. It had not been destroyed.

In the Beauport camp, Vaudreuil called a council of war, **Retreat of** attended by Bigot and the few surviving senior officers. The **French army** council decided to retreat up river—where supplies were anyway —and at 9.00 o'clock that night the army marched off up the east bank of the St. Charles river, leaving artillery and ammunition behind them for want of transport facilities. On the 17th of September, Vaudreuil met the Chevalier de Lévis, a senior French officer, and gave him command of the remains of Montcalm's forces. Food shortages prevented Lévis setting out for Quebec until the next morning, the 18th, but by then, it was too late to save the city. Quebec itself was close to starvation, and the British ships of the line were preparing to pound it into surrender.

The formal surrender of Quebec came on the morning of **Quebec** September 18, 1759, when the commander of the Quebec garrison, **September,** the Chevalier de Ramezay, signed terms of capitulation in the **1759**

British camp. The British marched in that evening and hoisted three Union Jacks in token of possession.

The town of Quebec had fallen, but a substantial army had still to be met and beaten. Lévis and Vaudreuil worked hard in Montreal, drilling and training their forces back into fighting order. In April of 1760, the French were still powerful enough to launch a dangerous counter-attack. They whipped the British, decimated by scurvy during the winter months, in the Battle of Ste. Foye just outside Quebec, and then proceeded to besiege the town itself. By the middle of May, however, this French effort was quickly broken up by the arrival of ships and men from Britain.

This was really the end of New France.

Montreal surrenders, September, 1760

In the meantime, General Amherst's army was moving slowly in the direction of Montreal. On September 9th, almost a year after the famous battle on the Plains, Vaudreuil and Lévis watched the British march into Montreal. What was left of the French army laid down its arms. But the French burnt their battle flags to save their honour.

New France had fought with courage and great gallantry, but she was now a British possession.

Treaty of Paris, 1763

The official close of the Seven Years' War came in February, 1763, with the signing of the *Treaty of Paris.*

The most important provisions of the Treaty are as follows:

All French possessions in North America, except Louisiana west of the Mississipi, became British. Britain also acquired the French West Indian islands of Dominica, Tobago and Grenada. All France managed to retain were two tiny islands off the south coast of Newfoundland—St. Pierre and Miquelon—which were to serve as "a shelter for French fishermen." (To this day they are French possessions.)

The former French territory of Louisiana, which lay west of the Mississippi, was granted to Spain.

Britain agreed to "grant the liberty of the Catholic religion to the inhabitants of Canada."

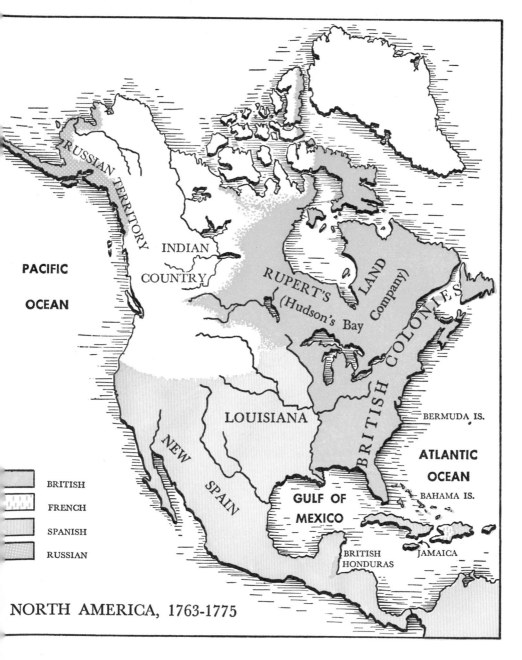

PACIFIC

OCEAN

RUSSIAN TERRITORY

INDIAN

COUNTRY

RUPERT'S LAND
(Hudson's Bay Company)

BRITISH COLONIES

LOUISIANA

BERMUDA IS.

ATLANTIC
OCEAN

NEW
SPAIN

GULF OF
MEXICO

BAHAMA IS.

BRITISH
HONDURAS

JAMAICA

BRITISH

FRENCH

SPANISH

RUSSIAN

NORTH AMERICA, 1763-1775

Britain agreed that for a period of eighteen months after the signing of the Treaty any French subjects wishing to leave Canada had the right to do so, taking away "their effects as well as their persons."

Britain agreed that "the subjects of France shall have the liberty of fishing and drying on a part of the coasts of the Island of Newfoundland." It was also agreed that the French had fishing rights in the Gulf of St. Lawrence and off the coasts of Nova Scotia.

Thus, Britain had won a tremendous sweep of empire, stretching from Hudson Bay all the way south to the Gulf of Mexico and from the Atlantic to the Mississippi. It was a gigantic area, occupied by thousands of Indians and French and British colonists, all of them needing wise and helpful government.

48

RESULTS OF THE WAR

After 1763, Great Britain was faced with the difficulties of ruling vast new North American territories, as well as the Thirteen Colonies along the Atlantic coast and her island possessions in the West Indies. In previous years, Great Britain had exercised a moderate control over her colonies, and had allowed them to develop customs and practices that the colonists themselves desired. However, with new lands to look after, largely Indian territory, Britain felt that the time had come when she must govern North America with greater care and attention. There would be no more Indian warfare. The fur trade and westward expansion would have to be closely controlled and disciplined.

The new land of Canada offered three big problems—fur-trading, the Indians and a French-speaking population. The first two were really a joint problem. The fur trade established by France was a most valuable business, but the western Indians, remaining loyal to France, did not trust the British conquerors who treated them in a very cold fashion. In addition, the Indians feared the flow of settlers pouring over the Appalachians and flooding Indian lands. It was, therefore, necessary to win the confidence of the tribes before the trade could continue to return its usual profits. A number of eager British traders arrived in Montreal with the purpose of making fortunes in furs. They hoped that the old French trading empire could be held together, that the former canoe routes could be used, and that the Indians could be won over as customers. With the help of French-speaking traders, guides and voyageurs, these adventurers began moving westward with cargoes of trade goods. But they were not helped by British agents and commandants at the western fur posts who had official orders to stop traders from giving presents to the Indians as the French had done. The traders were also forbidden to supply the Indians with gunpowder, something the Indians had to have in order to shoot game.

Problems of fur trade

Alexander Henry

The first to enter the western regions was Alexander Henry, a native of New Jersey, who, with a Frenchman as his partner, made contact with Indians in the areas around Lakes Superior and Michigan. These tribesmen traded with him, but they made it clear they had no love for the British. One Chippewa chieftain said:

Englishman, although you have conquered the French, you have not yet conquered us! We are not your slaves. These lakes, these woods, and mountains, were left to us by our ancestors. They are an inheritance and we will part with them to none.

A type of birch cupboard made in the eighteenth century by the craftsmen of New France. Constructed entirely of native wood, it is designed in the fashion of French furniture belonging to the period of King Louis XIII. Such cupboards were probably used by the habitants. The wealthy preferred more elaborate designs in their household furnishings, in the then popular Louis XV style shown on page 302.

The chief explained that the English had been able to win the war only because the French king, who was old and worn out with fighting, had fallen asleep. But his sleep would soon end. When he awakened, "What must become of you? He will destroy you utterly." The Chippewas had sent many of their braves to fight for the French. Many had been killed and their deaths, remaining unpaid in blood, was a duty of revenge left to those who still lived. The debt could be settled with the blood of the enemy—the British settlers crowding into the western lands. French traders worked hard to encourage the Indians in their belief that the "Father over the water would free his children again." Thus, in 1763, General Amherst had a war to deal with.

So strong were anti-British feelings, that Pontiac, a powerful Ottawa chieftain, was able to rally the western tribes against the British. A magnificent speaker, Pontiac inflamed the warriors with such statements as: **Pontiac fights the British**

And as for these British—these dogs dressed in red, who have come to rob you of your hunting grounds and drive away the game—you must lift the hatchet against them.

By 1763, well-organized war parties were attacking scattered British forts. These savage assaults were so successful that all British forts west of Niagara, with the single exception of Detroit, fell into Indian hands. Detroit, however, had to endure a six-month siege. At least 500 British soldiers were killed in this Indian uprising. As many as 2,000 colonists may have been slaughtered.

Alexander Henry was at Michilimackinac when it was attacked. The Indians there, pretending to be intent upon a game of lacrosse, rushed through the gate of the fort and fell upon the British. Henry's life was saved only because the attackers could not find him. He had hidden himself in a small room below a pile of "vessels of birch-bark used in the making of maple sugar."

Within a few months, Pontiac's campaign was over. It was a costly lesson for the British, so costly, that they had to find a better way of dealing with the Indians.

The first step taken by the British government to develop a new colonial policy came with the *Proclamation of 1763*. By this Proclamation, the western boundary of Quebec was set at the Ottawa River and a similar boundary for the thirteen colonies was created along the line of the Appalachian Mountains. British territory lying west of the two new boundaries was to be reserved only for the Indians and the fur trade. Such land was not to be open to all traders, but only to those granted trading licences by **Proclamation of 1763** one or other of the colonies. Furthermore, for at least some time to come, colonists were *not* to move into this territory to establish farms or settlements. Colonists could find new land and new homes in either Quebec or Nova Scotia.

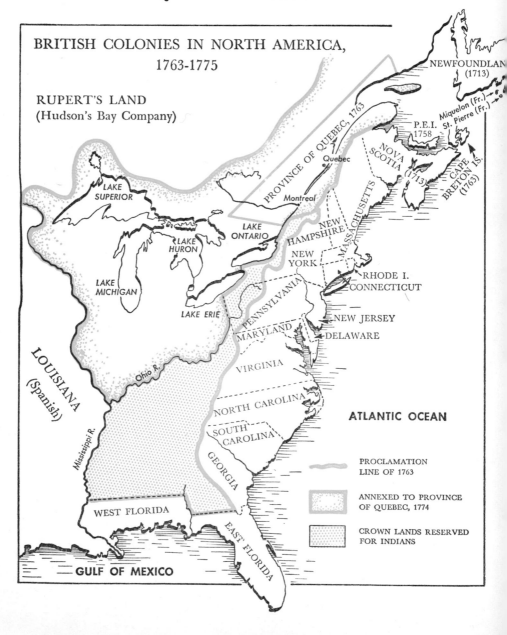

BRITISH COLONIES IN NORTH AMERICA,
1763-1775

RUPERT'S LAND
(Hudson's Bay Company)

NEWFOUNDLAN
(1713)

Miquelon (Fr.)
St. Pierre (Fr.)

P.E.I.
1758

PROVINCE OF QUEBEC, 1763

Quebec

NOVA
SCOTIA
(1713)

CAPE
BRETON IS.
(1763)

LAKE
SUPERIOR

Montreal

LAKE
ONTARIO

NEW
HAMPSHIRE

MASSACHUSETTS

LAKE
HURON

NEW
YORK

RHODE I.
CONNECTICUT

LAKE
MICHIGAN

PENNSYLVANIA

LAKE ERIE

NEW JERSEY

MARYLAND

DELAWARE

LOUISIANA
(Spanish)

Ohio R.

VIRGINIA

ATLANTIC OCEAN

NORTH CAROLINA

Mississippi R.

SOUTH
CAROLINA

GEORGIA

PROCLAMATION
LINE OF 1763

ANNEXED TO PROVINCE
OF QUEBEC, 1774

CROWN LANDS RESERVED
FOR INDIANS

WEST FLORIDA

EAST FLORIDA

GULF OF MEXICO

Although these arrangements may have been satisfactory to the Indians, they caused the greatest anger among the fur traders, and infuriated the colonists in Pennsylvania and Virginia who wished to settle the interior.

The Proclamation had a few vague things to say about government in Quebec, rather indefinite announcements regarding an elected assembly to be created "as soon as circumstances would admit." This proposal was acceptable to neither English nor French. The British merchants in Quebec wanted an elected assembly or government immediately, while the French were opposed to the idea of an assembly, because they feared the British would control it.

Habitant costume of the late eighteenth century was extremely colourful. The woman is wearing a straw hat with a cloth frill attached. Her summer dress and scarf are vivid with gaily coloured stripes and patterns. The man's warm winter costume includes leather leggings and a bright woollen sash. Habitants often wore shoes with removable soles fitted with iron spikes for moving over ice. For walking on slippery streets, cloth shoes and even stockings worn over ordinary shoes were employed.

Governor James Murray

Governor James Murray, one of Wolfe's brigadiers and the first British governor of Quebec, wisely believed that Great Britain had to treat the Quebecois with kindness and sympathy, allowing these people to retain their old customs, their own law and the Roman Catholic religion, and giving them some voice in their own government. Indeed, he believed such freedoms were absolutely necessary if Britain were to retain their loyalty.

Governor Murray saw to it that his officers and men were polite and courteous to the French. Troops billeted with French families were expressly ordered to display good manners and kindness. They were encouraged to share their meagre rations with their hosts. Above all, Murray defied and held at bay the demands of the merchant class to set up an assembly in which they, the merchants, could establish their own ideas of law and order. Murray knew they would interfere with the liberties of the French, and he steadily refused all requests for government by assembly. It is only now that Canadians are beginning to appreciate the contribution of this remarkable man. A few years ago a French-Canadian historian, Professor Arthur Maheux, wrote:

> Some day, when foolish animosities shall have ceased, Canadians of both tongues will have the features of James Murray cast in bronze, and will set up this figure as a symbol of the good relations which should exist amongst Canadians of every stock.

Quebec Act, 1774

Sir Guy Carleton, also one of Wolfe's senior officers, became the next governor of Quebec in 1766. Carleton, too, felt that various liberties should be offered to the Quebecois. He, too, fought off the merchants' demands for an assembly or provincial parliament. He, too, upheld the French-Canadian right to live in accordance with old customs and to worship in the manner of the Roman Catholic faith. It was largely through his and Murray's efforts that the Proclamation of 1763 was withdrawn and replaced by the *Quebec Act of 1774*. This famous document made a sincere effort to meet the social, political and economic difficulties which existed in Canada after 1760. The aim of the Quebec Act was to retain the loyalty of the Quebecois. Its most important rulings were as follows:

Religion: The right of French-speaking citizens to enjoy the "free exercise" of the Roman Catholic religion was officially confirmed. This was a very wise decision; to the habitant, his religion was a great concern in his daily life. Roman Catholic priests and officials were to receive their accustomed "Dues and Rights." The old French land tax or "tithe" for the support of the Church was reinstated.

Laws: The Province of Quebec was to have two sets of laws —British law in criminal cases and French law in civil matters, i.e., disputes as to property ownership or the rights and duties of a citizen. There was to be no interference with the old seigneurial system of land-holding. The seigneur would continue to enjoy his dues and rights.

Boundaries: The boundaries of Quebec were extended northeast to Labrador and westward to include the Great Lakes and a region bounded on the west by the Mississippi and on the south by the Ohio. This was a concession to the fury of the many Montreal traders who had been kept out of rich fur country by the Proclamation of 1763.

Government: There was to be no assembly. The Province was to be governed by a Council for the Affairs of the Province of Quebec appointed by the British government. The Council, under the direction of the Governor, would be composed of *both* French and British members. A special oath for Roman Catholics enabled the French-Canadians to become partners in government.

The Quebec Act undoubtedly pleased most of the French, particularly the seigneurs and the clergy who regained their old privileges. The habitants were less pleased. They would have been happy to break away from the seigneurial system, and they disliked the tithe which went to the support of their Church. However, there is every reason to believe that the provisions of this Act served to win and hold the loyalty of the Quebeçois. This loyalty was to be particularly vital during the turbulent period after 1774 in North America. The Montreal fur merchants were reasonably well satisfied with the Quebec Act for the fur trade once more was opened to them.

It was the people of the Thirteen Colonies who were greatly displeased by the contents of the Quebec Act.

Displeasure in the Thirteen Colonies

The boundaries of Quebec had been extended westward and southward, but little change was made in the boundaries of the Atlantic colonies, which were allowed only as far west as the Ohio. This meant, of course, that such colonies as Pennsylvania and Virginia had no chance to expand into the interior of the continent. They had fought for western expansion in the Seven Years' War. Now, the privileges of trade were being given to the ex-enemy. Another reason for dissatisfaction was the fact that the French-speaking citizens had been given special privileges. For example, not even in Britain at this time were Roman Catholic subjects allowed to hold public office. The Protestants of New England were particularly disturbed that the Roman Catholic Church should receive such consideration from the British government.

Growth in Nova Scotia

In the meantime, Nova Scotia was undergoing changes. This region, which had lost practically all its population through the expulsion of the Acadians, was desperately in need of settlers to clear the forests and operate the fisheries. Before the beginning of the Seven Years' War, there was some immigration from Great

In the eighteenth and nineteenth centuries, silversmiths were active in Quebec City and Montreal. Many of their products, such as chalices, baptismal basins and other religious silverwork, went to the churches of Quebec. Religious silver work was chiefly manufactured at Quebec, whilst the Montreal craftsmen concentrated on table silver and Indian trade goods. The silver bowl shown here was made by Dèlezenne, who worked from about 1740 to 1790, and was famed for the beauty and simplicity of his productions.

Until the coming of paved highways, travel in Canada was more comfortable in the winter months, since the rough, rutted roads became relatively smooth when frozen hard and covered with snow. In Quebec people used a variety of sleighs for winter journeys. The eighteenth-century sleigh shown here had a low-slung body with solid sides ending in iron-shod runners. Such vehicles were known as *carioles*. During the nineteenth century, these sleighs changed in design, acquiring lighter bodies raised on graceful runners.

Britain and Europe (notably the Germans who settled in Lunenburg and became fishermen and shipbuilders), but the outbreak of war cut off the flow of incomers. The population of Nova Scotia dwindled again in an alarming manner.

Before the close of the war, Governor Lawrence had offered free land to people who would settle in Nova Scotia. This offer was especially interesting to the New Englanders who had already settled New Hampshire, and other nearby areas. Nova Scotia therefore, was directly in line with this northward march of settlement. In consequence of Lawrence's offer, substantial numbers of New Englanders took over old Acadian farms along the Bay of Fundy, particularly in the Annapolis valley, while others created new fishing villages in the southern part of the province.

Before the end of the war, many of these new settlers requested the establishment of an elected assembly in which, as Englishmen, they would have a distinct say in their own affairs. Governor Lawrence did not receive this suggestion with any degree of enthusiasm. He believed an assembly would become a personal annoyance, perhaps bothersome, perhaps a handicap in time of war. Nevertheless, the British government instructed Lawrence to summon an assembly similar to those found in the other British colonies. Thus it was that in 1758, before the fall of Quebec, the first Canadian elected assembly held its first sessions in Halifax. Meeting year after year, the representatives of the people discussed common affairs and issued laws and regulations best suited to local conditions.

First Canadian elected assembly, 1758

The immigration programme continued to be successful. Between 1760 and 1775, the population of Nova Scotia jumped from 2,000 to 18,000 persons. Although the New Englanders made up the majority, there were other groups that came from England, Scotland, Ireland, France, Germany and Switzerland. In addition, as many as 2,000 Acadians returned to the province. More and more settlers moved into the lands bordering the Bay of Fundy, the Chignecto isthmus, the eastern areas of Nova Scotia and up into the rocky uplands of Cape Breton. So many Highland Scots entered Cape Breton that it became another Scotland, where only the Gaelic tongue was spoken.

By 1774, Nova Scotia held twice as many people as there had been at any time since the arrival of the French in 1604.

SUMMARY—SECTION VII

In 1756, fighting broke out in Europe between France, Great Britain and their respective allies. This conflict is known to history as The Seven Years' War, the war for empire. It brought British regular troops and Royal Navy warships to North America. It was these highly-trained and magnificently-disciplined forces, which, aided by British colonial forces, shattered the French Empire in North America within the space of four years. New France had successfully defended herself against British attack since 1689, but by 1756 there were too many miles of French territory to defend and too few Frenchmen to guard them.

At first, the generalship of Montcalm won a number of victories. In 1756, he took Fort Oswego. In 1757, he captured Fort William Henry and defeated an attacking British army at Fort Carillon (Ticonderoga). But by 1758, the British had arrived in North America in great numbers. Louisbourg, the guardian of the St. Lawrence, was besieged and taken. Fort Duquesne was captured. The British closed in on New France up the St. Lawrence, up the Lake Champlain route and up through the Niagara peninsula.

In 1759, the French suffered their main defeat at Quebec. After several weeks of siege, the city fell when Wolfe, in a surprise move, led his men onto the Plains of Abraham and in a European-style battle, defeated Montcalm's forces. The British occupied Quebec.

New France fought on for a few more months, even winning a battle outside Quebec, but all the odds were against her. In 1760, Montreal surrendered to vastly superior forces. New France from Labrador to the Floridas became a British possession. Britain owned North America from Hudson Bay to the Gulf of Mexico and from the Mississippi to the Atlantic.

In 1763, the western tribes under the leadership of Pontiac revolted against the British claim to settle their lands. After the revolt was crushed, Great Britain announced the Proclamation of 1763 which made the lands west of the Ottawa River and the Appalachian Mountains Indian land. This blocked off all westward colonial expansion.

After 1760, the inhabitants of New France were wisely governed by the British. The Roman Catholic Church, the seigneurial system and old habits and customs were not interfered with. No British form of government was imposed upon them. This policy was officially confirmed by the Quebec Act of 1774, which also created a Council of British and French members, acting with the Governor to rule Quebec.

In Nova Scotia, New Englanders, English, Scots, Irish and several European groups came to settle the colony. In addition, a few Acadian exiles returned to their former homes. By 1758, Nova Scotia had its own assembly, a group of men representing their fellow colonists. The assembly, working with the governor, discussed the affairs of the colony and issued the necessary laws and regulations.

EIGHT / *The American Revolution*

COLONIAL LIFE

THE SUGAR ACT OF 1764

THE STAMP ACT OF 1765

THE TOWNSHEND ACTS OF 1767

THE "BOSTON MASSACRE," 1770

THE "BOSTON TEA PARTY," 1773

THE "INTOLERABLE ACTS" OF 1774

THE CONTINENTAL CONGRESS

THE CLASH AT LEXINGTON, 1775

THE BATTLE OF BUNKER HILL, 1775

THE ATTACK ON QUEBEC, 1775

THE DECLARATION OF INDEPENDENCE, 1776

THE SURRENDER AT SARATOGA, 1777

FRANCE ENTERS THE WAR, 1778

CAMPAIGNS IN THE SOUTH

JOHN PAUL JONES

THE SURRENDER AT YORKTON, 1781

THE TREATY OF PARIS, 1783

THE CONSTITUTION OF THE UNITED STATES, 1788

GEORGE WASHINGTON BECOMES PRESIDENT, 1789

THE NEW CAPITAL OF THE UNITED STATES

49

LIFE IN THE THIRTEEN COLONIES

The Thirteen Colonies were largely composed of English people, but there were also important groups of Scots, Irish, Dutch, French, Germans and other Europeans. Between 1700 and 1763, the population increased tenfold—from 250,000 to 2,500,000. Two-thirds of these people were descendants of early settlers, while the remaining one-third were new arrivals.

Throughout the colonies agriculture was the most important **Agriculture** industry, but most colonists misused fertile land, practising none of the conservation measure that were used in later times.   Peter Kahn, the Swedish scientist who visited North America, wrote:

They had nothing to do but cut down the wood, put it in heaps and to clear the dead leaves away. They could then immediately proceed to ploughing, which in loose ground is very easy; and having sown their grain, they get a most plentiful harvest. This easy method of getting a crop spoiled the English and other European settlers, and induced them to adopt the same method of agriculture as the Indians; that is, to sow uncultivated grounds, as long as they will produce a crop without manuring.

Although colonial farming was unscientific, it nevertheless provided large stocks of food in the form of grains, vegetables, fruits and meats.   In the harsh climate of New England, where soil was neither abundant nor rich, the people could grow barely enough to feed themselves.   The New Englanders were forced to take to the sea to find an export.   They found it mainly in the codfish, which they salted or dried, and sold in the West Indies along with cargoes of New England lumber.   In the middle colonies, the "bread colonies" blessed with rich soil and navigable rivers, farming produced great quantities of wheat, flour and live-stock, all of which was exported to the West Indies. To the south, in Maryland and Virginia, tobacco was the vital product shipped to Britain and the West Indies, while in the Carolinas rice and indigo (a vegetable dye) were cultivated and traded abroad.

Industry   Industry was a much slower growth in the colonies, but in the towns were large numbers of craftsmen who manufactured cloth, shoes, wigs, hats, glass, leather goods, tools and a host of household articles. In time, some of these small industries were to develop into larger and more important businesses. Many of these manufactures were well designed, well made and extremely attractive in appearance.

Trade   Trading was the vital element in the life of the Thirteen Colonies.

Furs continued to find their way to Europe, but these were becoming a less important export in the total volume of trade. Timber for the manufacture of ships and masts was in constant demand by the British Navy, as were such other forests products as pitch, turpentine and resin. Crude iron, mined and smelted in the colonies, found ready acceptance in Britain. The West Indies provided an excellent market not only for food but for lumber used in the making of barrels, ships and buildings. Large stocks of barrels were required in the West Indies for the shipment of molasses, rum, sugar and tobacco.

Great Britain imported from her colonies the raw materials that she could not produce at home. This policy greatly assisted the southern colonies, but did little to help those lying to the north along the Atlantic coast. As a result, the New England colonies and the "bread colonies" were forced to find markets in the West Indies and in southern Europe. In so doing, they created several "triangular" trading routes which proved valuable and profitable. By one of these routes, food from the northern colonies was taken to France or the Mediterranean where it was exchanged for fruit and wines. These goods were then taken to Britain and exchanged for such manufactured items as fine textiles, furniture, hardware, paper and china, which were, in turn, carried back to the colonies.

During the seventeenth and eighteenth centuries, it was fashionable for men and women to wear wigs or "perukes" as they were often called. European soldiers of the period, too, wore powdered white wigs, even though these affairs were uncomfortable, particularly in warm weather. Wigs were so much in demand at this time that the craft of wig-making flourished in all the more important centres in colonial America. Here is a craftsman working on a short wig similar to those displayed in his window. This particular style was very fashionable in the latter half of the eighteenth century. The wigmaker was often a barber, and sometimes the local surgeon as well.

By another triangular route, ships with cargoes of timber and food sailed to the West Indies from the New England colonies where they were traded for sugar, molasses, tobacco and rum.   These latter were then taken to Great Britain and traded for manufactured goods.   By such methods, the colonies were able to sell their own surplus products and satisfy their need for British manufactures.

Much of the work in the colonies was done by indentured servants and negroes.

Indentured servants   The indentured servant was a European immigrant who agreed to work for a number of years in exchange for food, clothing and shelter in addition to the cost of his or her transportation across the Atlantic.   At the end of the period of indenture, these servants were free to go anywhere in the colonies and work for themselves.   In some colonies, an indentured servant received as much as fifty acres of land on achieving his freedom.   Thus, a man who started life in North America practically as a slave could become a landowner himself, and perhaps the employer of indentured servants.

Negro slaves   The negro occupied a much different and, often, a much worse position.   He was a slave, a worker owned and controlled by his master.   He could not look forward to a day of eventual freedom.   Negro slavery existed in the colonies as early as 1619, but it did not expand to any degree until the end of the seventeenth century.   After large plantations were created in the southern colonies, there was, of course, a great demand for negro workers.   Slaves were found in all the colonies, but by far the greatest number were in the south. In 1756, in Virginia, there were 173,000 white people and 120,000 negro slaves.   In South Carolina, the white citizens were outnumbered by negroes two to one.   At that time there were probably 400,000 negro slaves in all the colonies, and they composed about two-fifths of the total colonial population.

Slaves on the southern plantations were seldom badly treated. It was in their master's interest to keep them healthy and content to work in the tobacco fields.   However, they had no protection from the occasional evil owner.

One of the remarkable features of colonial life was the con- **Homes** struction of beautiful homes and handsome public buildings. Generally speaking, most buildings were made of materials readily available in the various communities. In New England and Virginia, trim houses were made of clapboard, and in such middle colonies as Pennsylvania wide use was made of stone and brick. During the eighteenth century, wealthy colonists favoured a style of English architecture known as *Georgian*. Elaborate doorways, flanked by tall, white pillars, were important features of this style. There were few architects in North America, but the colonial builders possessed enough skill to enable them to adapt European ideas to colonial conditions. In so doing, they created masterpieces of construction, which today are greatly admired.

The homes of the wealthy were luxuriously furnished, containing the finest furniture, drapes, rugs, pictures, chinaware and silver. Such famous furniture styles as Sheraton and Chippendale were imported from England. Mr. Josiah Wedgwood, the noted producer of English chinaware, said,

To the Continent we send an amazing quantity of white stoneware and some of the finer kinds; but for America we cannot make anything too rich or costly.

Few of the colonists lacked food. Wealthy families, of course, **Food** supplemented local products with expensive wines and other table products imported from Europe. The average colonist, however, was a farmer or a fisherman (sometimes both), who had to live on humbler fare. Corn bread, meat, fish and game formed the commonest items of diet in his home. His wife and daughters were skilled in the preservation of food; during the winter there was normally a supply of salted meat and preserves and vegetables. Due to hard work and an outdoor life, the colonist was a hearty eater and often a hearty drinker. The consumption of alcoholic beverages was surprisingly high. He was fond of such local drinks as hard cider, brandy and beer. Much of the rum he drank was manufactured in New England or imported from the West Indies.

When not working, the colonists amused themselves with a **Entertainment**

This beautiful eighteenth-century American house is built in a style of architecture known as "Georgian", named after the British kings of that period. The elegance of this home indicates how far the Atlantic colonies had progressed in the short space of one century. The house demonstrates a move away from a rough, pioneering way of life to that of a genteel, cultured society. Built in Virginia, about 1753, it is still in existence. It has four great chimneys, and many fireplaces heat all the main parts of the structure. One remarkable feature of its interior is the superb and elaborate panelling that decorates the walls of the rooms.

number of sports, games and entertainments. As might be expected, hunting and fishing were enjoyed in most places. In the south, where life was gayest, horse-racing, cock-fighting and card-playing were popular. Another activity was dancing, an amusement that was a part of most social events. On such occasions, the people danced away the night, swinging happily through horn-pipes, jigs, country dances or stately minuets to the accompaniment of bagpipes or violins.

As in Great Britain and other parts of Europe, the church **Education** played an important part in the early encouragement of colonial education. In the middle and southern states in particular, the religious denominations established church and parochial schools for their own children and also for orphans and poor children. However, in New England, schools were established in a different manner. As early as 1647, a Massachusetts law was passed requiring small villages to set up common schools (elementary) and larger centres to set up both common and grammar schools (secondary). This was the first time in history that English-speaking people required their own communities to create and support schools. This form of educational provision spread to the other New England colonies and gradually became part of life in those areas. In the middle colonies, schooling was not as universal as in New England. In the south, learning was generally limited to the children of wealthy landowners and professional men.

However, children in the Thirteen Colonies did not receive a satisfactory education. Sometimes they received none at all. While the children of well-to-do families attended private schools or academies, boys and girls from humble families were much less fortunate. Those who attended school had instruction for two or three months each year for a few years only in reading, writing, spelling and arithmetic. Thousands who did not attend school grew up lacking adequate training. Two-thirds of the women whose names appear on Massachusetts legal documents of the early 1700's could not write their own signatures.

Poor as school conditions were in the colonies, they were no worse, and perhaps better, than those existing in the Great Britain and Europe of that time.

50

THE ROAD TO REVOLUTION

Although the colonists enjoyed a prosperity and freedom that was unusual for their time, they became increasingly restless under British rule.   There were many reasons for this development. By the middle of the eighteenth century, many North Americans were five or six generations removed from their immigrant ancestors. They no longer thought along British lines. They were accustomed to making their own decisions and ordering their own lives.   They had become prosperous, independent farmers and merchants. They

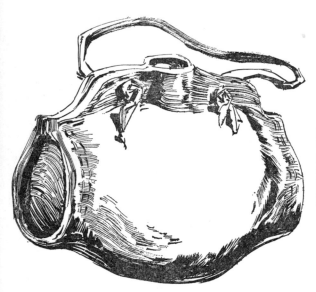

An eighteenth-century leather bottle or flask used for carrying liquids to work. When carried on journeys, it was hung from the saddle. Made of molded leather, the bottle was sturdy, watertight and probably kept liquids at their original temperature for a longer period of time than a metal flask.   Leather bottles were made in many different shapes and sizes.

had learned to govern themselves with little help or interference from Britain.   Until 1756, they had even fought wars, using only their own armed strength.   In addition, frontier life fostered a spirit of sturdy independence, and the colonists acted and thought differently from British politicians and officials.

Perhaps the factor which caused the greatest annoyance to the Thirteen Colonies was Britain's control of trade.

By means of various Acts of Trade and Navigation from 1651 on, such colonial products as sugar, tobacco, cotton and indigo had to be transported and traded in Britain, which lacked these commodities. Goods obtained from European countries sold at high prices in the colonies, because they had first to be taken to Britain where duty had to be paid on them. In this way, the price of non-British goods was raised, thus making the sale of British manufactures much easier.

Certain restrictions, too, were placed on manufacturing in the colonies, for it was feared that it might interfere with British industry. For example, the manufacture in North America of iron and steel or woollen goods was forbidden. Referring to this condition, Benjamin Franklin, the famous American writer, inventor and politician, wrote:

A colonist cannot make a button, a horseshoe, nor a hobnail but some sooty ironmonger or respectable button-maker of Britain shall bawl and squall that his honor's worship is . . . maltreated, injured, cheated and robbed by the rascally Americans.

Historians have long argued the benefit or harm that resulted **Unrest in the** from all these trade laws. Some declare that colonial prosperity **Thirteen Colonies** was caused by the trade laws—particularly the law that forbade a British merchant buying tobacco that was not grown in a British colony—while others say that prosperity could have been much greater if the British government had allowed greater freedom in trade, as in the case of colonial merchants forbidden to ship grain to Britain. Whatever the merits of each case, the fact remains that many colonists began to feel that they were being treated unfairly and that they were considered as second-class subjects.

After the Seven Years' War, Great Britain decided to station **Britain plans for** an army of 10,000 men in North America to defend the colonies **defence** against further Indian attacks or rebellions and to police her new territories. Property owners in Britain were already heavily taxed, and it was considered only fair that the colonists should share the cost of their own defence. The colonists, however, now that they were free of the French threat, could see no need for a standing army or the expense which it involved. Unfortunately, the strength of this colonial feeling was not appreciated by the British government.

Two acts were passed by Parliament to raise money in the colonies to meet the cost of the regiments of British soldiers in North America.

Sugar Act, 1764   The first, the *Sugar Act* of 1764, placed import duties on sugar, molasses, coffee, indigo, wines and a few other products. It actually halved an earlier duty, established in 1733, but provided effective means—revenue officials—to collect the tax money. What seemed even worse was that duties were to be paid in gold and silver, which were always scarce in the Thirteen Colonies. In the same year, the colonies were forbidden to issue paper money. Thus gold and silver was bound to become even more scarce. The colonists began to feel uneasy.

Stamp Act, 1765   The second, the *Stamp Act* of 1765, was the first attempt to raise revenue *within* the colonies. This Act required that stamps be placed on various documents and papers, notably wills, newspapers, contracts and licences. The stamp tax ranged from one cent on the smallest newspaper to several dollars on school and college diplomas. The colonists were outraged that such a tax should be ordered without consulting them or obtaining their consent.

An immediate result of the Stamp Act was many angry speeches in the colonial assemblies. Colonial merchants added to the general protest by refusing to buy British products until the Act was withdrawn. At the Stamp Act Congress of 1765, a meeting of delegates from nine colonies, it was declared that Britain had no right to tax districts which were not represented in the British Parliament. Only colonial assemblies, the delegates said, held such a right. To make matter even worse for the British government, merchants in England complained that they were losing a great deal of business in North America because merchants there were refusing to buy British goods.

The Stamp Act had to be repealed in 1766. As this was being done, Parliament declared that in the future the king and Parliament would legislate for the colonies "in all cases whatever."

However, hope of raising funds by other means was not given **Townshend Acts, 1767** up. The *Townshend Acts* of 1767 placed small duties on painters' colours, paper, glass, lead and tea. Again the colonists protested

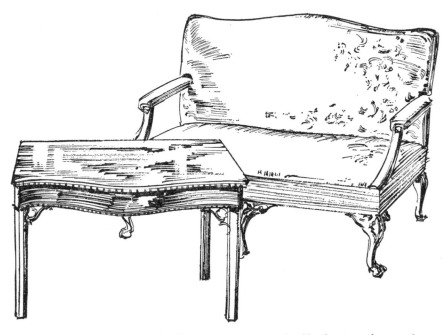

English furniture of the mid-eighteenth century period. The furniture designs of Thomas Chippendale, a cabinet-maker, dominated the entire English-speaking world of this time. Whereas French furniture of the period (Louis XV) possessed an easily-recognized line and shape, Chippendale's designs varied greatly. He borrowed freely from French, Chinese and Gothic designs in order to create his various patterns. The small sofa shown has a squarish back and simple lines, but also possesses curiously-curved legs that terminate in claw-and-ball feet. The side table, by contrast, is decorated in a Chinese manner.

loudly, and merchants refused to buy British goods. Some colonists, like Samuel Adams of Massachusetts, later a leading member of the Revolution, swore "to eat nothing, drink nothing, wear nothing" imported from Britain until the duties were dropped. The colonists refused to "buy British" and the sale of British

imports fell by almost two-thirds.   Surprised by this second out-
burst of colonial anger, in 1770, the British government dropped
the new duties, *except that on tea*.   This one item was retained
just to show that the mother country still claimed the right to
tax her colonies.

It was the duty remaining on tea that was to spark a
revolution.

Anti-British feeling still ran high in 1770 when two regiments
of British soldiers were ordered from Halifax to Boston.   These
soldiers were stationed in the centre of the city and encountered
considerable hostility.   On one occasion, a group of redcoats was
surrounded and taunted with such terms as "rascals" and "lobsters".   Not content with mere words, the Bostonians made snowballs and threw them at the soldiers.   In the confusion that followed, guns were fired and several colonists fell in the snow.   As
the story of this unfortunate event spread, it grew in the horror
of telling until people everywhere were talking of the "Boston
Massacre."

An American author, Samuel Goodrich, has given the following vivid account of the "Massacre":

"Boston   A great tumult broke out, between seven and eight o'clock, on
Massacre", the evening of the 5th of March (1770). The mob, armed with clubs,
1770   ran toward King Street crying, "Let us drive out these rascals! They
have no business here! Drive them out! Drive out the rascals!" About
this time some one cried out that the town had been set on fire. Then
the bells rang, and the crowd became greater, and more noisy; they
rushed furiously to the custom-house, and seeing an English soldier
standing there, shouted, "Kill him! Kill him!" The people attacked
him with snowballs, pieces of ice, and whatever they could find. The
sentinel called for the guard, and Captain Preston sent a corporal
with a few soldiers to defend him. They marched with their guns
loaded and the Captain followed them. They met a crowd of the
people, led by a giant negro, named Attucks; they brandished their
clubs, and pelted the soldiers with snowballs; abused them with all
manner of harsh words, shouted in their faces, surrounded them, and
challenged them to fire. At last, Attucks with twelve of his men, began
to strike upon their muskets with clubs, and cried out to the multitude, "Don't be afraid! They dare not fire—the miserable cowards!
Kill the rascals! Crush them under foot!" Attucks lifted his arm

against Captain Preston, and seized upon a bayonet. "They dare not fire!", shouted the mob again. At this instant firing began. The negro dropped dead upon the ground. The soldiers fired twice more. Three men were killed and others wounded. The mob dispersed but soon returned to pick up the bodies. The whole town was now in an uproar. Thousands of men, women and children, rushed through the streets; the sound of drums, and the cries of "To arms! To arms!" were heard from all quarters. The soldiers who had fired upon the people were arrested, and the governor, at last, persuaded the people to go home quietly. The slain citizens were buried with great ceremony, on the 8th. . . . The soldiers were soon after tried. Two were condemned and imprisoned; six of them were acquitted. . . . The irritated and unreasonable populace, if they could have had their way, would have torn the soldiers in pieces.

All the talk in the colonies of unfair taxes, of no representation in the British parliament, and of harsh oppression, exaggerated the true situation. The colonists had always paid various duties, so that the only new tax was the short-lived stamp tax. The colonies had never been represented in Parliament, nor, for that matter, were most of the people then living in Britain. There was no actual thought in Britain of "oppressing" the colonists, but merely of carrying out the trade practices of the time. However, trouble would ultimately have developed between Great Britain and the Thirteen Colonies no matter what conditions were. One old colonist undoubtedly spoke the truth when he remarked, "We always had governed ourselves and we always meant to." At any rate, from 1770 to 1773, there were few difficulties between Great Britain and her colonies. Having won relief from certain taxes, the colonists allowed the British to collect others.

It was the sole remaining tax, six cents per pound of tea, that caused trouble.

In 1772, the British Parliament passed the *Tea Act,* which **Tea Act, 1772** gave the sole right to sell tea in North America to the East India Company. This meant cheaper tea for the colonists, because the Company agreed to transport its tea to North America, and even when selling it with the six cents tax added, the Company could undersell the tea being smuggled in from Holland. But the colonists resented a tax they had not been consulted about, and many colonial merchants feared for their businesses, since only a few of them would be allowed to sell Company tea. Merchants in other businesses began to wonder when the British government would decide to make the same kind of arrangement for their goods and thus perhaps drive them out of business.

The colonists decided to refuse the tea.

"Boston Tea Party," 1773

East India Company ships from Britain were refused admittance to the harbours of New York and Philadelphia. At Charleston, two cargoes were pushed into warehouses and left untouched. Then, on December 16, 1773, occurred the famous "Boston Tea Party." One young colonist who took part in this affair described his adventures:

It was evening, and I immediately dressed myself in the costume of an Indian, equipped with a small hatchet and a club, and after having painted my face and hands with coal dust in the shop of a blacksmith, I repaired to Griffin's Wharf, where the ships lay that contained the tea. When I first appeared in the street, after being thus disguised, I fell in with many who were dressed, equipped and painted as I was, and who fell in with me, and marched in order to the place of our destination. The commander of the division to which I belonged, as soon as we were on board the ship, ordered me to go to the captain and demand of him the keys to the hatches and a dozen candles. I made the demand accordingly, and the captain promptly replied, and delivered the articles; but requested me at the same time to do no damage to the ship or rigging. We then were ordered by our commander to open the hatches and take out all the chests of tea and throw them overboard, and we immediately proceeded to execute his orders, first cutting and splitting the chests with our tomahawks so as to expose them to the effects of the water. In about three hours from the time we went aboard, we had thus broken and thrown overboard every tea chest to be found in the ship, while those in the other ships were disposing of tea at the same time. We were surrounded by British armed ships, but no attempt was made to resist us. We then quietly returned to our several homes, without having any conversation with each other or taking any measure to discover who were our associates.

All told, thousands of dollars worth of tea was destroyed.

The effects of the "Tea Party" were quickly felt in North America and in Britain. Many colonists thought that the raid on the Company ships in Boston harbour had been a foolish and

hasty action.   In Britain, friends of the colonists were keenly disappointed, while an angry government took stern measures.   A
series of laws, which the colonists called the "Intolerable Acts", **"Intolerable Acts"**
were passed.   By these Acts, the port of Boston was closed to all
shipping until the destroyed tea had been paid for; British officials
accused of violence in carrying out their duties were to be tried in
British, not colonial, courts; troops were quartered in Massachusetts towns; and Massachusetts had its rights of government
greatly reduced.   In addition, it was unfortunate that the Quebec
Act of 1774 was passed at this time.   The colonists regarded it as
one of the "Intolerable Acts" because it extended one boundary of
Quebec to the Ohio river and appeared to be an attempt to
exclude settlers from the western lands.   And did it not clamp a
firm British hand on Quebec affairs?

It was these Acts that began the Revolution.   Resentment
against them spread far beyond Massachusetts and began another
boycott of British goods.   The Acts also made many colonists
secretly collect arms and ammunition.

The British General Gage became the new governor of Massachusetts.   However, the people of the colony set up an independent government and made John Hancock, a Boston merchant,
their leader.   The colony then proceeded to raise an army of its
own.   Twelve thousand militia were enlisted, of whom two-thirds
were "Minutemen"—armed men ready to fight at a minute's notice. **Minutemen**

The British penalties placed on Massachusetts and the colonists' suspicion of the Quebec Act only served to unite the Thirteen Colonies in opposition against the mother country.   In
September, 1774, representatives from the colonies held a congress
at Philadelphia.   Of the delegates who attended, some believed
that strong action should be taken against Great Britain, but
others thought that their problems could be solved by peaceful
discussion.   However, the anti-British representatives at the *First* **First Continental Congress, 1774**
Continental Congress were so powerful that they swung feeling in
favour of a united and determined front.   It was agreed that all
trade with Britain should be stopped, and that a *Declaration of
Rights and Grievances* should be sent to King George III, begging

One of the most colourful incidents in the early period of the American Revolution was Paul Revere's ride to warn the people along the road to Lexington of the coming of British troops. Revere was a Boston silversmith of considerable skill and reputation. He was actually the official courier of the Massachusetts Provincial Assembly, which had pledged itself to watch every move of the British. The Assembly had arranged to light lanterns in the steeple of a Boston church to signal British troop movements; one lantern if the British were coming by land and two lanterns if they were moving by sea. Revere, who had stationed himself in a small town outside Boston, saw a single lantern glowing in the darkness and immediately rode off to warn the countryside. During the War of Independence, Paul Revere became a ranking officer in the militia. After the conflict was over, he returned to his business and became the greatest American silversmith of his time.

him to relieve them from Parliament's actions. The Declaration also stated that they wanted nothing more than the recognition of their right as Englishmen, particularly the right of being taxed only if represented in Parliament. Before ending their discussions, the delegates arranged to meet again the following May.

But the time for peaceful action had long passed. In April, 1775, General Gage, hearing that colonists were collecting food and ammunition at Concord, Massachusetts, sent 1,000 men to seek out and destroy these stores. The troops were ordered to go by way of Lexington so they might seize Samuel Adams and John Hancock who were visiting there. Paul Revere, a citizen of Boston and one of the "Indians" who raided the tea ships, seeing the departure of the British troops, took to his horse and galloped through the countryside, raising the alarm and rousing out the minutemen. At Lexington, he stopped to warn Samuel Adams and John Hancock that the British were approaching.

Paul Revere's ride.

Just before daybreak, the redcoats marched onto the village green at Lexington where they found a group of minutemen and local farmers awaiting them. In the skirmish that followed, eight colonists were killed and ten wounded. Pushing on to Concord, Gage's men destroyed the military stores there. By this time Massachusett's minutemen and militia were hurrying from all directions, converging on the British force. Shooting from behind rocks, trees, fences and buildings, they poured a damaging fire on the British regulars. Only with the help of a brigade of troops rushed out from Boston, did the redcoats reach the safety of the city. Nearly 300 of their comrades lay dead and dying along the road behind them.

Clash at Lexington, 1775

With the exchange of shots and the death of men on Lexington common, the quarrel between mother country and colonies changed to armed rebellion.

51

THE WAR OF INDEPENDENCE

Capture of Fort Ticonderoga, 1775   The news of Lexington and Concord spread and electrified the colonies. In May of 1775, a New England frontiersman, Ethan Allen, leading his "Green Mountain Boys," surprised and captured Fort Ticonderoga on Lake Champlain. It was an important victory, for a strong British fort had been taken and large quantities of ammunition and military stores had fallen into American hands. The following day, Allen and his men captured nearby Crown Point.

Second Continental Congress   In the same month, an assembly of colonial delegates, the *Second Continental Congress,* met at Philadelphia to plan their war for independence. An invitation to attend was sent to Quebec. Of course, British officials ignored the note. As a first step, the Congress appointed George Washington commander-in-chief of all American forces. The Congress than decided to ask the colonies for war supplies and troops, to send agents to France for loans of money, and to encourage rebellion in Quebec.

By June, General Gage was besieged in Boston by approximately 10,000 colonial regulars and militia, who surrounded the city on the land side. About 1,500 of this *Continental Army,* as it was called, managed to entrench themselves on an elevation known as Bunker Hill, which overlooked part of Boston. Fearing that the enemy might fire on the city, General Gage sent 3,000 **Battle of Bunker Hill, 1775** of his regulars to dislodge the colonials. Thus, on June 17, 1775, was fought the Battle of Bunker Hill, during which the colonists were forced to retire, but only after inflicting heavy losses. In the course of one and a half hours more than 1,000 of the redcoats were slain. The fact that their militia were able to deliver such a heavy blow gave renewed confidence to the fighting colonists. George Washington remarked, "The liberties of the country are safe."

Rumours reached the Congress that the British intended to send military expeditions southward from Quebec.   In consequence, an invasion of the province was organized.   Richard Montgomery led one force against Montreal and Benedict Arnold led another against Quebec.   Forts Chambly and St. John's and

A Pennsylvania rifleman of Washington's army. Unlike the regular soldier, this fighting man dressed in frontier fashion, wearing buckskin clothing, and was equipped with tomahawk and knife.   Many such men had spent their lives on the western frontiers and were experienced fighters and brilliant marksmen.   They possessed a firearm that gave them a decided edge in any fighting, the famous Pennsylvania rifle. This gun, designed by colonial gunsmiths, had a long barrel that gave steadiness and balance to the weapon and ensured great accuracy.   The British, with grim humour, called it "the most fatal widow and orphan-maker in the world."   At that time, no other hand weapon could match its accuracy and range.   A colonial rifleman killed a British general at the battle of Saratoga with one shot at 300 yards, probably one of the most amazing feats of the war. Regular troops under Washington did not employ the Pennsylvania rifle; they were issued with a gun similar to the British Brown Bess.

the city of Montreal fell to the colonists, but at Quebec it was a different story.   Arnold's men, after a difficult winter journey through the wilderness of northern Massachusetts, were badly-prepared and poorly-equipped to take the fortress-city.   On the last day of 1775, Arnold's force, by this time joined by Montgomery and his men, launched an attack in a blinding snowstorm. So sharp was the fire of the British defenders that the ragged advance of the invaders was beaten back and Montgomery was killed. Some hours later, the citizens of Quebec found the frozen bodies of some of their enemies in the snowdrifts. Pinned to their caps were bits of paper bearing the written words, "Liberty or Death!"

Despite a complete lack of artillery with which to breach walls, the surviving colonists maintained a siege of Quebec until May of 1776, when the British Navy arrived in time to land a fully-equipped army of 10,000 men.

The failure at Quebec was a disappointment to the revolutionary leaders; they had hoped that the colonies of Quebec and Nova Scotia might be persuaded or forced into rebellion against Great Britain. Neither of the northern colonies, however, displayed any desire to join the conflict. The habitant, his seigneur and the British officials had no desire to change the established order of life in Quebec. The province was reasonably satisfied by the Quebec Act of 1774. In Nova Scotia, the farmers and fishermen were too scattered and too busy making a bare living to join the rebellion. In both provinces, the merchants were more concerned with the fur trade or the provisioning of British fleets and armies to throw away good business opportunities.

Even late in 1775, the Thirteen Colonies had not thought of breaking away from the mother country to form a new nation. It is quite possible that had King George III and his advisers acted in a more sympathetic manner, the colonists themselves might have remained loyal. However, angered by what he considered treason, King George refused to accept the colonists' petition, declared the colonies to be entirely outside his protection, and ordered their ports under blockade by the British fleet. Yet the Congress still held back, unwilling to declare independence.

During the early months of 1776, fighting occurred in several places. There was a sharp skirmish in North Carolina between two groups of colonists, the *Whigs* who favoured revolution and the *Tories* who opposed it. The British Navy was repulsed in its attempt to capture Charleston in South Carolina. But the most important event was the siege of Boston by Washington and his troops with guns hauled from Ticonderoga through the winter snows. This resulted in the withdrawal of British forces from Boston to Halifax, and along with these troops went 900 citizens who wished to have no part in the rebellion.

By this time, many colonists were wondering why they should remain loyal subjects of King George III. They began to think that independence from Great Britain offered the only safety for their liberty. A pamphlet, *Common Sense,* by Thomas Paine, a newly-arrived English political writer, maintained that an evil Parliament, led by a stupid king, was interfering more and more with their lives and liberty. Thousands of copies of the pamphlet were sold and read. More and more colonists began to think of declaring themselves free of British control.

However, no doubt now remained in the minds of colonial leaders. The Thirteen Colonies must be free and independent. In June, 1776, Richard Henry Lee of Virginia introduced a resolution in the Continental Congress: "Resolved: that these United Colonies are, and of right ought to be, free and independent states." John Adams of Massachusetts seconded the resolution. A committee composed of Thomas Jefferson of Virginia, John Adams of Massachusetts, Benjamin Franklin of Pennsylvania, Roger Sherman of Connecticut and Robert L. Livingston of New York was appointed to draw up a declaration announcing why the United Colonies should be independent. Then the Congress would vote on the resolution. It was Thomas Jefferson, a shy young Virginian and a rather quiet member of the Congress, who was mainly responsible for drawing up the public statement of independence.

On July 4, 1776, John Hancock, as president of the Congress, **Declaration of Independence, 1776** signed the *Declaration of Independence* with a large bold signature, "large enough for the King of England to read without his spectacles." Then by way of celebration, citizens of Philadelphia rang the "Liberty Bell" in the old State House, and in New York, people knocked down a lead statue of George II, broke it up and melted it down for bullets.

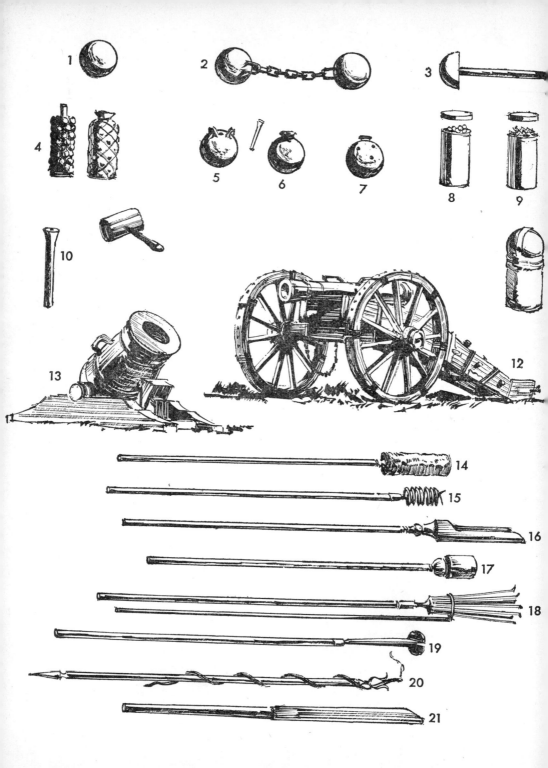

The science of artillery at the time of the American Revolution.   From the earliest days of gunnery, the type of shot fired was of the greatest importance, and the constant ambition of artillerymen was to develop more effective missiles.   By the middle of the eighteenth century, a wide range of shot was in use.   Here we see some of the commonest types: (1) is "round shot" of cast iron, sometimes called the cannon ball.   On occasion, it was heated before firing. (2) is "chain shot" and (3) is "bar shot".   Both were useful for such special purposes as destroying the rigging of ships.   Almost as common as round shot was (4) "grapeshot". Consisting of a number of small iron balls clustered around a wooden rod, the whole missile was bagged and netted.   When fired, the covering of the grapeshot burned away, allowing the balls to scatter.   (5) is a "shell" or "bomb". Similar in appearance to round shot, its hollow centre was packed with explosive. Its fuse is the small peg at the right which, after the gun was fired, was driven into a hole, thereby setting off the charge.   (6) is also an explosive shell, with a lip for holding it instead of the two small handles on (5).   (7), an incendiary bomb, was filled with pitch and other materials that burned fiercely.   The flames escaped through holes drilled in the shell case.   (8) and (9), "case shot," operated very much like grapeshot: (8) was loaded with lead balls, and (9) with metal scraps.   (10) is the enlargement of a fuse for (5).   Fuses were cut in various lengths to govern the time of explosion. A mallet, such as the one illustrated, was used to drive in the fuses.   (12), the field cannon, designed for mobility and ease of handling in battle, was one of the most useful and common artillery pieces of the eighteenth century.   Field cannon ranged in size from three to twenty-four pounders, the term "pounder" referring to the weight of cast iron shot fired. (13), the mortar, was another weapon in use at this time, and indeed throughout the whole history of artillery.   Unlike the cannon, which had a long, flat-curved line of fire, the mortar had a shorter range and a high, sharply-curved line of fire, which permitted shells to be dropped over walls and other obstacles.   The wheelless mortar sat on a flat heavy "bed" for the sake of stability, and was thus more difficult to move than a cannon.

The operation of loading and firing a cannon was accomplished by the use of several materials.   (14) is the "sponge," a long-handled wooden plug covered with lamb-skin.   It was dipped in water and then plunged into the mouth of the gun to extinguish any sparks remaining from the previous firing.   (15), the "wormer," was worked into the barrel like a giant corkscrew to draw out the bits of wadding stuck inside after firing.   Powder was then poured into the weapon by use of a ladle (16).   Next, wadding, composed of old cotton, waste rags or straw, was rammed down on top of the powder with a "rammer" (17).   Finally, the shot was put in and rammed down, but only after being cleaned and carefully inspected. Dirty shot could ruin a gun.   To fire the gun, a burning fuse was applied to a small "touchole" at the rear of the piece.   This fuse or "match" was often mounted on a "linstock" (20) that allowed the gunner to stand clear when firing.   (18) is a "cat" or searcher, used to discover dangerous holes or cracks in the barrel. (19) is a "scraper", a tool used to clean the barrel.   By the eighteenth century, powder was being packed in bags and loose powder ceased to be used.   A little later in time, the bag of powder, the wadding and the shot were all fastened together making a unit as shown in (11).   The "handspike" (21) was an iron-shod pole used to lift and manoeuvre the rear of the gun carriage, or to elevate the breech of the gun when adjusting the aim.

The Declaration of Independence is divided into three sections, the first of which states the belief of the revolutionary leaders:

that all men are created equal, that they are endowed by their Creator with certain inalienable Rights; that among these are Life, Liberty and the pursuit of Happiness; that to secure these rights, Governments are instituted among Men, deriving their just powers from the consent of the governed; that whenever any Form of Government becomes destructive of these ends, it is the Right of the People to alter or abolish it, and to institute new Government . . .

The second section of the Declaration lists a number of colonial grievances, while the third announces the birth of a new independent nation:

WE, THEREFORE, THE REPRESENTATIVES OF THE UNITED STATES OF AMERICA, in General Congress, Assembled . . . do in the Name, and by the authority of the good People of those Colonies, solemnly publish and declare, that these United Colonies are, and of right ought to be FREE AND INDEPENDENT STATES; that they are Absolved from all Allegiance to the British Crown . . . and that as Free and Independent states, they have full Power to levy War, conclude Peace, contract Alliances, establish Commerce, and to do all other Acts and things which Independent States may of right do . . .

There is no doubt that the Declaration was deliberately worded in such a manner as to win sympathy in Europe as well as support at home. For this reason, the document was not only a statement of intention, but itself became a strong influence in the success of the war. The Declaration divided the colonists into "Whigs" and "Tories," that is, rebels and those preferring to remain loyal to Great Britain. The Declaration also pleased two old enemies of Britain—France and Spain.

Delegates from all the colonies signed the Declaration, but this was no indication that all the colonists were pleased with their new condition. Many people in Massachusetts and Virginia were rebels, but in other areas large numbers of people remained loyal to Britain. Among these were officials, landholders, doctors, lawyers, ministers, wealthy merchants, prosperous farmers, politicians

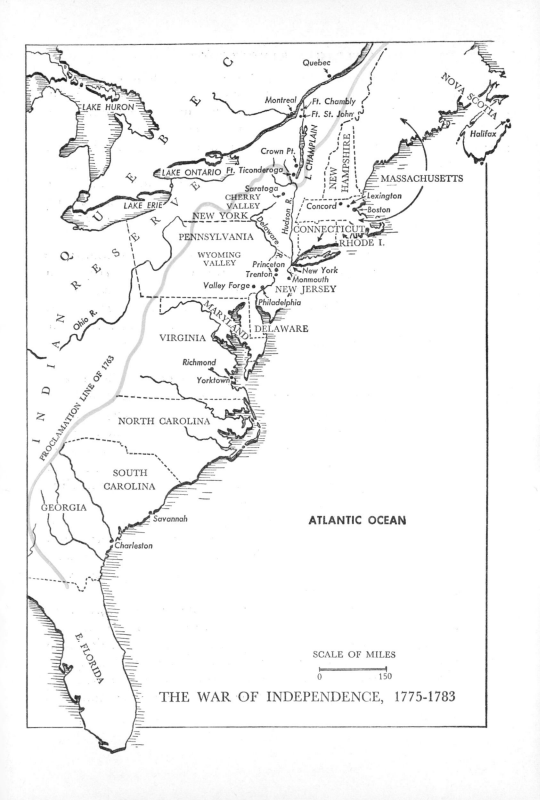

THE WAR OF INDEPENDENCE, 1775-1783

and some of the more humble citizens, all of whom were opposed to the break with Great Britain. Some of the Loyalists or Tories felt a sincere loyalty to the crown, while others were influenced by reason of their land, business, trade or official position.

Hardships of the Tories

In districts where the revolutionaries were in the majority, the Tories suffered seriously. Homes were burned, property destroyed, lands taken over and loyal families driven out of the community. Since in some regions the Tories were often wealthy persons and the rebels poor, the persecution of loyal colonists took on an unusual bitterness.

One of the surprising facts of the American Revolution is that the Tories were able to do so little for Britain. Why could not the thousands of Tories have offered strong resistance? There are several reasons. First, the Tories put too much faith in British military power; second, the British failed to make good use of the Tories; third, the rebels were much better organized than the Tories.

American military problems

The new government of the United Colonies or States faced many difficulties in maintaining war with Great Britain. Since the Congress had no power to raise taxes, there was a scarcity of money that left General Washington's men sadly short of food, uniforms, small arms, guns, ammunition and hospital supplies. In proportion to the total population of the country, the Continental Army was very small, a collection of state regiments and state militia, which varied on occasion from 3,000 to 90,000 men, but were only a few thousands at any one time. Washington himself was greatly discouraged by the lack of training and discipline among his militia men. They were mostly sharpshooting farmers and frontiersmen who excelled in guerilla fighting, but were unfitted for the European style of mass conflict.

Great Britain, too, was having trouble in the organization and conduct of the war. To begin with, she was fighting an expensive war 3,000 miles from home, a circumstance which made it necessary to maintain long lines of communication and supply. Officials in England and British military leaders in America seemed unable to cope with the difficulties of fighting in the forests of North America. The British plan was to blockade the Ameri- British plan of war can shores with ships, to capture coastal towns, and then invade the colonies one at a time. With the exception of Boston, British forces had no great difficulty in taking such key seaports as New York, Philadelphia and Charleston, but they found invasions of the interior difficult and dangerous moves.

Since the British could not invade the whole long coastline at one time, the War of Independence became a series of campaigns, first in New England, then in the middle states, and finally in the south.

After taking Boston, Washington moved his troops southward to New York where he expected the next British blow to fall. His guess was correct. However, the Americans suffered several defeats, in the course of which the British captured New York. Conditions became so serious for the Americans that Washington was forced to retreat across the Delaware River.

Confident that victory was almost won, the British commander, General Howe, sent Lord Cornwallis southward to occupy New Jersey. It was at this point that Washington showed his skill as a military commander. He made a number of swift and unexpected moves. In the closing days of 1776 and the early days of 1777, his men captured 1,000 British infantry at Trenton, N.J., and British defeats at Trenton and Princeton defeated another group at Princeton. Washington then withdrew his men into the highlands of New Jersey out of reach of Cornwallis. All the British could do was withdraw to New York.

In the spring of 1777, the Marquis de Lafayette, a young Marquis de Lafayette French nobleman and soldier, offered his services to the revolutionaries. He proved so skilful that he became one of Washington's generals. His devotion to the cause of freedom was so great that he equipped many of his troops at his own expense. Lafayette brought with him Baron de Kalb, a German officer who also became a general in the American forces. Later, Baron Steuben, a Prussian military engineer, joined Washington and made himself particularly useful by drilling and disciplining American troops.

In 1777, Major-General Burgoyne, the commander of a British army in Quebec, led his command south to join up with General

General
Burgoyne
surrenders at
Saratoga, 1777

Howe.   After re-capturing Crown Point and Ticonderoga, Burgoyne marched on south again, but a force of 1,000 American axemen felled trees across the only road that the British, burdened with artillery and supplies, could use to get to New York. The New England militia hemmed Burgoyne in on all sides, and sharpshooter rifles cut down the redcoat soldiers. Unable to advance or retreat, Burgoyne surrendered his army of 6,000 men at Saratoga.

British capture
Philadelphia,
1777

In the meantime, General Howe, knowing nothing of Burgoyne's movements, had moved southward to Philadelphia, which he captured that autumn. Washington, anxious to hold the enemy, set up winter camp at Valley Forge, a short distance west of Philadelphia. Desperately short of food supplies, clothing, shoes and stores of all kinds, his men spent a dreadful winter, marked by hardship, starvation and disease. An account of their suffering states:

> While Howe and his officers were living luxuriously in Philadelphia, Washington's men, naked and starving, were dying of putrid fever on the frozen hillsides of Valley Forge.

Washington and his men did not endure and suffer the winter of 1777-78 in vain. The news of Saratoga was the turning point of the war. It secured for the Americans the help of Britain's old enemy—France—who was sure that the United States could carry on an effective war. In February, 1778, France and the United

France and
Spain enter war,
1778

States signed a treaty of alliance against Great Britain. From now on, the Continental Army was largely supplied and paid with French gifts of money, and was reinforced by disciplined French regiments. In addition, other European nations—notably Spain—joined the war as allies of the Americans.

British leave
Philadelphia,
1778

News that a French fleet was being sent to the United States so alarmed the British that they decided to withdraw troops from Philadelphia and send them to New York. During this operation, 15,000 of the British forces were hurried across New Jersey. Washington tried to cut off their baggage-train at Monmouth, but due to the blundering of a senior American officer, the British made good their escape. The Battle of Monmouth was the last important engagement in the north. After 1778, most of the action took place in the south.

The Ferguson rifle. According to some historians, this gun could have altered the course of the American Revolution if it had been supplied to the British Army in any quantity. The firearm was a breech loader, that is, the trigger guard dropped down to permit the entrance of the bullet into the firing chamber. The only breech-loader to see service during the Revolution, the great advantage of the rifle was the speed with which it could be fired. A trained soldier could double the current rate of fire, shooting up to six shots per minute as against the Brown Bess capacity of three. In addition, the barrel was rifled for accuracy in much the same way as the famous Pennsylvania rifle. Yet another advantage of the Ferguson rifle was that it weighed three to four pounds less than any conventional hand gun of the time. Invented by a Major Patrick Ferguson in 1776, it was demonstrated before a group of British generals, who were so impressed, they established a sharpshooters' corps under Ferguson to fight in America. However, due to jealousy on the part of some senior officers, the rifle was never provided in large numbers to British soldiers.

Throughout the summer and autumn of 1778, there were several brutal raids and massacres by the British upon American settlers in the Wyoming Valley of Pennsylvania and the Cherry Valley of New York. This was the work of two important Tory leaders, Colonel John Butler, who led a troop of frontiersmen known as *Butler's Rangers*, and Sir John Johnson, who raised several Loyalist regiments. These forces were recruited mainly from Loyalist refugees at Niagara, men who had been driven from their homes in the colonies and thirsted for revenge. They did not hesitate to scalp American settlers. Both Butler and Johnson used Seneca and Mohawk Indians in this vicious frontier fighting. Although these hit-and-run affairs were daring adventures, they accomplished very little beyond destroying or carrying off cattle and crops that might have been useful to the Continental forces.

Raids and massacres, 1778

Late in 1778, the British decided that the Loyalists of the south were numerous enough to be of great help. In any case, the war in the north had become a stalemate. In December, Savannah, Georgia, was captured by the British and Charleston, South Carolina, was occupied in 1780. From 1778 to 1781, British armies marched into and across South Carolina, North Carolina and Virginia, their main forces never suffering defeat. However, the British were losing the war because they could not hold areas they conquered, nor could they protect their Loyalist helpers. The British were pinned to the coastal towns through which they were fed and armed.

British take Savannah and Charleston

At sea, there was little actual fighting during the War of Independence, but the conflict brought fame to an American naval officer, John Paul Jones, who commanded a squadron of ships lent by the French government and raided English shipping in their home waters. Jones raided British soil in 1778, defeated a British warship in a battle in 1779, and defeated three others in another engagement the same year. This American victory at sea was a blow to British prestige, and brought much pride and comfort to the rebels.

John Paul Jones

In the southern states, the war was approaching its climax.

Cornwallis, the British commander in the south, moved into Virginia and defeated an American force under Lafayette. Then Cornwallis returned to Yorktown on the coast to rest and refit his men. Learning of this situation, Washington acted swiftly, ordering American and French troops to Virginia. Caught between these land forces and a French fleet off the coast, Cornwallis was doomed unless he could escape by sea.

Surrender of Cornwallis, 1781

A British fleet attempting to relieve Cornwallis in September was driven off by the French. In October, Cornwallis, and 7,000 soldiers were forced to surrender. As the British general and his troops marched out to lay down their arms, a British band played "The World Turned Upside Down."

After this disaster, the British were ready to make peace.

52

THE STATES WIN
INDEPENDENCE

The sudden collapse of British power at Yorktown in 1781 **End of War, 1781** brought the War of Independence to a close. Peace negotiations did not begin until April 1782 because it took some time for France and her ally, Spain, to decide to stop fighting Britain.

During the peace talks at Paris, France, in which the Americans, Benjamin Franklin, John Adams and John Jay played a large part, Britain was determined to re-create good relations with her former colonies. For one thing, many British people had sympathized with the rebels throughout the war and wanted to see them gain the freedom they had fought for so long and at such cost. In addition, the British had not enjoyed fighting people of their own race. It was too much like brother fighting brother. Then again, Britain wanted peace to enjoy once more the American market where she had sold so many of her products and bought so much that she needed. The war had stopped all trade and commerce between Britain and the colonies, and people on both sides of the Atlantic were a great deal poorer as a result.

Great Britain, therefore, was happy to make peace with the Americans.

In the *Treaty of Paris,* finally drawn up and signed in 1783, **Treaty of Paris, 1783** Great Britain recognized the independence of the United States. Great Britain also agreed to recognize as the territory of the United States all lands lying between the Mississippi and the Atlantic and between the Province of Quebec and Florida. The American peacemakers had at first tried to obtain all British territory in North America, but this seemed to the British government too impudent a claim. Eventually, a common boundary between British and American territory was agreed upon. It ran from Nova Scotia in the east along a height of land that meets the St. Lawrence river. The boundary then followed the St.

NORTH AMERICA IN 1783

RUSSIAN TERRITORY

INDIAN COUNTRY

HUDSON'S BAY CO.

PROVINCE OF QUEBEC

NFLD.

NOVA SCOTIA

PACIFIC

OCEAN

SPANISH

TERRITORY

THE

UNITED

STATES

BERMUDA IS.

ATLANTIC

OCEAN

GULF
OF
MEXICO

BAHAMA IS.

BRITISH
HONDURAS

JAMAICA

BRITISH

AMERICAN

FRENCH

SPANISH

RUSSIAN

LAKE OF THE WOODS

LAKE SUPERIOR

Mississippi R.

LOUISIANA

LAKE MICHIGAN

LAKE HURON

CLAIMED BY MASS.

CLAIMED BY CONN.

CLAIMED BY VIRGINIA

Ohio R.

Mississippi R.

CLAIMED BY N.C.

CLAIMED BY S.C.

CLAIMED BY S.C. AND GEORGIA

CLAIMED BY GEORGIA

FLORIDA

QUEBEC

Quebec

Montreal

St. Lawrence R.

LAKE ONTARIO

LAKE ERIE

NEW YORK

VERMONT 1791

NEW HAMPSHIRE

MASSACHUSETTS

MASS.

CONN.

Portsmouth

Boston

Providence

RHODE I.

New Haven

PENNSYLVANIA

Philadelphia

New York

Princeton

NEW JERSEY

DELAWARE

MARYLAND

VIRGINIA

Williamsburg

NORTH CAROLINA

SOUTH CAROLINA

Charleston

GEORGIA

Savannah

ATLANTIC OCEAN

THE
UNITED STATES
IN 1783

GULF OF MEXICO

SCALE OF MILES

0   100   200

STATES HAVING NO
WESTERN CLAIMS

Lawrence to the Great Lakes and on to the Lake of the Woods, from whence it continued west to the Mississippi. Spain was recognized as owning East and West Florida and all lands west of the Mississippi. However, Cape Breton, the Gulf of St. Lawrence and Newfoundland remained in the British Empire.

The Americans were greatly pleased by the Treaty. They were now independent. They were free to move into the lands west and north of the Ohio river. They could again engage in the fur trade of the interior, and practically have it to themselves as soon as the British removed their garrisons from the western fur posts. The Americans also gained the right to fish in the waters off Nova Scotia and Newfoundland and come ashore along unsettled portions of these coasts.

However, the Treaty of Paris did not please everyone in North America.

The Indians, who had been promised life ownership of the lands west of the Ohio, had been betrayed. The Montreal fur traders suspected that the Americans would force them out of the Great Lakes area and the Mississippi valley. Perhaps worst of all, the Loyalists in the United States and those driven north to Canada during the war did not believe the half-promises of the American peacemakers to repay the Loyalist owners of homes that had been destroyed and land that had been taken over. The Loyalists still feared for their lives and property. What was to become of them? Did they have a future in the United States? Could they safely return from refuge in Canada?

53

THE FORMATION OF
THE UNITED STATES

The United States had won independence, but there was little unity or agreement for the future among the units of the nation. An American historian has described the situation thus:

> We were like a barrel made of thirteen stout staves, but yet without a single hoop to hold us together. The nation had no leader. It had only a Congress and that Congress was destitute of power.

The writer might have added that the nation did have a flag—voted by Congress in 1777. The flag was formed of thirteen stripes and a square bearing thirteen stars.

During the War of Independence, the Continental Congress had acted as a national government, but it had no actual legal power. Due to the pressures and dangers of war, the colonists had been willing to accept the authority of Congress, for they believed their future depended upon close co-operation. However, when the fighting was over, there was not the same feeling towards union among the states. Each state began to act as if it were an independent country with its own money, its own boundaries and its own import duties. The individual states did not trade with each other to any great extent. Citizens felt a greater loyalty to their own particular state than they did to the Philadelphia Congress. Each state, determined to go its own way, quarrelled with the others about trade, boundaries and money. One such dispute between Connecticut and Pennsylvania over land in the Wyoming valley almost led to war.

By 1787, things looked very serious. The British held fur trading posts in the north-west; the Spanish controlled the Indians of the south-west; Congress had no power to make foreign trade treaties acceptable to all the states; too many Americans were in debt as a result of the war and Congress was unable to raise money with which to carry on the business of government. The union was gradually falling apart.

Constitution of
the United
States, 1788 In 1787, again at Philadelphia, a convention of state representatives was called for the purpose of establishing a national government, a government for the entire country. For a period of months, this convention discussed, argued, and was at times divided by quarrels. After much debate, it produced a document known as the *Constitution of the United States,* a series of laws and regulations, which list the parts of government, indicate the powers and responsibilities of these parts, and make clear what the government may and may not do in its work of ruling the country.

The opening words of the Constitution indicate its purpose:

We, the People of the United States, in Order to form a more perfect Union, establish Justice, insure domestic Tranquility, provide for the common defence, promote the general Welfare and secure the Blessings of Liberty to ourselves and our Posterity, do ordain and establish this Constitution for the United States of America.

It was necessary, of course, to have the new constitution approved by each of the states before it could become law. At first, there was considerable opposition. Many states thought that too much power was being given to the central government. Many Americans began to wonder if they had thrown off British control only to face a new form of oppression. However, after much careful consideration, the states agreed in 1788 to accept the new plan of government.

The Constitution did what the War of Independence had failed to do—it truly united the thirteen states. John Adams put it neatly when he said, "The thirteen clocks all struck together."

The Constitution gave the United States a head of government to be known as the President. The Constitution gave Congress power to wage war and make peace, control relations with other nations, raise money for the purpose of government, coin money and regulate its value, establish courts of law, govern territory not yet made into states, enact laws necessary to the welfare of the nation, establish and maintain trade throughout the nation, and set up courts of law.

Congress, as established by the Constitution, is composed of the *House of Representatives* and the *Senate,* these assemblies corresponding to the House of Commons and the House of Lords in British government and the House of Commons and the Senate in Canadian government. The people of the United States have a voice in national government by electing to Congress members who act on their behalf in making laws.

Members of the House of Representatives, or *Congressmen* as they are called, are chosen by the people on the basis of a state's population, i.e., the greater the number of people in a state, then the greater the number of congressmen from that state elected to the House of Representatives. Members of the Senate, or *Senators* as they are called, are also elected by the people of a state, each state being allowed to choose two senators. This arrangement satisfied the demands of the large and small states, who had argued long and bitterly as to how many representatives each state should send to the national government. The Constitution also states that no measure can become law until it has been passed by a majority of votes in *both* the House of Representatives and in the Senate. The American people were never again going to be governed—and taxed—without the consent of their representatives. All laws passed are put into effect by the President and his *Cabinet,* a small group of *Secretaries* or advisers.

The central government established by the Constitution did not, of course, take away all rights belonging to state governments. It simply is a means by which representatives from each state can look after all matters which affect the welfare of *all* the states. Each state still retains the right to look after such local matters as education, housing, highways, etc. The members of state government are elected by the people of a state to make laws and regulations for the welfare of *their* state. This arrangement whereby a central or federal government rules the nation and various state governments rule the individual states is known as a *federal* system.

Political parties

When the new Congress of the United States met in the March and April of 1789, it contained two political parties: the *Federalists,* the representatives of the merchant, banker and manufacturing groups, who supported the Constitution and believed in strong central control, and, the *Anti-Federalists* or *Republicans,* the representatives of the southern planters, the small farmers of the back country and the labourers of the northern cities, who opposed the Constitution and believed that the greater power should remain with the states. Fortunately, both parties were willing to accept George Washington as the first President of the United States.

Nobody was very surprised at Washington's election to the Presidency. He was the one man of his time who was loved and trusted by the people. He had been a very able military leader and had stuck to the task of beating the British, even when winning the war seemed hopeless.

Washington did not want to become President. He wished to remain at his farm home, Mount Vernon in Virginia, and settle down to the work he liked so well—running a plantation. However, friends urged him to take the Presidency, and he bowed to their wishes.

In the April of 1789, Washington journeyed to New York. All along his route, people turned out to cheer him. They decorated the towns and villages in his honour. He travelled the last few miles from New Jersey by boat, and as he approached the New York shore, he heard the roar of cannons fired to celebrate his arrival.

George Washington becomes first President, 1789

On April 30th, George Washington stepped out onto the balcony of Federal Hall in Wall Street. Before the crowds of people listening to the ceremony of inauguration, he took the oath of office.

I do solemnly swear that I will faithfully execute the office of the President of the United States and will, to the best of my ability, preserve, protect and defend the Constitution of the United States.

In April, 1789, George Washington, after a triumphal procession from his home in Virginia, was sworn in as the first President of the United States. The ceremony of inauguration was held on the balcony of Federal Hall in New York, the oath of office being administered by the Chancellor of the State of New York. After the ceremony the Chancellor turned to the crowd assembled below the balcony and cried, "Long live George Washington, President of the United States!" The same cry, taken up by the multitude, thundered down Wall and Broad streets.

To assist him in solving the many problems facing the new nation, Washington appointed a cabinet of five well-known men. He made Thomas Jefferson his Secretary of State, Alexander Hamilton the Secretary of the Treasury, General Henry Knox the Secretary of War, Edmund Randolph the Attorney-General and John Jay the Chief Justice of the Supreme Court. In the meantime, Benjamin Franklin continued to represent the interests of the United States in Europe.

New import taxes
Since the national government had few funds to carry on its work, it was necessary to find means of raising money. To begin with, an import tax was placed on foreign ships bringing cargoes to American ports. This measure brought large sums of money into the Treasury, money which was used to pay national debts owing to France and other countries, to pay wages to American soldiers, and to pay debts owed by states to American citizens. This wise and honest policy, promoted by Alexander Hamilton, the Secretary of the Treasury, gained respect for the national government both at home and abroad.

Important developments
Other important developments included the first *census* or count of the population, the establishment of a national bank and a mint to coin money. The new bank and mint gave the United States a standard issue of money that was acceptable in every state. It was at this time that the currency was changed from pounds, shilling and pence, to dollars, dimes and cents.

The nation now had a government and a leader, but it lacked a capital. Philadelphia and New York had at various times been temporary homes for the revolutionary Congresses. What was now wanted was a place of permanent residence for the United States government. Everyone argued in favour of a different city. Even Congress could not make up its mind about an agreeable location. Eventually, after much argument, it was agreed that the new capital would be built on an area of ground along the Potomac river—which flowed past Mount Vernon, Washington's home.

By 1790, engineers were at work laying out the city. Major
Pierre L'Enfant, a French architect who had crossed the Atlantic
with Lafayette to fight for the Revolution, was given the responsibility of designing and building the new capital. L'Enfant
planned the city around the *Capitol* or Congress buildings and
the Presidential Mansion, known today as the White House. He
planned a city of broad avenues and beautiful public buildings,
all leading up to Capitol Hill. However, it was not until 1800
that the government moved into the Capitol, and even at that
time, only one wing of that building had been completed. The
city itself lacked private houses, and government officials and
people splashed about in the mud of the unpaved "avenues."
Congressmen lived in a few crowded boarding houses. But at least
the government of the United States had a permanent home.
Known initially as Federal City, it was later named Washington,
in honour of the saviour of the nation.

*Capital at
Washington,
1800*

SUMMARY—SECTION VIII

As a result of the Seven Years' War, Great Britain won a tremendous increase in North American territory. All French possessions in
North America, with the exception of Louisiana west of the Mississippi,
became part of a British Empire that stretched from Hudson Bay to the
Floridas.

British statesmen decided that their earlier policy of leaving the
colonies to look after their own affairs should be abandoned and
replaced by one of strict control. But events soon showed that it was
too late to do this. Each colony, excepting Quebec, was now accustomed to directing its own business.

Britain decided to station garrisons of troops in North America
to protect the Thirteen Colonies against attack by the Indians or the
Spanish. Between 1764 and 1770, a number of tax laws were passed
to raise money to support these garrisons. Convinced that they needed
no such protection, the colonists refused to pay some of the taxes, and

protested to the British Parliament that they should not be taxed without their approval and consent.

There were other troubles. In 1763, by royal proclamation, all settlement beyond the Appalachians was forbidden and all western land grants were withheld. The colonists protested that this order deprived them of the land "from sea to sea" guaranteed them in their charter rights. In 1764, the colonies were forbidden to issue paper money, and thus gold and silver coins promised to become scarcer than ever.

From 1770 to 1773, there was a period of good relations between the mother country and the colonies. Having won relief from certain taxes, the colonists allowed Britain to collect others. But in 1773, Parliament gave the British East India Company the sole right to sell tea in North America. However, there was a six cents a pound tax on tea which the colonists were unwilling to pay. At New York and Philadelphia, the tea ships were turned away from the harbours. At Boston, a few daring colonists boarded the tea ships and threw thousands of dollars worth of tea into the harbour. This incident is known as "The Boston Tea Party."

The British government, shocked and angered by this act of lawlessness, passed four acts in 1774—"The Intolerable Acts"—three of which restricted the liberties of the people of Massachusetts. Both sides were now very angry. Each misunderstood the feelings of the other. When the Quebec Act of 1774 was passed by the British Parliament, the colonists were further angered because this Act forbade them to enter the lands west of the Appalachians. The colonists began to collect arms. In 1775, when British troops tried to destroy military stores collected by Massachusetts colonists, shots were fired on both sides and the War of Independence began.

The colonists went to war unwillingly, for they still considered themselves loyal subjects of the king. They appealed to him for relief from Parliament. But the king refused to read their petitions. It was not until 1776, after months of fighting, that the colonists issued the Declaration of Independence, announcing that the United Colonies were free and independent.

The Americans won the war after eight years of fighting. Underestimating the willpower of the colonists, Britain never sent sufficient troops, never employed capable generals, and failed to use the Royal

Navy to good advantage. In 1781, the Americans, with French naval aid, defeated the last effective British force. By 1783, Britain agreed to peace terms and recognized the United States of America as a free and independent nation, with territory stretching all the way from the Great Lakes to the Gulf of Mexico, and from the Atlantic to the Mississippi.

In 1788, to govern the new nation, various political leaders drew up the Constitution of the United States, a document which outlines the powers, duties and responsibilities of the national and state governments. In 1789, George Washington became the first president of the United States.

NINE / *Growth in British North America*

THE UNITED EMPIRE LOYALISTS

SETTLEMENT IN NOVA SCOTIA

NEW BRUNSWICK BECOMES A PROVINCE, 1784

CAPE BRETON BECOMES A PROVINCE, 1784

SETTLEMENTS ALONG THE ST. LAWRENCE
AND THE LOWER LAKES

THE FUR TRADE MOVES WEST AND NORTH

THE NOR'WESTERS VERSUS THE HUDSON'S
BAY COMPANY

THE NORTH WEST COMPANY

JAY'S TREATY, 1794

VITUS BERING IN THE NORTH PACIFIC, 1741

THE SEA OTTER

CAPTAIN COOK ON THE PACIFIC COAST, 1778

THE JOHN MEARES INCIDENT, 1789

CAPTAIN VANCOUVER ON THE PACIFIC COAST,
1792-1794

ALEXANDER MACKENZIE

SIMON FRASER AND DAVID THOMPSON

THE CONSTITUTIONAL ACT OF 1791

UPPER AND LOWER CANADA

BRITISH NORTH AMERICA

54

THE UNITED EMPIRE
LOYALISTS

The American Revolution created the United States of America. It also created British North America.

The conflict between the Thirteen Colonies and Great Britain drove some British people out of the Atlantic colonies and into Nova Scotia and Quebec. These people were destined to build British North America, a second British Empire in the lands north of the United States.

Many persons living in the Thirteen Colonies had been opposed to the war with Britain. Those who supported the unity of the British Empire were labelled Tories by the rebellious colonists. When king and Parliament refused to recognize the Declaration of Independence, the Tories found themselves treated as traitors by their fellow Americans. During the War of Independence, many of these *United Empire Loyalists*, as they called United themselves, fought with the British against the Americans and, Loyalists as a result, their homes and properties were taken over. The Loyalists who stayed in the colonies and took no part in the actual fighting suffered injuries and insults.

By the terms of peace in 1783, Congress agreed to ask the states to restore or pay for Loyalist property taken over during the war, but the states refused to do so. Since most American communities were bitter and spiteful towards them, thousands of Loyalists left the colonies during and after the war. Most of them emigrated after the war, happy to accept the promises of the British government to give them grants of land, food rations and payments of money in proportion to what they claimed to have lost. They found their way to Europe, the British Isles, the West Indies, Newfoundland, Nova Scotia and Quebec.

379

It is not known precisely how many sought new homes in the northern colonies, but their number probably lay somewhere between 30,000 and 40,000. Among these Loyalists were professional men, government officials, wealthy planters and prosperous merchants, but the majority were persons without special wealth or influence — tradesmen, teachers, clergymen, storekeepers and farmers. There were, too, many discharged British soldiers who did not wish to remain among the hostile citizens of the United States.

Loyalists move northward   Starting early in 1783, Loyalists began moving northward. Large parties arrived in Nova Scotia at Halifax, Annapolis Royal and Port Rosway (re-named Shelburne). Most of the immigrants came from New York, New Jersey and Pennsylvania.

The Loyalists were chiefly of English, Scottish and Irish ancestry, although there were some of Dutch and German origin. About 2,000 negroes also sought refuge in the north. About three-quarters of all immigrating Loyalists arrived in Nova Scotia and approximately two-thirds of these remained to make permanent homes. The arrival of the Loyalists actually doubled the population of Nova Scotia.

Loyalists in Nova Scotia   Pleased to receive the new citizens, the Nova Scotia government provided land for the newcomers. Loyalists arriving without any means were fed at public expense, and tools for building and cultivating were provided for their use. Large land grants were made to disbanded soldiers and to groups of civilians, while smaller grants were made to other individuals. Some Loyalist families found homes near established settlements; others cleared land in the unpopulated areas of the St. John river valley, Cape Breton Island and Prince Edward Island (the former Ile St. Jean).

In May, 1783, Governor Parr of Nova Scotia wrote to the British government:

About 7,000 Refugees, including Women and Children, have just arrived from New York; upwards of 3,000 of them are clearing the Country and building a Town, agreeable to a regular Plan sent them, at Port Rosway, a most excellent Harbour, 33 Leagues from here W.S.W.; near 3,000 are gone to settle upon the River St. John in the Bay of Fundy; the remainder are gone to Annapolis Royal. I have hitherto done everything in my power to relieve the distresses of these poor unfortunate people.

Few of the wealthy or influential Loyalists who arrived in Nova Scotia remained as permanent settlers. However, those people who did stay were of good stock and somewhat better educated than the older residents of the colony. It was not long before some of them were seated in the colonial assembly and discussing provincial affairs. Loyalist energy was important in founding schools and in the creation of King's Colleges, one of which still exists as part of Dalhousie University, Halifax, another being the ancestor of the present University of New Brunswick at Fredericton.

In the beginning, relations between the Loyalists and the established residents of Nova Scotia were not always harmonious. The newcomers were inclined to feel a bit superior, sometimes referring to the original inhabitants as "bluenoses." As a result the "bluenoses" were quick to call the newcomers "refugees." Fortunately, this early ill-feeling was short lived. Both old and new citizens found they had to work in harmony to solve the problems that faced the colony.

Loyalists who settled on the Bay of Fundy near the mouth of the St. John River were an active independent group who soon demanded a government of their own. They had no wish to be governed by an assembly in Halifax. By 1784, they were so suc- **Birth** cessful in their demands that the province of New Brunswick was **of New** **Brunswick,** created. The new province extended from the St. Croix river **1784** to the Quebec boundary and met Nova Scotia at the old dividing line between French and English of the Isthmus of Chignecto.

The New Brunswickers quickly became prosperous. Up and down the St. John river, they cut down the forests of white pine and sold timber to Britain or used it to build sailing ships. All along the St. John river they cleared the ground, grew crops of wheat and potatoes, and raised fine herds of cattle.

Edward Winslow, a Loyalist from New England, played a most important part in gaining separate government for New

Eighteenth-century fire-fighting equipment. In many early settlements regulations were issued to deal with the threat of fire. Settlers were ordered to clean their chimneys regularly, to keep permanent ladders on their roofs, and place two buckets of water near their front door. The large fire engine shown above was given in 1784 to Loyalists at Shelburne, Nova Scotia, by King George III. It is an early hand-pump type, which remained in general use until well into the nineteenth century. Anywhere up to ten volunteer firefighters were needed to operate it during a fire, while more men formed a bucket chain to the nearest source of water. Note the leather bucket. The smaller fire engine also belongs to the same period. Although very crude, these machines could throw water a remarkable distance, some of them being able to project water to a height of 160 feet.

Brunswick. He must have had great hopes for the new province because in a letter he wrote:

> I cannot speak or write of that country about the river St. John without making use of extravagant expressions. . . I acknowledge myself to be a little romantic, but I will appeal to . . . others who have observed it without being so much in raptures, whether they ever beheld a more delightful grass country, better cattle, or better grain or more abundant crops.

By 1785, the trading post at the mouth of the St. John river was a growing city and was given the name of Saint John.

In 1784, Cape Breton, too, was given a government of its own, and Loyalists were invited to find homes there. In 1784 and 1785, some 3,000 arrived, and established themselves on the east side of Sydney harbour with its "valuable beaches" and conveniences for curing and storing fish. However, since land in Cape Breton was not granted freehold, many Loyalists went on to Quebec. Prince Edward Island, a separate province since 1769, also received several hundred Loyalist settlers, mainly farmers and disbanded soldiers.

The majority of Loyalists who settled in the east arrived by ship. But thousands crossed the borders of Quebec (shortly to be created the province of Lower Canada) after river journeys or difficult overland treks from western New York, western Pennsylvania and New Hampshire. Some reached Montreal and Quebec City by way of the Lake Champlain route; others moved into western Quebec (shortly to be created the province of Upper Canada) by crossing the Niagara and Detroit rivers. Some actually arrived during winter on horseback, or riding in sleighs loaded with food supplies, bedding and a few treasured articles from their former homes.

By the end of 1783, there were about 7,000 Loyalists in the province of Quebec, nearly all of whom lacked sufficient money, food or clothing. General Haldimand, Governor of Quebec, came to their aid. He bought Indian lands in the western regions of Quebec lying along the upper St. Lawrence and the eastern end of Lake Ontario, where his surveyors laid out fourteen new townships.

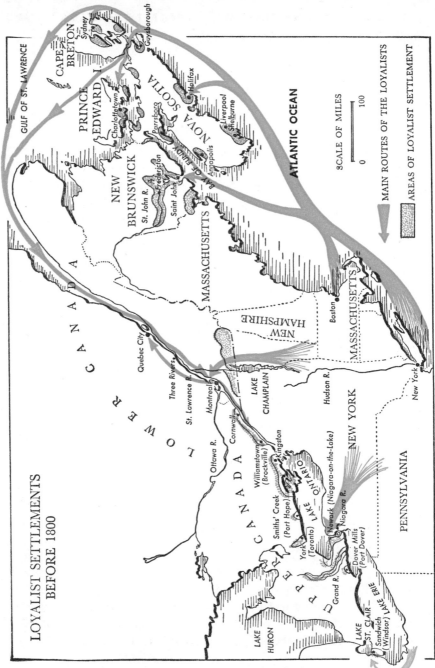

LOYALIST SETTLEMENTS
BEFORE 1800

SCALE OF MILES

0   100

MAIN ROUTES OF THE LOYALISTS

AREAS OF LOYALIST SETTLEMENT

ATLANTIC OCEAN

GULF OF ST. LAWRENCE

CAPE BRETON I.

Sydney

Guysborough

PRINCE EDWARD I.

Charlottetown

NOVA SCOTIA

Halifax

Parrsborg

Liverpool

Shelburne

Annapolis

BAY OF FUNDY

NEW BRUNSWICK

St. John R.

Fredericton

Saint John

MASSACHUSETTS

LOWER CANADA

Quebec City

Three Rivers

St. Lawrence R.

Montreal

Ottawa R.

Cornwall

Williamstown (Brockville)

Kingston

Smiths' Creek (Port Hope)

York (Toronto)

Newark (Niagara-on-the-Lake)

Niagara R.

Dover Mills (Port Dover)

Grand R.

Sandwich (Windsor)

LAKE ST. CLAIR

LAKE ERIE

LAKE HURON

UPPER CANADA

LAKE ONTARIO

LAKE CHAMPLAIN

NEW HAMPSHIRE

MASSACHUSETTS

Boston

Hudson R.

NEW YORK

New York

PENNSYLVANIA

In 1784, groups of Loyalists with supplies and equipment were transported in boats from Quebec to the areas of settlement. Such Loyalist officers as Colonel Stephen de Lancey, Sir John Johnson and Major Jessup, led the Loyalists and ex-soldiers under their charge by boat up the St. Lawrence to the new townships.

Sir John Johnson was the foremost Loyalist in Canada. In 1774, he had succeeded his father as superintendent of Indian Affairs in New York. The Mohawks in particular held him in great esteem. During the War of Independence, Sir John raised two battalions of the King's Royal Regiment of New York among his Loyalist friends in the Mohawk valley to fight the American rebels.

The newcomers were positioned in religious, racial and military groups. Sir John Johnson led one of his battalions, a mixture of Scots and Germans, to a new township on the upper St. Lawrence. The second battalion was settled near Cataraqui (Kingston). Roman Catholic Scots moved into one region. Protestant Scots occupied a neighbouring area. German Protestants settled next to them. English people accepted land grants along the Bay of Quinte. By the October of 1784, 4,000 persons were settled along the north-eastern shores of Lake Ontario and the upper St. Lawrence, and they had cleared over 1,000 acres of land. Log houses had been constructed, and some fall wheat was sown on the newly-cleared land. *Settlements west of Montreal*

Other smaller settlements had appeared earlier along the Niagara River. During the War of Independence, Fort Niagara on the east bank of the river had served as headquarters for Colonel John Butler and his Rangers. His men and their families lived in log barracks on the west bank. They were soon joined by hundreds of Loyalists who journeyed to the Niagara area from New York and Pennsylvania. By 1780, these people were living on land near the barracks and selling the wheat they grew to the Ranger companies and Loyalist regiments based at Fort Niagara. After the peace of 1783, the discharged Loyalists settled at Niagara on land granted them by Governor Haldimand. *Settlements at Niagara*

A Loyalist settler works his land along the shore of the upper St. Lawrence. In the background is his rude cabin of log construction. This typical early home, usually twenty feet in length and slightly less in width, was built of white oak or pine. At the corners of the structure the logs were interlocked or morticed. Large cracks between the logs were filled or "stubbed" with moss, mud, woodchips, and eventually with plaster. A great stone fireplace dominated one end of the cabin. Even this primitive house was superior to some of the homes built, for in a number of cases mere shacks were erected. In the background is a fleet of *bâteaux* carrying settlers further up river. The journey, made in fleets of up to twenty boats, was always difficult and dangerous due to various rapids. The old seigneury of Sorel, lying between Montreal and Quebec, served as base camp for these river expeditions.

Joseph Brant and the Mohawk Loyalists

The Six Nations—the Iroquois—remained loyal to Britain during the War of Independence. They took this stand chiefly through the influence of Sir John Johnson. Their great chief at that time was Thayendanegea, or Joseph Brant, as he is known to history. A Mohawk who had received a good British education, he enjoyed the confidence of his own people and many British officials. He led the tribes against the Americans in the War of Independence. After the war, Brant applied to the British for permission for his people to continue living under the protection of the British flag.   General Haldimand purchased land between Lakes Ontario, Erie and Huron from the Missisauga Indians, and gave a tract of land six miles wide along the length of the Grand River to the Mohawks and others of the Six Nations who wished to join them. Mohawks are living there today.

Since the Loyalist settlements were located within the bounds Problems of settlement of the Province of Quebec, land was held by *seigneurial tenure.* According to instructions received by Governor Haldimand from the British government:

> Land granted to the Loyalists is to be divided into distinct Seigneuries or Fiefs, to extend from two to four leagues in front, and from three to five leagues in depth, if situated upon a navigable river, otherwise to be run square, or in such shape and in such quantities, as shall be convenient and practicable.

According to the same instructions, land was to be allotted to individuals in the following manner:

> To every Master of a Family, One Hundred Acres, and Fifty Acres for each person of which his Family shall consist.
> To every single Man Fifty Acres.
> To every Non-Commissioned Officer of Our Forces reduced [honourably discharged] in Quebec Two Hundred Acres.
> To every private Man reduced as aforesaid One Hundred Acres.
> And for every Person in their Family Fifty Acres.

On first arriving in western Quebec, the Loyalists frequently lived in tents until they were given land upon which to build a home. The actual selection of farming lots was made when the settler drew a numbered slip of paper from a collection of slips made out by one of Haldimand's officials.

Some Loyalists, who were accustomed to frontier life, found no great difficulty in clearing land and building homes, but others, who had done little outdoor work, endured great hardship. Many a Loyalist woman hid her tears as she viewed the crude cabin her husband and sons were building.

In addition to land, the British government tried to supply the new settlers with food, tools, farm implements, seed, clothing and live-stock. The total cost of the whole operation was about

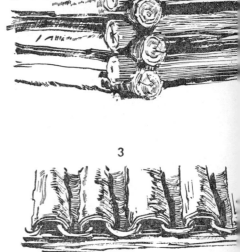

Types of Loyalist log construction. In (1), the squared log method, although slow, gave a more finished appearance to a house than (2), the cruder, round log construction. (3) is an example of roof construction commonly used in early dwellings. Basswood bark was so arranged that the convex and concave surfaces over-lapped. Working on the same principle as the tile roofs in Spanish colonies, the bark formed a sloping surface, which, with the aid of troughs, drained away rainwater.

$30,000,000, an expenditure of about $750 for each Loyalist. A list of goods requested for each family in a group settling near Cataraqui reads:

> Boards, Nails and Shingles . . . Eighty Squares of Window Glass . . . Arms & Ammunition, One Felling Ax, one Plough Shear & Coulter, Leather for Horse Collers, Two Spades, Three Iron Wedges, Fifteen Iron Harrow Teeth, Three Hoes, One Inch & half Inch Auger, Three Chisels (sorted), One Gouge, Three Gimblets, One Hand Saw & Files, One Nail Hammer, One Drawing Knife, One Frow for Splitting Shingles, Two Scythes & One Sickle, One Broad Ax, One Grind Stone allowed for every Three Families, One Years Clothing . . . Two Years Provisions . . . Two Horses, Two Cows and Six Sheep.

The arrival of United Empire Loyalists in the northern colonies created a British North America that was largely English-speaking and intensely loyal to Great Britain. Those who settled in western Quebec were not content with French civil law or the seigneurial system. They were soon to demand laws and land regulations more closely in keeping with British custom and tradition.

5 5

THE FUR EMPIRE OF
THE WEST

It is quite clear from the journals of Hudson's Bay Company servants that the British trader-adventurers who flocked into Canada behind Wolfe's army did not lose much time in exploiting the French fur trade. After the fall of Quebec in 1760, the elder Alexander Henry and other British adventurers made their way from Montreal into the old fur-trading empire of France. As early as the summer of 1761, the Indians reported to the factor of Moose Factory that the British were "as thick as Muskettos" on the streams flowing into James Bay.

By 1766, British traders had reached the southern part of Early British traders in the west La Vérendrye's domain — Lake Winnipeg, the Red river, the Assiniboine river and Lake Winnipegosis. They went into the Saskatchewan country, as Vérendrye had done, and discovered the rich, heavy winter pelts it produced. They learned the routes, crossroads and strategic portages of this vast region. On the Saskatchewan, the Montrealers heard of an area even wealthier in furs, a region where the plains ended and the forests began again, forests laced with streams and swamps and dotted with lakes. Beyond all this was the tundra—hundreds of square miles of streams, lakes and muskeg. In this tremendous area called the north-west, winter lengthened to seven, eight, nine months of the year—but furs were correspondingly heavy, rich and glossy-shining.

The Montrealers made plans to move in among the tribes— the Chipewyans, the Red Knives, the Dog Ribs, the Caribous and the Stoneys—living in the north-west. Two seasons of trading in these territories and a man could become rich. This was reason enough for going into these subarctic regions, two thousand miles beyond Grand Portage, which in turn was two thousand miles from Montreal. When they had succeeded in overcoming the hostility of the Indians, these men established a prosperous trade, which finally spread west to the Rockies and north to the barren lands bordering the Arctic.

The story of this heroic development is one of the most colourful tales in history. It tells of daring exploits, bold explorations and business successes without equal in the early history of this country.

Eighteenth-century British trade goods.   Grouped around a copper kettle are two kinds of knives, a powder horn and two axeheads.   The axeheads of this period were unlike those of the French (page 188), being counterbalanced for ease in handling.   The smaller objects are gun flints and silver ornaments.   These ornaments first appeared about 1765 and were a trading staple during the following fifty years.   Other trade goods in demand by tribesmen were woollen cloth and blankets, tobacco, thread, twine, silk and cotton handkerchiefs, nets, fish hooks and beads.

Two conditions favoured the ventures of the individual British traders working out of Montreal, the "Pedlars from Quebec" as the Hudson's Bay Company men contemptuously described them. First, they had at their disposal an ample supply of inexpensive trade goods—ammunition, hatchets, knives, blankets, beads and kettles. These articles were of better quality than those used in former years by the French traders. Second, the British were able to employ experienced French-Canadian *voyageurs,* canoemen who possessed the skill, knowledge and stamina to operate the long canoe routes that were to link Montreal and the lands hundreds of miles away in the north-west.

These British adventurers began to give themselves the proud title, *Nor'Westers,* signifying that they had the courage to live and trade in the wild country to the north and west of the Great Lakes. These independent businessmen were Scots, English, Yankee and French-Canadian, but the Scottish traders were by far the shrewdest and the most successful. In addition to Alexander Henry there were the Frobisher brothers, Joseph, Benjamin and Thomas, who traded on the Saskatchewan river, Peter Pond who established the first post in the Athabaska country, James McGill who had a particularly keen business sense and Simon McTavish who built a great fortune out of furs.

Nor' Westers

The Nor'Westers knew that by royal charter the Hudson's Bay Company had special trading rights in all the lands whose rivers drained into Hudson Bay, but that did not deter them from invading the richest fur lands on the continent. In fact, the Nor'Westers made bold plans to establish inland fur trading stations that would intercept Indians going down to Hudson Bay to trade their winter pelts.

As trade moved farther north and west, the difficulties of transportation increased and costs rose to high levels. It now took two seasons to get trade goods from Montreal to the Indians. To meet this challenge, the Nor'Westers developed an efficient transportation system, which served as the railway of its day. To make this system work smoothly and on schedule, they used brigades of birch-bark canoes and employed French-Canadian voyageurs.

Alexander Mackenzie, who was himself to become a famous Nor'Wester, has described the loading of canoes:

> The necessary number of canoes being purchased . . . the goods formed into packages, and the lakes and rivers free of ice, which they usually are in the beginning of May, they are then despatched from Lachine, eight miles above Montreal, with eight or ten men in each canoe, and their baggage, and sixty-five packages of goods, six hundred weight of biscuit, two hundred weight of pork, three bushels of pease, for the men's provisions; two oil-cloths to cover the goods, a sail, etc., a towing line, a kettle, and a sponge to bail out the water, with a quantity of gum and bark to repair the vessel. A European on seeing one of these slender vessels thus laden, heaped up, and sunk within six inches of the water, would think his fate inevitable in such a boat. . . .

Canoe transportation   The large freight canoes, thirty-five to forty feet in length, were capable of carrying from four to five tons of cargo. If these were remarkable watercraft, the men who operated them were equally so—the wiry voyageurs who paddled from dawn to dusk, stopping only for an occasional pipe of "tabac." Feathers stuck jauntily in their gay caps, the men swung their cedar paddles and sang the old songs of New France. At the portages, where it was necessary to unload and carry the packs, the voyageurs performed daily miracles of strength and endurance. On the trot, a voyageur could carry two packs, each weighing ninety pounds.

Up the Ottawa river, along the Mattawa river, across Lake Nipissing, down the French river to Georgian Bay, and then north across Lake Superior moved the big canoes, finally arriving at Grand Portage.

Grand Portage   Grand Portage, which lay forty miles south-west of present-day Fort William, became a most important place. It was here that *les canots du maître,* the freight canoes from Montreal, met *les canots du nord,* the lighter canoes from the north-west, that brought down cargoes of furs. After days of paddling, Grand Portage was a welcome sight to all tired travellers. As the Montreal canoes touched shore, there were shouts of welcome, the shaking of hands, the slapping of backs and the excited exchange of greetings among old friends.

Here at Grand Portage business arrangements were completed, cargoes were transferred and agreements were made between voyageurs and employers. Here the Montreal traders talked with *les hivernants,* their "wintering partners", who looked after business on the trading grounds of the far north-west. Taking advantage of their respite from work, the voyageurs enjoyed themselves in noisy, drinking celebrations.

Alexander Mackenzie has described the arrival of voyageurs from the north-west:

> The North men being arrived at Grand Portage, are regaled with bread, pork, butter, liquor and tobacco, and such as have not entered into agreements during the winter, which is customary, are contracted with, to return and perform the voyage for one, two or three years; their accounts are also settled and such as choose to send any of their money to Canada, receive drafts to transmit to their relatives or friends, and as soon as they can be got ready, which requires no more than a fortnight, they are again despatched to their respective departments.

When all business arrangements were completed, the *canots du maître* turned back toward Montreal loaded with furs, and the *canots du nord* turned north and west, laden with food supplies and trade goods.

At this time the Hudson's Bay Company had no such long canoe routes to maintain. Sailing ships transported goods and furs directly between Great Britain and the Bay. No further movement of trade goods was necessary because the Indians themselves travelled down the rivers to exchange their furs at the posts. However, the Company began to feel the effect of the vigorous efforts put forth by the Montrealers. As Nor'Wester posts appeared on the Saskatchewan and on Lake Athabaska in the north, the amount of furs moving toward the Bay was greatly reduced. In 1772, an employee of the Hudson's Bay Company, Matthew Cocking, was sent inland to gather information about the activities of the "Pedlars." More than surprised at what he

Rivalry with Hudson's Bay Company

saw, Cocking recommended that the Company should do everything to regain the trade which was being lost.   A report sent
to the head office in England stated:

> The Situation of your Affairs in this Country is very unpromising.
> I have not been indolent, I have gained certain Information of what
> is doing Inland, & think it is my duty to lay before you the success
> of my Enquiry. Your Trade at York Factory & Severn is greatly
> diminished, the Keskochewan (Saskatchewan) Indians Who are the
> support of it being intercepted by the Canadian Pedlars who are yearly
> Gaining fresh Influence over them by supplying them with Goods
> Inland. The Indians resort thither in the Winter for Ammunition &
> the whole body of the Natives build their Canoes not far distant
> from the residence of the Traders to whom they resort to Purchase
> Ammunition and other Articles in the Spring & finding they can
> procure Tobacco & other Necessarys so near & being kept in Liquor,
> every Inducement to visit the Company's Factorys is forgot, & the
> prime furs are picked out and traded, the refuse is tied up & brought
> down to us by the Leading Indians and their followers.

By 1774, the "Pedlars" were making such inroads on the
trade of York Factory that the Hudson's Bay Company sent
another trusted employee to establish its first inland trading post.
This man, Samuel Hearne, had already explored his way down
Founding of the Coppermine river to the Arctic Ocean.   Hearne founded
Cumberland Cumberland House, a post on the Saskatchewan river, not far
House from another trading station that had been erected two years
before by the Nor'Westers.

Cumberland House marks the beginning of what was to
become the most violent competition in fur trade history.

The Company, warned by Hearne that "sixty canoes came
inland from the Grand Portage in 1774", placed still more posts
in the interior to provide keen competition for the Montrealers.
As trade expanded even further north and further west into
the Athabaska country, the Nor'Westers found transportation
expenses rising to dangerous levels.   It was, in fact, becoming
increasingly difficult to compete on profitable terms with their
rivals on the Bay.

The Montrealers had co-operated with each other to a limited extent, but in the main tended to work as individuals or as

partners.   As a result there was a considerable amount of costly
and wasteful competition among themselves.   To go beyond the
Saskatchewan had been costly enough.   To go into the high north
would be costlier still.   It became obvious to the shrewder traders
that if they united to form a large company, they could reduce
expenses, increase profits and still keep ahead of the Hudson's
Bay Company which, at Cumberland House, was now doing busi-
ness in "Pedlar" territory.   In consequence, the *North West Com-* **North West**
pany was established by 1783 and was expanded in 1787.   By this **Company, 1783**
latter date, most of the leading traders of Montreal were in this
new company, which pooled its trade goods and whose members
agreed not to undercut each other's prices.

A canoe brigade travelling to Grand Portage on Lake Superior.   The famous
voyageur canoe was built using Indian methods of construction.   The ribs were made
of cedar or pine, durable woods that were readily available.   The birch-bark
sheathing was cut to a thickness of about one-eighth of an inch and the pieces sewn
together with spruce or cedar roots softened by boiling.   Joints were made watertight by applying spruce or tamarack gum, or a pitch made of resin and tallow.   The
canoe was amazingly light.   Even though used to carry four- and five-ton cargoes,
the craft itself weighed less than 500 pounds.   Sails, although dangerous on a boat
without a keel, were sometimes carried and used under favourable conditions.   The
tireless French-Canadian voyageur often paddled eighteen hours a day, sometimes
covering a distance of about one hundred miles.   In addition, he thought nothing
of the numerous portages, over which the entire cargo had to be carried.

The management of the North West Company was entrusted to the Frobisher brothers and Simon McTavish who were to be paid suitable commissions on all business transactions. Thus, the Montrealers formed a useful partnership with management placed in capable hands. In the beginning business flourished, as indicated in Alexander Mackenzie's journal:

In 1788 the gross amount of the adventure for the year did not exceed forty thousand pounds, but by the exertion, enterprise and industry of the proprietors, it was brought in eleven years, to triple that amount and upwards; yielding proportionate profits, and surpassing, in short, anything known in America.

Some idea of the extensive operations of the North West Company may be gained from the fact that the number of employees included fifty clerks, seventy-one interpreters, 1,120 voyageurs and thirty-five guides. In a good year the company was capable of handling the following quantities of furs: 106,000 beaver skins, 2,100 bear skins, 1,500 fox skins, 4,600 otter skins, 17,000 muskrat skins, 32,000 marten skins, 1,800 mink skins, 500 buffalo robes, 6,000 lynx skins, 600 wolverine skins, 1,650 fisher skins, 100 raccoon skins, 3,800 wolf skins, 700 elk skins, 750 deer skins and 1,200 deer skins dressed.

The North West Company was essentially a group of fur trading firms or individuals formed to avoid the evils of competition. It was a partnership of business interests and not a chartered company as was the Hudson's Bay Company. The North West Company owed its success largely to the fact that its "wintering partners", with a personal interest in the company, proved much more aggressive than the poorly-paid employees of the rival organization on the Bay.

British posts in American territory Further to the east, British traders were still using the posts south of the Great Lakes in what was legally American territory. They were able to do so only because British redcoats still occupied the fur posts. Britain which had signed away this territory in the treaty of 1783—insisted on maintaining post garrisons until the Americans saw fit to compensate Loyalist losses. However, Britain really held on to the fur posts to please the Montreal traders who objected to losing trade in the Great Lakes area, and also to pacify the Indians who insisted on retaining their hunting-grounds.

The Americans decided to push the British out.

The Indians, sensing trouble and angered by the entry over the years of American frontiersmen, rose against the Americans and defeated the first two armies sent against them.   However, at the battle of Fallen Timbers, the Americans crushed Indian resistance.

By this time, Britain and the United States were anxious to find a peaceful settlement.   Accordingly, the American government sent John Jay to London.   The result of the discussions was **Jay's Treaty, 1794** the signing, in 1794, of an agreement known as *Jay's Treaty*.   One of its most important terms was that Britain agreed to evacuate all posts located on American soil (i.e. in the area south of the Great Lakes), posts that she had promised to surrender in the treaty of 1783.

Thus, by Jay's Treaty, Montreal traders were eventually forced to withdraw from the region that had formed such a vital part of the old French fur trading empire.   In 1796, the last red-coats marched out of the territory of the United States.   From then on, fur traders journeyed to the lands spreading westward to the Rocky Mountains.

56

THE PACIFIC COAST

Although traders of the Hudson's Bay and North West Companies pushed far to the north and west, none of them had as yet crossed the mountains to the Western Sea.

Voyages of
Vitus Bering
However, the Pacific shores were known to a few daring European seamen, one of the earliest being a Danish navigator, Vitus Bering, who sailed in the service of the Russian government. Bering made two amazing journeys to North America, each of which involved a 6,000 mile overland trip from Europe to eastern Siberia, and then a voyage northward into the Pacific Ocean. In 1728, during the first voyage, he sailed through the waters now known as the Bering Sea and the Bering Strait, and in so doing disproved the ancient tale that Asia and America were joined together.

On his voyage of 1741, he skirted the coast of what is now northern British Columbia, made a landing (in Alaska) and then headed back toward Kamchatka by way of the Aleutian Islands. In the course of this second voyage he and his men discovered a sea animal that possessed a beautiful, soft, glossy fur—the sea otter. The great beauty and richness of its fur became its death warrant. After 1741, the sea otter was to be hunted down and killed by hunters in the same fierce manner that the beaver was pursued on the mainland. The demand for its skin, perhaps the finest of all furs, was to keep on rising until a good pelt sold for $2,000.

Russian traders moved eastward into the Aleutians and on to the north-west mainland of North America in search of the sea-otter pelts that found a ready market in China. Bering's explorations and the activities of these traders laid the foundations of Russia's later claim to the Aleutians and to Alaska.

Captain Cook's
Third Voyage,
1776-1779
Thirty-five years after Bering's second voyage, a great British navigator, Captain James Cook, began his famous third voyage of discovery, one which lasted from 1776 to 1779. Already well-

398

acquainted with the southern regions of the Pacific, Cook now turned to a careful exploration of the northern half of the great ocean. His prime purpose was to find a north-east passage to Europe, a passage that was believed to lie in the Arctic regions above North America.

Moving north and east from the Sandwich Islands (Hawaii), Cook sighted land to the north of California. As he sailed north, fog and bad weather prevented him from seeing the mouth of a large river (the Columbia) and also hid from him the entrance of a large strait (Juan de Fuca). He finally entered an inlet he called King George's Sound (Nootka Sound) off the west coast of what he thought was the mainland and what really was an island (Vancouver Island). Here he made such friendly contacts with **Sea otter trade** the Nootka Indians that a brisk trade in sea otter pelts suddenly developed. Cook and his men had not come prepared to engage in trade, and thus they had difficulty in finding items of barter to satisfy the Indians. Cook describes their difficulty in his journal:

> Our articles of traffic consisted for the most part of mere trifles and yet we were put to our shifts to find a constant supply even of these. Beads and such other toys, of which I still had some left, were in little estimation. Nothing would go down with our visitors but metal; and brass had, by this time, supplanted iron; being so eagerly sought after, that before we left the place, hardly a bit of it was left in the ship, except what belonged to our necessary instruments. Whole suits of clothing were stripped of every button; bureaus of their furniture and copper kettles, tin canisters, candlesticks, and the like went to wreck, so that our American friends here got greater medly and variety of things from us, than any other nation whom we had visited on the course of the voyage.

After a few days, Cook found out that the Indian trading system was carried on far back into the coastal interior. He noted that the Indians already had iron, brass and copper objects. He reasoned that they must have got metal goods by trading with Indians of the interior who had contact with Europeans. Cook guessed that the European traders were "in Mexico or Canada".

His second guess was the right one—the "Pedlars from Quebec." On the Pacific coast, an Englishman saw trade goods that had crossed the continent.

Captain James Cook at Nootka Sound, 1778. In the account of his last voyage there are some fine descriptions of what Cook saw. There are also some accurate pictures of life among the coastal Indians drawn by John Webber, the official artist of the expedition. The Indian lodges were made of hewn planks with roofs of loose removable boards. Light and fresh air could be admitted by moving or rearranging the loose boarding. Woodworking tools were entirely of stone or bone until after the arrival of European trade goods. Carved doorposts and totem poles were observed by Captain Cook, although totem poles did not reach their greatest development until the Indians possessed metal tools. Note the framework of poles used for drying fish.

Leaving Nootka Sound, Cook made for 60°N., a point, a mountain peak, noted on the mainland by Bering, and then examined an inlet (Cook's Inlet) to the west. Finding it to be a river exit, he sailed to the west along the coast and then turned north again through the Bering Strait into the Arctic Ocean. He was stopped by a solid barrier of ice and was forced to turn back. He had proved that there was no North-West Passage through the continent of North America. But the ice had barred him from finding out whether it was possible to sail east or west through the Arctic. He would have to try again the next year.

Captain Cook did not live to make that try; he was killed in a skirmish with natives in the Sandwich Islands in 1779. His officers and men, however, continued homewards, stopping off for a time in China. There, the seamen were astonished and delighted at the high prices offered for their stocks of sea otter pelts. Joyfully, the seamen exchanged their furs for the money so eagerly thrust upon them.

The standard garment amongst the Nootkas was a tunic made of pine or cedar-bark fibres plaited together. Men often wore it off one shoulder. A warm cloak, made from the skins of the bear, wolf or sea otter, was sometimes thrown over the tunic, as shown in this chief's costume. Fibre hats of a rather unusual design were worn. The hair was worn long and often heavily greased. On special occasions, the Indians would ornament their hair with bits of white down, held in place by pine gum.

When the record of Cook's voyages was published in 1784, it aroused keen interest in the sea otter. It was not long before the British were sailing the west coast of North America in search of the glossy pelts. American traders, too, hearing of the new opportunities, moved northward in their sailing ships.

Disturbed by the fact that foreigners were trading in waters which they considered their own, the Spanish sent ships to investigate the rush of foreigners to the North Pacific. A Spanish officer reported that in addition to the Russian ships in the far north there were eleven British vessels, eight American, two Portuguese and one French, all engaged in the sea otter trade. His report is particularly interesting because it contains a splendid description of the sea otter:

> The sea otter is an amphibious animal, but it lives almost continuously in the water, and it travels to a considerable distance from the shore. It can be seen sometimes far out to sea swimming rapidly, carrying its young at its breast, and at other times on its back, as long as they are unable to swim for themselves; in this way it goes from place to place, generally with no other object than to find the small fish which serve for its food. . . . The beauty of the skin varies according to the age of the animal. When they are a few months old, they are covered with whitish fur which is ugly; this they presently lose, and there then appears another type of fur, short and dark. When the otter comes to its full growth, it sheds this fur and becomes entirely black, and its skin is then at its most beautiful. . . . Experts agree in preferring otter skins which have very close fine hair, black and shiny, with silver strands here and there glistening on the neck and belly.

The Spanish had not settled north of California, but they still claimed the whole Pacific coast of North America along with trading privileges and rights of navigation. What authority then, they asked, had other nations sailing and trading in the north Pacific?

John Meares Incident, 1789 In 1789, to demonstrate the power behind their claims, the Spanish seized several British ships and a tiny trading post at Nootka Sound. John Meares, the owner of the post, reported his losses to the British government, which in turn forwarded a protest to Spain. There was so much anger in Britain over the Spanish raid that war seemed quite possible. Peaceful discussion, however, led to an agreement by which the Spanish promised to restore Meares' property and to recognize the British right to the sea otter trade in the Nootka Sound region.

In 1791, another British navigator, Captain George Vancouver, was sent by the British government to find a water passage through North America from the Pacific to the Atlantic. The

Pacific was by no means strange to him. He had sailed with
Captain Cook on the famous third voyage.

At Nootka Sound, Vancouver met and talked with the Spanish **George Vancouver and Don Quadra**
representative, Don Quadra. For several days, they talked over
the matter of the ownership of the area, but the two men, despite

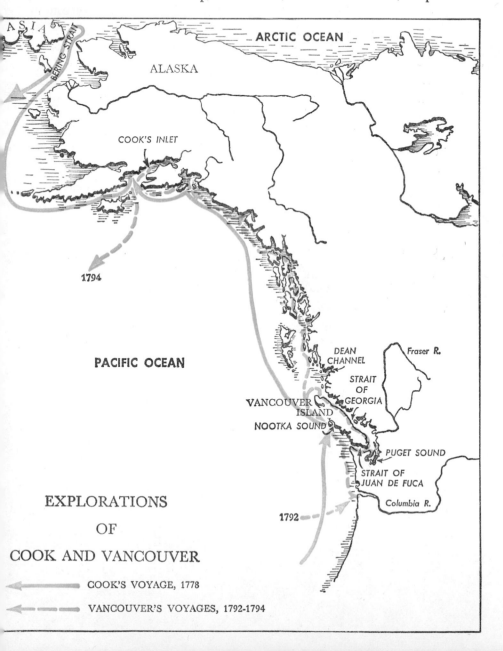

EXPLORATIONS

OF

COOK AND VANCOUVER

— COOK'S VOYAGE, 1778

--- VANCOUVER'S VOYAGES, 1792-1794

their mutual liking, were unable to work out a final settlement. Don Quadra was willing to hand back Meares' fort and a small bit of land, but Vancouver expected to get all the region surrounding Meares' property. The two parted friends, hoping that the problem would be solved by their respective governments. The Nootka problem was finally settled in 1795 when the Spanish government recognized British ownership of the Nootka region.

Vancouver charts Pacific coast, 1792-1794   However, Vancouver's voyage was by no means a failure. Between 1792 and 1794 he systematically explored and charted the northwestern coast of the continent. It was a magnificent piece of work, in the course of which Vancouver examined the Strait of Juan de Fuca, Puget Sound and the Strait of Georgia. He sailed around the large island behind Nootka Sound and called it "Quadra and Vancouver Island." But he couldn't find a water route into the interior.

Vancouver was unfortunate in other matters. He examined the mouth of a river, but claimed it for Britain too late. An American ship, the *Columbia,* commanded by a Captain Robert Gray, had discovered the river five months before and named it Columbia's River. At a later date, Vancouver failed to recognize an equally important river. When he saw very low land, apparently a swampy flat on the north shore of the Strait of Georgia, he had looked at, without knowing it, the mouth of what was to be called the Fraser river.

In June 1793, Vancouver was making soundings in a coastal inlet he called "Dean's Canal", now known as Dean Channel. Six weeks after Vancouver's departure, a Nor'Wester in a large, leaky canoe, manned by coastal Indians, came down the Bella Coola river into the salt water of Dean Channel.

5 7

THROUGH THE ROCKIES
TO THE PACIFIC

In 1789, Alexander Mackenzie was twenty-five years old. He had been a partner in the North West Company for four years and had been two years in the north country. In 1789, he built and operated Fort Chipewyan, a fur post on Lake Athabaska. Concerned with the tremendous cost of transporting goods and furs between his post and Montreal, Mackenzie hoped to find a water route from Lake Athabaska to the Pacific. If a short route could be discovered, then it would be possible to carry furs by canoe to the Pacific coast and from there to Britain by sailing ships. This would be a more efficient and inexpensive way of transporting furs over the thousands of miles between the north country and the London fur market.

However, Mackenzie was much more interested in exploration and discovery than in the fur trade. A restless, inquiring nature made it difficult for him to settle down to the monotonous routine of a northern fur post. After reading accounts of Captain Cook's third voyage in the Pacific, Mackenzie was more than anxious to get on with his own explorations. He set out for the Pacific Ocean. He was going to find Cook's Inlet at 60°N.

Without bothering to secure permission from the Company, he left Fort Chipewyan on Lake Athabaska in June, 1789, paddling northward in company with four voyageurs and a few Indians. On they went, down the Slave river, across Great Slave Lake and into the waters of a mighty river flowing westward. He was on his way to Cook's Inlet. On and on he travelled, week after week, but the river now led north. With the western mountains still in sight, he reached salt water—the Arctic Ocean. **Mackenzie reaches Arctic Ocean, 1789**

Greatly disheartened by the length of the river and its northward flow, Mackenzie named it *River Disappointment*. Today we are proud to call it the Mackenzie river, the longest river system in Canada. The journey of 1789 may have been a bitter one to

405

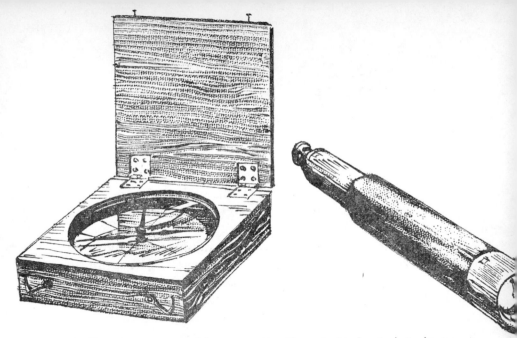

These instruments are of the type used by Alexander Mackenzie during his passage through the Rockies to the Pacific Ocean.   At the left is a pocket compass of 1790. By this date, most compasses were marked in degrees as well as points.   However, the telescope, similar to the one carried by Mackenzie, is thought to have been of too low a power for his needs.   His other instruments were generally inadequate even for his time.   They included a pocket sextant and a chronometer watch. The former was used to calculate latitude and the latter used to calculate longitude.

Mackenzie, but it actually was a very important piece of exploration that shed new light on North American geography. In a round trip of 102 days, Mackenzie and his men had made a journey of over 3,000 miles, but his route had not revealed a North-West passage. Mackenzie was now certain there was no truth in the idea of a waterway through the continent from the Pacific to the Atlantic.

Mackenzie did not give up hope of reaching the Pacific. He still had another route to test—the Peace river, which flowed out of the Rockies and into Lake Athabaska. In preparation for the exploration of this river, he spent a winter in England, where he obtained additional instruction and instruments for map-making.

By the spring of 1793 he was ready to begin his new adventure. With nine other men, he started up the turbulent Peace in a canoe twenty-five feet long, loaded down with 3,000 pounds of supplies and equipment.

ARCTIC OCEAN

Mackenzie R.

GREAT
BEAR LAKE

GREAT SLAVE LAKE

Slave R.

Fort Chipewyan

LAKE ATHABASKA

Peace R.

Parsnip R.

Blackwater R.

Athabaska R.

Bella
Coola R.

Fraser R.

VANCOUVER I.

PACIFIC

OCEAN

EXPLORATIONS

OF

ALEXANDER MACKENZIE

SCALE OF MILES

0   200   400

It was a difficult, frightening journey. The travellers were faced with boiling rapids, heartbreaking portages up and down cliff-like banks, and they were always conscious of the uncertainty of where they were heading and the constant danger of hostile Indians. Mackenzie was particularly horrified by the passage of the Peace River Canyon, which he described as "one white sheet of tumbling water." They moved westward on the Peace and then swung southward into one of its tributaries (the Parsnip). Reaching the headwaters of this stream, Mackenzie decided to cross overland to the upper reaches of another river (the Fraser).

Moving down it for some distance, he became uncertain that he was going in the right direction, changed his mind, and back-tracked to yet another river (the Blackwater), a western tributary of the Fraser. Up the Blackwater he paddled, and then marched overland to still another river (the Bella Coola). In borrowed canoes, the tattered, weary travellers pushed westward until they came to salt water.

Mackenzie reaches Pacific Ocean, 1793

Alexander Mackenzie experienced both pleasure and pain as he gazed at an ebbing tide in Dean Channel. He was pleased, of course, to be the first European to make the overland voyage to the Pacific, but he was bitterly disappointed that the "long, painful and perilous" way he had come was impossible to use as a fur route. He had hoped to find a portage of a few miles or up to half a day between Lake Athabaska and a smooth flowing river to the Pacific. Instead, he had discovered over 600 miles of wild mountain streams that are still barely navigable and for which his birch-bark canoes were totally unfitted.

Having calculated his latitude (50° 21' 48" north), Mackenzie marked the spot on which he stood. His journal states:

I now mixed up some vermillion in melted grease, and inscribed, in large characters, on the south-east face of the rock on which we had slept last night, this brief memorial—"Alexander Mackenzie, from Canada, by land, the twenty-second of July, one thousand seven hundred and ninety-three."

How amazed he would have been if Vancouver's ship had passed by while he was painting his proud message on the rock.

Activity increased on the Pacific coast. Russian traders were busy in Alaska and were eyeing the regions to the south. American traders and explorers were moving westward beyond the Mississippi towards the Pacific. In 1805, two of these, Meriwether Lewis and William Clark, actually crossed the Rockies and reached the mouth of the Columbia river. A Boston merchant, John Jacob Astor, quickly formed a fur company to trade in the Columbia region.

Lewis and Clark reach the Pacific, 1805

Realizing that other companies and nations had entered the race for furs, the North West Company made rapid plans to obtain a Pacific outlet for their furs. There was no time to be lost. In 1801 and 1802, North West Company attempts to cross the mountains failed. However, some years later, two Company men—Simon Fraser and David Thompson—succeeded.

During 1805 and 1806, Simon Fraser, a partner in the North West Company, established three posts on the upper reaches of two mountain rivers (the Peace and the Fraser) in what is now central British Columbia. The earliest of these posts, Fort McLeod, was the first European settlement west of the Rockies. Fraser was trying to work his way through to the coast by going down the Columbia river—if he could find it.

Fraser so admired the wild mountain beauty to the east of Fort McLeod that he called it *New Caledonia,* New Scotland, in memory of his mother's homeland. In 1807, Fraser began looking for the Columbia again, the river he knew would lead him to the Pacific, because every other river he tried led him elsewhere.

In 1808, Fraser set out with a party of twenty-three men to trace the route of what he guessed was the Columbia. In beginning this journey, he had no idea what a wild, perilous adventure it was to be. Day after day the canoes fought white rapids and hurtled through dark canyons. Fraser speaks of tremendous "gulphs and whirlpools . . . ready every moment to swallow a canoe with its contents and the people on board." Some five hundred miles later, Fraser and his men saw the Strait of Georgia and mountains on an island (Vancouver Island) across the water. When Fraser had calculated his position, he knew by Vancouver's charts that he was still north of the mouth of the Columbia.

Like Mackenzie, Simon Fraser was bitterly disappointed by failure. To begin with, the very fury of this mountain waterway made it impossible as a fur route to the Pacific. In addition, he had discovered that this was still not the Columbia. The North West Company had again been unable to find a Pacific outlet. Nevertheless, history records that in the exploration of the Fraser river, the fur trader had completed one of the most hazardous expeditions ever made on this continent.

Simon Fraser explores the Fraser River, 1808

In 1808, Simon Fraser made one of the most daring canoe voyages in the history of exploration. Fraser describes his passage through a narrow canyon in these words: *The water which rolls down this extraordinary passage in tumultuous waves and with great velocity had a frightful appearance . . . Once engaged, the die was cast, and the great difficulty consisted of keeping the canoes clear of the precipice on one side and of the gulfs formed by the waves on the other.*

David Thompson, the second of the two men sent over the Rockies, was originally an employee of the Hudson's Bay Company. But, because he was not free to explore, he resigned and joined the North West Company where, in the course of trading he was encouraged to travel, to explore, to survey and to draw up maps of various regions in western Canada.

Between the years 1797 and 1807 he had made a series of long journeys that took him from the Great Lakes and the headwaters of the Mississippi to the Rockies and north to the Peace and Athabaska rivers.   So it was that with all this travel and experience behind him, David Thompson, in 1807, made his way into what is now the south-eastern part of British Columbia.   There, on the upper reaches of a large river he called "The Kootenae," he built a trading post, Kootenay House.

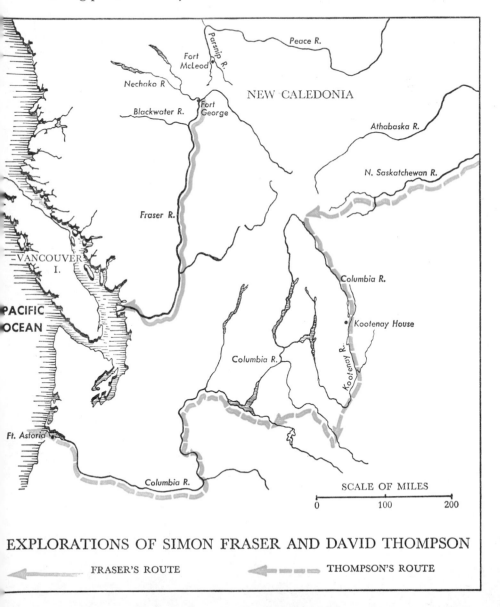

EXPLORATIONS OF SIMON FRASER AND DAVID THOMPSON

⟵ FRASER'S ROUTE   ⟵ --- --- ⟶ THOMPSON'S ROUTE

David
Thompson
explores the
Columbia,
1808-1811

Thompson had no idea on what river he was located, but he was determined to find out. He planned a careful, scientific examination of its whole length and its tributaries. In 1807, he ascended the river to its source, taking his time and paying much attention to trade with the Indians. He surveyed and mapped as he established posts on the upper "Kootenae" and its tributaries.

In 1811, when he eventually arrived at the mouth of this river, he was shocked to find a freshly-constructed fort on the left bank, flying the American flag. John Jacob Astor's American Company had sailed around Cape Horn and established Fort Astoria while Thompson was making his painstaking way up and down the river valley. It was the Columbia, and Astor's men had got there just four months ahead of Thompson.

Astor, however, found himself unable to compete with the vigorous Canadian traders. In 1813, he sold his post to the North West Company. This gave the Nor'Westers substantial control of the Pacific coast trade from the Columbia to Alaska.

David Thompson achieved much more than the exploration of the Columbia River. In the course of his trading ventures, he penetrated far into the present states of Montana, Idaho and Washington. His most important contribution to North American

Thompson's
map of the
North West

geography was the creation of his great map of the "North West." In 1813 and 1814, he worked almost continuously on the preparation of this amazing piece of work for the North West Company. (This was by no means the end of his explorations. In 1816, he was engaged by the International Boundary Commission to survey the boundary between Canada and the United States from St. Regis, Quebec, to the north-west corner of Lake of the Woods. He spent ten years in this work.)

Dr. J. B. Tyrell, a twentieth-century geologist and historian, writing of David Thompson, states:

David Thompson was the greatest land geographer who ever lived. . . . With extraordinary accuracy he placed on the map the main routes of natural travel in one million two hundred thousand square miles of Canada (approximately one-third of Canada's land area) and five hundred thousand square miles of the United States (about one-sixth of the U.S.) . . . Study of his journals shows that on foot, by canoe and on horseback he covered fifty-five thousand miles.

The searchings of Mackenzie, Fraser and Thompson had pushed the trade of the North West Company from Montreal to the Pacific Ocean. In 1794, the historic fur lands of the Great Lakes had been lost to the Americans by Jay's treaty. The North West Company had more than balanced this loss by opening up the west and carrying Britain's trade claims through the prairies and the high north and on to the Pacific coast by means of the Columbia river.

58

THE TWO CANADAS

While fur traders were moving further and further west across the continent, vital political events were taking place in the east.

Unrest among the Loyalists
The Loyalists who had settled along the St. Lawrence and the lower lakes were dissatisfied with the seigneurial system and with French civil law, both of which had been retained by the Quebec Act of 1774. The Loyalists were chiefly concerned with the problems of owning their own land, building homes, and constructing mills to grind grain. Accustomed to freehold land and British law, they were not prepared to live under an ancient land system and an unfamiliar code of law.

Unrest among the merchants
The British merchants of Montreal were even more dissatisfied. They disliked living in a province which, having no elected assembly, was ruled by a governor and his council. They were ambitious, aggressive men, many of them wealthy, who desired some say in government. In 1783 and 1784, they signed petitions requesting that the Quebec Act be repealed, except for those rights given French-Canadians regarding religion and property. The merchants asked for English law and an assembly elected by the people. Unfortunately, in their enthusiasm for change, the merchants claimed they spoke for the French-Canadians and for all English-speaking citizens. This was an error. The French-Canadians soon let it be known that they desired no changes in the Quebec Act. They feared that an alteration of the Act or a repeal of the Act would weaken their position. What is more, they did not appreciate the worth of English law, of trial by jury or an elected assembly with progressive ideas. French-Canadians opposed trial by jury because they suspected it would be useful only to the powerful and the wealthy. They opposed an elected assembly because they believed it would only serve to raise property taxes.

414

The Loyalists, too, expressed some disagreement with the requests made by the merchants. As a result, the new settlers drew up their own petitions, asking for English law, local courts, and assistance in the establishment of schools, roads, mills and churches.

While in the older, settled sections of British North America furniture of great beauty was being created (page 302), in the newly-settled areas of western Quebec (Upper Canada) people had little time to make anything but the simplest, and the most practical items of furniture. The pine chair shown above was made in 1785 by an early colonist living near the settlement of York. The seat is woven of split elm-bark. The cradle, too, would be difficult to beat for sheer simplicity and utility. Even these plain pieces of furniture were much better than those found in many an early pioneer home, where at times tree stumps served as chairs, and beds were constructed from a few poles. Sleeping on such beds must have been very uncomfortable, for in place of mattresses, the colonists normally used a pile of spruce boughs, or a bed-tick stuffed with leaves, moss or straw.

Their most striking demand, however, was for a separate government to rule the new settlements west of Montreal. The differences between the requests of the Loyalists and those of the merchants tended to split the English-speaking people into two groups.

As time went by, the demands for change became louder and more frequent. They caused considerable concern to the British government, because there arose the difficult question as to how it was possible to satisfy the English-speaking residents of Quebec without causing resentment among the French-Canadians. Great Britain was uncertain of what should be done. She had suffered a bitter experience during the American Revolution, and she was particularly anxious to avoid a blunder in British North America.

An early nineteenth-century box stove. The box type stove of this period was very popular since it gave a much more efficient heat for warmth and cooking than the open fireplace of many pioneer homes. The particular stove illustrated was used by the same family for over one hundred years. It was considered so valuable, that during the war of 1812, it was hidden at the bottom of a creek to prevent its being stolen by looting soldiers. This stove was manufactured by the earliest iron foundry in Canada, St. Maurice Forges, Quebec, a business established in 1737.

Various solutions were proposed by the British. It was suggested that Quebec, Nova Scotia, Prince Edward Island and Newfoundland should be united into one large colony or province. Then it was argued that these provinces were too far apart for any satisfactory union. In the end, it was not union but further division which was recognized when the British Parliament passed the *Constitutional Act* or *Canada Act* of 1791.

Constitutional Act, 1791

Following the Act of 1791, Quebec was divided into two parts —the eastern province of *Lower Canada* and the western province of *Upper Canada*.   The Ottawa river became the boundary between the two provinces, a boundary that placed most of the French-speaking citizens in Lower Canada and most of the English-speaking citizens in Upper Canada.

In addition to creating an entirely new province, the Act introduced important changes.   Land in Upper Canada was to be granted *freehold,* that is, ownership was given freely and permanently to the settler without his having to pay any rents or duties. In Lower Canada the old seigneurial system was to remain in force, except in the case of new grants when the applicant desired the freehold arrangement.

Because of the demands made by the English-speaking citizens, the Act also introduced alterations in the form of government.   Upper Canada was to have a governor and an elected assembly of at least sixteen members and Lower Canada a governor and an elected assembly of at least fifty members.   In addition to these assemblies or "lower houses" as they are sometimes called, the provinces were to have legislative councils or "upper houses" that would work under the direction of the provincial governor and his executive council.   Legislative and executive councils would be composed of men appointed by the governors of the two provinces. Laws would be made and passed by the assemblies and legislative councils.   The laws would be enforced by the governors and their executive councils. The Act also set aside land equal to one-seventh of all future lands owned by the Crown in each province for the purpose of supporting and maintaining a Protestant Church. All rents from these "clergy reserves" would be paid to a Protestant Church.

The chief purpose of the Constitutional Act was to permit the French and the British to work out their own problems by using political and land systems familiar and acceptable to each race. The British government hoped that in time the French-Canadians would recognize the superiority of British customs and usage and give up their own traditions and practices.   In this hope the government was to be disappointed; in Lower Canada the French-Canadians clung with determination to the ways they loved and respected.

In Upper Canada, events moved quickly.

**John Graves
Simcoe**   John Graves Simcoe was appointed the first Lieutenant-Governor of Upper Canada. A British officer who had commanded the Queen's Rangers in the War of Independence, Simcoe was a fiercely energetic man and a strong Loyalist. He was determined to do everything possible to recompense his fellow Loyalists for their losses in the United States during and after the War of Independence. He intended to see them settled on their own land, producing large, healthy crops, and their affairs carefully controlled by the government of Upper Canada. In short, he aimed to create a little Britain.

In July, 1792, Simcoe arrived at Niagara (now Niagara-on-the-Lake), which for a short time served as the capital of the province. Disliking the word "Niagara", Simcoe renamed the place Newark. It was there that he presided over the first government to meet in Upper Canada.

**First assembly
in Upper
Canada, 1792**   The first provincial assembly or legislature of Upper Canada was held on September 17th, 1792, in Freemasons' Hall and Butler's Barracks, two of four buildings, which in former years had been erected at Niagara. They were crude structures, little better than the first rough cabins built by the early pioneers. Opening day of the first legislature was an exciting one for the people of the region. Discharged soldiers, new settlers and some Iroquois, all in holiday attire, gathered to witness the event. Governor Simcoe, dressed in a uniform of scarlet and gold, rode in accompanied by a guard of honour of the Northumberland Fusiliers. Mrs. Simcoe was no less magnificent in appearance; she wore a dress of white satin brocaded with wreaths of flowers. The governor and his lady made a deep impression upon the watching men and women.

In beginning his address to the legislative council and the sixteen assembly men, Simcoe said:

Honourable gentlemen of the Legislative Council and gentlemen of the House of Assembly;—I have summoned you together under the authority of an Act of Parliament of Great Britain, passed in the last year, which has established the British Constitution and all the forms which secure and maintain it in this distant country.

The governor had complete faith in the future of the new province and its people, for he went on to say:

The Natural advantages of the Province of Upper Canada are inferior to none on this side of the Atlantic. There can be no separate interest through its whole extent. The British form of government has prepared the way for its speedy colonization, and I trust that your fostering care will improve the favourable situation, and that a numerous and agricultural people will speedily take possession of a soil and climate, which, under British law and the munificence with which His Majesty has granted the lands of the Crown, offer such manifest and peculiar encouragements.

The first session of the assembly lasted only a month, but in that time no less than eight acts were passed. These provided for British civil law, trial by jury, the erection of courthouses in four districts, and a toll was fixed for millers for their services in grinding grain.

Since Newark, the capital, lay next door to American territory, it was considered a dangerous location if war should break out with the United States. Governor Simcoe wished to move the provincial capital to a site now occupied by the city of London, Ont., but the Governor-General, Lord Dorchester, refused permission. It was finally decided that the new capital should be located on the north shore of Lake Ontario at Toronto Bay: its natural harbour could easily be fortified against American attack. Accordingly, in 1794, Simcoe transferred the seat of government to **New capital** Toronto Bay, and the settlement which arose there he named York **at York, 1794** in honour of the Duke of York, a son of King George III.

Governor Simcoe decided that York should become a model settlement built along British lines, but in his time it was little more than a military centre. Two hundred men of the Queen's Rangers were put to work erecting buildings and constructing roads. In a comparatively short time, they built barracks, block-houses, a powder magazine, wharves and a bridge. Castle Frank, overlooking the Don river, was built as a summer residence for the Simcoes, and in 1796, work was begun on the Parliament Buildings.

Governor Simcoe inspects the construction of a blockhouse at Fort York, 1793. The blockhouse survives to this day, being one of the few buildings to escape destruction during the American invasion of 1813. Block houses were of squared log construction similar to the Loyalist type seen on page 386.

**Roads in
Upper Canada**
In Upper Canada, the construction of roads was of the greatest importance to both settlement and defence. One of the most important pieces of work accomplished was the laying out of Yonge Street, a roadway leading north through the forest from

York to Lake Simcoe. It was begun by the Queen's Rangers. This remarkable roadway, which has since become a busy highway, was named in honour of an old friend of Simcoe's, Sir George Yonge, at that time the British Secretary of State for War. Simcoe decided upon another line of communication leading across the province from Montreal to Detroit, but only a small portion of it was completed before Simcoe's term of office ended in 1796. This road, known as Dundas Street or Governor's Road, linked the western end of Lake Ontario with York, but it was some years before it stretched all the way from Montreal to Detroit.

Yonge Street in modern Toronto and Dundas Street in modern London are still considered the "main streets" of those cities.

Although progress had been made, York was still a small backwoods community in 1796. One traveller has described it as:

> a dreary dismal place, not even possessing the characteristics of a village. There is no church, schoolhouse, nor in fact any of the ordinary signs of civilization. There is no inn: and those travellers who have no friends to go to, pitch a tent and live there while they remain.

Loyalists settlers in Upper and Lower Canada were soon **New immigrants for Upper and Lower Canada** joined by a steady stream of immigrants, all eager to secure land and establish homes. Among the newcomers were sturdy Scots who settled in the eastern part of Upper Canada, in the counties of Stormont and Glengarry. By 1800, nearly every Highland clan in Scotland had members living in Upper Canada. Scots were by no means the only people to arrive as new settlers. Americans, too, flocked in. The governments of both Upper and Lower Canada extended cordial invitations to Americans to settle in the provinces. Upon swearing an oath of allegiance to the Crown, an applicant could obtain 200 acres of free land. In addition, the son or daughter of a Loyalist could claim 200 acres without payment of the usual purchase fee. Disbanded officers could claim twenty-five times as much land.

As a result, large numbers of people crossed the border, became British subjects, and secured land.   In Lower Canada the new settlers chose to live chiefly in the "Eastern Townships", which lie to the east of Montreal. Loyalists and immigrants from the United States gradually took up land along Lakes Erie, Ontario and St. Clair, pushing back the forest from the edge of the waters.   Transportation and travel was still largely by water, since the building of roads was a costly and laborious operation. Shortly after 1800, however, good roads linked York, Kingston and Montreal, and on these roads stage coaches operated on more or less regular schedules.

So rapid was the growth of settlement, that shortly after 1800 the population of Lower Canada had trebled, and Upper Canada had increased almost tenfold—all this within the fifty-five years since the meeting of British and French on the Plains of Abraham.

59

LIFE IN THE NORTHERN COLONIES

The new settlers in the northern colonies were so fully occupied with the production of food, clothing and housing that they had little time for amusements and entertainment. It is difficult today to appreciate how much hard, heartbreaking work was required to clear land, plough the soil, erect homes and provide food and clothing for the pioneer family. These tasks had to be tackled with the simplest tools and were accomplished only at the cost of unceasing labour.

Fortunately, settlers were often able to combine their work **Pioneer** and social activity. With no electrical power, gasoline engines **co-operation** or powerful machinery to ease many heavy tasks, they found it helpful to work together in groups. Gatherings of settlers, organized to accomplish a particular task, were known as *bees*. At these events, parties of local people were able to complete a surprising amount of work in a short period, and afterwards enjoy such activities as dancing, skating or sleighing. Bees were common in various parts of North America; in New Brunswick and the United States they were known as "frolics." That the pioneers loved these gatherings is apparent, for in many communities they were organized on almost any excuse. An early writer remarks that:

> people in the woods have a craze for giving and going to bees, and run to them with as much eagerness as a peasant runs to a race-course or a fair.

Without the spirit of co-operation that existed among the pioneers, settlement would undoubtedly have progressed at a slower pace and would have been an even more dismal and

423

depressing activity. New-comers in Upper Canada were often welcomed by the people of the district who arranged a bee to construct their house or clear their first plot of land.

Logging bees   Since the felling and removal of trees was such a laborious and slow process, the logging bee became a vital part of pioneer life. At such an event, men from perhaps twenty miles around gathered at the farm of one settler, bringing with them tools and teams of oxen. After the first underbrush had been cleared away, trees were felled, their limbs cut off, and the trunks hauled away by oxen to be cut into logs. Then, men with handspikes pulled, pushed, and lifted until the logs were arranged in great piles six to eight feet in height. Dry branches, bark and evergreen boughs were placed about each pile and the whole mass set on fire. Millions of dollars worth of valuable pine, cedar, oak, walnut and maple were destroyed in this manner, but the settler could do little else. He required cleared land to sow his crops.

Once the work of the day was finished, the men settled down to an evening's relaxation. The hours of heavy labour seemed to have had little effect upon their energy, for after a large meal they were ready for some amusement. At such times and in most places drinking was considered an important part of entertainment. A short poem written by a Mr. Dundas Moodie relates that:

> There was a man in our town,
> In our town, in our town—
> There was a man in our town,
> He made a logging bee;
> And he bought lots of whisky,
> To make the loggers frisky,
> At his logging bee.

Unfortunately, the serving of whisky and other alcoholic drinks often turned loggings bees into disgraceful, drunken brawls, marked by quarrels and fist fights. As the piles of logs crackled and glowed in the darkness, the night was filled with the sound of wild songs and the bellows of angry men. Many a pioneer couple regretted their helpers when they counted the cost of entertainment and the damage done to home, chinaware and furniture. Not all logging bees, of course, were riotous affairs, because in some communities the men were able to work together without engaging in rowdy, boisterous behaviour.

After the logging bee, great numbers of tree stumps, dotted the newly-cleared land. Although the stumps occupied good land, they were not considered an immediate problem and were removed over a period of time. Hardwood stumps were often left in the earth for from seven to fifteen years since the process of rotting aided the work of removal. Some stumps were chopped out or burned, others being uprooted by oxen. Blasting was sometimes employed in particularly difficult cases. In parts of modern Ontario, there are still stump fences, formed in the days of the stumping bees. Shown above is the broad-wheeled stump wagon, sometimes used for hauling stumps away from the fields.

Barn raising bees were frequent occurrences. Every pioneer **Barn raising** needed such a building and it was impossible for him to erect the **bees** framework himself. On these occasions the men often were divided into two teams, each of which was responsible for raising one-half of the framework. In the exciting competition which followed, the teams worked at top speed, each trying to finish first. Urged on by the cheers of women, children and older men, the workers performed miracles of strength and endurance.

The family whose barn was being raised was expected to provide food and entertainment for all their helpers. Since sometimes one hundred people were in attendance, vast quantities of food were required. An early description of a barn raising states that in addition to great numbers of pies and cakes, the following were served at a single meal:

> a roast pig and a boiled leg of mutton, a dish of fish, a large cold mutton pie, cold ham and cold roast mutton, mashed potatoes and beans and carrots, a large rice pudding, a large bread-and-butter pudding, and currant and gooseberry tarts.

Other bees

There were numerous other types of communal projects such as building a store, a church or a mill, and of course pulling tree stumps, ploughing land, harvesting grain and building stone or rail fences. The women, too, held their own bees for quilting, spinning, weaving and preserving. At times there were double bees during which the men worked at some outdoor task and the women engaged in a household project. Husking bees were of particular interest to the young folks because these events took on the true flavour of a party. The husking bee was held during the evening in a barn illuminated by the flickering glow of candles or lanterns suspended from the walls. The task was to strip the husks from ears of corn piled high on the barn floor. When a young man discovered a red ear of corn, he earned the right to kiss the young lady sitting next to him. The finding of a red ear caused shouts of laughter and a great deal of good-natured joking.

Most bees ended in a dance held either in the house or the barn. To the music of a fiddle, young folks whirled through the energetic pioneer dances, and it is said that many a grandfather forgot his rheumatism when a lively tune was struck.

Amusements

Numerous amusements enjoyed by pioneer men and boys were connected with feats of strength. This was only natural, for strength was an important matter in the hard struggle with the uncleared forest, primitive farming methods, the cold winters and the ever-present threat of hunger. As a result, whenever men or boys collected together in groups, they liked nothing better than to test their strength against each other. They engaged in wrestling, lifting stones, throwing weights and pulling mightily in a tug-of-war. On some occasions men of unusual strength brought shouts of admiration by lifting a heavy log or the end of a wagon. Contests that required strength, skill and endurance sometimes took the form of felling trees or cutting logs at astonishing speed. Most communities, therefore, had recognized champions in wrestling, lifting, throwing, sawing and chopping. Even small boys imitated their elders in the hope that they too might some day be champions.

Hunting and fishing in most districts not only provided essential food but served as popular sports. In the early days of settlement deer were so plentiful that it was not uncommon for a family to have half a dozen of these animals hanging in the barn after a successful hunt. Wild pigeons in enormous flocks offered easy prey for men with guns or for fowlers with their wide nets. Hundreds of pigeons could be procured in the course of a single day. In many districts the birds were cleaned, salted and stored away for winter use.

Pioneer people, many of them living in isolated areas, undoubtedly took great pleasure in visiting their friends and relatives. At times, visits were short Sunday afternoon affairs made to the house of a neighbour; at other times they involved difficult journeys and extended periods of stay. The organization of surprise parties, too, seems to have been of particular delight. A birthday or an anniversary was often sufficient excuse to set the women baking and cooking. Then, on the selected day, a group of families would arrive unannounced at the home of the person being honoured. With peals of laughter and shouts of merriment they would rap on the door and troop in laden with food and gifts.

Town life differed quite considerably from that of country districts. Most of the towns in Upper Canada grew very slowly despite the fact that the population of the province was increasing. In 1794, the largest town, Kingston, had only 345 citizens, while York and Newark had even fewer.

Early nineteenth-century dairy equipment. At the left are a three-legged milking stool, a wooden dipper called a "noggin" and a wooden pail. The large object in the centre is a dash churn, an early butter-making implement. The handle was plunged up and down through the cream contained inside, causing globules of butter to form. The one-legged stool was used when milking fidgety cows, and a stave-handled pail was also useful in making a quick "getaway." A wooden butter bowl containing two rolls of butter is shown at the right, together with a fifty-pound butter "firkin", used in packing butter for winter use. Behind the dairy articles is a typical log barn of the period. Many of these barns are still standing today. Nineteenth-century barns were usually lower and narrower than those of later times.

As might be expected, town life imitated that of English cities. This was especially true of Kingston, York and Newark, where government officials and military officers were stationed. These persons, along with wealthy merchants and some professional people, made up the "upper class" of the province. These people considered themselves superior beings, associated only with members of their own class, and entertained amongst themselves. They engaged in riding, horse-racing, shooting, cricket, cards, chess and dancing.

Some citizens living in the villages and towns participated in so-called sports that today are forbidden by law. Dog-fighting, for example, was a popular pastime among the rougher men and boys. Dogs were kept by these people not for their friendly qualities or hunting skill, but because they were fierce, savage fighters. Dog-fights were arranged by the owners, and bets were placed on the outcome. Cock-fights, too, were organized in a similar manner.

During such special events as fairs, the old British spectacles of bull-baiting and bear-baiting were sometimes witnessed. In these cruel events fierce dogs were set loose in an enclosure to fight with bears or bulls, while onlookers laughed and cheered. However, it was only a few citizens who enjoyed these savage scenes. Many sought pleasure in the more wholesome activities of skating, snowshoeing, tobogganing, curling, sleighing, swimming, boating, canoeing, hunting and wrestling.

Inns and taverns played a great part in the early development of social life in Canada. The genial inn-keeper was frequently the most popular and highly-respected man in his community. He was more than a business man; he was a friendly host who extended a warm welcome and entertained his guests with jovial conversation. Persons travelling by stage-coach enjoyed hearty dinners and spent merry evenings around the fireplaces of the inns scattered along the stage routes. Inns and taverns not only served travellers, but acted as community centres for local people. They were the obvious places to hold smaller dinners, political banquets, meetings, political rallies, elections and many other activities. Before church buildings were erected, many a religious service was held in a tavern.

The descriptions of social life in this chapter apply largely to Upper Canada, but much of what has been said applies equally well to life in the English-speaking settlements in Lower Canada, Nova Scotia and New Brunswick.

This lantern of the late eighteenth or early nineteenth century was made of perforated tin. Inside was a single candle, held firmly by a metal holder. Smoke escaped through a small chimney in the top. Such lanterns, probably designed for use around barns and stables, had at this time been in use for about two hundred years without major changes.

Life in Lower Canada   In Lower Canada the habitants continued to live in accordance with old customs, tilling their narrow fields, and passing their lives within the boundaries of the seigneuries. The conquest of Quebec by the British and the arrival of the Loyalists had remarkably little effect upon their way of life. Refusing to be absorbed by the new-comers, the French-Canadians continued to speak their own language and to worship as they always had done. Priests of the Roman Catholic Church still remained important, respected personages who wielded great influence throughout the numerous parishes.

Life in the towns and cities of Lower Canada continued as gay and lively as it had been in former years when the French flag flew over New France. Quebec City, a trade centre, grew slowly larger, but remained essentially French. Montreal, however, became the headquarters of aggressive British traders and merchants, who brought their own customs, their own traditions and their own ways of doing business.   Montreal, with a population of 22,000 by 1801, became the financial capital of the northern provinces and the centre of the commercial system of the St. Lawrence.   It was the Montreal merchants who dominated the import and export trades.   It was the Montreal merchants who handled the fur trade and, in so doing, built immense fortunes.

60

BRITISH NORTH AMERICA IN 1800

By 1800, Newfoundland was still a fishing colony, its population scattered in tiny settlements along the coastline. There was little if any chance of agriculture on the rocky, heavily-forested island. Similarly, the inhabitants of Cape Breton Island depended upon the sea for a living. Only on Prince Edward Island, with its rich, reddish soil, did farming become the main activity.

Maritime Colonies

In the 1790's, settlement in Nova Scotia and New Brunswick still took place along the coast and in the larger river valleys. Farming was the principal occupation in the few fertile regions, but many people looked to the sea for their main source of income. Poor soil and vast forest areas — particularly in New Brunswick—forced the inhabitants to combine a little farming or timber cutting with an active life on the fishing grounds.

During the summer months husbands were busy at sea while their wives and children looked after the farm work as best they could. Some men engaged in fishing a few miles off the coast; others were gone for weeks on the Grand Banks. When the boats returned with fresh catches, whole families turned out to assist in cleaning, salting, and laying out the fish on the wooden "flakes" which stretched along the shores.

Shipbuilding and trade

The men of these provinces also built ships. There was plenty of fine timber at hand, and there were craftsmen with the skill to build staunch vessels. Settlers who had come from New England brought with them experience in the design and construction of both small boats and large ships. In consequence, the schooners they built were admired for their speed and seaworthiness. Ships were built not only for local use but for sale in Europe and the West Indies. By 1800, shipbuilders in Nova Scotia and New Brunswick were producing vessels, loading them with lumber, and sending them off to Britain where both ships and cargoes were sold.

The Durham boat. A flat-bottomed barge with a rounded bow and square stern, the Durham boat was normally eighty to ninety feet in length. When running downstream, it could carry a cargo of about thirty-five tons, nearly ten times that of the earlier *bâteau*. Basically a cargo carrier, practically no accommodation was made on the Durham boat for passengers. Nevertheless, great numbers of travellers found it the best available means of transportation, even though they had to sleep in the open air on any clear spot to be found among the many items of cargo. The mast of the Durham boat was jointed about four feet above the level of the deck and thus could be lowered when passing under bridges. A tremendous lower boom on the sail actually rested on deck and carried the canvas well beyond the vessel's side. Note the tremendous size of the rudder.

Every year, trade with Britain increased due to her steady demand for fish and timber. New Brunswick in particular benefited from the timber trade and shipbuilding. This province had enormous forests that supplied pine for spars and masts. A document of 1809, referring to Charlotte County, New Brunswick, states:

> ... the great demand for this article [pine timber] the last season and the consequent high price, induced every exertion to be directed to this object and there are now twenty Thousand Tons of squared pine timber ready for market, two-thirds more than has been obtained in any other season prior to the last, with the logs sufficient to employ Forty saws in the different mills within the County.

The West Indies also became a valuable market for the products of the eastern provinces. After the War of Independence, American ships were not permitted to trade with these British island colonies, thus giving a tremendous opportunity to traders in Nova Scotia and New Brunswick. So it was that schooners went south with cargoes of fish, flour, pork and lumber. The West Indian colonies were not entirely satisfied with this arrangement, because neither the eastern provinces nor the two Canadas could provide sufficient food to meet the needs of the islands. As a result, there was much smuggling of food from the United States. Nevertheless, Nova Scotia and New Brunswick gained considerably from this trading market where sugar and molasses were so easily obtained.

The eastern provinces were still so widely separated from Upper and Lower Canada that an overland journey between the two regions was a long and sometimes adventurous trip. It actually proved much simpler for New Brunswick and Nova Scotia to trade with Britain and the West Indies than with their sister provinces to the west.

The St. Lawrence river continued to dominate the economic life of the northern colonies.

Highway of the St. Lawrence The fur trade came down to the St. Lawrence ports. Settlements grew up along the river borders. The river was a highway of trade and travel. Well before the coming of the Loyalists, Quebec felt the vigorous stirring of British trade which brought dozens of ships up the St. Lawrence. Quebec City remained the chief port of the province, but ships of up to 400 tons made their way to Montreal in spite of the hazards of river navigation. In addition to sailing ships, there were small flat-bottomed

Canadian timber rafts of the eighteenth century sometimes started as small individual rafts 800 miles from their destination. Then, as they floated next to one another in a widening river, the rafts were joined together to form a gigantic stretch of timber. Flags were raised and sails unfurled. A large number of men lived on board in huts and shelters where they slept and ate their meals. Pine and oak were the most commonly-cut timber, and the rafts normally combined both types of wood, the pine helping to keep the heavier oak afloat. Merchants in Upper Canada used these timber rafts to ship such products as pork, potash and flour. The rafts were quite capable of carrying several hundred barrels of goods at one time.

bâteaux carrying loads of wheat, flour, meat and potash—the ashes of maple, birch and beech wood. Large quantities of potash were required in Europe where it was used to bleach cotton and to make soap.

The Ottawa river became the great lumber river. Enormous **Lumber** rafts of white pine, skilfully managed by rivermen, floated majestically down to Quebec City, which became a shipbuilding centre. Because of its size, Canadian pine was acknowledged the best wood for masts and bowsprits. Because of its lightness and freedom from knots, it was also put to decorative uses.

Farming in Lower Canada   Although the habitants of Lower Canada changed little in their basic habits and traditions, they did learn some valuable lessons in agriculture from the British and other newcomers. The French-Canadians had been accustomed to growing such specialized crops as peas and beans, all the while neglecting many vegetables. Potatoes, for example, had been entirely ignored during the French regime, but because British authorities encouraged the planting and marketing of this vegetable, large crops were soon grown. As early as 1770, on the Ile d'Orleans, farmers were producing thousands of bushels of potatoes each year. In addition to potatoes, other vegetables were raised on habitant farms—cauliflower, broccoli, turnips, celery, spinach and lettuce.

The French *Calèche*. This was probably the first public vehicle to travel the roads of Canada. Two-wheeled, with a collapsible top, the *calèche* was described by some travellers as being a "gig upon grasshopper springs with a seat for two passengers." Quebec used the European system of travelling in stages between stations or posts where there were frequent changes of horses. There were at one time twenty-four such posts between Quebec City and Montreal. Each *maître de poste*, post manager, was required to keep four *calèches* for summer use and four sleighs or *carioles* for winter travel.

The fact that French-Canadians found a ready market in the towns for their farm products encouraged many of them to plant an even greater variety of crops and to further increase their yields. This is indicated by the organization of one farm which was offered for sale in 1771:

> . . . 7 acres in front and 32 in depth, of which upwards of 60 acres is cleared and on which is sow'd 25 Bushels of Wheat, 16 Bushels of Oats, one acre of Irish Potatoes, and Half an Acre of English turnips, also a good Kitchen Garden, and the whole being well fenced in.

In addition to the crops listed, this same farm had livestock in the form of oxen, cows, horses, pigs and poultry.

The seigneurial system continued in Lower Canada although it was slowly becoming unpopular. It was, in fact, a type of landholding avoided by British settlers. Then, too, the French-Canadians themselves were disturbed when they realized Loyalists and other settlers were receiving grants of land free of rents and duties. An ancient system which had proved its worth in the early days of French settlement, the seigneurial system had now passed its period of usefulness. The seigneurs enjoyed far less power and prestige than they did when the French governors and intendants were in control, and in consequence, some of the seigneurs actually sold their lands and returned to France. While it is true that the seigneurial system was dying before 1800, it continued in use for another half century.

In Upper Canada the settlers found fertile soil well suited **Farming in Upper Canada** to the production of vegetables, fruits and grains. They carried on a mixed type of farming—some crops and a few cattle—but wheat gradually became the most important product. In 1794, the Bishop of Quebec, after a visit to Upper Canada, spoke of "the fine crops of grain which the new lands everywhere produce." Governor Simcoe was particularly pleased by this development. It had been his hope that, since Lower Canada could not supply enough grain for its own support, Upper Canada would be capable of supplying flour to its neighbour and also become "a granary for England."

F. D.–15

Many settlers, ignorant of efficient farming methods, tilled the soil wastefully and used no fertilizer to enrich the fields, but the land's basic richness produced good crops year after year. A farmer planting a bushel and a half of wheat per acre could expect to reap twenty-five to thirty-five bushels—and often did. Wheat was not the only grain produced. Farmers grew buckwheat, rye, Indian corn and some oats. Turnip crops proved useful as winter feed for livestock. Maple sugar and syrup were prepared for family use, and molasses was made from pumpkins. Apple trees thrived in various districts, and in 1793 cherries and peaches were being cultivated in the Niagara Peninsula. However, wheat was still the only crop produced in sufficient quantities to allow of export.

Labour

Most farmers in Upper Canada were forced to do all their own work. They could not afford to pay the high wages demanded by workers. A hired man working on a farm during the harvest season expected to be paid daily wages equivalent to the value of one bushel of wheat. A few of the Loyalists brought their slaves with them when they moved into the province; some of these workers were used in the homes and in the fields. An advertisement appearing in the *Upper Canada Gazette* in the year 1800 reads:

> To be sold—A healthy, strong Negro Woman, about 30 years of age; understands cookery, laundry and taking care of poultry. N.B.— She can dress ladies' hair.

Kingston, largest town in Upper Canada

Kingston, which at this time was the largest town in Upper Canada, had a surprising number of shops and small businesses. In 1810, the town boasted a printing office, a tannery, a small carriage factory, a sawmill, a grist-mill, a harness-making shop, a boot-making shop, a kiln for the manufacture of bricks, a jewellery store and a tailoring establishment, all these in addition to the ordinary types of stores and shops.

*   *   *

Thus, there was an eager stir of activity in the settlements scattered all the way from the Atlantic coast to the shores of Lake St. Clair. There were fishing boats on the coastal waters and axes at work in the forest. Cabins were being built in clearings, and villages and towns were slowly growing. Sailboats were moving up and down the St. Lawrence, and stage-coaches were rattling along the roads. Ripe golden wheat was waving in the fields, and women were baking and cooking in their kitchens.

It was a bustling, vigorous, active time. Here were Englishmen, Frenchmen, Scots, Irishmen, Germans, Yankees, Dutchmen and many others, all absorbed in the work of making a home, earning a living, and raising a family. Sometimes they were rough, crude and even cruel, but they were everlastingly courageous, and endured the hardships born of the endless forests, the bitter winters and the constant threat of hunger. These were the men of steel and the women of faith who wrested a livelihood from the waters and wildernesses of British North America. These were the men and women who laid the foundations of this fair domain, this Dominion of Canada.

SUMMARY—SECTION IX

The War of Independence was a civil war as well as a war against Great Britain. In every colony there were colonists who refused to forswear their allegiance to the king. After the Declaration of Independence had been adopted, these colonists or Loyalists were regarded and treated as traitors. Many left the country for Canada or Britain as soon as the war began. The greater number of Loyalists endured insult and the loss of personal property during the war. After peace terms were signed in 1783, Loyalists were brought to Canada by the British Government. They settled in Nova Scotia, Cape Breton Island and Prince Edward Island, established New Brunswick, and also found homes in Quebec and in the western regions of Quebec. These last settlers were to create the province of Upper Canada, now known as Ontario.

The American Revolution had not interrupted the fur trade. As far back as 1766, British traders from Montreal had reached La Vérendrye's domain, the Lake Winnipeg area. These Montrealers cut deeply into the Hudson's Bay Company trade as they moved up the Saskatchewan and onto the plains. The Montreal "Pedlars" pushed so far into the north-west that it now took them two seasons to ship goods to Indian customers. Thus, they built fur posts where they wintered, and in the short summer seasons trade goods arrived at these posts from Grand Portage and bundles of furs were taken back to Grand Portage and later sent on to Montreal. Individual traders, tired of competing with each other for small profits and realizing that a big business organization and methods were necessary, began to think of uniting into a company. In 1775, 1778 and 1779, a trading company was formed in which traders pooled their goods, shared expenses, and took out an equal profit. The final combination of 1787, composed of eight partnerships, was called the North West Company. While the pioneers were making their way into western Quebec, the North West Company was exploring the western territories of the future nation of Canada.

The last geographic problem was to find a water route to the Western Sea—the Pacific Ocean. Captain James Cook was just ahead of the fur traders. Cook's task in 1778 was to find a North-East passage to Europe. He failed to do so, but he did meet west coast Indians. He made his way as far north as the Bering Strait but was forced back by Arctic ice. Captain George Vancouver, ordered to find a water route through the continent of North America, sailed through the strait of Juan de Fuca and up the Georgia Strait behind the island (Vancouver) missed by Cook. He charted the northwest coastline but could not find a waterway to the east. Vancouver missed an important river—the Fraser—and he also failed to claim the Columbia river for Britain quickly enough — an American did so five months before Vancouver.

However, as yet, no one had made his way overland to the Pacific.

The North West Company was seeking a way to the Pacific to gain a share in the sea otter trade which Russian traders seemed to be enjoying. In addition, with transport costs to and from Montreal still costing too much money, if the Company found a transport route through the mountains, furs could be sent to the Pacific where ships would freight them direct to markets in the West Indies, the United States and Europe. Alexander Mackenzie, aware of these business ambitions, but moved more strongly by a simple desire to find a way to the Pacific, pioneered the way, mistakenly to the Arctic Ocean and later, successfully, to the west coast. He didn't find a practical water route through the mountains, but he was the first European to make his way through the Rocky Mountains and the first to reach the Pacific overland.

Still seeking a way to the rich sea otter trade of the coast, the Company sent men into the mountains in 1801 and 1802. They failed to find a way to the sea. The Company sent Simon Fraser into the mountains in 1805 and 1806, but it was 1808 before Fraser reached salt water at the Strait of Georgia. He had been looking for the Columbia and had failed to find it. The river he had just descended was impossible to use as a fur route. David Thompson finally reached the Columbia and its mouth in 1811, but American fur traders were there before him and were busy buying pelts. The race to the Pacific was over.

Further to the east, the fur trade suffered from the commercial interests of the United States. In 1783, in the treaty of Paris, British statesmen agreed to a boundary line between the United States and British North American possessions that followed the water boundary of the St. Lawrence river and the Great Lakes to the Lake of the Woods and then ran due west to the Mississippi. This agreement cut off the Montreal fur merchants from the fur trade of the Great Lakes region, and denied Indians the hunting-grounds promised them by the 1763 Proclamation. However, British troops stayed on in these territories to guard against Indian uprisings (and Montreal traders still journeyed into the territories to trade with the Indians). The Indians did rise— against the American settlers who flooded into the lower Great Lakes area and claimed land for themselves. By 1794, the Americans finally defeated the Indians and demanded that the British leave as they had promised. By Jay's Treaty in 1794, the redcoats were obliged to leave the western fur posts. American competition gradually drove the Montrealers north above and beyond the lakes.

In the east, British North America was born of the American Revolution. By 1800, there were six provinces. (Newfoundland was still a fishing colony.) Cape Breton Island depended on the sea for its livelihood. Prince Edward Island supported several farming communities. Nova Scotia and New Brunswick, heavily-settled by United Empire Loyalists, were prospering areas, the former engaged in fishing, shipbuilding and a steady West Indies trade, the latter also busy building and exporting lumber. In 1791, the Constitutional Act or Canada Act created the provinces of Upper and Lower Canada.

The Loyalist migrations into the upper St. Lawrence valley had brought British habits and customs to the wilderness. The Loyalists wanted to hold their own land under English law, worship after the Church of England manner, and elect their own representatives. They wished to be as free from seigneurial rule, French law and the influence of the Roman Catholic Church as were the Maritime provinces. The Act of 1791 recognized that the old province of Quebec was now largely divided by race, language and location into English- and French-speaking areas. Quebec was divided along the line of the Ottawa river into the two provinces of Upper and Lower Canada. The privileges guaranteed the people of Quebec in 1774 remained intact. In Upper Canada, land was to be held by freehold tenure, and land was reserved for the support of a Protestant clergy. Each province was allowed representative assemblies, although councils, appointed by the governor-general, ruled each assembly.

By 1800, British North America was producing fish, lumber and ships in the Maritime provinces and lumber, furs and wheat in the St. Lawrence region. These northern colonies were beginning to establish trade with the West Indies and with Great Britain. All these activities were the beginnings of a nation.

APPENDIX

Stories From the Past

Many stories of North America's early years have been told and retold so often that it is now very difficult to decide which are true, which are partly true, and which are just stories made up to please a boy or girl, or perhaps a grown-up. A few such stories still find their way into history books and appear as facts. Sometimes, years pass before somebody discovers that they are just legends, tales about famous people or simple folk or strange events, tales told or written about so many times that they have often been accepted as the truth.

All that need be said about the following stories is that there is *much* truth in all of them. It is not important that some of them have been added to or changed by a storyteller's imagination. They tell us a great deal about the people, Indian and European, who lived, worked and fought—and died—in North America many, many years ago. They tell us a great deal about past times and places. In a way, they are a part of history.

* * * * *

THE HAPPY HUNTING-GROUNDS

The Indian tribes of North America had no special teachers of religion. It was the "medicine-man" who acted as a priest or minister, and reminded them of Manitou, the Great Spirit, who had created the earth and everything on it. The medicine-man was the story-teller who spoke or sang the tribal stories of the powers of the Great Spirit. One of these stories is that of the Happy Hunting-Grounds.

The Great Spirit smiled upon his children in sunshine and shower and frowned upon them in fierce storms and whirlwinds. He created lesser spirits, evil spirits, who caused pain, sickness, trouble and death, but he also created the good spirits that helped the hunter in the chase and brought health and happiness. Finally, he had prepared for his children a "Happy Hunting-Ground" where everyone would go after death. There, beautiful birds sang, and deer, bears and buffaloes roamed magnificent plains, whilst many fish swam in clear, fresh waters. The brave Indian could live there with his family and hunt game all day without ever wearying. But the cowardly Indian would return from the chase tired and empty-handed. He would be made to feel ashamed of his cowardice when he was given food by the good Indian.

In the very beginning, all Indians lived in this wonderful land, but were so busy playing and shouting that the Great Spirit could get no rest because of the noise they made. Besides, there were no evil spirits in the Happy Hunting-Grounds, and they could not learn to be brave unless they suffered the pains and troubles of the world. So the Great Spirit made a large basket in which he placed the Indians, carefully covering them so they could not see the trail by which he took them to the earth. He left them there and promised that when they had become brave and fearless, and after they had died, they would again be carried to the Happy Hunting-Grounds and there dwell for "so many moons that all the needles on the greatest pine tree would not tell them all."

HIAWATHA

There are many Iroquois legends about the great Mohawk warrior chieftain, Hiawatha, who played a great part in creating the League of the Iroquois. Here is the great tale of his wisdom and strength:

One day, the mighty Ta-ren-ya-wa-gon, the holder of the heavens, who afterwards became a man, the wise Hiawatha, looked out from the entrance of the Happy Hunting-Grounds. He saw men and women in the forest, moaning with terror, because all their relatives and friends had been slain by giants and fierce monsters. He went quickly to their aid and led them all to a safe place deep in the forest. He gave to all the people corn, beans, squash, potatoes and tobacco, and also dogs with which to hunt game. He named some of the people Te-ha-wro-gah (divided speech, i.e., a strange tongue—the Mohawks), and showed them where to build their villages. He led the rest to where the trees of the forest were of great size, and settled some of them there. He told them that they would be called Ne-ha-wre-ta-go (the Oneida). He then led the others toward the setting sun till they came to a mountain, which he called O-nun-da-ga-o-na-ga (on the hills), where he named some the Onondaga and told them to settle. He led the others many days' journey to the west, to the shores of a lake he called Go-ya-gah (mountain rising from the water), where he bade some of them settle, calling them the Cayuga. Then, with those that were left, Ta-ren-ya-wa-gon continued toward the sunset until they all came to a mountain near the lake, Ga-nun-da-gwa, and here he told them they should dwell. He gave them the name, Te-ho-ne-noy-hent (guarding the door—the Seneca).

But many people were not content to stay where the holder of the heavens had bidden them to live, and they ran away toward the setting sun until they came to a great river, which they crossed on a wild grape vine. But when the last ones were crossing, the vine broke and none could ever return. (This is an account of the presence of the Indians beyond the Mississippi.)

Then Hiawatha instructed each tribe in a distinctive skill. To the Seneca, he gave the power of swift feet, and they were able to outrun any animal in the forest. The Cayuga became skilled in the use of the canoe, and glided over the waters more rapidly than the skimming birds. The Onondaga were taught the laws of the Great Spirit. The Oneida became skilful makers of weapons, builders of houses and weavers of baskets. The Mohawk were shown how to shoot arrows with deadly aim and how to catch fish with ease and efficiency.

Hiawatha showed all his people the skills of hunting and agriculture. He showed them which plants were poisonous and which were safe to eat. He gave them good government.

Then Ta-ren-ya-wa-gon decided to live with his people. He assumed the form of a man and chose an Onondaga maiden as his wife. When he had done this, he was named Hiawatha, and became the leader of the tribes.

LEGENDS OF THE ALGONKIAN INDIANS

The Indians living along the shores of the Gulf of St. Lawrence and in what are now the Maritime provinces of Canada held many strong beliefs.

When the northern lights flashed across the sky, the Indians believed that the changing colours were caused by the spirits of their dead relatives and friends holding joy dances in the upper world, the bright robes of the dancers swirling and swishing through the sky. When thunder rumbled, accompanied by gusts of wind, it was because a huge bird was beating its way across the heavens; it was the flash and gleam of its eyes that produced the lightning.

There are also numerous tales that centre round two brothers, one of whom was good and the other bad. The one brother created all that was good and beautiful in the world, whilst the other was responsible for everything evil and unpleasant. The brothers were always in conflict with each other, until finally, the good brother, Glooskap by name, succeeded in defeating and vanquishing his brother.

Glooskap was a benefactor of his people in many ways. He taught them to build canoes and tepees, to trap wild animals, to raise crops, and to make sugar from the maple tree. Of course, he had many enemies—wizards, witches and demons, all of whom lived in the clouds and often came down to earth to burn his home or kill his friends. He spent much of his life battling them.

Finally, he left his old haunts and journeyed far away into the setting sun. All nature mourned his going. The pine trees sighed in the breeze. The bull-frogs croaked in dismay. The whippoorwills called sadly, "He is gone! He is gone!" The owls asked, "Whoo-oo? Whoo-oo?" To which the tree toads replied, "Glooskap, Glooskap." The Indians mourned long and loudly for their lost protector and champion.

ANCIENT ESKIMO LEGENDS

The Eskimos believed that there was a great spirit called Torngak, who controlled their lives, their fortunes and their health. If he was angry with them, they sought to please him by having their *angakoks* or medicine-men play on magic drums and sing his praises. They also believed in a Great Seal Mother who lived in the moon. When the hunting was poor, the Eskimos asked the angakok to appeal to the great Moon-Mother to drop a seal or two into nearby waters, so that other seals might be attracted to the vicinity and thus provide good hunting.

The Eskimos believed angakok tales of giants and dwarfs that dwelt beneath the ground, and of whom a mere glimpse was considered a bad omen. An *amulet* or lucky charm worn or carried by a person was often sufficient to ward off evil spirits. The amulet might be a fish fin, a bird's claw, a caribou's ear, a bear's paw or any one of a hundred other items said to bring good luck to the wearer.

Ancient Eskimo tales were nearly always about some remarkable display of human strength and bravery against the wildness of the northern winter or the animals of the Arctic, or plain misfortune of some kind or other. A good example is the tale of Popoluk, the Bear Man.

Popoluk was rather tall for an Eskimo—nearly six feet in height. He was an expert seal hunter. He had the patience to sit at a "breathing-hole" out in the ice for hours or even days on end, until a seal came up to breathe. Popoluk never missed a seal.

One winter, his village was starving. There was no game or fish to be caught. The angakok appealed for help to Torngak, the great spirit, who told him that the strongest and best hunter must be sent to a distant island, where he would be rewarded with a seal. Whom else could they send but Popoluk?

Setting off with his dogs and *komatik* or sled, the hunter reached the island, where he caught an enormous seal, the largest he had seen that season. Just as he was about to load it on the komatik, the howling of his dogs warned him of danger. A polar bear was approaching. Seizing his knife, Popoluk lunged for the bear, while his dogs attacked from the rear. The bear was clever and shot out a clawed hand to sweep Popoluk to the ground, but the Eskimo had already ducked and jumped forward to grab the bear's throat. Luckily, the bear stumbled over the body of the seal and fell, whereupon the dogs tore at its head, giving Popoluk a chance to thrust his knife again and again into the bear's body. The Eskimo staggered away from the dying bear to sit down on the komatik and get his strength back.

When he brought the bear and the seal back to his village, his wife proudly skinned the bear, cured the hide, and fashioned it into a great coat for her husband. From then on, he wore it on every occasion, and wherever he went, people shouted, "There is Popoluk, the Bear Man!"

CHRISTOPHER COLUMBUS AND THE EGG

Christopher Columbus received many honours and awards after his discovery of America. Several members of the Spanish court envied him his success. It is said that on one occasion, during a court banquet, some noblemen proclaimed loudly that, after all, the voyage of Columbus had not been particularly important. Any one of them, they said, might have accomplished the same feat.

Columbus calmly took an egg from a dish on the table and suggested that each clever fellow should be able to stand the egg on one end. They all tried, but no one succeeded.

Columbus then took the egg, broke one end slightly, and thus stood it on one end.

The courtiers all cried, "Why I could have done that!"

"Yes, if the thought had struck you," replied Columbus, "and if the thought had struck you, you might have discovered America."

SIR WALTER RALEIGH AND TOBACCO

The use of tobacco by the Indians probably dates from a period early in their history. It was usually smoked in pipes or in cigar form, although the Aztecs of South America employed nostril tubes for inhaling the smoke through the nose.

In 1559, a Spaniard imported some tobacco plants from Mexico. Six years later, tobacco found its way to England. Sir Walter Raleigh and Sir Frances Drake took to pipe smoking and helped to popularize its use in England.

According to legend, one of Raleigh's servants was astonished when he first saw his master smoking. Thinking the nobleman was in danger of being burned, the servant soaked him with a pailful of water.

CAPTAIN JOHN SMITH AND POCAHONTAS

Captain John Smith is thought to have once escaped death through the courage and kindness of a young Indian girl named Pocahontas. The incident took place during one of his journeys away from the settlement of Jamestown, Virginia, when he was captured by Indians. Taken before their chief, Powhatan, who sat upon a crude throne in a huge lodge, the prisoner was warmly welcomed, kindly treated and entertained to a great feast.

However, the friendly atmosphere changed when a large stone was carried into the lodge and placed on the ground. Captain Smith was seized by several warriors and his head was forced down upon the top of the stone.   Other warriors seized war clubs and raised them high above their heads in preparation for the kill.

At this crucial moment, Pocahontas, the chief's favourite daughter, ran to the captive, took his head in her arms and laid her face on his. Looking steadily at her father, she begged that Captain Smith's life be spared. Rather regretfully, Powhatan agreed, and two days later the captive was set free on condition that he send gifts to the chief and his daughter.   On his return to Jamestown, Captain Smith was only too pleased to send presents to the young Indian girl and her father.

Pocahontas later married a young English settler, John Rolfe, who took her to England in the year 1616. She died there after giving birth to a son, who later settled in Virginia.

A LEGEND OF THE ST. LAWRENCE

Every Quebec town and village along the banks of the St. Lawrence river has its stories of the past. The people of Quebec dearly love an old tale of Indian raiding or ghostly happenings.

Although the fear of Iroquois attack was a real one for many years, there was one fear that often disturbed the habitant more—the evil power of the Witch of the St. Lawrence. The Indians called her Matshi Skoueou.   She had no dwelling-place or home.   Instead, she wandered up and down the length of the great river. At night, when everything was cool and quiet and the will-o'-the-wisps danced eerily over marsh and swampland, the Witch circled round the tiny settlements, a horrid creature of great size, with sea-green eyes, long black hair, and a copper-hued skin. She was usually dressed in white, and a ghastly blue flame flared above her head. She was supposed to be in league with the Iroquois, a sort of advance scout, looking for settlements that they could attack. The atrocities and cruelties of the Indians were not to be compared with the terrible behaviour of the Witch, as the following story of a habitant family demonstrates:

A man called Houel met with a serious accident whilst on his way from his farm to the town of Quebec to settle some business matters. As soon as they heard of his misfortune, his wife and eight-year-old son set out with a canoeman to go to him.   It was late in the evening when they started down the St. Lawrence, and at this period, the Iroquois were rumoured to be on the warpath.

The boy, who had been sleeping by his mother's side, suddenly wakened and gazed over the waters of the river.

"Mother," he whispered, "do you see that woman over there? Look, she's dressed all in white. She's walking on the water."

His mother looked all round but could see nothing except the gently flowing water.

"Go to sleep, my child," she said. "There is nothing there. It will soon be morning."

However, the canoeman was alarmed by the boy's vision. "Maybe the boy is right. Perhaps it is Matshi Skoueou, leading the Iroquois to attack a seigneury."

They had not gone far when they discovered other canoes in their immediate vicinity. The canoeman, himself an Indian, recognized them as an Iroquois war party.

A shot rang out, and then another, and another. In the struggle that followed, the canoeman and the mother and her son were pitched out of their canoe into the river and lost each other in the watery darkness. When the canoeman reached shore, he began looking for his passengers. For a long time he searched without finding them. Suddenly, he heard voices. Creeping towards a group of trees, he saw Iroquois warriors moving off into the forest, leaving a woman and a boy hanging from a tree. The woman, the mother, was dead, but her son was still alive. When he had been cut down, he told the canoeman how the White Witch had led the Iroquois to them in the water and how she had danced and laughed while the Indians, following the Witch's instructions, killed his mother.

FATHER MARQUETTE AND THE MANITOU

A number of interesting legends are told about the life of Father Marquette, the famous priest-explorer. One of these is the story of Marquette's capture by a band of Chippewa Indians. After being held for a short time, the priest escaped with the help of the chieftain's daughter, but was recaptured.

Realizing that the Indians would undoubtedly kill him now, Father Marquette looked about desperately for another chance to escape. His eyes fell upon an ugly, wooden idol, known to the Indians as "Manitou." Standing up straight and looking at their leader, Chief White Otter, the priest said, "I shall pray my God to burn this idol."

White Otter, laughing aloud, cried, "If your God can do that, I shall set you free!"

Father Marquette immediately held up over his head a crucifix, to which was attached a small magnifying glass. He held the glass firmly so that the bright rays of the sun would be focused on the wooden side of the idol. A tiny curl of blue smoke arose, the air was filled with a burning odour, an orange flame flickered, and finally, Manitou was covered with leaping flames.

Chief White Otter and his warriors, trembling in fear, fell down before Father Marquette and begged his forgiveness.

A DREAMING MATCH

Sir William Johnson, appointed superintendent of Indian Affairs for New York in 1755, once received some elegant new suits from England. A Mohawk chief named Hendrick admired the suits greatly, but at first said nothing about them. However, within a few days, the chief called on Sir William and reported that he had had a special dream in which he had been given one of his fine suits. Sir William took the hint and presented Hendrick with one of the best suits.

Some time later, Sir William, who happened to find himself in the chief's company, remarked that he also had had a dream, a dream in which Hendrick had granted him 5,000 acres of land along the Mohawk River. The chief presented Sir William with the land immediately, but in doing so, remarked: "Sir William, I will never dream again with you; you dream too hard for me."

A STRANGE ESCAPE FROM TORTURE

During the British expedition against Fort Duquesne in 1758, a number of soldiers belonging to a Highland regiment were captured by Indians. One of the captives, Allan Macpherson, was forced to watch as several of his companions were tortured to death. Realizing that it would soon be his turn to suffer torture, Macpherson said that if his life were spared for a few more minutes, he would reveal the secret of a medicine that allowed the skin to stand the strongest blow from a tomahawk or sword. Seeing that he had aroused the curiosity of the Indians, he asked permission to look in the forest for the necessary berries. He promised that after making the medicine, he would allow the strongest warrior to strike him.

When permission was granted, the young Highlander picked berries, boiled them in a pot, and rubbed his neck with the juice. Then, laying his head upon a log, he asked that the most powerful of the braves should strike his neck with a tomahawk. An Indian stepped forward and levelled a mighty blow, which struck off the soldier's head.

Realizing what had been done, the Indians were ashamed of being so easily cheated of a victim, but expressed admiration of the manner in which their prisoner had escaped lingering torture. They were so impressed that they inflicted no injuries on the remaining prisoners.

MAJOR-GENERAL WOLFE

The story has long been told that in the early hours of September 13th, 1759, as Wolfe and his troops rowed towards the Anse au Foulon to wade ashore and climb up the cliffs to the Heights of Abraham, Wolfe recited an English poem, *Elegy in a Country Churchyard*. Wolfe, the tale goes, spoke the lines in a low tone as his boat moved down river to his appointment with glory and death. The following verse of the poem is often quoted in connection with this legend:

"The boast of heraldry, the pomp of pow'r,
   And all that beauty, all that wealth e'er gave,
Awaits alike th' inevitable hour.
   The paths of glory lead but to the grave."

As his recital ended, the commander is reputed to have said, "Gentlemen, I would rather have written these lines than take Quebec."

Modern historical research reveals that Wolfe may have gone to visit some of his posts on the night before the battle, and that in the course of his tour he may have recited the poem and made his remark about preferring to be the author of the poem. Another version of the tale states the poem was read to him, and then he made his comment.

Both accounts of the story say the incident occurred on the evening of the 12th. This seems reasonable. After all, what general, depending upon silence and surprise, is going to approach a battle area quoting poetry, when, only a few hours previously he had ordered strict silence upon the part of everyone sharing a risky venture?

CHIEF JOSEPH BRANT IN ENGLAND

In 1785, Chief Joseph Brant of the Mohawks paid a second visit to Great Britain and was again welcomed as a loyal and honoured subject of the king. In the course of his stay, he was received by the king and lavishly entertained by several noble families. However, during a masquerade ball held in London, he is said to have been the author of a humorous incident. Brant arrived at the affair dressed in the full war regalia of a Mohawk chieftain. One of the guests, thinking the visitor was a friend disguised in costume, approached Brant and playfully pulled his nose, but the guest was astonished when he found he had actually tugged at a real nose and not at a mask. Seeing an opportunity to have some fun, Brant screamed out a loud warwhoop and lifted a knife high over his head. Then, seizing the surprised offender, he pretended that he was about to scalp him on the spot. The remaining guests, alarmed by the scene, hurried from the room and were persuaded to return only after the Mohawk chieftain laughingly explained that he was having a joke at the expense of the terrified guest.

BENJAMIN FRANKLIN'S TOAST

Some years after the American Revolution, Benjamin Franklin was dining in company with the British and French ambassadors. In the course of the evening, a number of toasts were drunk. The British ambassador is said to have stood and remarked, "To England, the sun whose bright beams enlighten and fructify the remotest corners of the earth."

The French ambassador, glowing with national pride, said, "To France, the moon whose mild, steady and cheering rays are the delight of all nations; consoling them in darkness, and making their dreariness beautiful."

The story goes that Benjamin Franklin then arose and with his usual dignity said, "To George Washington, the Joshua, who commanded the sun and the moon to stand still; and they obeyed him."

INDEX OF ILLUSTRATIONS

Collective index entries have been made as follows:

AGRICULTURE

ARCHITECTURE
   GENERAL
   CHURCHES

BATTLES AND ENGAGEMENTS

COSTUME

FORTS

FURNITURE

HOUSEHOLD ARTICLES

INDIAN TRIBES
   GENERAL
   COSTUME
   DWELLINGS
   WEAPONS

MILITARY AFFAIRS
   NAVAL
   UNIFORMS
   WEAPONS

TRANSPORTATION
   LAND
   WATER

A

Acadians (expulsion of), 262
AGRICULTURE
   Dairy equipment, early 19th cent., 428
   Loyalist farming, 386
   Ploughing (17th cent. New France), 211
   Seigneurial system in New France, 180-181
   Stump removing, 425
   Tobacco growing (Virginia), 129
ARCHITECTURE
   GENERAL
   L'Habitation, Port Royal, 58-59
   L'Habitation, Quebec, 65
   House (Quebec City), 166
   House, Georgian style, circa 1753, 340
   House, Jesuit, 1637 (Sillery, Que.), 91
   House ("salt-box"), 1686 (New England), 137
   Log house construction, 388
   Old Ship Meeting House (Massachusetts), 135
   CHURCHES
   Notre Dame des Victoires (Quebec), 231
   St. Paul's (Halifax), 253

B

Baking in New France, 177
BATTLES AND ENGAGEMENTS
   Braddock being ambushed near Fort Duquesne, 280
   Champlain attacks an Onondaga village, 76
   Louisbourg under bombardment, 1745, 248
   Louisbourg under bombardment, 1758, 295
   Siege of Quebec, 1759, 309
Beaver hat, 265
Beaver trapping, 272
Bigot, Intendant, 300
Bolas, 35
Boundary marker, 150
Brides (en route to Virginia), 131

C

Candle-making, 154
Canoe (Iroquois), 31
Cartier, Jacques (at Stadacona), 51
Cook, Captain James, 400
COSTUME
   Beaver hat, 265
   English costume, early 17th cent., 131
   French costume, circa 1665, 175
   Habitant, late 18th cent., 327
   Jesuit missionary, 101
   Viking, 42
   Wig-making, 337
   Coureur de bois, 199

D

Dollard, Adam, 109
Drum (Iroquois), 111

E

Eskimo, 38

F

Fire-fighting equipment, 18th cent., 382
First inhabitants of North America, 6-7
Flask, leather, 18th cent., 342
FORTS
  Amsterdam, 143
  Louisbourg, 244
  Ste. Marie, 106-107
  Ville Marie (Montreal), 96
  William Henry, 286
  York (Toronto), 420
Fraser, Simon, 410
French settlers (wintering with Indians, 1628-1629), 88
Frontenac, Count (expedition to Cataraqui, 1673), 196-197
Frontenac, Count (expedition against the Iroquois, 1696), 234-235
Fur brigade, 395
FURNITURE
  Canape (settee), French, circa 1750, 302
  Chair, Acadian, 257
  Chair, French, circa 1600, 93
  Chair, French, circa 1680, 93
  Chair, Upper Canada, 1785, 415
  Cradle, Upper Canada, circa 1785, 415
  Cupboard, birch, 18th cent., New France, 324
  Game table, French, circa 1750, 302
  Lowboy (dressing-table), French, circa 1650, 93
  Military field desk, 278
  Sofa, English (Chippendale), 345
  Table, English (Chippendale), 345

G

Gazette (Halifax), 255

H

L'Habitation (Port Royal and Quebec), See ARCHITECTURE
Halifax, 1750, 253
Hébert, Louis, 80
HOUSEHOLD ARTICLES
  Candles, 154
  Fire-scoop, 174
  Outdoor bakeoven, 152
  Spice-grinder, 18th cent., 294
  Stove, cast-iron, 19th cent., 416
  Sugar-cutters, 18th cent., 294

Table utensils, 17th cent., New England, 141
Tools, carpentry, French, 18th cent., 84
Hudson's Bay Company trading post, 223
Hudson's Bay Company trading token, 225

I

INDIAN TRIBES
  GENERAL
  Adze (Iroquois), 29
  Iroquois villages destroyed by French, 170-171
  Maple sugaring, 26
  Travois (Plains Indians), 20
  COSTUME
  Iroquois, 30
  Iroquois, 67
  Mandan, 268
  Nootka, 401
  Tlinkit mask, 11
  DWELLINGS
  Algonkian wigwam, 24
  Blackfoot tipi, 20
  Iroquois lodge, 30
  Mandan lodge, 269
  Tsimshian lodge, 12-13
  WEAPONS
  Blow-gun (Iroquois), 32
  Bow and arrow (Huron), 76
  Shield (Sioux), 17

J

Joliet, Louis, 203

K

Kayak (Eskimo), 38

L

Lachine massacre, 1689, 214
Lantern, 18th-19th cent., 430
Lighting ("cresset"), 17th-19th cent., 127
Liquor trade, 165
Loyalist settler, 386

M

Maisonneuve, Sieur de, 96
Maple sugaring (Algonkian Indians), 26
Marquette, Father Jacques, 203
Mask (Tlinkit), 11

MILITARY AFFAIRS *(See also*
BATTLES AND ENGAGEMENTS)
NAVAL
Wolfe's troops disembark above
Quebec, 1759, 314
Warship, British, circa 1710, 238
Warships, British, circa 1759, 314-315
UNIFORMS
American, Pennsylvania rifleman, 1775, 353
British, Black Watch regiment, 1758, 288
French, Carignan-Salières regiment, 1664, 169
French, infantryman, circa 1746, 247
French, musketeer, circa 1609, 68
WEAPONS
Artillery ammunition, circa 1780, 256
Cannon (French garrison gun), circa 1650-1700, 229
Cannon (field), circa 1780, 356
Gunnery, tools and methods of, circa 1780, 356
Matchlock, French, circa 1530-1550, 52
Matchlock, French, circa 1600-1620, 68
Mortar, circa 1780, 356
Musket, British *(Brown Bess),* 1758, 288
Musket, French (Charleville), 1746, 247
Rifle, American (Pennsylvania), 1775, 353
Rifle, British (Ferguson), 1776, 363

N
Navigation instruments (telescope and compass) 1790, 406
New Amsterdam (street scene), 146
Newfoundland (disputes over settlement), 121

O
Order of Good Cheer, 61
Oven (outdoor, Pennsylvania), 17th cent., 152

P
Pilgrims (Thanksgiving celebration), 138-139
Portaging (canoe), 71

Q
Quebec, ruins of, 1759, 316

R
Radisson, Pierre and Groselliers, Sieur de, 192
Revere, Paul, 350

S
Seigneurial system, 180-181
Ship-steering apparatus, circa 1703, 240
Ships, *See* TRANSPORTATION
Silver work, 330
Simcoe, John Graves, 420
Stump removing (Upper Canada), 425

T
Talon, Jean, 175
Timber rafts, 435
Tobacco, *See* AGRICULTURE
Trade goods, British, 390
Trade goods, French, 188

TRANSPORTATION
LAND
Calèche (small carriage), 436
Cariole (sleigh), 331
Travois, 20
WATER
Canoe (Iroquois), 31
Canoe brigade (fur traders), 395
Durham boat, 433
Kayak (Eskimo), 38
Ship, 15th cent., 47
Ship ("ketch"), 17th cent., 118
Ship-steering apparatus, circa 1703, 240

V
Viking, 42

W
War drum (Iroquois), 111
Washington, George (sworn in as President, 1789), 373
Well (sweep type), 149
West Indies (smuggling operations), 159
Wig-making, 337
Windmill, 17th cent. (New France), 184
Wolfe's headquarters at Montmorency, 308

INDEX

The following subjects have been grouped together for convenient reference:

Cities, Towns, and Villages
Forts and Trading Posts
Governors—British
Governors—French
Indian Groups
Indian Tribes
Intendants
Lakes
Rivers
Ships
Statutes
Treaties
Wars

A

Abercrombie, General, 286-289
Acadia, 57, 86, 90, 230, 236, 237, 239, 244, 245, 256-263, 330-332
Acadians, expulsion of, 256-263
Acts, *See* Statutes
Adams, John, 355, 370
Adams, Samuel, 345, 351
Agriculture, 7, 129, 130, 140, 148, 149, 158, 176, 177, 335, 336, 436, 437, 438
Aix-la-Chapelle, *See* Treaties
Alaska, 3, 398
Aleutian Islands, 3, 398
Alexander, Sir William, 86
Algonkian Indians, *See* Indian groups
Allen, Ethan, 352
American Revolution, *See* Wars
Amherst, General Jeffrey, 290-297, 304, 320, 325

Anse au Foulon (Wolfe's Cove), 312-316
Anti-Federalists, 372
Arctic Ocean, 405
Argenson, *See* Governors—French
Arnold, Benedict, 353
Astor, John Jacob, 408, 412
Astoria, *See* Forts and Trading Posts
Avagour, *See* Governors—French

B

Bahama Islands, 156
Baltimore, Lord, 148-150
Barbados, 158
Baronets of Nova Scotia, 86
Battles,
  Bunker Hill, 352
  Fallen Timbers, 397
  Fort Duquesne, 277, 279
  Lexington, 351
  Monmouth, 361-363

Battles (*cont'd*)

Montmorency, 309-310
Plains of Abraham, 312-318
Princeton, 361
Saratoga, 362
Ticonderoga, 286-283
Trenton, 361
Yorkton, 364
Bay of Quinte, 76
Baye Sainct Laurens, 49
Beauport Shore, 306, 309, 315, 316, 319
"Bees", 423-426
Beaver, 55, 178, 220, 221, 222, 275
Beaver hats, 220-222
Bering, Vitus, 398
Bermuda Islands, 132
Biencourt, Charles de, 62
Bigot, François, *See* Intendants
Bison (buffalo), 16-18
Bjarni, *See* Herjulfson
"Black Robes," 83, 202, *See also* Jesuits
Bolas, 35
"Boston Massacre," 346-347
"Boston Teaparty," 348-349
Bougainville, Louis-Antoine de, 301-302, 306, 317, 319
Bourgeoys, Marguerite, 97
Bradford, William, 138
Brant, Chief Joseph (Thayendan-egea), 386, 453
Braddock, General, 278-280
Brébeuf, Father Jean de, 83, 90, 104-105
British North America, 379-439
Brûlé, Etienne, 75, 77
Buffalo, *See* Bison
Burgoyne, Major-General, 361-362
Butler, Colonel John, 363, 385
Butler's Rangers, 363, 385

C

Cabot, John, 46-47, 117, 145
Cahiagué, 75
Canada Act, *See* Constitutional Act

Cape Breton Island (*See also* Ile Royale), 46-47, 239, 383, 432
Capitol, 375
Card money, 212-213
Caribbean Sea, 44
Carignan-Saliéres regiment, 168-169, 172, 174
Carleton, Sir Guy, *See* Governors— British
Cartier, Jacques, 49-52
Carteret, Sir George, 191
Carver, John, 134, 136, 138
Castle Frank, 420
Cataraqui, *See* Forts and Trading Posts
Champlain, Madame de, 81-82
Champlain, Samuel de, 56-62, 64-92
Chebucto, 252
Chequamegon Bay, 190
Cherry Valley, 363
Chesapeake Bay, 126-127, 149
Chicago portage, 206
Christian Island (*Ile St. Joseph*), 106
Cities, Towns, and Villages
Albany, 142, 198
Annapolis, 237, 380
Beaubassin, 259
Boston, 140
Charleston, 364
Concord, 351
Detroit, 213
Halifax, 252-255, 259, 332, 346, 380
Haverhill, 237
Jamestown, 127, 128, 130, 132
Kingston, 385, 428-429, 438
Lexington, 351
Montreal (*Ville Marie*), 94-48, **108**, 113, 185, 199, 205, 215, **267**, 305, 320, 323, 329, 353, **383**, 395, 397, 414, 430, 431
New Amsterdam (*See also* New York City), 142-143, 145-147
New Orleans, 209, 242
New York City, 143, 147, 361, 372
Newark, 418-419, 429

Niagara, *See* Newark

Philadelphia, 152-154

Plymouth, 136

Port Rosway, *See* Shelburne

Quebec, 64-66, 173, 185, 189, 190, 194, 238-239, 298, 303, 305, 311, 353, 354

Quebec, Sieges of, 87-90, 304-311, 353-354

Saint John, 383

St. John's (Newfoundland), 51

Salem, 140

Salmon Falls, 229

Schenectady, 229

Shelburne, 380

Sydney, 383

Three Rivers, 189, 305

Washington, 375

Williamsburg, 132

York (Toronto), 419-422, 429

Clark, William, 408

Clergy Reserves, 417

Cocking, Matthew, 393-394

Columbus, Christopher, 44

Common Sense, 355

Company of New France, 84-85, 87, 167

Congés, 199

Congregation of the Sisters of Notre Dame, 97

Constitution of the United States of America, 370-373

Continental Army, 352, 360, 363

Continental Congresses, 349, 352-353, 355, 369

Cook, Captain James, 306, 390-401

Cook's Inlet, 400, 405

Cornwallis, Governor Edward, 254, 257-260

Cornwallis, Lord, 361, 364

Corte Reale, Gaspar, 47

Courcelle, *See* Governors—French

Coureurs de bois, 198-200, 213

Cumberland House, 394

D

Dalhousie University, 381

Daniel, Father, 103-104

D'Argenson, *See* Governors—French

D'Avagour, *See* Governors—French

De Courcelle, *See* Governors — French

Declaration of Independence, 355, 358, 379

Declaration of Rights and Grievances, 349, 351

Dean Channel, 404, 408

De Denonville, *See* Governors — French

Deerfield, massacre of, 237

De la Barre, *See* Governors—French

De Lancey, Colonel Stephen, 385

De Meulles, Jacques, *See* Intendants

De Mezy, *See* Governors—French

De Monts, Sieur de, 57-62, 64, 66

De Tracy, Sieur, 168-172

De Troyes, Chevalier Pierre, 225

Dorchester, Lord, *See* Governors—British

Dollard, Adam, 108-113

Drake, Sir Bernard, 119

Drake, Sir Francis, 124

Drucour, Augustin de, 291-295

"Dry" fishery, 117-119

Duchesneau, Jacques, *See* Intendants, 210

Dundas Street, 421

Durham boat, 433

Dutch colony, *See* New Netherlands

Duval, Jean, 65, 66

E

Eastern Townships, 422

English colonies (*See also* United States) of America, 117-160, 200, 240, 275-280, 323-331, 335-341, 342-351, 352-355

Eric the Red, 41
Ericson, Leif, 42, 43
Eskimos, 34-39
Evangeline, 256
Executive council, 417

F

Farming, *See* Agriculture
Federalists, 372
Filles du Roi, See "King's
 Daughters"
Five Nations, 32
Fishing, 10, 23, 29, 36, 45, 55, 117-
 123, 140, 178, 227, 243, 320, 368,
 432
"Fishing admirals," 120, 123
Forts and Trading Posts
 Albany, 220, 225
 Astoria, 412
 Beauséjour, 260
 Carillon (*See also* Ticonderoga),
  285-289
 Cataraqui (*See also* Fort Fronte-
  nac), 195-198, 204
 Chambly, 353
 Charles (*See also* Rupert's
  House), 191-192, 220, 225
 Chequamagon, 242
 Chipewayan, 405
 Crown Point, 362
 Detroit, 242, 325
 Duquesne, 277-279, 451
 Edward, 285
 Frontenac (*See also* Cataraqui),
  212-213
 Kaministiquia, 242
 Kootenay House, 411
 La Reine, 267
 Lawrence, 260
 Louisbourg, 242-251, 276, 290-297
 Loyal, 229
 Maurepas, 266
 McLeod, 409
 Michilimackinac, 242
 Moose, 220, 225
 Necessity, 277

Nelson, *See* York Factory
Niagara, 213, 242, 325, 385
Orange, 142
Oswego, 284-285
Rupert's House, 220
St. Charles, 266
St. John's (Quebec), 353
St. Louis, 212
St. Pierre, 266
Severn, 220
Tadoussac, 55-56
The Pas, 271
Ticonderoga, 352
William (Newfoundland), 123
William Henry, 285
York Factory, 220, 222, 224, 271,
 273
Franklin, Benjamin, 343, 355, 374,
 453
Fraser, Simon, 409
Freehold tenure, 417
Frobisher brothers, 391, 396
Frontenac, Count, *See* Governors—
 French
Fur trade, 55-56, 72, 74, 103, 140,
 144, 172, 178, 186, 188-193, 205,
 206, 213, 219-226, 227, 251, 264-
 274, 275, 323-325, 336, 389-396,
 398, 399, 402

G

Gabarus Bay, 291
Gage, General, 349-352
Gazette, The Halifax, 255
Georgia, Strait of, 404
Georgian Bay, 75
Gilbert, Sir Humphrey, 119, 124
Glaciers, 3, 4
Glengarry County, 421
Governors—British
 Carleton, Sir Guy, 328
 Dorchester, Lord, 419
 Haldimand, General, 383, 385,
  387
 Murray, James, 328

Governors—French
  D'Argenson, 163, 189
  D'Avagour, 164, 165
  De Courcelle, 168, 169, 176
  De Denonville, 213, 215, 223
  De Frontenac, 194-200, 210-211, 215, 227-236
  De la Barre, 212
  De Montmagny, 93
  De Vaudreuil, 283-285, 299, 319-320
Governor's Road, *See* Dundas Street
Grand Banks, 45, 47
Grand Portage, 265, 390, 392, 393, 394
Grand Pré, 260-261
Grand Seminaire, 167
Grand Sault (*See also* Lachine Rapids), 72
Gray, Captain Robert, 404
Greater Antilles, 23
Green Bay, 202, 204
"Green" fishery, 117
Greenland, 41-43
"Green Mountain Boys", 352
Groseilliers, Sieur des, 187-193
Gulf of Mexico, 44, 206

H

Habitation (Port Royal), 58
Habitation (Quebec), 64-65, 79
Haldimand, General, *See* Governors —British
Hamilton, Alexander, 374
Hancock, John, 349, 351, 355
Hawkins, John, 124
Hearne, Samuel, 394
Hébert, Louis, 79-81
Henday, Anthony, 271-274
Henry, Alexander, 324-325, 389, 391
Herjulfson, Bjarni, 41
Hiawatha, 32
Hochelaga, 49, 50
Howe, General, 361-362

Hudson, Henry, 72, 142, 219
Hudson's Bay Company, 193, 219-226, 266, 271-274, 391, 393-395
Huronia, 75, 77, 99-107
Huron missions, 99-107

I

Ice ages, 3-5
Igloo, 36
Ile d'Orleans, 306-307
Ile Royale (*See also* Cape Breton Island), 239, 247-248, 252, 290-297
Ile St. Jean (*See also* Prince Edward Island), 239, 380, 432
Immigration, 330, 332, 421
Indian groups
  Algonkian, 22-27, 55
  Eastern forests, 23-27
  Iroquoian, 28-33
  Pacific coast, 9-15
  Plains, 17-21
Indian tribes
  Algonquins, 23-27, 66-70, 71-73, 79, 108-113
  Andastes, 172, 198, 211
  Arawak, 156
  Assiniboine, 17-21, 223-224
  Bella Coola, 9-15
  Beothuk, 23, 121-122
  Blackfoot, 17-21, 272-273
  Blood, 17-21
  Carantouan, 75, 77
  Carib, 156
  Cayuga, 28-33
  Chippewa, 23-27, 264, 324
  Coast Salish, 9-15
  Cree, 17-21, 23-27, 190, 223, 266, 268, 271, 274
  Gros Ventre, 17-21
  Haida, 9-15
  Huron, 28-33, 66-70, 71, 74-78, 79, 99-107, 108-113, 188
  Iroquois, *See* League of the Iroquois
  Kwakiutl, 9-15
  Mandan, 264, 267-269

Indian Tribes (*cont'd*)
  Malecite, 23-27
  Micmac, 23-27, 52, 259
  Missisauga, 387
  Mohawk, 28-33, 170-172, 363, 385,
    386, 387
  Montagnais, 23-27, 66-70, 79
  Naskapi, 23-27
  Neutral, 28-33
  Nootka, 9-15, 399-400
  Objibwa, 23-27
  Oneida, 28-33
  Onondaga, 28-33, 75
  Ottawa, 188, 190
  Piegan, 17-21
  Seneca, 28-33, 213, 363
  Sioux, 16-21, 190, 264, 266
  Tlinkit, 9-15
  Tobacco, 28-33
  Tsimshian, 9-15
  Tuscarora, 29-33
Inns, 429, 430
Intendant, office of, 173
Intendants
  Bigot, Francois, 299-301
  De Meulles, Jacques, 212
  Duchesneau, Jacques, 210
  Talon, Jean, 173-178, 201
International Boundary
  Commission, 412
Iroquois, *See* League of the
  Iroquois

J

Jamaica, 158
James Bay, 191
Jay, John, 374, 397
Jefferson, Thomas, 355, 374
Jemeraye, *See* La Jemeraye
Jessup, Major, 385
Jesuit
  College (Quebec) 83
  Missions, 99-107
  Order, 82, 83, 90, 210
  Relations, 94, 176

Jogues, Father Isaac, 187
Johnson, Sir John, 363, 385
Johnson, Sir William, 451
Joliet, Louis, 84, 201-204
Jones, John Paul, 364
Juan de Fuca, Strait of, 404

K

Karlsefni, 43
Kayak, 35, 37-39
Kelsey, Henry, 222-224
King's College (New Brunswick),
  381
King's College (Nova Scotia), 381
"King's Daughters" (*Filles du Roi*),
  174-175
Kirke, David, 87, 89-90
Kootenay House, *See* Forts and
  Trading Posts

L

La Barre, *See* Governors—French
La Chine, 204
Lachine massacre, 214-215
Lachine Rapids (*See also Grand
  Sault*), 75
Lafayette, Marquis de, 361
Lakes
  Allumette, 73, 75
  Athabaska, 393
  Cedar, 267
  Champlain, 69
  Erie, 201
  George, 69
  Great Lakes, 50, 187-188, 190, 198,
    202, 204, 206, 264, 276, 324, 396
  Great Slave, 405
  Huron, 187
  Kawartha Lakes, 76
  Lake of the Woods, 266, 368
  Michigan, 187
  Nipigon, 265

Nipissing, 75
Oneida, 76
Ontario, 76
Rainy, 266
Superior, 187
Winnipeg, 224
Winnipegosis, 224
La Jemeraye, 265
Lalemant, Father Charles, 83, 104-105
La Salle, Robert Cavelier de, 195, 201, 204-209
La Tour, Charles, 62, 86, 87
Laval, Bishop, 163-167, 210
La Vérendrye family, 264-270
Lawrence, Colonel Charles, 260, 290, 331, 332
League of the Iroquois, 32, 33, 66-70, 74-77, 95, 96, 102-107, 108-113, 166, 168-172, 178, 195-198, 211-215, 228-230, 232-234, 239, 386-387
Lee, Richard Henry, 355
Legislative assembly, 417
Legislative council, 417
Leif, See Ericson
Levis, Chevalier de, 319-320
Le Loutre, Abbé, 259
Le Moyne, Pierre, Sieur d'Iberville, 225-226
L'Enfant, Pierre, 375
Le Jeune, Paul, 90
Lescarbot, Marc, 60
Lesser Antilles, 156, 158
Lewis, Meriwether, 408
Liquor trade, 72, 163-164, 210
Livingston, Robert L., 355
London Company, 126, 130
Long Sault Rapids, 108-113
Louisiana, 206, 209, 320
Lower Canada, 417, 421-422, 430-431, 434-437
Loyalists, See United Empire Loyalists
Lumbering, 178

M

McGill, James, 391
Mackenzie, Alexander, 396, 405
McTavish, Simon, 391, 396
Mance, Jeanne, 95-97
Maisonneuve, Sieur de, 94-98
Manhattan Island, 142-143
Marquette, Father Jacques, 202-204, 450
Mason-Dixon Line, 150
Massasoit, Chief, 137,139
Massachusetts Bay Company, 140
Massé, Father Enemond, 83
Matagorda Bay, 207-209
Mayflower Compact, 136
Meares, John, 402
Meulles, Jacques de, See Intendants
Minas Basin, 256, 260
Minutemen, 349, 351
Miquelon, 320
Montcalm, Major-General, 283-289, 299-303, 306, 312-318
Montgomery, Richard, 353-354
Montmagny, See Governors—French
Mont Royal, le, 49
Murray, See Governors—British

N

New Brunswick, 239, 246, 259, 381, 383, 423, 430, 432-434
New Caledonia, 409
Newfoundland, 45-46, 51, 117-123, 237, 239, 242, 432
New France, 48, 64-113, 163, 215, 227-236, 237-241, 242-245, 276, 283-289, 290-297, 319-322
New Netherlands, 142-147, 165, 178
New Netherlands Company, 142
Nootka Sound, 399, 400, 402-404
North Carolina, 354, 364
North West Company, 395, 396, 405-413
Nor'Westers, 391-396
Nova Scotia, 86, 241, 244-246, 251, 252-255, 256-263, 330-332, 337, 354, 380-381, 432, 434

O

Ohio Company, 277
Ontario, province of, *See* Upper Canada
Order of the Baronets of Nova Scotia, 86
Ordre du Bons Temps, 60-63

P

Pacific Ocean, *See* Western Sea
Paine, Thomas, 355
Patroon system, 144
Peace treaties, *See* Treaties
"Pedlars from Quebec", 391-396, 394, 399
Pemmican, 18
Penn, William, 151-155
Pepperell, Colonel William, 247-249
Petit Seminaire, 167
Phips, Sir William, 230, 231
Pilgrim Fathers, 133-141
Pilotte, 97
Pitt, William, 289-290, 304
Plantations, 130, 158
Playing card money, 212-213
Plymouth Company, 126
Pocahontas, 448, 449
Point aux Péres, 308
Point Lévis, 308
Pond, Peter, 391
Pontiac Rebellion, 325
Potlach, 14
Port Royal (*See also* Annapolis), 58-63, 79, 86, 87, 230, 237
Poutrincourt, Sieur de, 57-62
Prince Edward Island (*See also* Ile St. Jean), 239, 383, 432
Proclamation of 1763, 325-328
Puget Sound, 404
Puritans, 133-141

Q

Quadra, Don, 403, 404
Quakers, 151-155
Quebec, province of, 319-322, 325-329, 383-388, 414-417 *See also* Lower Canada
Queen's Rangers, 418-419

R

Radisson, Pierre Esprit, 187-193
Raleigh, Sir Walter, 126, 448
Ramezy, Chevalier de, 319-320
Récollet Order, 74, 79, 82-83
Relations, See Jesuit *Relations*
Revere, Paul, 350-351
Rivers
  Arkansas, 203
  Bella Coola, 408
  Blackwater, 408
  Columbia, 404, 410-412
  Coppermine, 394
  Delaware, 151
  Don, 420
  Fox, 187
  Fraser, 409
  French, 75
  Grand, 387
  Hudson, 142
  Illinois, 204-206
  James, 127
  Kootenay, 411
  Mackenzie, 405
  Mattawa, 75
  Missisguash, 259-260
  Mississippi, 201-209, 239, 264, 275, 320, 365
  Missouri, 202, 267
  Montmorency, 309-310
  Niagara, 385
  Ohio, 202
  Onondaga, 235
  Ottawa, 50, 73, 74-75, 108-113, 189, 325, 392, 417, 435
  Parsnip, 407
  Peace, 406
  Pigeon, 265

Potomac, 148
Richelieu (River of the Iroquois),
    68, 168
Rupert, 191
Saguenay, 55
St. Charles, 305
St. John, 381, 383
St. Lawrence, 49, 385, 434-435
Saskatchewan, 267-268
Slave, 405
Winnipeg, 266
Wisconsin, 202
Roanoke Island, 126
Roberval, Sieur de, 50-51
Rocky Mountains, 224, 269, 272
Rolfe, John, 129, 130
Rupert, Prince, 191
Rupert's Land, 193
Russians, 398, 402
Ryswick, *See* Treaties

S

Sachems, 33
Scolp, John, 45
Saint Croix Island, 57-58
St. Ignace, 104, 105
Sainte Marie, 101-107
St. Pierre, 320
San Salvador Island (later Watling
    Island), 156-157
Saunders, Vice-Admiral Charles, 305
Sea otter, 398, 402
Seigneurial system, 179-185, 329, 387
Seigneurial tenure, 387
Separatists, 133-141
Sherman, Roger, 355
Shipbuilding, 140, 336, 381, 432, 435
Ships
    Blessing of the Bay, 140
    Columbia, 404
    Discovery, 126
    Eaglet, 191
    Falcon, 124
    Godspeed, 126
    Griffon, 206
    Half-moon, 142, 252-255
    Matthew, 46-47
    Mayflower, 134-137
    Nonsuch, 191
    Pelican, 225-226
    Speedwell, 134
    Squirrel, 126
    Susan Comfort, 126
Siberia, 5
Simcoe, John Graves, 418, 419-421
Sisters of Notre Dame, *See* Congre-
    gation of the Sisters of Notre
    Dame
Six Nations, 32
Skrellings, 43
Slaves, 130, 158, 338
Smith, Captain John, 128, 134, 448,
    449
Society of Jesus, 83
Society of Our Lady of Montreal, 94
Somers, Admiral Sir George, 132
Squanto, 137-138
Stadacona, 49, 50, 64
Standish, Miles, 135, 137
Statutes
    Constitutional Act (Canada Act),
        416-417
    "Intolerable Acts," 349
    Quebec Act, 328-330, 349
    Stamp Act, 344
    Sugar Act, 344
    Tea Act, 347-348
    "Townshend Acts," 345
Stormont County, 421
Stuvyesant, Peter, 145-147
Sugar, 158-159

T

Tadoussac, *See* Forts and Trading
    Posts
Taverns, 429-430
Thanksgiving Day, 139, 140
Thirteen Colonies, *See* English
    Colonies
Thompson, David, 410-413

Tipi, 19
Tithes, 167
Tobacco, 129-132, 149, 156, 158, 243, 336, 338, 448
Toboggan, 26
Tories, 354, 358, 360, *See Also* United Empire Loyalists
Totem poles, 15
Trade goods, Indian, 222, 390
Trading posts, *See* Forts and Trading Posts
Travois, 20
Treaties
    Jay's Treaty, 397, 413
    Peace of Ryswick, 236
    Treaty of Aix-la-Chapelle, 250-251
    Treaty of Paris (1763), 320, 322
    Treaty of Paris (1783), 365-368
    Treaty of Utrecht, 239, 241
Troyes, *See* De Troyes

U

Ulu, 37
Umiak, 37-38
United Empire Loyalists, 379-388, 414-422
United States of America, 365-368, 369-375
University of New Brunswick, 381
Upper Canada, 417-422, 423-430, 437-438
Upper Canada Gazette, 438
Ursuline Sisters, 94
Utrecht, *See* Treaties

V

Valley Forge, 362
Vancouver, Captain George, 402-404
Vancouver Island, 404

Vaudreuil, Marquis de, *See* Governors—French
Verchéres, Madeleine de, 232-234
Verrazano, Giovanni de, 47
Vignau, Nicolas, 72-73
Vikings, 41-43
Ville Marie, See Cities, Towns, and Villages—Montreal
Vimont, Father, 95
Voyageurs, 183, 391

W

Wall Street, 143
Wars
    American Revolution (War of Independence), 342-368
    Queen Anne's War, 237-241
    King George's War, 246-251
    King William's War, 227-236
    Seven Years' War, 283-332
Washington, George, 277-279, 352, 360-362, 364, 372, 373
Western Sea (Pacific Ocean), 50, 264-270, 405-413
West Indies, 44, 156-160, 200, 243, 320, 336
Whigs, 354, 358
Wigwam, 24
Winslow, Edward, 381, 382
Winslow, Lieutenant-Colonel John, 261
Wolfe, Major-General James, 290-295, 304-318, 452
Wyoming Valley, 363

Y

Yankee, 141
Yonge Street, 420-421
York, Duke of, 145

THE RIVALS

LAKE SUPERIOR

Sault Ste. Marie

Michilimackinac

LAKE NIPISSING

Ottawa R.

Ft. Mackinac

GEORGIAN BAY

LAKE MICHIGAN

LAKE HURON

Montreal

Ft. St. J

F R A N C E

Ft. Frontenac

St. Lawrence R.

L CHAMPL

Ft. Rouillé (later York)

LAKE ONTARIO

Ft. Oswego

Ft. Ontario

Ft. Frédér

Ft. Carill

LAKE ST. CLAIR

Ft. Pontchartrain (later Ft. Detroit)

Ft. St. Joseph

Ft. Niagara

Ft. William Henry

Ft. Stanwix

Ft. Edwar

Ft. Herkimer

NEW YORK

Albany

LAKE ERIE

Ft. Presqu'Ile

Ft. Le Boeuf

Ft. Venango

Hudson R.

Ft. Miami

Ft. Sandusky

N E W

M O U N T A I N S

Susquehanna R.

Ft. Augusta

Delaware R.

New York

Ft. Duquesne (later Ft. Pitt)

PENNSYLVANIA

Ft. Harris

Philadelphia

NEW JERSEY

Ohio R.

Ft. Bedford

Ft. Necessity

Ft. Cumberland

A P P A L A C H I A N

Potomac R.

MARYLAND

DELAWARE

DELAWARE

VIRGINIA

Mt. Vernon

James R.

Richmond

CHESAPEAKE BAY

N

SCALE OF MILES

0   50   100